The New Natural Resource

The New Natural Resource

Knowledge Development, Society and Economics

HANS CHRISTIAN GARMANN JOHNSEN

University of Agder, Norway

Routledge
Taylor & Francis Group

LONDON AND NEW YORK

First published 2014 by Gower Publishing

Published 2016 by Routledge
2 Park Square, Milton Park, Abingdon, Oxon OX14 4RN
711 Third Avenue, New York, NY 10017, USA

First Issued in Paperback 2016

Routledge is an imprint of the Taylor & Francis Group, an informa business

Gower Applied Business Research
Our programme provides leaders, practitioners, scholars and researchers with thought provoking, cutting edge books that combine conceptual insights, interdisciplinary rigour and practical relevance in key areas of business and management.

British Library Cataloguing in Publication Data
A catalogue record for this book is available from the British Library.

The Library of Congress has cataloged the printed edition as follows:
Johnsen, Hans Chr. Garmann, 1955–
   The new natural resource : knowledge development, society and economics / by Hans Christian Garmann Johnsen.
      pages cm
   Includes bibliographical references and index.
   ISBN 978-1-4724-2343-6 (hardback)
   1. Knowledge, Sociology of. 2. Information society. 3. Knowledge economy. I. Title.
   HM651.J64 2014
   306.4'2–dc23
                                                                    2013048216

ISBN 9781472423436 (hbk)
ISBN 9781138228085 (pbk)

Contents

PART II   KNOWLEDGE IN SOCIAL STRUCTURES

List of Figures and Tables

Figures

Tables

About the Author

Hans Christian Garmann Johnsen is a professor in the Faculty of Economics and Social Sciences at the University of Agder in Norway and an adjunct professor at Gjøvik University College. Professor Garmann Johnsen is a specialist in the study of working life and innovation and is the Centre Leader at the Centre for Advanced Studies in Regional Innovation Strategies (RIS) at Agder. He has an MBA from the Norwegian School of Economics and Business Administration and gained his PhD at the Copenhagen Business School. He has been a visiting scholar and fellow at several universities including UC Berkeley and Cornell in the USA and Kingston University in the UK. For 15 years Garmann Johnsen has been involved in a national research programme into collaborative innovation. He has written and presented papers and authored journal articles published worldwide. He also co-edited the book, *Creating Collaborative Advantage*.

Foreword and Acknowledgements

I have worked on the following text for several years; however, it is due to study leaves in 2013 that I have been able to make it into a book. The starting point of the book was firstly reflections I did in the late 1990s on how the new, open-world situation with globalisation, new information technology and without the iron curtain had created new conditions for social development. Secondly, during the 2000s I became more and more interested in the knowledge economy and knowledge organisations: how are they different from more traditional organisations? This eventually led me deeper into a reflection on what is knowledge. The present book is the outcome of these reflections.

I have this year had the chance to sit and write in different places, for which I am grateful. This includes visits to the Centre Franco-Norvegien en Sciences Sociales et Humaines in Paris in January, to the Norwegian Centre at UC Berkeley in the USA in February and March, to the Department of Strategic Management and Globalisation at CBS in Copenhagen, Denmark in April, and finally I had the chance to pull the whole thing together at Metochi at Lesvos in Greece in October. In addition, a scholarship from Norsk Faglig Forfatterforening has been helpful.

Three chapters have been published in earlier works: Chapter 6: 'Knowledge Organisations: Developing Knowledge in Practice', is published in Holbek, Kristiansen and Randøy (eds) (2013) *Management for Progress*; Chapter 7: 'Cultural Knowledge and Market Development', is published in Knudsen, H. et al. (red.) (2012) *Mysterion* (Oslo: Novus Forlag); Chapter 8: 'Modernist Criticisms and Development of Social Knowledge', is published in *Sosiologisk Årbok* (2013) (Oslo: Novus Forlag).

Although responsibility for all opinions and shortcomings in the following text is completely my own, I should like to thank colleagues that directly and indirectly have contributed with stimulating comments and discussion. Among these are Hans Helof Grelland, Jan Pavlik, Ingrid Garmann Johnsen, Christian Garmann Johnsen, Jonny Holbek, Jon P. Knudsen, Dag G. Aasland, Lars Peder Nordbakken, Nicolai J. Foss, Roger Normann, Olav Eikeland, Øyvind Pålshaugen and Harald Knudsen. I would also like to thank the University of Agder, Department for Work Life and Innovation, which has provided the opportunity for me to work on these ideas. In particular I need to thank Professor Richard Ennals. Without his continuous and critical support, this book would never have been written.

Hans Christian Garmann Johnsen
Lillesand

Knowledge and Society: An Introduction

Introduction

This book is based on a very simple idea: that *knowledge is inherently a social phenomenon*. This idea implies that I need to address society and the social processes, in order to understand how knowledge develops. Understanding knowledge is a comprehensive task. The construction of knowledge is dependent on the mechanisms of social and political deliberation. I therefore argue that liberal, democratic society is a precondition for the soundness of knowledge development.

The argument I will develop in this book says that knowledge is developed in and between different social domains: political processes, markets, organisations, social groups, public administration, or private association. In knowledge society, it seems that, in particular, science and art have become important contributors to social development. I therefore in particular discuss how science and art make knowledge, and how this knowledge is influencing society.

If my treatise has a thesis, it is that knowledge development is a complex, often long-term, process. In knowledge society, although knowledge is a main resource for development, we should not expect to have knowledge about everything. This is not and should not be possible. We should be more concerned with the processes of producing knowledge, because we are so dependent on them. That requires more and deeper understanding of knowledge development processes in different areas of society. To understand these processes is complex. There are not only different theories of knowledge development; there are also, as I will show, different theories of theories of knowledge development. In arguing that, I refer to different thinkers in the field. Two of them in particular have inspired me. They are in some sense antagonists, but in the sense I use them here, they supplement each other. The two are Friedrich A. Hayek and Jürgen Habermas – one Austrian, the other German, one growing up around the First World War, the other around the Second World War. Both have had a tremendous impact on Western society in the second half of the twentieth century, and both have pioneered our understanding of knowledge in society.

All arguments represent a reduction of the phenomena in question. Social science, philosophy, history of ideas, political and economic theory, to mention some, all strive to understand certain phenomena related to human life and existence in society. As these are complex matters, something beyond what we can understand in its totality, all these attempts to understand them, including my own, have limitations. Also, making arguments is like erecting a construction. One argument assumes another and leads to a third. They are steps in a construction, building on other arguments and leading to further arguments. Therefore each attempt ends up as a certain building.

This is what I will try to do here. In my construction I see society along certain dimensions, as indicated by Figure I.1.

Figure I.1 tries to illustrate the relation between the social domains I discuss. First we have the subject, which is each of us. We form opinions and engage in knowledge development. Secondly we have different social processes that I, for simplicity, divide into two: society and market. The reason for this division is that I see the market as a more structured form of interaction than society at large. Thirdly we have the state, which differs from the others, as it is a structure that represents the law, can limit the others and has the capacity to implement decisions to an extent that exceeds the other domains. It can restrict or encourage knowledge development.

I will try to show that, in order to understand *the type* of knowledge society that Western societies are developing towards, we need to understand *how* knowledge is developed. In order to make this argument, I have divided the book in three. In the first part I present, through three chapters, some assumptions on individuals and society that are fundamental to the issues of how knowledge develops as a social phenomenon. In the second part, I present five studies of different aspects of knowledge development in science and art and their relation to social change and market processes. In the third part I try, through three chapters, to be more normative in arguing how society ought to be organised in order to support knowledge development.

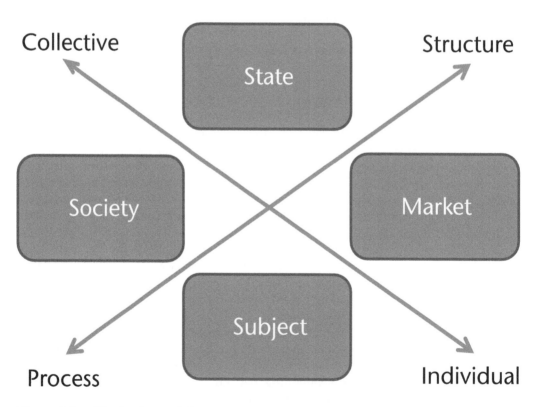

Figure I.1   The basic model

Background

The background for my discussion is what has been called a development towards a knowledge society. This development has implications for how we understand the individual in society, the economy and the market, social and cultural processes, the role of social structures, institutions and organisations, and democracy and the political processes. As knowledge is a certain kind of resource, different from physical resources, it plays a different role in society than physical resources, and it thereby has an impact on how we understand economic and social processes, and how we organise them. The book discusses how knowledge is developed in social processes.

Knowledge has become a buzzword. Increasingly in the public discourse there are references to knowledge economy, knowledge society, knowledge workers and knowledge organisations. The argument is that knowledge is becoming the main economic resource, replacing natural resources that drove the Industrial Revolution. The new knowledge economy is driven by knowledge development, innovation and highly skilled employees. Increasing investment in higher education and in universities is in line with this strategy and understanding. Florida argues about the new production of knowledge and creativity:

> The shift to knowledge-based capitalism represents an epochal transition in the nature of advanced economies and societies. Ever since the transition from feudalism to capitalism, the basic source of productivity, value and economic growth has been physical labour and manual skill. In the knowledge-intensive organization, intelligence and intellectual labour replaces physical labour as the fundamental source of value and profit. (Florida, 1995)

There is a call for new forms of interaction between public sector, university, research and business. Nowotny, Scott and Gibbons (2001) have talked about the *new production of knowledge*, implying a new institutional relation between business and academia. They are expected in collaboration to produce the type of innovative economic development that the new knowledge economy demands. Leydesdorff (2006) argues that the 'triple helix' between public administration, university and industry is a key motor in knowledge development. Related to this there is an increasing demand for knowledge management in organisations. Organisations now formulate knowledge strategies and discuss what knowledge resources they possess.

In normative terms, this signifies new ways of organising knowledge development processes between universities and business. In descriptive terms, we can see the emergence of new governance structures, new organisational forms between university and business, and more practice-based ways of organising education. This implies overcoming traditional dilemmas related to roles (such as the role of the researcher) and institutional understanding (such as the role of the university, or new arenas for university/business collaboration) in the regional context.

Knowledge and Collaboration

It has been argued that in the globalised economy, local aspects achieve new significance. This has inspired efforts to develop collaboration between companies at a local and regional level and what is called territorial innovation models (Moulaert and Sekia, 2003).

It has also led to changing roles of institutions, as regions are forced to become more active in developing economic strategies and supporting business development. Michael Porter argues that:

> *A cluster is a geographically proximate group of interconnected companies and associated institutions in a particular field, linked by commonalities and complementarities. The geographic scope of a cluster can range from a single city or state to a country or even a network of neighbouring countries. (Porter, 1998)*

Among others, this challenges the traditional role of universities, but also of public administration. In the book *Creating Collaborative Advantage*, Johnsen and Ennals (2012) proposed four typologies for understanding collaboration. These four typologies differ in whether they are coordination related or change related, and also to what extent they are based on *solving problems* or based on common learning and understanding. Collaboration can be seen as a coordination of interests (plus sum game) or as negotiations. Coordination can also be seen as dialogic collaboration in order to reach a common interpretation and understanding. Collaboration can be aimed at radical change based on common beliefs, conviction and ideology, such as a political movement, while pragmatic collaboration can be established order to create a *common good* or conformity (community).

Knowledge is related to communication, learning and collaboration. Johnsen and Ennals (2012) argue that one of the main reasons why collaboration gives advantage is through the *knowledge that is developed in collaborative structures*. This argument is based on some theoretical as well as empirical observations. The empirical observations refer to cases of collaborative structures, for example collaborative arenas between business and university. Theoretically, we can distinguish collaboration from transaction or negotiations. It can be argued that collaborative arenas are not transactional arenas, that is, arenas for transfer of real resources. Collaboration is foremost a social practice, an arena for sharing of interest and knowledge and for exchange of ideas and opinions. The idea of that book was to develop theoretically the argument that collaborative arenas develop knowledge.

Phillip Cooke (2002) argues that there is a new type of growth dynamic in the new knowledge-based economy. It develops in ways that are different from the more traditional economy. Soft institutional infrastructure and un-traded interdependencies, institutional thickness, learning, networking, reduced transaction costs, associated economy, stability and risk reduction, participation, trust and social stability seem to be more relevant in the new economy (such as ICT) compared with the more traditional economy (Parker and Tamaschke, 2005). However, this is a paradox, since the new, knowledge-based economy, such as the ICT sector, is typically characterised by what Clayton Christensen (1997) has called *disruptive technologies*, that is, quick and powerful technological changes that threaten the existing enterprises.

Although it is generally agreed is that there is no easy solution to enhance knowledge development and innovation, it is an ambition to find ways to do so, and literatures about these issues are found in many fields. Geography studies (Cooke, 2002) have increasingly used a systems perspective in order to understand innovation. They see innovation as a result of a particular configuration of institutions in the region. Management and organisation theory (Nonaka and Takeuchi, 1995; Tsoukas, 2005) have discussed innovations as interactive learning processes between different competencies within the firm. Furthermore, organisational and management structures within companies (Holbek, 1988), as well as structures between companies (Porter, 1998), seem to influence the ability to innovate.

Also within philosophy (McKelvey, 2002; Fuller, 2002) we find arguments on what encourages innovation, with an emphasis on understanding the knowledge development part of innovation. Work-sociology (Gustavsen, 2004) has discussed innovation both as larger systems, such as regional development coalitions, and as participatory incremental innovation and learning processes at work.

The perspective on knowledge economy has a strong standing in applied economic geography (Lundvall, 2002; Rodrigues, 2002) and in the university/region debates (Nowotny et al., 2001; Amin and Cohendet, 2004). This literature argues normatively for closer cooperation between different partners in the innovation system, such as businesses, networks of businesses, policymakers and universities. It is a way of thinking about innovation that has influenced the discussion of clusters, university and enterprise cooperation in a regional context, which we have referred to as the Triple Helix model (Etzkowitz and Leydesdorff, 2000).

The innovation literature gives references to innovation in both a broad (innovation system) and narrow (internal innovation processes in organisations) perspective. Furthermore, innovations are discussed as emergent and planned, incremental and radical, as a result of creative internal processes, or as a result of outside pressure.

Some examples: Cooke (2002) makes the same distinction as Schumpeter between *exploration* (knowledge for development) and *exploitation* (knowledge for commercialisation). He uses this distinction to argue that different types of knowledge play different roles in different types or phases of innovation. Triple Helix, Mode-2 and Regional Innovation System are examples of this systems perspective on innovation (Etzkowitz and Leydesdorff, 2000; Nowotny et al., 2001; Lundvall, 2002; Rodrigues, 2002). Yet another approach to innovation is represented by Michael Porter and his analysis of business climate (Porter, 1990). His ideas are somewhat in opposition to, but can also be combined with, Florida's idea on a people climate for creativity (Florida, 2002). Both sets of ideas focus on interaction and relations and how different norms and attitudes are important for innovation. This system of innovation literature argues that there are systemic effects beyond the individual actor or unit (firm, or agencies) that define how innovation happens. Clusters, learning networks, regional and national innovation systems are examples of use of systemic arguments in innovation theory.

The knowledge management and knowledge economy literature often refers to knowledge development as a result of interrelations between different knowledge forms, in particular the interrelation between codified and uncodified knowledge (Nonaka and Takeuchi, 1995; Spender, 1997; Amin and Cohendet, 2004). Much of this innovation literature is inspired by a dualist conception of knowledge (Ryle, 1949; Polanyi, 1966). Enterprise development literature often takes as a point of departure an emphasis on locally communicated and intersubjective generated knowledge (Mintzberg, Ahlstrand, and Lampel, 1998).

None of these perspectives are able to fully explain either if there is something special that we might call the knowledge economy, or what particular mechanisms explain innovation in this new economy. Together with colleagues (Johnsen, Karlsen, Normann and Fosse, 2009), I have asked for a deeper philosophical discussion of the concept of knowledge like the one offered by Fuller (2002) as a foundation for the theories of knowledge management (Foss, 2005) and the knowledge economy.

If we look at the available literature discussing knowledge development and knowledge management, it is hard to find a consistent description of what knowledge is and how it is developed. Much knowledge management literature is either adopted from the former technology management literature, from the former organisational learning or human resource management literature. Furthermore, this literature to a small extent communicates with the literature on sociology of knowledge, the literature on organisation of universities (higher education) or with the innovation literature discussing the new production of knowledge. This discourse only to a small extent communicates with the philosophy of science discourse on how science makes knowledge. Therefore, I argue here, that there is a need for a framework in which insights from these different discourses can be brought together, or at least communicate with each other.

Philosophical Roots

The development towards what we refer to as a knowledge society was a theme already in Daniel Bell's 1973 book *The Coming of the Post-Industrial Society*. J.-F. Lyotard wrote about it in his book *The Postmodern Condition: A report on knowledge* from 1979 (Lyotard, 1984). Peter F. Drucker's 1993 book *Post-Capitalist Society* has had a large impact on thinking on management and organisations, and many of the features of this new condition were described by Manuel Castells in 1996 in *The Rise of the Network Society*. Knowledge management is today a large field of academic research, as well as having practical implications. The purpose of this book is to take a broader view on knowledge management and try to establish a more comprehensive picture of the cultural, social, political and economic changes that the advances of knowledge in society imply.

The development of the modern conception of the *knowledge society* can be traced far beyond the works of Bell, Lyotard, Drucker and Castells. We might see it as an emergent conceptualisation, developed in an attempt to catch some specific feature of modern and modernist society. In his book *The Philosophical Discourses of Modernity* (1987), Jürgen Habermas argues that Georg Wilhelm Friedrich Hegel (1770–1831) was the first major philosopher to understand the inherent dynamics and contradictions of modern society. The tension between *structural instrumentality* and *subjective reflexivity* defines the individual in modern society, its quest for meaning and its alienation. This is a theme developed within critical theory and criticism of modern society. Another reference might be Auguste Comte (1798–1857) and his work that he started to publish in 1830 and completed in 1842 under the title *Cours de philosophie positive* (Comte, 1988). In this work, Comte spelled out how he sees that society has gone from a theological state, via a metaphysical state towards a positive state. The positive state is a society based on scientific truth. It is a society where true science reaches for the ultimate truth. Science has replaced religion as a foundation for society.

Philosophically, there is another line of thought that has roots back to phenomenology, interpretive sociology and pragmatic philosophy, found in the works of Michael Polanyi, *Personal Knowledge: Towards a post critical philosophy* (1958) and *The Tacit Dimension* (1966), in A.J. Ayer's *Language, Truth and Logic* (1947), and John Searle's work *Speech Acts* (1969). This treatment makes a dualism between private and public knowledge, tacit and explicit knowledge, and between knowing *what* and knowing *that*. I will argue below that these dualisms have strong limitations in order to understand what knowledge is.

There is another tradition related to what is called Austrian Economics, where knowledge is acknowledged as an important economic factor. The two works by Frederic von Hayek – *Knowledge and Economics* (1937) and *The Use of Knowledge in Society* (1945) – argue that the emphasis on knowledge has severe implications for how we understand the possibility and limits of economic planning.

Finally, I will emphasise the works within the tradition called sociology of knowledge, which have argued that knowledge somehow is socially constructed. It is a tradition that derives from Karl Marx and his argument that the material condition of production in society defines the ideological superstructure of society. This argument, developed further by Max Scheler (1973), and not least in Karl Mannheim's 1929 work *Ideology and Utopia: An introduction to the sociology of knowledge* (Mannheim, 1979), formed the background of a considerable academic discussion that has impacted our understanding of the social construction of knowledge, our belief in scientific knowledge and our understanding of the role of scientific knowledge in society.

Knowledge has many forms and is formed in many ways. The economist Fritz Machlup (1984) argued that knowledge is probably easier to classify than to define. He argues for five types of knowledge: practical knowledge, intellectual knowledge, small talk, spiritual knowledge and unwanted knowledge. Practical knowledge includes professional knowledge, business knowledge, workman's knowledge, political knowledge, household knowledge and other practical knowledge. The core of Machlup's analysis is that society has different knowledge domains, but also that they are interrelated. The complicated question is how they interact.

Beyond Dualisms

My interest is to discuss how the emphasis on knowledge impacts on how we understand the individual in society, the economy and the market, the social and cultural processes, the role of social structures, institutions and organisations and democracy and the political processes.

What does this imply? Let me briefly relate it to the areas I have mentioned. For our understanding of *the individual in society*, an emphasis on knowledge brings the private, subjective understanding and reflexivity to the foreground. Knowledge is inherently something we have in our mind, not something we take on (such as physical resources). Knowledge is social, but individuals as actors in the social process impact what knowledge is. Emphasis on knowledge means acknowledging personality, as Chris Argyris discussed in his 1965 book *Personality and Organization*, or more generally the human mind or *the human condition* as Hannah Arendt discussed it in her 1958 book.

How does knowledge imply changes in our understanding of *the economy and the market*? First of all, knowledge is not a scarce resource. Contrary to conventional economic theory, the possibility to possess knowledge and make knowledge into a private good is less meaningful than its parallels with physical goods. This means that scarcity, as a major condition for price formation, is less present in a knowledge economy than in a conventional commodity economy. The perspective of the employee, the worker, also changes as we go from a commodity economy to a knowledge economy.

Knowledge workers possess knowledge and are not only means of production, but also owners of the capital stock of the organisation they work in. This has an impact on employer–employee relations and the dynamic of the market. From an economic perspective, the emphasis is increasingly on how knowledge is developed, how it is shared and how it is utilised.

How does our emphasis on knowledge impact on how we think about *the social and cultural processes*? One major discussion in social science is about what Peter L. Berger and Thomas Luckmann, in their book published in 1966, called *The Social Construction of Reality* (Berger and Luckmann, 1991). As society increasingly emphasises knowledge products, the process by which knowledge is constructed comes to the forefront. Some have argued that society thereby resembles the field of fashion and art, with new trends popping up constantly. In urban planning, one recognises that people do not only settle where it is convenient, but more and more where it is *trendy*. Contrary to the industrial towns of the modern area, modern urban planning has to be alert to fashions and trends. Trends and styles imply that things become popular, but also fade from social focus quicker than before. People are less bound to their traditional values. Children of a working-class family do not inherit their parents' political views, their lifestyle or their relations to the local grocer. This implies that new types of shop, new types of social interaction and new types of opinion develop faster and less predictably than in the earlier modern or in the pre-modern area.

So how does this impact *the role of social structures*? First of all, there is a general trend in knowledge societies to develop less hierarchal structures. The reason for this is that the monopoly on resources, which allowed a monopoly on power and, subsequently, produced hierarchical social structures, is altered. As they become more educated, people possess knowledge themselves. Today a person can check the diagnosis given by her physician on the Internet. Together with the knowledge society, we see that the idea of administration changes in the direction of being more alert to costumer demands, more service minded and more exposed to competition. However, together with these changes, there is also the question of how the opinions and ideas in the mind of people are influenced by structural dimensions in society. To what extent does structure create new monopolies of power, for example in the form of expert knowledge? To what extent is society transparent and allows knowledge to be exchanged? Are there structural conditions that have to be in place in order to supervise knowledge development? These are normative and factual questions facing the modern knowledge society. They have an impact on issues such as to what extent the Internet should be supervised and to what extent intellectual property rights should be granted.

Institutions and organisations are influenced by the development of the knowledge society. As knowledge is possessed by people, by employees and is more accessible in the public sphere, the older hierarchical systems or organisations change. The knowledge management literature tries to capture these changes and what they imply for management practice. Knowledge workers like to be motivated, to have flexibility and to have influence on their own work situation, and so on. These are conditions that management have to comply with. But also at an institutional level we see changes. The role of institutions and the borderline between them are moving. Universities are increasingly supposed to play a role as part of a system for innovation; public administrations are increasingly defined as service institutions; and businesses are increasingly asked to take social responsibility. These institutional changes imply redefinition of the purpose of the institution, and so it implies new communicative processes in understanding the identity of work. These changes also have more substantial impacts. In the case of universities, the changes we see challenge our understanding of what is science, what is research and what is the relation between science and society.

The development of a knowledge society also has an impact on *democracy and the political processes*. Electors are less loyal to a certain political party than they were a generation ago. The political and ideological positions are less fixed and parties change their profile more often. Much of these changes can be related to the general individualisation in society. As the knowledge society challenges individual reflexivity, it also loosens those cultural/historical fixed bonds to political ideology. As the children to a lesser degree inherit the family grocer, so it is also the case with the political party.

It is argued here that knowledge development and knowledge formation play an important role in all these processes. This makes it important to ask *what knowledge is and how knowledge is developed and distributed*. Something becomes knowledge when it is recognised as such, which implies that knowledge is neither mere information nor purely beliefs. Knowledge is a combination of insights and facts on the one hand and meaning on the other. Subsequently, what we want to know about knowledge is how it is developed, how it is distributed and what implications that has for human conditions and structures and institutions in society. This implies that *knowledge is not the same as truth*.

So I will have to bridge different discourses, such as that of knowledge in natural science and insights from social science. Peter Winch argued many years ago that there probably is no similarity between the two, which means that social and political phenomena can only be understood and interpreted through concepts and propositions that themselves are influenced by social features such as prejudice, consensus dominance and individual expectations (Winch, 1958). Social science is, in other words, the science of interpreting interpretations.

If this limit to interpretations is acknowledged, a reasonable attitude to take is for the researcher to clarify their position and express the normative foundation of their analysis. So let me express mine: my own concern is what I call the liberal argument; how liberal, democratic society, based on the values of individual freedom, the market economy, the system of rule of law and a social order of pluralism and tolerance enhance knowledge development.

My Concept of Knowledge

It is not my intention to describe the nature of the knowledge society (Stehr, 1994). Nor is it to discuss this as sociology of knowledge or a cultural theory or anthropology (McCarthy, 1996). Sociology of knowledge society and cultural theory both represent important insights into knowledge society and how society makes knowledge. But their independent variable is respectively societal development (Stehr, 1994) or culture (McCarthy, 1996). My *independent* and at the same time *dependent* variable is knowledge. My intention is to try to understand what knowledge is, how it is developed and what it does.

A book with the title *Knowledge and Society* was published by Arnold B. Levison in 1974. It is a book that deals primarily with the philosophies of social science. My treatment is larger in scope than mere philosophy of social science, but I also think that we can learn a lot about knowledge development by looking at how science makes knowledge. I discuss this in Chapter 4.

Knowledge, for me, is a *neutral* concept. There might be knowledge that I disagree with. I might regard it as wrong or false, but it might still be knowledge. However, as not all claims and statements are knowledge, there have to be (social) procedures that sort out mere fantasies from knowledge (Chisholm, 1977; Pritchard, 2014). These procedures can be understood as *communicative rationality*. It opens discussion on false consciousness, the need for critical theory and democratic dialogue (McCarthy, 1996; Adorno and Horkheimer, 2010).

I will try to develop a perspective on knowledge where I claim that knowledge is primarily a social phenomenon. Knowledge is what is (socially) regarded as a right understanding of things. Knowledge is not the same as an opinion. Saying it is social also implies that there are warrants to knowledge. The social process somehow sorts out what is knowledge in relation to lies, fantasies, deliriums or meaninglessness. From this it follows that knowledge is a meaning-related phenomenon. Knowledge is not the same as truth. Saying that there are socially warranted understandings of things that we hold as knowledge does not mean that they are true. However, as knowledge is distinguished from fantasies or opinions, there has to be some sort of truth procedures or validity procedures in order for something to be knowledge.

Neither is knowledge just fact. Facts are not knowledge. Facts become knowledge when they are subject to some sort of interpretation. One could say that knowledge is facts plus meaning, but that would be too simple. Knowledge is something we know, or we think we know. However, knowledge is not something personal. I think the expression *personal knowledge* is something of a paradox, or contradiction. I see knowledge as something social. I can have opinions about something that differs from the socially accepted knowledge, but my opinion only becomes knowledge when it is exposed and formulated as a statement or a position that has been accepted as meaningful. I therefore argue that tacit knowledge is something of a contradiction. Also, I believe, the idea that society holds tacit knowledge in the form of culture is a wrong use of the term. Culture has in it many implicit elements, such as patterns of behaviour or rules of conduct, many of which are valuable to society, but it only becomes knowledge when it is exposed and deliberately understood and discussed as knowledge.

Knowledge is different from skills or routines. Skills and routines might be the result of former knowledge. One could say that former knowledge is imbedded in routines or skills or culture. However, these things are not in themselves knowledge. Knowledge is social, explicit warrants to truth, but not truth itself.

This concept of knowledge allows us to discuss the question about whether the mentality in society is a product of material conditions (determinism) or whether our mentality defines our understanding of the physical world (idealism). It allows us to discuss Bourdieu's concept of symbolism in society (Bourdieu, 1993). It also allows us to discuss Hayek's concept of knowledge in the economy (Hayek, 1937; 1945). For instance, is there a distinction between different kinds of knowledge, and do we know if the market produces the right or acceptable kind of knowledge?

This conception of knowledge therefore has many advantages. Firstly, it allows us to differentiate knowledge from other things such as beliefs, culture, routines, skills, opinions, truth and facts. All these can be discussed in relation to knowledge, many of them are based on knowledge, but none of these are knowledge themselves.

Secondly, this concept of knowledge brings us above the type of dualism that has been predominant in management and economic discourses on knowledge (Johnsen et al. 2009). These dualisms between local and universal knowledge, implicit and explicit knowledge, and scientific and practical knowledge, have, as I see it, done harm to developing knowledge about knowledge, rather than illuminating the field. It has created some either/or discussions that conceal the social nature of knowledge.

Thirdly, this concept of knowledge that I try to develop here allows us to discuss the cost of knowledge, investment in knowledge, trusting knowledge, cheating on knowledge and lying. It is also a concept that can help us understand why we always see new knowledge or need to make new investment in knowledge. As knowledge is related to the world and to facts that are constant, but also to our understanding and interpretation that is shifting, knowledge has the characteristic that it is never fixed.

Conclusion

The theme of this book is how knowledge is developed in social processes. I argue here that knowledge is not an objective entity, established once and for all. Knowledge development is interrelated with values, norms, perceptions and interpretations. In these knowledge development processes I will try to explain what the mechanisms are by which knowledge becomes legitimate, true and relevant.

I have called this an academic essay. I find the essay as a form suitable for my task. T.W. Adorno observed many years ago that the essay as a form is different from a more scientific treatment. The essay starts with some generally acknowledged (and not necessarily scientific!) truths and leaves the discussion before it is closed, without reaching some philosophical end (Adorno, 1958). In this way the essay manages to throw some light on the issues raised, open the debate and not conclude or close the discussion. My ambitions are well within these limits.

I have chosen to cover a wide range of topics. That implies that I cannot go deeply into each topic. It also implies that I cannot be very precise on many discussions on how to interpret certain theories and scholars' work. I make rough reference for instance to Schumpeter, knowing well that Schumpeter changed many of his opinions over his lifetime, knowing that he sometimes contradicted himself and knowing that there are different interpretations of his work. I cannot go into all this. So, when I refer to Schumpeter, I use some of his ideas for my own purpose. It will hopefully become clear from my reasoning what part I am using, and why. Also, one of the main points I make is that knowledge develops in discussions and discourses. I have tried to reflect this in my writing by presenting discussions and competing theories and opinions about the topic I discuss.

Based on this, the structure of this book is as follows. The intention is to comment on knowledge development in relation to the following dimensions: the individual in society, the economy and the market, the social and cultural processes, the role of social structures, institutions and organisations, and democracy and the political processes. This is done through the following chapters.

In Part I: 'The Epistemological Foundation of Knowledge', I try to present some positions that are used in the further development of my argument. In Chapter 1: 'Sociology of Knowledge Development', I introduce the sociology of knowledge perspective. In Chapter 2: 'Subjective Reflexivity and Knowledge', I argue that our conception of the individual is central to the discussion of knowledge. I present three perspectives on individual perception: the pure logic of choice, pragmatic socialisation and subjective reflexivity. I discuss how these have an impact on how we understand knowledge formation processes. In Chapter 3: 'Communicative Rationality', I discuss a core mechanism in evaluating the truthfulness of knowledge.

In Part II: 'Knowledge in Social Structures', I present five studies in knowledge development. These are: how science makes knowledge; economic thought, market and knowledge; knowledge organisations: developing knowledge in practice; cultural knowledge and market development; and modernist criticisms and development of social knowledge.

In Part III: 'Knowledge Development in a Liberal Society', I present three chapters that try to discuss implications for social and political organisation. In Chapter 9: 'Knowledge, Market and Social Justice', I discuss the normative aspect of society, with a special emphasis on social justice. I present four perspectives: the naturalist order perspective, the rationalist perspective, the humanist perspective and the discursive perspective. I discuss how these four have different understandings of justice and thereby what is valid knowledge. In Chapter 10: 'Knowledge, Social Systems and Legal Order', I discuss the legal order and the constitution of society, and in Chapter 11: 'Knowledge and Democracy', I discuss the political order. I discuss the distinctions between four visions of the political order: libertarian, republican, communitarian and deliberate democracy.

The Epistemological Foundation of Knowledge

In this part I present three chapters that are intended to form a foundation for the further discussion in the book. Firstly, I try to give my account of the concept of sociology of knowledge. I argue for an understanding of this concept that is in line with my further argument in this book. Secondly, I discuss the theory of the mind. This is important in relation to how we model the individual in our theorising on society. I argue for a position that allows us to appreciate the subjectivity of the individual and to avoid a reductionism in the understanding of people in society. Thirdly, I discuss the concept of communicative rationality. This concept is at the core of the argument in this book and therefore I have to define it before I move on to discussing particular areas of knowledge development.

1 *Sociology of Knowledge Development*

Introduction

The literature on knowledge society, knowledge economy and knowledge organisations emphasises how we can influence knowledge development, through education, investments in research and innovation or through clever organising and development of incentives and motivation. But what is the relationship between how we organise (the social process) and the knowledge that is developed? This, in short, is the issue that sociology of knowledge discusses. However, this discussion is more controversial than it might first appear, because the knowledge in question is not only everyday, practical knowledge, but is largely related to how we come to know things in the first place, or how we develop the fundamental schemes by which we interpret the world around us. So is knowledge socially determined?

Critics have worried that the sociology of knowledge, which implies a contextual view on knowledge, would lead to a form of relativism that undermines the objective value of a democratic society. Because knowledge is the product of social and historical processes, according to the sociology of knowledge, it provides no basis for defending a democratic society as more true and objective compared with other forms of social organisation. However, this argument relies on a misconception which the present chapter is intended to correct. Rather than undermining the value of democracy, sociology of knowledge emphasises the necessity of an open society that permits the production of knowledge. It is precisely because knowledge is the product of a social context that we need an open and democratic society. But in order to develop this argument, we first need to get a better understanding on the nature of the sociology of knowledge.

I will trace the root of sociology of knowledge in three different yet closely connected intellectual traditions – German materialism, French structuralism and American pragmatism. Rather than providing a comprehensive account of these traditions, we will show how they all are views embedded in a social and historical context. Furthermore, we need to take a closer look at the arguments against sociology of knowledge. Based on the conceptual basis developed by tracing the root of sociology of knowledge, I will develop the argument that production of knowledge has a social dimension, but this does not necessarily imply political relativism. This is the case because knowledge is not a homogeneous phenomenon, but takes various forms and shapes.

I will argue in this chapter that the sociology of knowledge has two rather distinct versions, which somehow confuses the debate. On the one hand, the sociology of knowledge has been seen as an epistemology, or a theory about theory. The focus has been on *what is knowledge*? That is, a theory about knowledge. On the other hand, it has been seen as sociology. That is, as a theory of how social groups form knowledge and how knowledge plays a role in structuring social groups and social behaviour, often discussed as social epistemology (Haddock, Millar, and Pritchard, 2010; Goldman and Whitcomb, 2011). In this chapter I will try to present the two, but also to discuss how they relate to each other and what that implies. In relation to the epistemological perspective, we might ask: how can sociology of knowledge help us understand *production of knowledge*? What do we know about the production of knowledge process and value-creation?

If we take the more sociological perspective, we might ask: what do we know about the optimal number and type of institutions in a *production of knowledge process*? What do social sciences know about the relation between institutions in a production of knowledge process? What do we know about organising and managing production of knowledge processes in and between institutions? What do we know about learning and knowledge flows in and between institutions, and its effect on production of knowledge processes and innovation?

The Roots of Sociology of Knowledge: Materialism, Structuralism and Pragmatism

I could start the argument with reference to the late Wittgenstein (2001) and argue that already, by writing, I am taking on a social organisation (language), and by writing in English, I even take on a language that is not my native language. In order to make myself understood, I move into a context of meaning that I will have to comply with. The argument that knowledge is somehow influenced by social organisation is therefore not new. Arguments in that direction can be found in English empiricism (Locke), in the Scottish enlightenment (Smith, Hume), in German idealism (Hegel) and German materialism (Marx). With the development of a sociological science (Spencer, Durkheim, Weber), this perspective became more empirically founded. A classical study is Durkheim and Mauss's study of primitive cultures, where they discovered that religious claims paralleled social organisation in the tribe: religion mirrors society, rather than the opposite (Durkheim and Mauss, 1903; for a discussion see Bloor, 2005).

McCarthy (1996) argues that there have been stages in the development of the sociology of knowledge. There have also been different positions within this line of thought. Marx founded his ideas on materialism. Scheler (1973) and Berger and Luckmann (1991) had a reference to phenomenology. Mannheim tried to develop a concept of ideology. In Durkheim (1902), Weber's (1978) sociology of knowledge is discussed as cultural theory. Merton tries to frame the field within mainstream sociology. Holzner (1968) and Luhmann (2013b) take a structuralist and systems theory perspective and Knorr-Cetina (1999) and Lave and Wenger (1991) discuss sociology of knowledge related to organisation theory.

DeGré (1943) sees sociology of knowledge in the context of stratification: how social groups use knowledge in the sense of ideology to oppress, create resentments and aggression. He also argues for a German (Marx, Nietzsche, Scheler) and a non-German (Durkheim, Mead, Pareto) contribution to the discourse. DeGré argued that Nietzsche, Scheler, Pareto/Sorel, Durkheim and Znaniecki were the main contributors to the sociology of knowledge. Robert Merton (1951) mentions in particular the contribution of Marx, Scheler, Mannheim, Durkheim and Sorokin. Below I divide this discussion into three: the German, the French and the American tradition.

The German Tradition: between Idealism and Materialism

G.F. von Hegel would often be referred to as a main source for the idea that mental structures and knowledge are formed by a nation's specific historical development. As a sort of opposition to this, Karl Marx argued that knowledge is not only materially based; it is also contextual (local and time specific). However, the deeper question is to what extent I am aware of my own knowledge. Marx's study of German ideology (Marx, 1845), stands out as a clear exposition of this perspective. Marx studied the ideological justification of social order in relation to the organisation of production.

> The production of ideas, of conceptions, of consciousness, is at first directly interwoven with the material activity and the material intercourse of men, the language of real life. Conceiving, thinking, the mental intercourse of men, appear at this stage as the direct efflux of their material behaviour. The same applies to mental production as expressed in the language of politics, laws, morality, religion, metaphysics, etc. of a people. Men are the producers of their conceptions, ideas, etc. – real, active men, as they are conditioned by a definite development of their productive forces and of the intercourse corresponding to these, up to its furthest forms. (Marx, 2000)

Jürgen Habermas (1974) presented an argument about this, in line with the critical theory tradition. Habermas starts out by challenging the Marxist universal theory of historical materialism. This theory claims both to be objective in origin and universal in application. Against this, Habermas argues:

> Critique understands that its claims to validity can be verified only in the successful process of enlightenment, and that means: in the practical discourse of those concerned. (Habermas, 1974, p. 2)

One could argue that this position focuses on local practice and local knowledge. However, the fact is that the inherent dialectics of the critical approach implies that one recognises what is criticised, in this case theory. Habermas's point is therefore not one of arguing against general and universal knowledge or theory, rather to argue that theory has to be understood in a special way in social science, as a way of objectivising knowledge in line with Popper (1979b) and Nozick (2001).

Habermas argues along three dimensions – the empirical aspect, the epistemological aspect and the methodological aspect – and comes up with mainly three sets of arguments. The empirical aspect implies that theory has to relate to the general, empirical reality. Habermas (1974) talks about the dual relationship between theory and practice: on the one hand a social practice that makes theorising possible, on the other hand political practice that makes theorising meaningful. Stability of social practice is a necessary precondition for social theorising, *invariance* in Robert Nozick's term (Nozick, 2001). Habermas is not a critic of theory; rather he argues in line with Popper that the social and system world have ontological status (Habermas, 1997; Popper, 1979b). Based on this general understanding, one has to see social theorising in relation to structural conditions in society. As these change, so does the focus of social theory; that is, in modern (post-modern?) society this has brought issues of legitimacy up in front of societal understanding.

The phenomenologist Max Ferdinand Scheler (1874–1928) coined the concept sociology of knowledge in the 1920s. His programme was to develop an argument that would balance an essentialist/*a priori* position on the one hand and a social construction of knowledge on the other (Scheler, 1973). By developing such an argument, he would be able to distinguish between variance and invariance in knowledge formation in society. Scheler, as a phenomenologist, believed in truth and in a fundamental and transcendent order in society.

This programme was heavily criticised by Karl Mannheim (1929). Mannheim makes the argument that ideology (the basic belief system in society) is socially constructed. There is no truth beyond what is socially constructed. Karl Mannheim (1893–1947), with his work *Ideologie und Utopie* (1929) (translated and published in England as *Ideology and Utopia* in 1936), is often referred to as the core, founding text in this field (Mannheim, 1979). He traces the roots and sources of the sociology of knowledge back to Marx and Nietzsche. His argument is that these authors discuss the social and material preconditions and determinations of ideology. Nietzsche's main contribution is to deconstruct and question the concept of knowledge as such. As Foucault writes:

> It is for this reason that in Nietzsche we find the constantly recurring idea that knowledge is at the same time the most generalized and most particular things. Knowledge simplifies, possesses over differences, lumps things together, without any justification in regard to truth. It follows that knowledge is always a misconstruction [méconnaissance]. Moreover, it is always something that is aimed, maliciously, insidiously, and aggressively, at something like a single combat, a tête-à-tête, a dual is set up, contrived, between man and what he knows. There is always something in knowledge that is analogous to the dual and accounts for the fact that it is always singular. That is the contradictory character of knowledge, as it is defined in the Nietzsche texts that seem to contradict on another – generalizing and always singular. (Foucault, 1973, p. 14)

Mannheim's work from 1929 is an interesting and useful account of some of the preconditions and principles that the sociology of knowledge has to comply with. Mannheim, long before social constructivism became a popular phrase and point of (self) reference in the discourse of knowledge, identifies the difficulties that follow from the fact that a sociology of knowledge both has to deal with: (a) which knowledge is constructed in a particular situation; and (b) how to define validity (and truth) over and above the situational knowledge construction. I believe that these are the two large and interconnected questions and challenges that the sociology of knowledge has to address.

The anthropology of knowledge formation was heavily criticised by Mannheim as utterly speculative. In this, Mannheim resembles the Marxist position that all knowledge has a material (social) basis. Merton's way out of this dilemma is not to take a stand on everything there is to be said about knowledge construction, but rather to restrain the scope of the sociological investigation into knowledge formation processes (that is, as a form of cultural analysis). Subsequently, in Merton we might see the conversion of the field of sociology of knowledge, from comprehensive theory formation to a more limited agenda of a disciplinary discourse.

Berger and Luckmann in their *The Social Construction of Reality: A treatise in the sociology of knowledge* (1966) actually went back to Mannheim's broader perspective and discussed how the main belief systems in society (notably religion) are constructed. However, they added other sociological insights into this, such as structural-functionalism and social psychology. They take as a starting point of their analysis the phenomenology of the social world, inspired by Alfred Schutz. Our immediate understandings of social order (rules, norms, routines, structures) are objectivised through, among others, social practice and language. Furthermore, some of these structures are institutionalised and legitimised, and society invests a lot in maintaining some of these structures (for instance, religious rituals). These structures have a socialising effect, and are internalised in people's self-understanding and identity. Berger and Luckmann described a *social mechanism* on the macro level by which *societies internalise beliefs* and through that create structures. Also, they explain how these beliefs become interlocked and self-concealing. They are challenged when immediate, everyday practice and experience contradict these structures and norms. Subsequently, Berger and Luckmann's theory is very well able to explain how traditional and religious societies are challenged by modernism and plural ways of life.

One could see this German discussion as a questioning of the foundation of our knowledge. It is reflected in the work of Adorno and Horkheimer. In their *Dialectic of Enlightenment* ([1944] 2010) they discuss how our understanding of the world can be distorted. Taking Nazism as their main target, they try to explain how mass deception and delusion is possible. They see it as a result of limits to enlightenment and also as an argument for critical theory. How is it that we develop false consciousness, and how do we know that what we believe in, and take as true, actually is true? Actually, this was also the question posed by Mannheim.

French Structuralism

French structuralism refers to works inspired by Ferdinand de Saussure, but can also be associated with the works of the anthropologist Claude Lévi-Strauss and later the sociologist Pierre Bourdieu (Bourdieu, 1990). Structuralism is a perspective that sees our thinking in terms of frames of references and symbolism. This is an elaboration of the discussion of symbolic systems and structures (Durkheim, Talcott Parsons, Pareto, and Berger and Luckmann) on how society forms knowledge through socialisation. This is also a reference to post-structuralist thinkers such as Derrida, Foucault and Lyotard. In their work, the idea of discourse and language as structuring the way we think is central. One can see the world as a multitude of language games (grammars) that are not automatically transcendent and not linked to 'facts'. Foucault, in *The Archaeology of Knowledge* (1989), argues for a constructivist perspective in the sense that we can understand some functional structures of development.

If one were to say something overall about this perspective it would be that individuals have to be understood as part of a larger whole. Bourdieu's work on social structuration, not least his concept of social field and social capital, is illustrative in this respect (Bourdieu, 1993). Individual knowledge as well as individual language refers to a larger system that defines some of the frames for individual understanding. For example, one could see Thomas Kuhn's concept of *paradigms* in science as an example of such structural processes. Lévi-Strauss's work in anthropology also has links to concepts of meaning that can be interpreted as parallel to the concept of hermeneutics (Taylor, 1971).

American Pragmatism

American pragmatism relates to both William James and his objection to *a priori* knowledge (James, 1978) and to Richard Rorty (1979) and his rejection of knowledge as a mirror of nature. Both imply a practical and contextual perspective on knowledge. One of the insights from pragmatism is how knowledge is constructed from interpretation of signs, impressions and dialogues. Insights into the formation of local knowledge (Clifford James Geertz (1926–2006)) also relate to this pragmatic perspective (Geertz, 2000). Therefore it links up with hermeneutics (Gadamer, 2006).

   Robert A. Merton's essay 'The Sociology of Knowledge' from 1945 (Merton, 2005) and his *Social theory and social structure* from 1951 represent a point of reference in this development of sociology of knowledge. What Merton did was to define the sociology of knowledge as a sub-theme of general sociological theory, thereby going back to Durkheim. By doing that, he defined the sociology of knowledge as (and thereby reduced it to) one (among many) sociological perspective and, furthermore, defined the prerequisites that such a perspective needed to have in order to be researchable. Robert Merton therefore presents a critique of relativism (knowledge as culture):

> *Knowledge has often come to be assimilated to the term 'culture' so that not only the exact sciences but ethical convictions, epistemological postulates, material predications, synthetic judgements, political beliefs, the categories of thought, eschatological doxies, moral norms, ontological assumptions, and observations of empirical facts are more or less indiscriminately held to be 'existential conditioned'. (Merton, [1945] 2005, p. 45)*

Robert Merton defined the sociology of knowledge as:

> *Systematic consideration of the social factors in the acquisition, diffusion and growth of knowledge … . (Merton, 1951, p. 247)*

Mannheim had argued, in line with Merton, that the sociology of knowledge does not pretend to explain everything about knowledge, not even to argue that social processes are the only sources of knowledge. However, Merton in his 1951 treatment of the subject is rather critical of some interpretations that Mannheim's analysis might be compatible with, notably some sort of historicist, determinist and relativist argument. Merton prefers to interpret Mannheim in a more pragmatic way, as holding the view that:

> *… thought is seen as but one among many types of activity, as inevitably linked with experience, as understandable only in its relations to noncognitive experience, as stimulated by obstacles and temporary frustrating situations, as involving abstract concepts which must be constantly reexamined in the light of their implications for concrete particulars, as valid only so long as it rests upon an experimental foundation. (Merton, 1951, p. 264)*

Merton (1951) proposes the following questions/challenges that a theory of sociology of knowledge must answer: where is the existential basis of mental productions located, for example in the social structure or in the culture? What mental productions are being sociologically analysed, which spheres, at what level of abstraction? How are mental productions related to the existential basis such as causal, functional or symbolic factors or conditions in society? Also, I would argue that a sociology of knowledge needs to answer: what is the purpose or rationale for this process, what does it lead to or contribute to, and when and where does the process happen, for example on occasions where personal, existential issues are integrated with historical events? In short, how is it that our individual construction of meaning is linked to collective social events?

What Merton (1951) tries to do is to limit the scope of the sociological approach to *practical knowledge construction*, thereby ignoring the ideological/epistemological part of the discussion. Max Scheler (1973), with his phenomenological point of departure, had tried to retain a structure of reasoning where he combined a social construction process of knowledge at one level and an essential development of knowledge at another. He developed what has been called a philosophical anthropology, arguing that the *a priori* knowledge did not limit itself to abstract categories as argued by Kant, but also material ones.

Knowledge System

Holzner, in his 1968 book, makes much of the same argument as Merton. He poses three critical arguments against the Marxist position: firstly, the un-reflected dualism between ideas and real life. This dualism assumes these as mutually exclusive categories, whereas experience tells us that they are interrelated. Secondly, the use of large constructions such as stages in history and social classes, which make it almost impossible to scrutinise the empirical data. And thirdly, the epistemology implied in this reasoning, assuming that both subjects are victims of sociological processes while the researcher himself is outside this epistemology (able to grasp *the big picture*).

Holzner rather argues for a sociology of knowledge that: (1) investigates the socio-cultural processes which shape the construction of reality, (2) identifies the effects of modes of reality construction on social structure, and (3) looks into the distribution of reality constructs in the social structure (Holzner, 1968, p. 18). Holzner furthermore (and to some extent in line with Berger and Luckmann (1991)) deliberately argues for a position on the construction of social reality (sociology of knowledge) that draws on phenomenology (like Alfred Schütz (1972) and Merleau-Ponty (1994)), traditional sociology (structuralism and systems theory) and social psychology (William James, pragmatism). Furthermore, he argues that he should like to avoid the larger debates on the development of our perception of reality as such, but rather have a more limited agenda of situational analysis of the *formation of (everyday?) knowledge*. Subsequently, Merton and Holzner's approach allows us to change the dependent variable, so to speak; the issue at stake is not *how* knowledge is constructed in society, but which type of knowledge is constructed in society (and, we might add, in specific situations)? This last formulation allows us to look at socially constructed knowledge without implying a complete epistemology.

Holzner's argument is that society, deliberately or indirectly, *controls actions*. The constructions of knowledge are thereby a product of *constraints* in interactions. Holzner argues that knowledge influence action, so that controlling knowledge is a way to regulate society. There are three main areas of control: *orientations*, *situations* and *communication*. Orientation is controlled through cultural socialisation, education and rules. Situations are controlled through rituals and norms and expectation related to different roles:

what is appropriate to do at work, in the church or in class? And communication is controlled both directly, in limiting information flows, but also indirectly through the type of normative references inherent in the language.

These control mechanisms have to be seen in relation to the underlying theory of how we as humans learn and are socialised. The micro process Holzner refers to is that of social and development psychologies, where rewards, punishments and recognitions are the main factors in forming the child's social orientation. As adults we meet these mechanisms again, as cognitively developed frames of references that we reproduce in our actions. Networks and epistemic communities are *regulative systems* that presuppose compliance with rules and norms. They develop in parallel with identity formations and thereby there is a sort of self-closing, auto-poetic process by which social structuring is reinforced. This point, as we shall see, was taken up and elaborated upon by Niklas Luhmann.

The core claim of the sociology of knowledge is that social organisation influences what is perceived as knowledge. A strong claim would imply that all knowledge is a function of social organisation; a weak claim would argue that social organisation has some influence on what is regarded as valid knowledge. A rejection of the sociology of knowledge would argue that knowledge is universal or *a priori* in relation to a specific social context. A weak claim will accept some *a prioristic* and some universality, but still argue that organisations, institutions and social processes influence what is regarded as valid, interesting and social facts.

However, Berger and Luckmann's *The Social Construction of Reality – A treatise in the sociology of knowledge* (Berger and Luckmann, 1991), which became a bestseller after its publication in 1966, takes the discussion back to the epistemological level. They discuss the development of our belief system. In their review of the field, they remark that:

> ... American sociologists, who have in the main looked upon the discipline as a marginal speciality with a persistent European flavour. (Berger and Luckmann, 1991, p. 16)

Although this work of Berger and Luckmann is a milestone in the field, it is important to note that their treatise is not intended as a theory of science, or a new epistemology. Their work is mainly within the classical sociological tradition (Durkheim and Weber). I therefore believe that Thomas Kuhn's work on science from 1962, *The Structure of Scientific Revolutions*, could be seen as a parallel development in the field, which addresses the epistemological aspect of seeing science as a social construction (Kuhn, 1970). See Chapter 4 – 'How Science Makes Knowledge'. Kuhn's argument that even science develops within self-referring belief systems, what he calls *paradigms*, leads to a rethinking of what science is.

Elements of the Sociology of Knowledge

To summarise the discussion so far: McCarthy (1996) sees the achievement of sociology of knowledge within three main areas of philosophy – German materialism, French structuralism and American pragmatism. From German materialism we have the argument that there is a need of critical theory because of the development of false consciousness. Ideology could be seen as a result of material, social organisation (Kårl Marx and Karl Mannheim). Marx had shown how the organisation of production leads to belief systems.

However, with Nietzsche (*The Genealogy of Morals* and *Beyond Good and Bad*) the origin of beliefs, ideology and resentment is not to be found in any material base.

One might argue that the field of anthropology (Lévi-Strauss, Margret Mead: see McCarthy, 1996) was devoted to the relation between society and knowledge, but at the same time the original focus of sociology of knowledge (study of ideology and the discourse on the foundation of knowledge as such) came in the background. Sociology of knowledge leads to different arguments against objectivity, but also to the claim by Nietzsche that there are no truths and all beliefs are constructed, more or less like illusions. Versions of this position are seen in post-modernism, in relativism and in what is often referred to as social constructivism. In line with this argument, but slightly different, is the critical theory position. This position holds that social science has a normative role of correcting society. The researcher has a specific social role in ensuring that voices are not suppressed, that false consciousness does not develop, and that truth is not silenced. Another social position, but again slightly different, is the linguistic/communicative turn, which questions the truth in language. As language is a social medium, so will social science be, as it uses language.

When Nico Stehr and Volker Meja picked up the topic in an anthology in 1984 (*Society and Knowledge – Contemporary perspectives on the sociology of knowledge*), they argued that after a decade of decline, there was a renewed interest in this field of study. What we might regard as new perspectives in this field that emerged during the 1980s was the merging of communicative (linguistic) theory with sociology and micro-sociological studies of knowledge formation (at workplaces, in science, and so on). Out of this grew concepts such as communities of practice (Lave and Wenger, 1991), epistemic communities (Knorr-Cetina, 1999) and to some extent knowledge management.

The original discussion had a stronger emphasis on the formation of the more 'fundamental belief systems' than you find in contemporary treatises. Rather than fundamental beliefs, sociology of knowledge has in the last decade been concerned with how interpretation and choices are influenced by how we organise economic and social activity. If we look at some of the contributions from the 1990s, Stehr (1994) discusses how we can conceptualise the knowledge society and, not least, the role of expert knowledge. McCarthy (1996) sees knowledge as culture and discusses it in terms of the post-modern turn. One basic concept she refers to is society as symbol driven (Lévi-Strauss and Bourdieu). Therefore, there are many different conceptualisations of knowledge, even within the sociology of knowledge discourse. Roughly speaking, both epistemological and ontological issues are debated.

Table 1.1   Different kinds of views on science and types of phenomenon

Epistemology/ Ontology	Accessed through universal methods	Accessed through contextual, local knowledge
Phenomenon as universal, stable and repeatable	Knowledge as objective truth reached through universal methods	General knowledge applied in a unique, local situation
Phenomenon as situational, conditional	Knowledge of the local seen in perspective of the general	Local knowledge subject to interpretation

Table 1.1 is constructed along two dimensions: epistemology and ontology. It describes situations of combinations of these two. If we have access to knowledge through methods (realist epistemology) and what we try to understand is stable and universal (ontology), pure positivist science makes sense. In the other extreme, if we only have our subjective understanding of impressions and what we try to understand is situational, our knowledge is more interpretive. It illustrates how one can think of knowledge in different forms and be able to combine situations of rational and non-rational explanations of knowledge.

The Discontenders of Sociology of Knowledge: Hayek and the Fear of Relativism

F.A. Hayek (1944) opposed the attempts to develop a sociological theory of knowledge. Living in Europe in the 1930s and 1940s, where ideological delusion and propaganda were leading whole nations into disarray, he and many others naturally argued that knowledge is and should be something above social construction and manipulation. Hayek, rightfully as I see it, saw a sociological theory of knowledge at that time as an assault on reason, on individualism and on a liberal society. He therefore saw Mannheim's sociology of knowledge, as it was presented in *Ideology and Utopia* (1929), as a relativistic argument leading to totalitarianism, hence Mannheim's communism, and argument against reason and a modern, liberal and democratic society.

The same position was taken by Karl Popper, Hayek's contemporary, who in *The Open Society and its Enemies* identifies sociology of knowledge and Mannheim as a threat against a liberal, open society (Popper, 1945). Peter Sloterdijk, in *The Art of Philosophy* (2012), makes much of the same argument against sociology of knowledge. He argues that, as knowledge has been associated with or linked to interests, knowledge has degenerated from its former position as theoretical and reflexive activity into a form of commodity, or as he describes it: a catastrophe for pure theory. Jürgen Habermas, who argued for the relation between knowledge and interests, is also mainly concerned about how to retain rationality under these modern conditions. It is a project that in many ways is similar to that of Popper (1945) and Hayek (1944) (Mulkey, 2005).

Znaniecki (1940) argued strongly against sociology of knowledge that was intended as a science of science. Such a perspective would imply to question sociology as a science itself. He would rather see sociology of knowledge as a sub-division of general sociology, in the same way as there is sociology of family or sociology of religion. But, as he also observes, this implies that as a sociologist, you observe the relation between social structuring and knowledge, but you do not discuss the truthfulness or validity of the knowledge possessed by these sub-systems. The validity of your research is related to how you observe the social system, not an evaluation of the social systems themselves.

In observing social systems and knowledge, he argues that one can start out with two assumptions: on the one hand, one can assume that the social system selects certain types of knowledge, that is, you are allowed into these sub-systems if you possess certain types of knowledge; on the other hand, you can see the relation in terms of social systems that form the type of knowledge their members have. Niclas Luhmann (1995) with his general systems theory sees this as more interrelated.

Holzner (1968) uses the framework of sociology of knowledge to discuss two structural features of modern society: expert systems and ideologies. Expert systems or professional work group systems exist very much on the basis of controlling information. Their logic of working and prevailing follows the general system of control and reinforcement. Society allows expert systems to develop because they are regarded as essential to certain knowledge and wealth. Ideologies, likewise, are general norm systems aimed at legitimising a certain power structure in society. They are systems that define who we are and who they are, who's inside and who's outside. Subsequently, ideologies will always exist as long as there are social groups, and these groups (by their nature) have to define some consistent formulations that give the group identity.

This perspective is in line with classical sociology: how social differentiation, rationalisation and meaning is developed (Max Weber, Alfred Schutz, Robert A. Merton). The structure of systems helps us understand how power structures are developed in order to control knowledge. A systems perspective would see the knowledge transformation in society (Berger and Luckmann, Bell, Holzner and Marx, Lyotard, Castells, Florida) as a transformation from traditional, modern society to post-industrial or post-modern society, information society, knowledge society, implying changes in the role of expert systems.

For Luhmann (2013a and b), the differentiation of society in expert systems is a precondition for the advances of knowledge. The systems perspective is important in order to understand processes within a system, such as social capital and how power structures are developed in order to control knowledge, as we see in expert systems, hierarchy and norm systems. The development of expert systems and the development of knowledge society go hand in hand. However, Luhmann's conception of systems and sub-systems is dynamic (open). Social systems are self-referential (auto-poetic) in the sense that a system constitutes and reproduces itself. A system exists as a result of an ability to identify *we* and the *others*. A system, like a firm or an organisation, frames and interprets external changes in order to sustain as a system. The major processes of reproduction are communication, integration and interpretation (reformulation of identity). Luhmann thereby tries to avoid the rigidity and determinism of a functional theory.

The Habermas/Luhmann dispute (Holub, 1991) relates to the formative role of communication: can the communicative situation bring in critical perspectives beyond the framework of the communication (ideology or values)? The Weber and Habermas position in the individual–society discussion is about avoiding the reduction of individuality to collective entity.

Mulkey (2005) asks if science is a cultural product: can we combine sociology of knowledge with universalism? The discussion of science has to relate to the ontology of the phenomenon one is investigating: unchangeable, repeatable phenomena should appear in the same way with any method. Changeable, interpretable phenomena must appear differently at different times in different contexts and through different methods.

Bershady (1973) refers to Parsons' critique of *historicism*. He argues that Parsons in *Wissensociologi* sees the same problem of relativism as is the case of German historicism. The argument against sociology of knowledge is then a replica of the argument against the German historical school and the *historiker streit*. This argument is parallel to arguments found in Popper and Hayek, and lies at the bottom of their distaste for the sociology of knowledge argument. However, there are some interesting observations in both Hayek and Popper, more in their works perhaps than in the objectivism of Parsons that argues in favour of subjectivism. Subsequently, this position of Hayek and Popper will have to show how subjectivism and objectivism can be combined in social theorising.

Table 1.2   Individual and social knowledge

	Individual	Society
Knowledge as constant	Seeking certainty, truth, meaning	Certainty here is institutionalised, but the social system should always be challenged in order not to be totalitarian Certainty in procedures and underlying principles rather than specific interest-related knowledge
Knowledge as changing	Changing knowledge refers to learning and improvement in conditions	Society should allow for change, but along procedures regarded as decent, fair and meaningful (democratic processes)

Source: Based on Bershady (1973).

A core question will be how these and other factors influence the production of knowledge; a more fundamental question will be, is all knowledge equally social? A more applied question will be, what particular knowledge is produced in a certain social context? A question related to a larger system perspective will be, how is knowledge made at a local level in a local context transformed through the social system into more general knowledge (for example, a local group of scientists that have their knowledge assessed through peer review)?

But a weak claim implies some special challenges. If all knowledge were defined by organisation and social interaction, this would be all we had to investigate. If society is only partly influencing knowledge creation and only in certain situations and at certain times, and perhaps only some sort of knowledge, we need to define and defend arguments about what, how and where this is.

Table 1.3   Knowledge types: degrees of relativism

Knowledge type/ Discourse form	Local, immediate, situational knowledge	General, invariant, fundamental knowledge
Problem-solving in a particular context	Small group, finding their way; routines, copying, adaptation	Not meaningful, although all individuals reflect on the more fundamental issues in their daily activity; ethical reflection, personal values
Large, societal discourses	Not meaningful, although also the larger discourses relate to local stories; legitimacy through local cases	Long time, large system changes of perception and understanding. Institutionalised structures for deciding legitimate knowledge, challenging through political processes and competing knowledge institutions in society

The questions that the sociology of knowledge perspective raises are: what knowledge is produced in different contexts? How can we explain that particular kind of knowledge? What is the relation between this knowledge and the larger knowledge systems (what discourses do they relate to, where do they find legitimacy)? Fuller (2002) argues that in the knowledge society, the main carrier of legitimacy becomes knowledge; that is, holding the right knowledge, rather than having the right material position, becomes more important and is defining what gives recognition and success in society. This implies that there are categories of knowledge: some more general and fundamental than others.

Is there an economics of knowledge, that is, a rationale for why certain types of knowledge are chosen? Is there also an economics of scale (Fuller, in Stehr and Meja, 2005) of knowledge, that is, good reasons for why some knowledge is chosen by many agents across transactions? Habermas's project is about how to retain rationality (rationalism) in a modern (modernist, post-modern) society. Taking Hegel as a point of departure, he sees the modern society (modernity) as the dialectic between two forces or perspectives: on the one hand, the rational reconstructions of structure based on reason and on the other hand individuality have replaced myths, religion and metaphysics. This development from the renaissance culminates in the Kantian rational philosophy. On the other hand, it involves the recognition of *subjectivity* that in a society based on rationalisation, differentiation and instrumentalisation finds it hard to find meaning. Alienation in the attempt to replace metaphysics with subjective reflection is the core of the sort of restlessness that was exposed later in modernist art. Romanticism already exposed this dialectic: on the one hand, the realisation of subjective sentiments as legitimate (the revolutions in 1830 and 1848); on the other hand, the reconstruction of a democratic society based on order, structure and binding norms.

Conclusion

In this chapter I have tried to present the discourse of sociology of knowledge and discussed how this discourse can help us understand knowledge formation in society. I have tried to address the epistemological aspect and asked: how can these discussions help us understand *production of knowledge*? What do we know about the production of knowledge process and value creation? I have also addressed the more purely sociological aspects and asked: what do we know about the optimal number and type of institutions in production of knowledge processes? What do social sciences know about the relation between institutions in production of knowledge processes? What do we know about organising and managing production of knowledge processes in and between institutions? What do we know about learning and knowledge flows in and between institutions, and its effect on production of knowledge processes and innovation?

As I see it, sociology of knowledge gives valuable insight into knowledge formation in society. My main thesis is that some, but not all, knowledge is a cultural product, produced in a field of social relations, interests, power and structures. However, one of the main challenges with this perspective is that it has an insufficient definition of its dependent variable: knowledge. Roughly speaking, I would argue that there are different kinds of knowledge. Some forms of knowledge are local, time- and place-specific, some are partial. But there are also more universal forms of knowledge.

I have tried to discuss how social processes affect the production of knowledge. We have seen that sociology of knowledge can imply both objectivism and relativism. These are two interpretations or traditions. Even though Rorty or Foucault could be identified with relativism, this relativism is at the same time their argument for a democratic society. That is also why Adorno and Horkheimer (2010) talk about the dialectics of enlightenment. They point out that some modernism has not been to the advantage of society, while others have. They want to rule out false enlightenment.

As I will discuss in Chapter 8 on Modernist Criticisms and Development of Social Knowledge, how many concepts that are of a universal nature might be contested in their application. We might agree that liberty is better than being coerced, but we might disagree what this implies in practice. An illustrating case is how President Obama, in his inauguration speech in January 2013, as a black president celebrated the foresight of the Founding Fathers and their Bill of Rights, knowing very well that the same Founding Fathers accepted slavery.

Habermas, in line with many other social scientists and philosophers, would remind us that no system can observe itself. Can the sociology of knowledge also refer to the sociology of knowledge; how do we know something about the social processes' impact on knowledge, if that is only mirroring our own organisation and social structure? An implication of this is that we have to adopt some sort of meta theory that we cannot prove in itself. Günter Dux (2005) argues that there is an inconsistency between, firstly, a philosophy that will argue that certainty is impossible, secondly, a sociology that will observe society (and try to make true claims) and, thirdly, a psychology that will tell us that humans need constants and structures in order to construct consistency and meaning. For example: most of us are aware of the arbitrary character of many of the categorisations we use in daily life, but we still use them as if they referred to real things and seldom expose the uncertainty they imply. I return to these issues in Chapter 3 on communicative rationality.

2 *Subjective Reflexivity and Knowledge*

Introduction

The conceptualisation of the individual is important in a treatise on knowledge. Put differently, if we are to understand knowledge development in society, we need to understand how individuals form knowledge, that is, how we come to know things. In the debate on this there are different positions. I will discuss three positions – the pure logic of choice, pragmatic socialisation and subjective reflexivity – and I mainly relate them to organisational theory.

When one reviews theories and debates on how individual perception operates, what defines us as human beings and how we come to have knowledge of the world – often referred to as theory of the mind – one is struck by the fact that this has been and is an ideological battlefield. The reason for this is easy to understand. If you have a certain idea of what society should look like, how it should operate and be managed, it has to correspond with your idea of the human being in that society.

As I discussed in the previous chapter, McCarthy (1996), in her treaties on knowledge society, refers to three traditions: German materialism, French rationalism and American pragmatism. They all have their distinct and different epistemologies, that is, understanding of the mental processes in society. They are thereby distinct theories of knowledge development in society. Likewise, some of the ideological struggles within liberal thinking, such as the natural rights theorists versus republican liberals, refer to the theory of mind, as I will argue below. In another example, Habermas has developed a concept of *communicative rationality*, which I will discuss in Chapter 3. In developing this concept, Habermas had to distance himself from Hegel's theory of mind (Habermas, 1987). Also famous is Vilfredo Pareto (1848–1923), who wrote a major sociological treatise with the title *Trattato Di Sociologia Generale* in 1916, which got the English title *The Mind and Society* when it was translated in 1935 (Pareto, 1983). One of the main arguments in this treatise is the discussion of the implication of irrationality at an individual level and how it influences the political processes at society level.

Theory of mind is not only important as a foundation for theory of society; it is also relevant in theories on economy and organisation. If we are to form a theory of motivation, for example, we need to know how motivation works. If we are to form a theory of demand, we need to know how consumers make choices, and, consequently, how they perceive the world. As will be argued in Chapter 5, one of the controversies in the development of economic thought has been over the theoretical assumptions of the individual.

Therefore there is a lot at stake when we develop a theory of the individual and how individuals make knowledge. How should we pursue that? I could try to discuss the different theories and argue which is the right one. I could also just present one assumption and make the claim that this is the right one. Of course there are theories of the mind that I find problematic, either because I see them as contradictory or because they are in conflict with values I hold. I could form an attack on something I believe to be completely wrong, as John Searle in his 2004 book *Mind: A brief introduction* does, when he calls Descartes' dual mind theory 'a disaster'.

What I will try to do is to take a sort of meta-perspective, where I acknowledge different opinions on the theory of the mind and discuss how each of them gives some insight into the formation of knowledge. A reference could be Habermas and his concept of *subject-centred reason*. For Habermas, what characterises modernity is the increased necessity for individual *reflexivity* (Habermas, 1987). Another concept might be the Lacanian form of Marxism, that is, a form of Marxism based on Freud's psychology. It is an argument that leads to what we might call a *social psychology*. A third version might be the pragmatic position, to see individual learning mainly in terms of impressions and challenges in the social sphere. Related to this concept is the idea of a *social mind*. A fourth version might be the neo-classical concept of *rationality*, making it possible to model individual decision-making in economics. Finally, I will point at the concept of *subjectivity*, a concept that models the individual in a more idiosyncratic form than the other concepts.

These five concepts of individual knowledge formation are based on different philosophical assumptions and also have different implications when it comes to understanding knowledge formation in society. They give different answers to questions such as: what is the mental and social process by which we come to form opinions about things? Why do I believe what I believe, and how, if at all, can I assume that my beliefs are right? I try to acknowledge insights from different positions, but I will at the same time try to argue for a position that places a lot of faith in the individual's ability to reflect and form their own knowledge.

In order to make the discussion comprehensible, I will group the different positions into three main groups. The first group I will call *the pure logic of choice*. This group refers, among other things, to theories that refer to themselves as *rationality*, *rational choice* or *methodological individualism*. Also in this group we find *behaviourism*. The second, and to some extent opposite to the first group, I will call *pragmatic socialisation*. In this group we find theories on social psychology (post-structuralism) and social mind (pragmatism). The third group I will refer to as *subjective reflexivity*. Here we find theories such as individual reflexivity (Habermas) and subjectivity (dualism, sensationalism and phenomenology). Some will object to this lumping together of philosophical positions. However, the intention is not to present a philosophical treaty of the mind, but to develop some operating concepts that correspond with the discussion in the rest of the book.

The Body–Mind Problem

The particular part of the philosophy of mind that I will be referring to is the so-called body–mind problem (Searle, 2004): how do we form our opinions about the external world?

The issue here is whether there are mental processes prior to, and independent from, the external world. There is also the issue of how to establish knowledge about the non-sensational mental process. I will refer to phenomenology that deals with this problem. My aim is to study the consequences for theory construction that follows from the two standpoints respectively: does it have any consequences for our reasoning on social phenomena whether individual knowledge is established purely by sensation and, alternatively, that there are non-physically-based mental processes?

The two concepts of mind can, in this rough classification, be termed *monism* and *dualism* (McGinn, 1997, p. 6). Monism is also known as empiricism, sensationalism or behaviourism. The essence of this concept is that everything that is in the mind has come there through sensation of some sort. Therefore, monism is reductionism; all classes of facts or statements can be reduced to another class of fact or statement.

Dualism, on the other hand, is not reductionism, since the idea is that mental phenomena relate to two separate realms: the mental realm and the physical (external) realm (Foster, 1991, p. 1). Dualism is the main element in the philosophy of Descartes – man's need to speculate over his existence and his ability to understand the external physical world in a correct way come from the fact that his mental realm is ontologically separate from the physical world. There is an interrelation between the two realms.

The discussions between monists and dualists have gone on for a long time. Attempts to reconcile the two views have been made (McGinn, 1997; Pettit, 1993). The one aspect of this discussion that is relevant for us here is whether there are any consequences for individual attitude and behaviour that follows from taking one or the other view. Why should we suspect that? Well, logically, from a monist point of view, our knowledge of the external world must correspond with our experience with that world. Non-experienced knowledge cannot exist. At its extreme, one could classify this position as socially deterministic (Popper, 1979a, p. 178). On the other hand, if we take the dualist position, we have the problem of how to separate our knowledge of the external world from purely mental knowledge. How do we interpret the impressions we get from the external world? And what if we have some mental knowledge that exceeds the knowledge of the external world? A positive answer to these last questions would lead to an idealistic position.

A way to deal with these questions, without having to go into the extensive philosophical debate that they represent, is to compare the position that philosophers from different sides of the debate take on more applied issues. If they all take the same view on some practical level, despite their fundamental differences, we can suppose that this fundamental difference has no practical consequences. However, the outcome of this discussion is not obvious. If there is a systematic difference between the two schools on more applied issues, we may conclude that an important reason for this is their fundamental difference in their concept of the mind. If there is no difference on the applied level, the more applied problems seem to be unaffected by the fundamental difference. However, this last result may also follow, if the difference within the school is as obvious as between schools.

Why might it be that a fundamental difference in the theory of the mind does not reveal itself in different positions on more applied issues? One solution would be to say that although monists claim that everything in the mind came there by sensation, they could still argue that the mere complexity of these impressions makes it impossible to trace the relation between sensation and action of some particular kind. This complexity implics that on a more applied, practical level, it is impossible to spot the difference between monists and dualists.

CONCEPTUAL REFERENCES: MONISTS, DUALISTS AND INTENTIONALISTS

Let us see how this works out in practice. I will study this by using J. Searle, A.J. Ayer and Gilbert Ryle as representatives for the monism, Karl Popper and John Foster as representatives for dualism, and Colin McGinn and Phillip Pettit as representatives for an intermediate position that they call *intentionalism*. The question I ask is what do these philosophers say about the following issues: knowledge about the self, identity, freedom of will and consciousness?

Ryle (1990) rejects the argument that there is some dual mental process. A dual mental process could be that, firstly, there is a process by which a person decides to will something, and secondly, a process for the execution of this will. Ryle also makes it clear that the mental process is not mechanistic. He claims that there is no separate process of will formation, and no mechanistic stimulus–response mechanism. Searle (2004) argues that even if there were such processes, they would be impossible to identify, because the whole process by which we perceive the world is so complex, including chemistry in the brain and neurological processes. Consequently, the theory about the freedom of will is one where individuals, in a practical situation, make a decision that is both an articulation of his will and the execution of it.

What then constitutes the self, the 'I'? According to Ryle, the 'I' is constituted by the same process by which I constitute 'you'. This means that there is some higher-order reasoning, by which we are able to characterise and constitute phenomena around us, and this ordering device is the same as (and not different from, as the dualists would claim) the ordering device we use to understand our self. This view corresponds with the view of Giddens (1984). They both argue that the process of understanding our own mental process is parallel to the one of understanding the same process in other human beings.

Free will is consequently something that is easier to observe than to explain. The dualist John Foster argues, contrary to Ryle, Giddens and Ayer, that humans have both a physical and a non-physical mental process, and that in order to understand how they work, you have to understand the attachment between the two. It follows from this that human experience is the same for two persons only if it is attached to the same mental consciousness. In other words, in order to understand the world around us, we should be looking for some pattern, order and structure that represent the same reference for all minds. The experience of space and time might be such patterns. However, each person develops his own private mental biography and, for that reason, no two persons will be totally the same.

On freedom of will, Foster argues that in order for the concept to have any meaning, it must imply that

> the subject himself is, at the time of its occurrence, directly causally responsible for his decisions. (Foster, 1991, p. 273)

This means that it is no other prior condition that can be the cause of this act. Freedom of will must ultimately mean that the subject himself has a unique mental state from where the will is created. Popper, although a proclaimed dualist, emphasises in *Epistemology Without a Knowing Subject* (Popper, 1979a) the social, biological and evolutionary aspect of mind. Popper's system is complicated, since he operates with the distinction between three worlds that are only loosely coupled: world 1 is the world of physical objects, world 2 is the world of mental states and world 3 is the world of objective contents of thought (Popper, 1979a, p. 106ff). Popper further argues that these worlds are autonomous (ontological independent), which means that they are not made by us but can be discovered by us. In Popper's theory, these three worlds interrelate, but the one cannot be reduced to any of the others. By this way of arguing, Popper aims at defending the autonomous mind from materialism (being merely a product of the physical world). At the same time he defends the world of ideas (world 3) from being merely a product of our deliberate construction or manipulation.

The mental process relates to world 2, while most of the human action is within world 3. In this thinking (as with Habermas), the language is essential to link the internal mental process (world 2) to external action (world 3). Popper therefore indicates that the discussion of the mind might be related to the distinction between the practical and the purely theoretical world, or to world 3 and world 1, as he calls it. World 3 is the socially constructed world of myths and stories.

Although McGinn (1997) represents a position that tries to bridge the dualist and the monist position, he argues that consciousness is a genuine novelty in the architecture of species, the fact that makes people different from machines or animals:

> The nature of consciousness is a mystery in the sense that it is beyond human powers of theory construction, yet it is no sense in which it is inherently miraculous. (McGinn, 1997, p. 42)

The consciousness, and the will it represents, is linked to action through embodiment. In McGinn's theory, the mental substance has a means–end relation to the body. Following this, McGinn argues that the self is a unitary phenomenon, not to be divided, and different from what we call identity. While the self is something unique for one particular person, identity might be this same person's attachment to the external world. While the self is unchanging, identity is not.

Pettit (1993) has a different way of reasoning. His method is not to discuss how the mind functions, but how the mind has to function in order to be a mind. He makes an essential distinction between intentionality and thought. A system might be intentional without having thought. Intentional states might be beliefs, habits or desires. The execution of these might be both thoughtful and thoughtless. Therefore, the distinction between thinking and non-thinking entities is important. People are the only thoughtful intentional agents. But where does thought come from? Pettit says little about this. What he develops is a list of criteria and implications of being thoughtful. The requirement of thought is to practise intentional assent and to practise rule-following. But these two requirements are both related to prior and future actions. Action, then, seems to be important in order to explain thought.

METHODOLOGICAL INDIVIDUALISM

When social science theory refers to *methodological individualism*, it implies a reductionist and deductionist claim – all social phenomena must be explainable by either reducing them to, or deducing them from, individual action or intention. The questions that this raises are, firstly, what is the practical meaning of this reductionist/deductionist claim in a complex, developing world? Social phenomena may some time ago have been intended and created by individuals, while they now are institutionalised, and it is impossible to trace them back to their intention. Secondly, what do we mean by individual? Why not, for instance, reduce all social phenomena to neurological processes within the human brain?

The first question relates to the current status of inter-subjective phenomena. Nozick (1977; 1993) claims that in a Robinson Crusoe-world an individual may act rationally or intentionally in his play against nature. However, in a two-or-more-person world, where the intention and expectations of one person affect the intention and expectations of the other, the question of rationality and individuality is more complicated. Nozick observes further that:

> Institutions don't disappear overnight, for they are embodied in the modes of behaviour which don't alter overnight. (Nozick, 1977)

In the same mood, Giddens argues that *structuration theory* (the theory of interception between individual action and social structure) is not incompatible with methodological individualism. This is partly so because, as he argues, methodological individualism is a vague term, and partly because the structuration theory is different from structuralism and functionalism (Giddens, 1984, p. 208). For example, Elster (1989) writes:

> I believe that both norms and self-interest enter into the proximate explanations of action. To some extent, the selection of the norm to which one subscribes can also be explained by self-interest. Even if the belief in the norm is sincere, the choice of one norm among the many that could be relevant may be an unconscious act dictated by self-interest. Or one might follow the norm out of fear of the sanctions that would be triggered by violation. But I do not believe that self-interest provides the full explanation for adherence to norms. There must be some further explanation, X, of why norms exist. (Elster, 1989)

We can identify some problems with the term methodological individualism. They might be summed up in these five issues:

1. Reduction and deduction are not the same. If they are different, something has to either be added during deduction, or it cannot be reduced.
2. Reduction opens the question of reduction to what? Neurological processes?
3. There is the question of time. In what time-span must phenomena be reducible or deducible? Example – can a deterministic system be compatible with methodological individualism? Yes, if it is determined from within (the individual). No, if it is determined from the outside (collective).
4. The status of man-to-man situations, versus man-to-things situations.
5. Individualism as an ontological phenomenon versus a reductive phenomenon.

This implies that methodological individualism is not a term that can make a distinction between dualists, monists and intentionalists. They are all compatible with some form of individualism. While dualism would acknowledge the existence of non-experienced mental processes, monists would treat this as higher-order reasoning. While the self in dualism is distinctly different from identity, the two runs into one in monism. Also, intentionalists regard the self as unique. However, they emphasise the practical means–end rationality of human action. Only dualists would meet a strict definition that requires complete autonomy of the individual (Nagel, 1979, p. 542). But then, following Nozick (1977), we would only be able to deal with man-to-things-situations. Nozick argues that methodological individualism is the only reasonable position to take, because institutions are always dependent variables (individuals are the prime mover).

In the following, I will refer to the intentional (intentionalist) position as the *pure logic of choice*, the monist position as *pragmatic socialisation* and the autonomous (dualist) position as *subjective reflexivity*.

The Pure Logic of Choice

A pure logic of choice conception sees individuals as rational agents optimising their possessions. It is a concept that assumes that agent as decision-maker, and thereby one that has rights, and can make decisions. It is relevant to refer this to the concept of *individual natural rights*. This was a concept used among others by John Locke in his argument against despotism in Britain. But even Locke recognised that reference to natural rights was not sufficient for reconstruction of a liberal civil society (see Chapter 9). Rights were mainly a negative argument. In a more modern treatise of rationality and rights (Nozick, 1974; 1993), the potentials and limitations of this argument have been explored. One of the interesting aspects of Robert Nozick's (1993) argument is that myths and belief are treated as rational phenomena. This means that irrationality is part of rationality as long as it serves some function. Another approach to rationality is presented by discourse theory, elaborated mainly within the neo-Marxist tradition (Skirbekk, 1993). According to this tradition, rationality is defined by the framework of communicative action. That means that rationality is some characteristics of the discourse process and is built into the system of communication. I discuss this in the next chapter.

INCENTIVES

Let us assume that the core of logic of choice is to calculate decisions. An example of such a simple rational model would be a stimulus–response model. The most common simple incentive models are drafted according to the assumption that individuals respond to contracts and incentives, so-called static contracts. The agent in these models trades off effort against wages. Prendergast (1999) and Gibbons (1998) defend the idea that effort will increase by use of economic incentives. They refer to empirical studies on the matter. However, they remind us that most of these studies refer to simple-task situations.

We can extend this simple model in different ways. We could look at multi-tasks (Holmström and Milgrom, 1991). The general argument is that in multi-task situations, you need to be able to identify each task element and the principal needs to establish one incentive per task. Theoretically, one could construct vectors to each task and establish a multiple index of performance. However, in such a case, the principal would not be able to monitor the relative effort by the agent provided to each task-element. The use of economic (price) incentive schemes in multi-task situations, where there is a combination of easy measured and ambiguous elements, could turn out to be altogether counterproductive (Holmström and Milgrom, 1991).

Do these two models make a distinction between different types of action by the agent? No, they do not focus on how the agent performs his or her job, or his or her motives, and thoughts. The incentive models mainly focus on outcome (effort). Therefore, in the cases where there is a discrepancy between measurability of quantity and quality, and where quantity is more easily measured while quality is more important, incentive schemes are not suitable (Holmström and Milgrom, 1991).

CALCULATION AND GAMES

Another way of understanding rationality and the pure logic of choice is to look at game situations. Let us look at repeated prisoner's dilemma (PD) games (Ullman-Margalit, 1977; Leibenstein, 1987, p. 66). The game says that if both parts (let's call them Y and Z) go from conflict to cooperation, both will have a gain. However, if one party cooperates and the other chooses conflict, the party that conflicts will have an extra gain. There is a risk of cooperation, but a mutual gain as well.

This might look a little different in the perspective of an ongoing relation, so-called repeated game situation. Kreps (1990) argues that reputation and repeated interaction might restrain people from cheating, shrinking or acting hazardously. In this case, we could argue that there is a situational element. According to a simple decision of optimisation, one type of action might be chosen. However, if the individual considers this decision in a wider situational context, a different decision is reached.

If a PD game runs only once, and person Z believes that person Y will cooperate, person Z will be able to gain from conflict. With rational expectations, Y would probably not take that risk, and would choose a conflicting attitude as well. In a repeated game, Z is facing a different decision problem, now Z has to compare the present value of conflict to the present value of continuous cooperation. The example illustrates that in a repeated game situation, the trust in others' behaviour is dependent on what value is put on future expected rewards. If one does not bother with future events, or if one is insecure about what rewards one might expect in the future, one will tend to base the decisions more on the present situation than on the future.

Related to an organisational context, one could argue that company cultures, in order to play the function of stimulating long-term investment in relationships by the employee, subsequently have to be convincing (Kreps, 1990; Prendergast, 1999). In the opposite case, a breakdown of company culture tends to induce opportunistic behaviour by the employees. The problem with a PD-game solution is that if one party goes for conflict, the cooperation solution totally collapses. There is no middle way. Gibbons (1998) proposes a relationship contract in this case, in order to signal the company's intention to honour long-term relations and mutual cooperation and development.

THE PURE LOGIC OF CHOICE AND KNOWLEDGE

The conceptualisation of the individual in terms of pure logic of choice implies two reductions: the reduction of the reflexive processes and the reduction of the situational or contextual conditions. This is a theory that brings both down to a level that one is able to overview and conceptualise, and bring forward choice alternatives that are distinct. Knowledge, we could say, is thereby reduced to choice situations and calculations.

Pragmatic Socialisation

Pragmatism is one position that opposes any form of *a priori*. The argument is that nothing of content could be in the mind before we were born. As Searle argues, the whole point in arguing this is to remove the mystery of mind. He argues for a conceptualisation of the mind that relates it to the real world here and now (Searle, 2004). However, one can also argue that this implies some sort of social determinism of the mind. This is first of all an argument against John Locke and his theory of *tabula rasa*. If this idea of *tabula rasa* is true, our consciousness is determined by our surroundings or milieu, because there are no autonomous inner contents in our mind which could resist the influences coming from the external world. This applies also to David Hume (our ideas are formed on the basis of given impressions), and to all forms of empiricism and associationist psychology. One reference to this is the laws of association, which automatically lead to the forming of notions, concepts and memories. It culminates in behavioural psychology, which annihilates human consciousness and reduces man to a deterministic system of inputs and outputs. It is monism in my terms, because it is a form of naturalisation of human psyche. Searle (2004) argues for what he calls *some sort of functionalism*. Our mind, action, choices are somehow determined by social and other factors. I will refer to this as *pragmatic socialisation*.

THE SOCIAL MIND

As already argued, the more conventional sociological challenge to the autonomous mind theory (the ontology of the self) comes from positions that emphasise the sociality of the mind. There are different readings of the social mind theory. In one reading, the self is social in the sense that it is constituted socially:

> The constitution of the 'I' comes about only via the 'discourse of the Other' – that is, through the acquisition of language – but the 'I' has to be related to the body as a sphere of action. [...] 'Conscious' is sometimes used to refer to circumstances in which people pay attention to events going on around them in such a way as to relate their activity to those events. In other words, it refers to the reflexive monitoring of conduct by human agents, largely in the sense of what I have called practical consciousness. (Giddens, 1984, p. 43)

In the social-constructivist model, social processes have identity-formation consequences. In Giddens' (1984, p. 45) words, we can talk about a discursive consciousness. The problem with Giddens' concept of a discursive self is that it presents no mechanism by which the self is not in the process of change. In order to find philosophical backing for their approach, we can refer to thinkers such as George Herbert Mead and Merleau-Ponty. Mead was a pragmatist in the American tradition. The main perspective in his philosophy was that, firstly, the individual is *created* through a social process and, secondly, that the individual *creates* society. Mead therefore represents a particular blend of monism and social constructivism. Mead writes:

> While minds and selves are essentially social products, products or phenomena of the social side of human experience, the psychological mechanism underlying experience is far from irrelevant – indeed is indispensable – to their genesis and existence; for individual experience and behaviour is, of course, psychologically basic to social experience and behaviour: the processes

and mechanisms of the latter (including those which are essential to the origin and existence of minds and selves) are dependent physiologically upon the processes and mechanisms of the former, and upon the social functioning of these. (Mead, 1962, p. 1)

I want to point out, however, that even when we come to the discussion of such 'inner' experience, we can approach it from the point of view of the behaviourist, provided that that we do not too narrowly conceive this point of view. What one must insist upon, is that objectively observable behaviour finds expression within the individual, not in the sense of being in another world, a subjective world, but in the sense of being within his organism. (Mead, 1962, p. 5)

To start with:

We are not, in social psychology, building up the behaviour of the social group in terms of the behaviour of the separate individuals composing it; rather, we are starting out with a given social whole of complex group activity, into which we analyse (as elements) the behaviour of each of the separate individuals composing it. (Mead, 1962, p. 7)

Giddens has built his argument into a larger model. He writes:

Freud divides the psychic organisation of the individual into three, divisions represented in English by the unfortunate terms 'id', 'ego' and 'super-ego'. I do not believe these terms are particularly useful, and shall instead substitute the threefold division suggested in the stratification model: basic security system, practical and discursive consciousness. (Giddens, 1984, p. 41)

He writes:

Ordinary day-to-day life – in greater or less degree according to context and vagaries of individual personality – involves an ontological security expressing an autonomy of bodily control within predictable routines. The psychological origins of ontological security are to be found in basic anxiety-controlling mechanisms [...], hierarchically ordered as components of personality. The generation of feelings of trust in others, as the deepest-lying element of the basic security system, depends substantially upon predictable and caring routines established by parental figures. (Giddens, 1984, p. 50)

This model of Giddens creates a relation between the individual autonomy on the one hand and the individual relation to others on the other. How can we model this situation? Mead writes:

The game is then an illustration of the situation out of which an organised personality arises. In so far as the child does take the attitude of the other and allows that attitude of the other to determine the thing he is going to do with reference to a common end, he is becoming an organic member of society. He is taking over the moral of that society, and is becoming an essential member of it. He belongs to it so far as he does allow the attitude of the other that he takes to control his own immediate expression. What is involved here is some sort of an organised process. That which is expressed in terms of the game is, of course, being continually expressed in the social life of the child, but this wider process goes beyond the immediate experience of the child himself. (Mead, 1962, p. 159)

Merlau-Ponty was a phenomenologist who emphasised the embodiment dimension in the development of the self. For a concentrated expression of Merleau-Ponty's perspective about the mind and the body, I will cite the following:

> To sum up, what we have discovered through the study of motility, is a new meaning of the word 'meaning'. The great strength of intellectualist psychology and idealist philosophy comes from their having no difficulty in showing that perception and thought have an intrinsic significance and cannot be explained in terms of the external association of fortuitously agglomerated contents. The Cognito was the coming of self-awareness of this inner core. But all meaning was ipso facto conceived as an act of thought, as the work of the pure I, and although rationalism easily refuted empiricism, it was itself unable to account for the variety of experience, for the element of senselessness in it, for the contingency of contents. Bodily experience forces us to acknowledge an imposition of meaning which is not the work of a universal constituting consciousness, a meaning which clings to certain contents. My body is that meaningful core which behaves like a general function, and which nevertheless exists, and is susceptible to disease. In it we learn to know the union of essence and existence which we shall find again in perception generally, and which we shall then have to describe more fully. (Merleau-Ponty, 1989, p. 147)

Not all social constructivism would follow this approach. However, the structuration theory of Anthony Giddens has much in common with the social psychology of Mead and Merleau-Ponty, although Giddens emphasises that he does not agree with Mead that the 'I' is, so to say, *created* through the social process. Rather, Giddens prefers to see the expression of the 'I' as a social phenomenon (Giddens, 1984, p. 43). Likewise, Giddens is sceptical regarding the extent of Merleau-Ponty's argument. However, in principle, Giddens, although more moderate, is concerned with the same perspective.

Mead and Merleau-Ponty are more specific than Giddens about the philosophy of mind. What Merleau-Ponty does is to give an account of what embodiment implies; it is related to the practical level of awareness. Mead, on the other hand, declared himself a *behaviourist*. At the same time, Mead qualified this term: man is not an animal that responds blindly to external stimuli. When man is confronted with the external social world, he is able to make his own judgement. The mechanism Mead is presenting is one where the twin activities of being formed by society and forming society are integrated.

Also, Mead (1962) is concerned with games and their implications. Mead's main argument is that the individual (in this case a child) involves games as part of their development in social terms. This involvement is linked both to their understanding of others, their understanding of social rules, and their forming of their own self. At first sight, at least, it seems that Mead is talking about a game as a process that exceeds the formal implications in Nozick's theory. Games are in this context related to the development of scripts, or natural (ontological) forms. The individual's participation in games influences its understanding of these scripts and forms.

When Giddens (1984) and social constructivists such as Berger and Luckmann (1991) are able to combine the insight of Mead and Merleau-Ponty, it is due to a very important step they make in their argument. They limit their analysis to the individual perception of practical knowledge. The point where this leads us is a comprehensive model where both the constitution of the self, including autonomy, the development of the self and relation to others (the basic security system), and the relation between the self and the bodily expression are incorporated. If we add to this Mead's emphasis on symbolic expression in the discourse, we have established the main elements of the social constructivism perspective.

This early discovery by Mead anticipated what has later been called the cognitive revolution. The term cognitive revolution is ambiguous, but refers mainly to the discovery of mental processes that could form the basis for artificial intelligence and, subsequently, the development of computer processing (Bruner, 1990, p. 6). The main discovery was that intelligence does not operate in terms of solving the almost endless equations in order to make decisions. Rather, it operated in terms of patterns, scripts and symbols. The ability to recognise patterns and develop cognitive scripts and maps are essential mental processes.

CONFORMITY

What are the consequences of this perspective for organisation theory? Maehr and Kleiber (1985) argue that persons invest in certain activities depending on the meaning these activities has to them. Meaning is also composed of three interrelated (situational) conditions: goals, self-concepts and action possibilities. One can imagine some typical types of situation where the response to individual, external incentives is different.

Also customs represent a motivating force that arises from the individual striving for coherence and justification. Customs emerge from the individual desire to align behaviour, conviction and emotions tightly with another. Individuals have preferences for patterned behaviour, for acting according to their convictions, and for forming their convictions according to what they are experiencing (Schlicht, 1998). If this is so, we might argue that there is a meta-preference for conformism that transforms (endogenously) actual experience, through conviction, to alignment of behaviour according to customs. Individuals form meaning systems related to the context by which they are socialised.

This is observed in organisation theory. Kreps (1997) argues that there might be situations where norms are internalised in the sense that adherence to these norms is a good in itself. This leads to the argument of intrinsic motivation. The explanation Kreps (1997) gives is that people adhere to certain norms (and not others), not for reasons of (repeated games like) calculation, but simply because some norms are endogenous (part of their utility function) and others are not. Taking intrinsic motivation seriously means having a more subtle understanding of people's individual systems of values and norms.

A clue to this theme could be Habermas's concepts of life-worlds: certain norms are related to certain life-worlds. In the intimate, family-like life-world, opportunistic behaviour is not accepted, while it might be accepted in the more remote, abstract market systems. Following this rough classification, one could explain the seemingly paradoxical finding that extrinsic rewards reduce motivation by arguing in the following way: if in a team situation, a certain set of norms have evolved as the team members develop family-like, intimate relations, the introduction of extrinsic incentives and reward systems might jeopardise this intimate life-world and activate the more opportunistic behaviour of the market system.

There can be situations known as bandwagon effects (Leibenstein, 1987. Bandwagon effects imply more elastic responses to external changes than what the sum of individual action implies. Bandwagon effects reinforce those tendencies that are already there. Consequently, bandwagon effects might explain how customs are maintained. A combination of game-based effects and bandwagon effects might explain why certain norms are (seemingly) internalised. Bandwagon effects explain why a certain norm that has been established through a coordination game mechanism is maintained and reinforced. This two-sided pressure is difficult to explain in a theory of individual action where only the individual disutility is present.

Maehr and Kleiber (1985) talk about meaning systems and personal investment. This is a conception that adds to the personal dimensions, such as Etzioni's (1961, p. 10) concept of value-loaded personal meaning systems, Bandura's (1986, p. 454) concept of cognitive meaning-system, intensity of preferences (Etzioni, 1961; Kuran, 1995), complexity and maturity (Schütz, 1972), which gives a link to the self-realisation theme and communicative action (Habermas, 1997).

In all these examples, we do not explain why people adhere to certain norms, only what the effects are when they do. People might be snobs (deliberately choosing what the best does), or for their own reasons choose to be non-conformist. These choices are not explained as such in the theories we have referred to here. Culture has the function of framing. Culture as such is a neutral concept in relation to the contents of the norms. For instance, a cultural system needs symbols, it is dependent on participation, there has to be a communication and information provision, and it probably must be related to some comprehensive structures (reward system and ranking). In short, a culture will sort out what is regarded as appropriate from non-appropriate action within an organisation.

Economists have been trying to incorporate these effects into their models. The most fundamental of these attempts has been to redefine the neo-classical notion of preferences (Becker 1996; Bowles 1998). Making preferences endogenous means that the individual actor is not as sovereign in their choices, as we would assume in a neo-classical model. It implies that social conditions somehow influence choice. However, the trick of making preferences endogenous does imply a broadened concept of preferences, one that could be criticised.

PRAGMATIC SOCIALISATION AND KNOWLEDGE FORMATION

In pragmatic socialisation, we can talk about a perspective that implies a reduction of the mental process but a complex perspective on situation and context. The theory tries to reduce complexity in mental processes in order to be able to see some patterns in how the individual relates to complex situations. One could say that this perspective allows for complexities of knowledge in social situations, but a reductive perspective on the individual's processing of the knowledge.

Subjective Reflexivity

Autonomistic theories of the individual are found in Descartes, Kant, Brentano and Husserl. According to these theories, there exists an autonomous ego – self-reflecting (Descartes), or transcendental (Kant and Husserl) – or that there exist intentional acts, which are not submitted to natural causality (Brentano). Precisely this is the basis of human autonomy according to them. Hegel, as I will argue below, represents a special case here.

These principles constitute a sphere of spirit or *Geist* (in German), which does not depend on empirical circumstances and forms the basis for our dominance over external and inner nature and instincts and also for our resistance to empirical social and political pressures (like Kant's categorical imperative). These theories are dualistic in my terms.

This group of theories enables to consider individuals in organisation as free autonomous units which can be determined from the outside only to a certain degree. In relation to explaining organisations, it implies the method of understanding dialogue and other forms of interaction rather than presenting a deterministic theory.

F.A. Hayek, particularly in his last work on evolution (Hayek, 1988), is trying to combine the individualistic approach of classical liberalism with a collectivistic approach of evolution similar to that found in Herbert Spencer (1981 (1850), p. 367ff) and Joseph Schumpeter (1976 (1942), p. 121ff). John Rawls has made considerable effort in order to argue (or even prove) that there is a rational (freely chosen) social order that has some humanistic features (Rawls, 1971, p. 11). A more than a century-old idealistic tradition within democratic theory has been taken up by philosophers such as Loren Lomasky, where human development and flourishing is supposed to be a major driving force in social development (Lomasky, 1987, p. 16). French idealist tradition, for instance Emmanuel Lévinas (1972) following Henri Bergson, has argued that creativity and social order develops not in the individual mind, but when the individual is involved with other individuals. In all these approaches there is an appreciation of subjective reflexivity.

THE ANTIGONE MYTH

As a starting point for this discussion, I will refer to the Antigone myth, because that is one of Hegel's references in his *Phenomenology of Mind* (Hegel, 1966). In his play *Antigone*, Sophocles tells the myth of the two brothers of Antigone, Eteocles and Polyneikes (children of King Oedipus), who fought and killed each other during the struggle over the rule of Thebes. King Kreon of Thebes ordered the body of Eteocles, who defended the city, to be buried, while his brother Polyneikes, who attacked the city, was to lay unburied on the ground (a cruel destiny according to Greek mythology). Anybody trying to bury the body would be punished with death. The sister, Antigone, the future wife of King Kreon's son, disobeys the king's order. She buries the body and is sentenced to death. The king orders, against the general mood of the people, that she be locked in a cave. Here she takes her own life. The king's son kills himself in anger over his father. King Kreon's wife does the same over the loss of her son. King Kreon falls into endless despair, and so the tragedy ends.

Antigone is in this myth torn between duty, her inner consciousness and the laws of society. The act to follow one's own consciousness is, according to Hegel, the realisation of oneself. Self-existence only comes about through acting and thereby realisation of the self. But the act happens within a social, ethical context and can therefore not be the full realisation of the inner self.

From this process of duty and guilt, starts a complicated discussion of the interrelation between the individual consciousness and the social, ethical reality. In the case of the family, these two levels can more easily be intervened and reconciled than in the case of the whole society. Antigone and Polyneikes share, so to speak, the same spirit. (In fact, Antigone did not have any real choice, because her life strategy already had destined her to take the position she did.) In the case of society, Hegel does in fact speak of a public spirit, and argues in favour of balancing this spirit with the individual consciousness. Latour (1993) sees Antigone as the impossibility in self-realisation.

Organisation theory has only a superficial attitude to these issues. Reference to terms such as company spirit, emotional labour and organisational learning is made without the sincere discussion of Hegel about these terms (Argyris and Schön, 1996, p. 6). What does it imply to talk about a company spirit, what kind of ethical issues are at stake in emotional labour, how do we perceive the individual within the organisation? How often is the term guilt used within organisation theory? In general, it seems to be the case that organisation theory has avoided philosophy, and instead looked to psychology in order to develop its behavioural foundation. G.W.F. Hegel writes:

> *Acting expresses precisely the unity of reality and the substance; it expresses the fact that actuality is not an accident for the essential element, but that, in union with that element, it is given to no right which is not true right. On account of this actuality, and on account of its deed ethical consciousness must acknowledge its opposite as its own actuality; it must acknowledge its guilt. (Hegel, 1966, p. 491)*

Hegel goes far to indicate the interrelation between the inner life and the ethical sphere. One reflection from the discussion of Antigone is that more complicated ethical and related issues arise as we are more involved in a situation. Some people's values and opinions creates issues that are not present in other people's minds when they do not hold the same values. Hegel's inner consciousness can be interpreted as anti-liberal.

Eudonomy in the Aristotelian sense meant to be a sound politician that, in modern terms, is a social-minded individual. The Aristotelian concept of eudonomy is not individualised, but rather a form of essentialism similar to what is later found in Hegel. The idea is that existence is supposed to actualise some essence or meaning that is prior to existence. This idea was reversed in the existential philosophy, where existence was supposed to be prior to essence. Both these ideas are anti-liberal in the pure empiricist sense.

Also the argument of human flourishing, which we can find in early writings such as Mill, has been termed neo-Aristotelian with reference to the Aristotle treatise of the human good. As Gray (1989) has pointed out, there is very little reason to regard Aristotle as a liberal. In fact, he did not have any sympathy for the pluralist way of life in the modern liberal sense of the word. That is why he saw no conflict between prudence and morals, between values and rights. Aristotle seems to have assumed that there are some universal concepts of prudence and that these are all in accordance with morals. It is only on this totalitarian assumption that the human flourishing argument makes sense, and therefore it is inadequate as a liberal argument.

Habermas argues on the other hand explicitly that his conceptualisation of the autonomous self is not of this Hegelian kind where there is a predefined consciousness that stands in a conflicting relation to society (Habermas 1997, p. 81). The main arguments Habermas presents against this Hegelian construction is firstly that it does not present us with a reflective mind and secondly that it portrays society as a fixed and not a discursive entity. As I will elaborate further in the next chapter, one of the main arguments of Habermas is how reflexivity is developed under conditions of modernity.

PHENOMENOLOGY AND SENSORY ORDER

Phenomenology in the Husserl sense claims that laws of thought are ambiguous and might reflect the regularity in the thought world, or they might mean the standards by which we decide whether a person uses their perception and mental capability properly. Phenomenology in Hegel and Husserl's sense is thinking about thinking, or reflections on reflections. Phenomenology is reasoning about the nature of things and the qualities that real things have to have in order to be able to perceive and reason about them.

Hayek refers to the central idea of phenomenology, that there is both a physical and a mental world, and that we perceive the world through our psychological mechanisms. Our mental order contains ordering devices and ordering patterns that help us perceive the world. But the world that we see is only the psychological world; even logic is a psychological phenomenon (Copleston, 1985, vol. VII, p. 432). This is phenomenology in the Ernst Mach sense. Edmund Husserl called this psychologism – the idea that fundamental laws are mere psychological generalisations.

Hayek admits that the development of his thoughts have been influenced by Ernst Mach and his theory of sensation (Hayek, 1976c, p. 176). However, Hayek points out that there is an important difference between his theory and that of the phenomenologist's: the evolutionary theory of sensation. As long as our ability to understand the world is in constant change, it is impossible to establish absolute knowledge about the physical world. Our knowledge of the physical world will have to be general knowledge. Hayek therefore criticises what he calls psychological rationalism: that we can manipulate and construct the physical world.

Related to Hayek's thoughts are the ideas of his cousin, Ludwig Wittgenstein. The idea of a non-verbal or pre-verbal conversation leads very easily to the notion of tacit knowledge (Polanyi) (ref. Bloor, 1983, p. 120). This is related to the idea of evolution since tacit knowledge has grown through an evolutionary process. The evolution of order is in Hayek's context both a mental and a social process, which brings us to the problem of social equilibrium.

Hayek elaborated his physiological theory in a book published in 1952, *The Sensory Order*. However, we know from his biography that the main elements in this theory were developed more than 20 years earlier, and we may therefore assume that Hayek had these thoughts in mind when he wrote about equilibrium. Some quotations from this book will help to clarify his position:

> *The gradual evolution of the mental order involves thus a gradual approximation to the order which in the external world exists between the stimuli evoking the impulses which 'represent' them in the central nervous system. But while conceptual thinking has long been recognised as a process of continuous reorganization of the (supposedly constant) elements of the phenomenal world, a recognition which makes their arrangement correspond more perfectly with experience, we have been led to the conclusion that the qualitative elements of which the phenomenal world is built up, and the whole order of the sensory qualities, are themselves subject to continues change. (Hayek, 1952, p. 107)*

What is important here is that Hayek on the one hand makes a distinction between the physical world and the sensory world, but on the other hand, he says that our sensory world is not only a question of how we are able to perceive the physical world, but rather, that the perceptive function of our sensory world is formed by the experience of the physical world. On the other hand, the ability to perceive the physical world is limited by the structures and maps of the mental world:

> *This means that we can know only such kinds of events that show a certain degree of regularity in their occurrence in relations to others, and that we could not know anything about events*

which occur in a completely irregular manner. The fact that the world which we know seems wholly an orderly world may thus be merely a result of the method by which we perceive it. Everything which we can perceive we perceive necessarily as an element of a class of events which obey certain regularities. (Hayek, 1952, p. 176)

Subjective reflexivity should imply that we see the human mind capable of making assessment of situations in ways that bring together different kinds of information and experiences from a non-deterministic point of view. This is in line with Alfred Schütz, who writes:

Here we are not referring to differences between the personal standpoints from which different people look at the world but to the fundamental difference between my interpretation of my own subjective experience (self interpretation) and my interpretation of the subjective experience to someone else. What is given to both the acting self and the interpreting observer is not only the single meaningful act and the context or configuration of meaning to which it belongs but the whole social world in fully differentiated perspectives. Only through this insight can one understand how the other self is grasped as an ideal type in the sense we have just discussed. (Schütz, 1972, p. 8)

This means that there are some aspects of human living (life-world) that are, and in my mind should be, inaccessible to social processes and also that there is possibly always an element of strategic thinking (role-playing), even in an involved situation. Further I will argue that, by acknowledging this, we can have a better discussion about what knowledge from the human life-world is possible and relevant in the social discourse. The inner contradiction between the uniqueness of impressions and the comprehension and meaning-construction of knowledge is something we have to comply with (Weber, 1978; Schütz, 1972; Mead, 1962; Merleau-Ponty, 1989).

SUBJECTIVE REFLEXIVITY AND KNOWLEDGE FORMATION

The subjective reflexive perspective on knowledge implies that one retains a complex view both on the situation and contexts that knowledge is part of, and the individual processing of knowledge. This means that we cannot model these situations in simple models. There is a complex set of knowledge and a multitude of processing activities that makes the outcome of a particular knowledge situation undetermined. Only at a more general and abstract level can we model these relations.

The Mind and Society: How Can We Theorise Individuals in Society?

I have argued that we can identify different positions on the theory of the mind, and on how individuals process knowledge. The three models or categories I have presented give very different explanations of this. In the pure logic of choice model, individuals calculate gains and losses according to preferences. In the pragmatic socialisation model, sociality and the social process are important factors as forming norms and meaning systems. In the subjective reflection model, the individual choices are based on inner values and opinions. I have also argued that there are crossovers between the three. Habermas has increasingly referred to pragmatism, and the phenomenology of Lévinas can be read within a pragmatic set of thinking (Craig, 2010), to mention some. This is not to argue that the differences do not mean anything, because their differences are really fundamental. Rather, the purpose is to see that some new perspectives might appear if one has a dialogue between the positions.

Knowledge formation is based on both individual reflection and the social processes it plays into. The social order is a result of individual action, but it is not a totalitarian order, it cannot be a result of the deliberate design of only some individuals. Rather, as has been stressed by Hayek, it has to be some sort of un-designed result of individual action.

A social theory is a classification and categorisation of social events (Glaser and Strauss, 1967, p. 36), which means that we in theorising remove ourselves from the unique, subjective life-world. If we reject any classification, and/or only report the subject's idiosyncratic experience (phenomenology), I think we basically will have defined ourselves out of the scientific discourse. Subjective knowledge, even reflexive subjectivity, is mediated in the social discourse. A subjective story is true in its own right. But this subjective account might from another perspective be wrong or untrue.

I follow Bourdieu in *The Logic of Practice* (1990) when he argues that (A) social science is basically a reflection over practice. One of his fields of study, symbolic action in society, can illustrate this. His reflections on symbolic action lead him to develop concepts such as symbolic capital, and the role of symbolic systems on structuring of society. (B) Our ability to understand practice is actually dependent on the theoretical concepts and perspectives that we have. Better theories and better and deeper conceptual understandings will allow us to also understand practice better. (C) Social science is in itself a practice. In order to understand the theoretical universe of social science, and how science make sense of practice, we also have to understand that much of what we observe in practice also points back to social science as a practice.

So, is there an essential difference between practical knowledge and theoretical knowledge? This distinction is important in relation to Habermas's theory of communicative action. It points at the issue of whether there is a theoretical entity prior to practical action: in other words, is theory superior to practice?

Barry Smith writes:

> *Practical knowledge has been brought to the attention of philosophers in recent times, on the one hand by Ryle, with his distinction between knowing how and knowing that, and on the other hand by Heidegger, whose philosophy rests centrally on a view of the structure of our ordinary experience as determined primarily by the hierarchies of interdependent objects of use (tools, equipment) with which we are continually bound up in our everyday activities. (Smith, 1986, p. 22)*

The reflective practitioner (Schön, 1983) and situated learning (Amin and Roberts, 2008b) emphasise the importance and superiority of practice and locally developed knowledge. See also Göranzon and Ennals (2006) on practical knowledge. However, research must have categories that guide your mind, but that will also characterise your induction. I return to these issues in Chapter 6 on knowledge organisations.

How can a researcher in practical terms look for and identify more universal, scientific knowledge (Johnsen, 2013)? Methodological debates are about finding methods for more valid and true knowledge. Sociological studies are focused on the patterns of action and organisational forms and structures that are involved when scientists do their research. But, there are different conceptualisations of the actor in social and economic theory. Coleman (1975) argues that:

> [...] the perfectly competitive market is a paradigm of individually rational, noncooperative, unconstrained social interaction. Each .agent is motivated only by a desire to maximize his or her utility function. (Coleman, 1975)

Furthermore he writes:

> [...] the morality that makes competition possible is itself a collective good. It follows, then, that co-operative, collective action, in this case the provision of morality, is logically prior to competition. (Coleman, 1975)

This also has epistemological aspects because, if it is so that organisational forms and ways of working have influence on research, it implies that it will also have influence on what is regarded as valid and true (see Mulkey 2005). Hayek writes:

> If we can agree that the economic problem of society is mainly one of rapid adaptation to changes in the particular circumstances of time and place, it would seem to follow that the ultimate decisions must be left to the people who are familiar with these circumstances, who know directly of the relevant changes and of the resources immediately available to meet them. [...] But the 'man on the spot' cannot decide solely on the basis of his limited but intimate knowledge of the facts of his immediate surroundings. There still remains the problem of communicating to him such further information as he needs to fit his decisions into the whole pattern of changes of the larger economic system. (Hayek, 1945)

How can true knowledge about the other be generalised or converted into more general knowledge about humans and society and still be respectful to the person we observed and their subjective personhood? Hayek (1967) and Krugman (1991) argue that complex phenomena can be approached with simple models. A predominant example would be the market equilibrium model that has a very strong explanatory power in spite of its simplicity. Another example could be Granovetter's theory of strength of weak ties in networks (Granovetter, 1983). Simple models and simple mechanisms in models help us see some generic aspects of a complex reality. So simple models in social science does not have to imply a reductionist or deterministic view of the individual. A very different strategy would be Clifford Geertz's thick description (Geertz, 1973). A thick description is used to identify the uniqueness and context specificity of a phenomenon. It is a meaningful strategy when what you want to explain is the unique locale and the interplay of a complex set of factors. In between these two strategies one can think of more context-specific models of a different kind.

A NEW YORK PICTURE

I have a picture on my computer taken while I was in New York City, taken in the park at New York Public Library. It shows the park, the library and the typical Manhattan skyline.

I can hardly see myself in the picture on my computer. However, I can zoom in on different areas of the picture. When I do, I get a close look at myself sitting at one of the coffee tables in the park, the skyline disappears, and so does the public library. The only things left in the picture are myself and a women sitting by another table in the park. Anybody with no insight into the situation could have interpreted from the picture that there was some sort of relation or dialogue going on between the woman and myself.

When I presented this picture in a class, a student commented that she thought that the woman and myself had had a quarrel. In the picture we are both alert, but the truth is that we are not attending to each other, and not looking at the same thing. In fact, I have no idea who she is. However, this is not obvious when you only interpret the picture. As I zoom in even more, I am the only one present in the picture. It could have been taken almost anywhere, and it gives the impression that I am sitting alone in a quiet place, contemplating. Nothing tells the spectator that this is in the middle of Manhattan. As I zoom out again, I am back to the city skyline, to the structure of the city where no single individuals or small details are identifiable.

Involvement is partly a process of zooming in, looking into details and trying to understand the other. I think that close, engaged involvement gives us access to intimate, detailed knowledge that we probably would not be able to see in other ways. But at the same time, it does so at the expense of other knowledge, such as overview or *the big picture*. However, I will argue that we can also see a greater picture in the small, intimate scene.

How to establish a relation between subjective, involved knowledge and social, true knowledge depends on what perspective one has on what is objective, true knowledge. Roughly speaking one can argue that there are two extreme positions: a relativistic and an absolutistic (Blackburn, 2011. The problem with the relativistic position is that we never get beyond the local, subjective story. There is nothing substantial beyond the subjective world (life-world), what are beyond that are different language games (Lyotard, 1979). Absolutists and realists (Nagel, 1979) will criticise relativism as meaningless and argue that there is an objective reality that subjective accounts have to comply with. This objectivity thereby represents a scale or standard on which one can evaluate the trueness of the subjective story. However, this absolute truth could be a treat to individuality. An in-between position, inspired by Weber, argues for inter-subjectivity as the basis for collective entities. Searle (1995) is among those who argues for such an inter-subjective position.

As a theoretical framework for discussing this, I will in the following use Habermas (1997) and his distinction between the life-world, the social world and the system world. The argument will be that involvement brings us closer to what we might call the life-world: our inner, subjective experience. Furthermore, I argue that scientific knowledge belongs to both the social world and the system world. When a researcher gets intimate, personal (life-world) knowledge through involvement, they have to convert and communicate this knowledge to the scientific community. I will later, in Chapter 4 'How Science Makes Knowledge', try to argue how knowledge from the life-world is converted or transferred into social, systemic scientific knowledge. In Table 2.1 I have tried to indicate how different combinations of type of involvement and situations produce different kinds or areas of knowledge.

Table 2.1   Transformation of knowledge

Transformation	from involved ...	to non-involved
from person ...	1) Knowledge of intimate experiences	3) Knowledge of the more general human experience that this exemplifies
to situation	2) Knowledge of the circumstances of this episode take place, what made it possible	4) Knowledge of what general learning can be made from this event that is relevant for other people (that they might identify with) and could appear in similar situations

Table 2.1 tries to illustrate how both involved, intimate knowledge can be combined with more general knowledge dependent on how you choose to see and engage yourself in a situation. We see different things when we are involved than when we are not involved; we see some things more clearly, and leave other things out, but we might also misinterpret what we see. Involvement changes the focus and the substance of what we perceive.

The subjective story we learn through involvement might be false. Internal validity will not automatically imply external validity. So we need to establish a relation between this subjective, involved knowledge and what we can verify as true knowledge. Secondly, one can argue that those who have been involved in knowledge-creation bring this knowledge (story) to the scientific community and thereby there is an interpretation which in practice is a sort of external validity test.

Honneth, who is using Hegel as a reference when he, in his *Kampf um anerkennung* (1992), argues that recognition at a personal level is transformed into a social and structural level of society. This transformation implies that a similar phenomenon takes a new form as we go from one social level to the other. There is a sort of translation of the phenomenon into a new form. This is methodically in line with Habermas (1997), although the two disagree on the ontological status of the different levels. I therefore use this roughly as an approach to discussing how involved knowledge is transformed into scientific knowledge.

In Honneth's analysis of recognition (Honneth, 1992), he argues that self-confidence in the intimate private domain parallels recognition in the social domain, and that love and affection in the private domain parallel solidarity in the social domain. I believe that this is a valuable and meaningful way of arguing. It implies that we do not argue that the one phenomenon is reduced to the other, for example that solidarity is the same as love. Rather we argue for a transformation that shows the relevance of one phenomenon in relation to another.

While the simple model in social science is able to say something about generic features of social processes, and the thick description is useful in order to understand the local, specific and unique in a phenomenon, the context-specific models can easily fall into the intermediate category of neither being general enough nor being specific enough. These are issues and dilemmas we have to live with.

Conclusion

In this chapter I have discussed the implication of theories of the mind for knowledge development. I have talked about degrees of reductions in conceptualisation of knowledge formation, both in relation to the individual and in relation to the context and situation the individual is in.

I have presented two philosophical positions on the theory of the mind: monism and dualism. And, I have discussed there different conceptualisations on the individual–society relation: the pure logic of choice, pragmatic socialisation and subjective reflexivity. I have tried to argue for an individual–society relation that does not represent a reduction of the subject.

Based on the argument that we in terms of subjective reflexivity are facing rather complex knowledge formation processes, I discussed in the last part of the chapter how we can theorise and research knowledge development under these conditions.

3 Communicative Rationality

Introduction

In this chapter I will discuss the concept of *communicative rationality*. In short, this is a concept developed by Jürgen Habermas in response to the challenge of establishing rationality and reason in the public domain under conditions of subjective reflexivity.

Habermas distinguishes between three major structures: life-world, social world and system world. Life-world is posed by the individual, immediate and existential experience. It is our subjective and private world. The social world is the intersubjective, collective reality that we are part of, and the system world is the set of governing structures that are relatively fixed, and at least outside of what we, with our immediate action, can change.

Habermas (1997) argues that the intention to reach mutual understanding is the main way of developing co-action in communicative processes. Development is a matter of mutual adjustment. An alternative to mutual adjustment is one-sided design and adjustment without a communication process. The reflexive, autonomous individual is central to Habermas's argument. This gives Habermas's theory a distinct character in relation to how we conceive social development, the role of dissent and the role of communication and culture in society.

The question is how to maintain rationality under conditions of subjective reflexivity. I have structured the chapter in the following way: (a) the background for Habermas's argument, (b) the concept of communicative rationality, (c) the structure of an ideal talk situation, and (d) communicative rationality and social deliberation.

The Background for Habermas's Argument

Jürgen Habermas was born in Düsseldorf, Germany, in 1929. He is one of the most important sociological thinkers in the last century. Among his most important works are *Strukturwandel der Öffentlichkeit: Untersuchung zu eiener kategorie der bürgerlichen Gesellschaft* from 1962 (Habermas, 1991), *Theori des Kommunikativen Handelns*, published in two volumes in 1981 (Habermas, 1997) and *Faktizität und Geltung: Beiträge zur Discurstheorie des Rechts und des democratischen Rechtsstaats*, published in 1992 (Habermas, 1998).

Habermas argues that the two classical sociologists George Herbert Mead and Emile Durkheim have influenced him. From Mead he has adapted the communication-theoretic reformulation of social-action theory, while from Durkheim he has taken the approach on linking social action with integration of the social system. In other words, the Habermas theory-building stretches from the individual intention and action level to the total social system level. He has through this writing covered different aspects of this wide field of analysis.

Habermas's theorising plays into the post-war field of ideological differences. In this, he attempts to bridge controversies. One such position is neo-Marxists. In short, this position would argue that: (1) the individual is realised through interaction with others (the group); (2) the destiny of the group is therefore very important for individual development; (3) the group naturally constructs its own (bourgeois) reality (= life-world); (4) there is an ideal reality which is un-influenced by (3) and which forms the basis for critique of (3) (= the life-world). On the other hand, you have the liberal position, which argues that: (1) the individual is autonomic; (2) the individual lives in society; (3) the destiny of the individual is therefore independent of society – although society might have an influence on the individual, the individual is able to place itself outside society; (4) ideal reality comprises autonomous individuals that cooperate peacefully.

CRITICAL THEORY

Habermas adheres to critical theory, the political programme of the Frankfurter School (Horcheimer, Adorno and Marcuse). This position has had an impact on Western thought and has contributed to our understanding of the democratic process. Adorno and Horkheimer (2010) launched critical attacks on the idea of enlightenment. Habermas has within this programme developed the function and meaning of discourse, its constitutional elements and relations, and criteria of validity. In his later writings, Habermas is taking on an almost Humean perspective on democratic development, integrating universalistic and particularistic arguments. He has encouraged liberal values such as the open-endedness of a discourse process, expanded the experience of those who participate, emphasising pluralism and a peaceful exchange of ideas.

This leads to some ideal conceptions of, for instance, discourse: the discourse as a revival of an ideal talk situation (non-dominant, non-interfered discourse). The ideal or essence is an ahistorical phenomenon that discloses how things are in their pure, un-socialised form, prior to social development. Critical theory tends to see society as an artefact; in bourgeois society, this has led to alienation and materialisation. The real/ideal/essential human relation is revealed in a face-to-face society, undisturbed by these bourgeois values and the subsequent alienation and materialisation. Ideal life-world is a small, close, tribal society.

Critical theory distances itself from totalitarian political ideologies. However, critical theory argues that there are features of modern, conventional, bourgeois society that might be improved. Habermas subscribes critical discussion and open public discussion as a means to improve society. One of the implications of this interpretation of critical theory is therefore openness and public engagement, in previously closed or private spheres of society.

UNDERLYING PRINCIPLES IN HABERMAS'S THINKING

Habermas tries to bring his argument beyond the life-world and shows how a liberal society based on the rule of law can comply with subjective reflexivity in the life-world. He is a subjectivist in the sense that he presupposes in his theory sovereign autonomous individuals that are able to interpret social situations and make subjective decisions. In this respect, he departs from the traditional Marxist materialists. A key concept in Habermas's thinking is *rationality*. To Habermas, the individual is in general regarded as rational. However, there are different rationality contexts. Rationality does not mean only one way of acting (for example, always to maximise material outcome, what I have called pure logic of choice) in transactions; rather it is a reference to different systems of validity (Habermas, 1997, p. 329).

Any community of discourse, or discourse in a small group, will, if it lasts for some time or expands to many people, reach a point where there is a need to regulate the discursive behaviour of the participants. This diverted discourse will have the form of bargain (strategic action) because it has a particular aim – to create conditions for further discourse. The bargain will by nature lead to laws or administrative arrangements that restrict some action and reduce complexity. However, it is central to Habermas's argument that the validity of this type of authority is open to constant re-evaluation in the moral/ethical discourse. Through this, legitimacy is established.

What is the nature of the creation of legal *validity*? First of all, the de facto validity of a law is determined by that degree to which the law is acted on. This de facto implementation is one of the main criteria of legitimacy. According to Habermas (1998, p. 168), we can perceive this process of legal validity as a discourse. The way Habermas understands this process is that any spontaneous (moral, ethical) discourse at some point will reach a point where there is a need to have a procedurally regulative bargain.

Integration is another key word in Habermas's thinking. He is concerned with reflective individuals, but he is also concerned about individual identity, in the sense that the individual realises itself under the condition of shared inter-subjectivity. In more simple words, one could say the individuals are, on one hand, sovereign, and on the other they are supposed to play a role in communication with others and through that integrate themselves with others. There is a voluntary link between the individual and society. Habermas's duality theory of the self implies that there is an autonomous self. Still, Habermas argues that communication represents the link by which individuals interrelate with their fellow citizens. He argues that features of the communicative process may explain individual attitude in a certain situation.

Jürgen Habermas, in his *On the Pragmatics of Social Interaction* (Habermas, 1984), distinguishes between different social theories – that of atomistic versus holistic theories – and he also distinguishes between modes of action: behavioural, strategic and communicative. These terms allow us to set up a matrix of different social action explanations, ranging from behavioural psychology, via interpretivist sociology, to structural-functionalistic approaches. One can choose to see these as explanations that manage to capture different aspects of social interaction, subsequently an argument for a multi-level analysis of social developmental processes.

To apply such an approach requires a set of discussion and arguments. Firstly at a personal/individual level, we have to argue that organisation and context have (a certain) impact on action. A core idea here is what Weber discussed as different rationalities, and others more specifically have discussed as the distinction between self-interested, rational behaviour and norm-based and tradition-bound behaviour.

A second level of analysis will be that of institutions and their impact on behaviour. Can institutions change and form action and, if so, how and in what direction? Are there configurations of institutions that are favourable to a certain form of action?

This discussion will in theoretical terms address organisational theory, institutional economics and classical sociological debates on institutions, systems and behaviour.

A third level of theoretical discussion will have to address the more normative, output side of social action. Saying that certain contexts and institutional set-ups influence behaviour does not tell us anything about the implication of this for, let's say, economic development. We will need to introduce theories on innovation and economic development in order to understand what might be possible implications of different ways of organising the economy. A concept for understanding the interplay between different institutions and social processes at different levels, as pointed out among others by Manuel Castells (1996), is that of *communication and knowledge*.

INTERPRETIVE SOCIOLOGY

Communicative action must be understood as a symbolic mediated interaction, as learned skills and as inter-subjectivity. This leads to the meta-theoretical position of communicative action. Jürgen Habermas (1997) developed a social theory that allows both for individual, rational action (individual level) and at the same time to see individual rational action in a larger social structure (holistic theory). In other words, Habermas wants to avoid the individual being reduced to some sort of determined factor in a holistic theory, and at the same time he wants to avoid society being reduced to subjectivity.

By arguing about rationality, Habermas likes to develop a concept of action that both has the inner, purposeful dimension in it, but also at the same time addresses spheres that have other claims to validity: that is, action is the one thing that binds different parts of society together, because action addresses different spheres of society at the same time. Habermas argues against a causal link between context and action. His concept of discourse and communicative action implies that there is room for discussion and development of arguments. Communicative action implies being involved in communication, and in the process of validating arguments and reconsidering one's own arguments and beliefs. It is possible for the individual to distract himself from immediate emphasis of interests.

As I have already indicated, Habermas distances himself both from the predominantly Hegelian and Marxist and the predominantly social constructivist perspective. Habermas is a dualist in the sense that he maintains the ontological independence of the three worlds – the world of objects, the social world and the self. In strategic action this independence is of no significance, as Habermas argues, because the individual acts on an objective and socially defined reality, exploring its potentials. The concept of interests belongs to this mode of action. It is when it comes to communicative action that the ontological independence of the three worlds becomes significant. That is so because communicative action is related to our interpretation of the three worlds. We interpret them first of all through communication, which in itself is a social phenomenon.

The Concept of Communicative Rationality

An actor approaches the objective world (world 1) with statements that can be evaluated according to truthfulness, the social world (world 3) with statements that can be evaluated according to legitimacy and to the subjective world (world 2) with statements or experiences where the actor has privileged access and that can be evaluated according to authenticity (Habermas 1997, p. 100). These three worlds are in Habermas's theory ontologically different (autonomous) but can be conceived according to their different validity claims. Validity claims represent our main tool for constructing meaning and understanding about the three worlds. Furthermore, our subjective world is where we, through our meaning construction, conceive and interpret the social and objective world.

Habermas wants to defend the individual or the social world from being reduced to the physical world (materialism). Habermas's reconstruction of Popper (1979a) introduces a second dimension to the ontological separation of the three worlds. Habermas argues, in line with Popper, that the linguistic or communicative dimension has to be taken into account. In his argument an actor has relations to the three worlds through communication, that is, through different types of validity claims.

This simple threefold division represents an analytic form that gives us permission to interpret a number of challenges in our speech acts. One challenge is to establish a set of rules for the speech act. In Habermas's analysis, these will vary, depending on the specific system one enters into. In the life-world, we will seek the authentic, in the social world, we deal with a set of social norms, while in the system world closer challenges that appear more or less strict are provided. We can distinguish between something that is meaningful or meaningless (life-world), is ethically acceptable or unethical (social world) and right or wrong (system world).

We can consider the rules of discourse (constitution) based on criteria such as openness, fairness, representativeness and plurality. Different discourses are different validity claims. Habermas therefore distinguishes between three discourses:

1. moral discourse: discourse for greater mutual understanding
2. ethical discourse: discourse on rules for discourse
3. pragmatic discourse: allocate interests.

THREE DISCOURSES IN SOCIAL DEVELOPMENT

How can we perceive communicative action in a development perspective? Following the argument already given, it is the process of interpretation, that is, the process of engaging in a discourse of mutual understanding and meaning construction. The autonomous, reflective individual is a precondition in social development. Relevant for the understanding of these development processes are three concepts: *communication*, *reflection* and *participation*.

Individuals in a communicative process are part of a discourse. To communicate is not only to speak, but to speak within a social order and set of norms and rules. Habermas uses the concept of discourse to characterise different communicative situations according to their norms and rules and the content of the communicative process itself. Habermas defines the three different discourses in the following way:

> *In moral discourse, the ethnocentric perspective of a particular collectivity expands into the comprehensive perspective of an unlimited communication community, all of whose members put themselves in each individual's situation, worldview, and self-understanding, and together practice an ideal role taking (as understood by G.H. Mead). (Habermas, 1998, p. 162)*

> *In pragmatic discourses, we test the expediency of strategies under the presupposition that we do know what we want. In ethical-political discourses, we reassure ourselves of a configuration*

of values under the presupposition that we do not yet know what we really want. In this kind
of discourse, we can justify programs insofar as they are expedient and, taken as a whole, good
for us. (Habermas, 1998, p. 161)

In addition to emphasising the difference in characteristics of these three discourses, Habermas argues that they play different roles in a development process. Moral discourse is characterised by an open-ended debate with a high level of self-expression, typically in a process of development and reaching new understanding. Ethical-procedural discourse occurs when a relation is to persist over time and there is a need for regulative norms. Pragmatic discourse is needed when rules are institutionalised and the discursive process is about negotiating over interests. All in all these three discourses can be regarded as stages in a process of legitimacy.

One should keep in mind all the time that reaching understanding does not mean developing the same personal opinion. Reaching understanding means agreement on how to define a phenomenon, not on what is the personal meaning or opinion of the phenomenon. This is important, because in discourses we always assume that there is room for dissent. We even assume that norms and rules that have been agreed upon through discourse always can be challenged and discussed in a discourse.

What is it that makes an individual respond in a specifically responsive way? At one level, this may have to do with common identity formation during discourses. Habermas (1998, p. 18) argues along these lines, but at the same time he warns us that the identity formation might reduce plurality in the discourse (Rehg, 1998). Common identity is therefore not the essential aspect of discourse. Rather, it is the process by which a new argument becomes accepted by others that is the characteristic of a good discursive process. This process of acceptance is related to *validity* and *objectivity* of arguments.

There are different validity claims, depending on situation. In an expressive speech act, for example, validity is related to authenticity, in a scientific discourse to truth. Furthermore, there is probably an individual moral code of fairness and values that has to be accepted in order for an individual to resume a dialogue.

MORAL DISCOURSE

Moral discourse is a discourse where we try to reach mutual understanding. Habermas (1997) talks about reflection and interpretation as an important part of the process of being involved (self-reflection and meaning). He is also critical of the deconstruction of this reflection since this is a phenomenon beyond our observation. What we can observe is the outcome of the reflection and meaning created by this process of reflection: how individuals act according to the meaning they have constructed. Furthermore, Habermas argues that there are (at least) two types of action: actions aimed at reaching success (instrumental and strategic action) and action aimed at reaching understanding (communicative action).

It is central to Habermas's idea of democratic dialogue and critical discourse to make a distinction between different types of acts, foremost of which is the distinction between strategic and communicative action. What makes his distinction important is that it refers to the individual attitude towards that acting situation.[1]

---

1   Habermas writes: 'We call an action oriented to success instrumental when we consider it under the aspect of following technical rules of action, and assess the efficiency of an intervention into a complex of circumstances

There is also a distinct duality in Habermas's theory of action between the objective (system world and social world) and the subjective (life-world). Strategic action is more related to the social and system world, while communicative action is more related to the life-world of the individual. Communicative action implies that the individual is willing to reconsider their values and beliefs.

Moral has a social dimension (social moral norms). This implies that there has to be some sort of mediating between subjective moral and moral norms. But involved in this, Habermas wants to develop a theory where moral rightness is not only corresponding to contextual social moral norms, but also to a larger claim of truth. As Habermas notes, the moral language game consists of (1) judgements about how we ought to behave, (2) assenting or dissenting response and (3) reasons by which the assenting or dissenting partners can justify their attitudes. This means that the moral language game both points at the subjectivity of the matter, the social norm in the matter, but also a reference to reason or truth (justification). This is what Habermas refers to as the Janus-face of moral discourse.

ETHICAL-PROCEDURAL DISCOURSE

Habermas (1997) describes the historical development from pre-conventional via conventional to post-conventional situation. The pre-conventional situation is related to an authoritarian system where interests activate co-operation. In conventional action, roles are more predominant and norms are guiding the activity. While in the post-conventional situation, action is related to discourse. It is supposed that these three levels of convention are related to an increasing level of rationality (Skirbekk, 1993). The assumption is that critical discourse will remove irrationality since reality will dominate discourse, while authority tends to increase primitivity, mysticism and symbolism. Towards an authoritarian system, loyalty, relation to tribe, organisation of group, egocentrism and obedience of order are important ethical elements. While in the discourse situation, voluntary interaction, respect of procedures and striving at truth are essential elements. In between these two extremes, there is conventionalism, where norms and the feeling of duty are essential (Habermas, 1988, p. 176).

The authoritarian system has to balance between the use of force and the appeal to interests. In the conventional situation on the one hand there are *roles*, on the other hand there are *norms*. While in the post-conventional situation there is the relation between form and content: the rules and the process of striving at truth. However, if we look at the whole scheme there is a tendency of development from a closed system to an open-ended system.

---

and events. We call an action oriented to success strategic when we consider it under the aspect of following rules of rational choice, and assess the efficiency of influencing the decisions of a rational opponent. Instrumental action can be connected with and subordinated to social interaction of a different type, – for example, as the 'task elements' of social roles; strategic actions are social actions by themselves. By contrast I speak of communicative action whenever the actions of the agents involved are coordinated, not through egocentric calculation and success but through acts of reaching understanding' (Habermas, 1997, p. 285). He writes: 'The expressive attitude of a subject who reveals a thought, makes known a wish, expresses a feeling, who exposes a bit of his subjectivity before the eyes of others, is distinct in a characteristic way from the objectivating attitude of a manipulating or observing subject towards things and events, and from the conformative (or nonconformative) attitude of a participant in interaction toward normative expectations. Moreover, we also connect expressive utterance with a criticizable validity claim, namely the claim of truthfulness or sincerity. Thus subjective worlds, as domains of noncommonality with privileged access, can also be drawn into public communication' (Habermas 1997, p. 52).

The three stages – pre-conventional, conventional and post-conventional – might be interpreted, not as a successive development, but rather as parallel processes: as open and closed processes that run parallel in an organisation and in society. Society can at one stage both have open-ended critical discourse and authoritarian leadership.

The authoritarian system, as a closed system, tends to focus on balancing authority and interests. In order to be able to enforce its will, people are encouraged to organise into social groups. The reason for this is of course to remove individuality in order to be able to enforce authority. This orientation towards groups and tribes are less important in a conventional situation. The conventional situation is more universal and rests on *norms* and roles. However, even in this system there is a fear of individuality. Conformity gives stability to this system, and conformity and the feeling of duty, to some extent, takes the place of authority.

Habermas disagrees that there are any causal links between context and action independent of interpretation. In Habermas's perspective, the individual will be able to understand the necessity of formal structures, rules and power without being alienated. Fairness of rules and commitment to ethical standards are aspects of context that will influence interpretation.

Habermas (1998, p. 8) also sees the function of formal rules as to stabilise the instability that might result from discussion where individual interests do not produce coordinated solutions and that therefore threatens to ruin social stability and progress. As institutions are *functional* in a sense that creates an underlying tension in individuals' relation to them, contextual design has in normative terms to be made so as to make it meaningful for individuals to be involved.

This is relevant for the workplace, since that is a functional context. By definition it is therefore a type of context that induces non-involved strategic action (alienation). In order to change this, in order to induce involved, communicative action, the context has to meet formal requirements. That is, formal structures (for instance that secure participation), the use of power and general culture of trust have to correspond with normative ideals of involvement. Foremost of these are fair norms. The ethical-procedural discourse is the process of developing these fair norms.

PRAGMATIC DISCOURSE

Pragmatic discourse involves practising interests, negotiating and making social choices within a set of rules. In the following I will discuss some challenges to this type of discourse.

Table 3.1   Strategic and communicative interaction

Strategic interaction	Communicative interaction
Roles and norm-regulated action	Discourse
Coordination of interests	Integration via talks and development of a common-world perspective
Duty, norm and role conformity	Autonomy, reflexive norm basis and the search for universal procedures

Source: Based on Habermas (2003).

For example, organisational culture has been argued to have impact on involvement. However, there is no necessary link between the concept of involvement in communicative change processes and organisational culture. The communicative dimension in Habermas's system is a direct contrast to the conventional idea of common culture and common values. For Habermas (1988), communication and dialogue do not require common norms in the sense of predefined and comprehensive values and goals. Rather, communication in the sense of an unconstrained dialogue requires some open-ended universal rules of just conduct. To the extent that common culture means more equality and less dissent, it will be contrary to communicative processes.

Downscaled to an organisational level, we might question the logic of *common culture* as a denominator for committed and involved action. Involvement in a post-conventional communicative system of non-common values means by definition to be honest, reflexive and open to rational discussion. On the other hand, it is rather obvious that a functional relation in the form of an organisation needs to have some common cultural denominators. Somehow, the plurality of individual meanings and arguments has to be restricted by cultural values, norms in order for decisions and common actions to be made (Rehg, 1998).

Habermas's communicative theory is based on the fact that interests are not a pre-political phenomenon. That is, Habermas sees democracy not primarily as a negotiation arena for predefined interests. Rather, interests are developed and formulated and reformulated in a discourse. With that, a division between two types of action emerges – communicative action and strategic action. Communicative action is aimed at own understanding and articulation of own interests in a critical discourse with others. There are also arenas for strategic action distinguished by interest articulation and interest negotiations, but these are distinctly different from communicative arenas.

In a descriptive perspective, we should ask ourselves if it in fact is like this – that communicative action is different from strategic action. A relation we should explore is whether communicative arenas as the dialogue conferences, as they are practised in businesses, have managed to reach the communicative type of action. Further, we could look closer both on the frames for the dialogue (the arena) and on the communicative competence – in other words, whether the qualifications for communicative action are present. According to Habermas the difference between the two strategies – strategic and communicative interaction – may be described as shown in Table 3.1.

It may be claimed as a hypothesis that change of organisation via collective representation and cultural development represents a thinking with basis in a typical strategic interaction thinking, while the dialogue and the communicative change presupposes a communicative perspective on the organisation as social system.

LEGITIMACY

Discourses are playing together in larger systems that provide legitimacy. We can also distinguish between different epistemological positions (our knowledge and ability to understand reality). To engage in communicative action is to try to reach coordination and common understanding on the first two of these elements in the speech act. That is, communicative action does not mean coordinating individual meaning, values and beliefs. Communicative action aims at reaching a common, valid description of a phenomenon that is true and legitimate. It is this process of finding a true and legitimate description of a phenomenon in a communicative action that is referred to as the process of interpretation.

The process of interpretation, that is, of finding mutual and valid descriptions of the objective and the social world, presupposes a subject. This subject can, as we have seen, relate to the social and objective worlds in different ways characterised by different types of act. The subject exists in their life-world. Habermas, however, does not ascribe to the subject characteristics such as identity or alienation. That is so because of the subject's ontological independence. However, there is a coupling between the self and the social world, as the meaning construction through communicative action is the way the individual builds relation between themselves and the social world.

When the subject is involved in the social world, they take part in a communicative process. The outcome of this process is a new, better and/or common interpretation of phenomenon in the world that surrounds us. The process of reaching common understanding (as distinct from common meaning or beliefs) takes part in a social process within a set of norms and rules – in a discourse. In order to understand the process of interpretation, we need to understand the working of different discourses.

This challenge can be perceived as a parallel to the researcher's attempt to make meaning in social research. With reference to Skjervheim (Habermas, 1997, p. 111) and his positivist critique, Habermas argues that the researcher both has a performative (participatory) and an objectifying purpose in relation to the field. What the researcher does is to communicate and thereby make valid their observation. It is brought from the researcher's life-world as experience to the attention and validation by others. It is individuals themselves (and the researcher) that make sense of and interpret action, and subsequently bridge different types of expression. This process of interpretation is often built into a pre-structured social reality, which give special meaning to the act. Thereby one integrates meaning and structure.

RATIONALITY

The core of Habermas's project in communicative action has been to develop a theory of rationality that allows us both to discuss meaning and attention, and to address the development of modern society. Modernity, in Habermas's sense, means the development of more complex relations between different spheres of society, more diversified institutional arrangements and, by that, new conditions for the individual. The traditional Marxist position developed an inconceivable conflict between individual and the capitalist production system. A theory of rationality must be able to address this in a constructive way.

Rationality, then, understood as communicative action, allows the individual to relate to different spheres with different strategies: communicative, norm obedient or strategic. Such an understanding of rationality allows us to analyse complex relations between different institutional arrangements. It also allows us to see the individual, intentions and meaning in relation to larger institutional structures.

Habermas tries to show how this general framework allows us to address contemporary societal issues, such as different societal discourses and development of the private versus public sphere. He asks: how can we perceive modern society in its institutional form and, not least, how can we perceive the development dynamics in modern, democratic society? He starts with the argument that neither of the two predominant approaches, the individual (Hobbes) and the holistic (Hegel), works in a modern, complex society (Habermas, 1998). A modern society is complex beyond the individual action. It cannot be expected that any individual can take all parts of the environment that they act within into account when they act. On the other hand, a state solution to that problem is not feasible. The idea of a rational, omnipotent state breaks down when we approach a complex society. This poses a challenge. As Habermas writes:

> *This explains the attractiveness of the only option that seems to remain open: the brash denial of reason altogether, whether in the dramatic form of a post-Nietzschean critique of reason or in the more sober variety of a systems functionalism that neutralizes anything that, from the participant perspective, appears obligatory or at all meaningful. Anyone in the human science not absolutely committed to a counterintuitive approach will find this solution rather unattractive as well. For this reason, I have taken a different approach with the theory of communicative action, replacing practical reason with a communicative one. This involves more than a change of terminology. (Habermas, 1998, p. 3)*

So, as can be read from this, Habermas's project is to argue that there is something in between individual rationality (pure logic of choice) and determinism. This in-between is communicative action. Why is this in between? It is so because communication is not an individual but a collective phenomenon. As we communicate, we make ourselves understandable to others. We engage in a social process. And we use language that is a social phenomenon, not an individual one.

From this, Habermas elaborates the perspective of life-world and local knowledge, and argues that this cannot be the whole story. The normative of the subjective world is not in itself a sufficient justification for rightness and truth. Individual, subjective action plays into a larger entity and gets its rightness from this. There are some sort of *facts* out there. So the project becomes one of linking the subjective, individual world (norm) with that of the larger social/structural and institutional environment (fact). This is the project, to explore the area between facts and norms.

LIFE-WORLD AS A POINT OF DEPARTURE

Habermas wants further to bridge his micro theory of communicative action to the larger institutional changes. An act can be defined according to its purpose/intention. An act is the result of the meeting between this intention and the external, social world. This social world gives meaning to the act. In this respect, Habermas includes in his conception of the individual life-world, the social world and the system world. He argues:

> *The lifeworld, of which institutions form a part, comes into view as a complex of interpreting cultural traditions, social norms, and personal identities. (Habermas, 1998, p. 23)*

Staring from the life-world, Habermas goes on to explore language as an interrelation and social process, and, further, he introduces the concept of law. The argument for going beyond the life-world is that the individual cannot handle the complexity in the environment and needs some stability in order to act. The everyday communication is 'formless, free-floating' (Habermas, 1998, p. 38). It needs some more structure to be reasonable and effective. Law, then, emerges from below, and is constantly challenged from below. This emergent perspective on law sees the law as an institutionalised, power system organised by the state (top–down). These two aspects of law create the tension and dynamics of the development of a modern, complex societal system. How, then, can reason be built into this process?

Habermas (2003) re-addresses the philosophical preconditions for his thinking, especially the problem of identifying truth. He discusses the concept of moral rightness versus truth. Habermas starts out with the Aristotelian concept of different types of knowledge, such as phronesis and episteme (or practice and theory). These concepts indicate that the two are ontologically different. Habermas wants to root his theory of moral in the individual and in the individual intention and action. At the same time, moral has a social dimension (social moral norms). This implies that there has to be some sort of mediating between subjective moral and moral norms. But involved in this, Habermas wants to develop a theory where moral rightness does not only correspond to contextual social moral norms, but also to a larger claim of truth.

Habermas then discusses if moral can be reduced to something else: could we understand it in systems terms, as a natural part of a social system, or could we understand it in anthropological terms as a contextual phenomenon? Habermas's discussion here is intended to fence off these positions; he does not want to reduce moral discourse to something else.

The next step in his argument is to introduce language and the linguistic term; the fact that all moral and ethical utterance as well as truth claims have to express themselves in a common language implies at a structural level that they interlink. In this sense, truth is in the utter end of this discursive activity:

> *Accordingly, a proposition is true if it withstands all attempts to invalidate it under the rigorous condition of rational discourse. (Habermas, 2003, p. 251)*

This truths claim is really a Kantian one: a universality claim. But it also establishes a continuum between different discourses and different validity claims. There are less rigid claims to moral rightness than to truth, but they are both to be considered in relation to validity claims. This means that we might socially agree on something that is not necessarily true, but that might in that respect be right. What the relevant language game is, and what the relevant validity claim should be, need to be discussed in relation to the issue involved: is it only personal (authenticity), is it contextual (social norm, right) or is it universal (claims to true)?

The Structure of an Ideal Talk Situation

Communication brings the three worlds together. When we communicate, we interpret, form beliefs, reflect and develop meaning related to a phenomenon. We may think of this in terms of a speech act. A speech act will normally contain three elements – one element that identifies the object, a second element that ascribes to the object certain characteristics and a third element that indicates my own meaning, value or position towards the phenomenon. The first of these elements belongs to the objective world and is validated according to truthfulness, the second relates to the social world and is validated according to legitimacy, while the third relates to the subject itself and is validated according to authenticity.

One way of perceiving the relation between the individual and the social order is within the context of a game. A game can be interpreted both in mental terms, such as intentionality, and in formal terms reflecting the logic of choice (Nozick, 1993, p. 145). Basically, there are two types of logic involved, both of the formal type. One sort of formal logic is of the type: if I choose A to B, I did not choose B to A. The other sort of formal logic is of the type: by choosing A to B, I have accepted the logic of choosing, and subsequently a lot of other formal rules.

A parallel to language could be made. By speaking, we are involved in two different sets of rules – the rules of *semantics* related to interpretation and the logic of the argument, and the rules of *syntax*, related to the formal rules of the language itself (Popper, 1979b). To be engaged in a game, then, is to be involved in the formal logic of choice. As Nozick observes, the revealing of this type of formal logic can bring us a lot closer to the understanding of individual choice. But it still cannot say very much about our initial choice of A to B (Nozick 1993, p. 150).

Hayek (1976b) has offered some indications of his answer to this problem. He has said that equilibrium occurs when each individual actor is in equilibrium in relation to present situations and expectations, and when there is compatibility between one actor's and all the other actors' plans. Insight into other people's plans and expectations (*verstehen*) is consequently a precondition for the type of economic *game* that leads to equilibrium.

Generalised, one could say that the central element that explains the efficiency of the natural order is that it contains complex information – that is, more complex information than any single individual could ever control. Hayek's argument has been called a rule-utilitarian argument. It has as a principle that utility is measured, not by the *end result* of individual action, but by the *potential* of actualising individual knowledge. It is the *open-endedness* and general nature of the natural order that bear this potential.

But how can an individual gain insight into the plans and expectations of others? The answer, of course, is that they cannot. There has to be some sort of medium by which the expectations and plans of individuals is transformed into information to others. The question is: how is this process operating? Theories treat different aspects of this coordination problem. Tacit knowledge, ideal types, institutions and norms might be regarded as *ordering devices* in the social process.[2] Habermas's argument is that this can be sorted in an ideal talk situation.

THE IDEAL TALK SITUATION

Although moral development in an *ideal* discourse is the background for Habermas's moral theory, most discourse analysis relates to the discourse elements in a society where even authoritarian structures are present (Fairclough, 1993). It can be observed that authority, meaning and symbols, features of the pre-conventional situation, are brought into the discourse, although the general expectation is that the critical discourse will rule out these features (Skirbekk, 1993). However, as the critical discourse will rule out some types of action, it will tend to activate others, for instance self-expression,

---

2   The inter-subjective world of structures, roles and functions is important, and does have some coordinating effect. And, if that is all there is in the coordination problem, its solution might be sought within the discipline of hermeneutics or institutionalism. But I am not sure that this was Hayek's intention.

self-promotion, hegemony and strategic action (Fairclough, 1993). In a non-ideal discursive situation, there might be ethical (moral) implications of these activities. The main question will be: how can we be sure that a discourse without any authoritarian norms will have a self-controlling effect and lead to more rationality, that is, to a more correct approach to reality (in other words, lead to learning)? One answer might be to point at the inherent feature of this discourse process: the idea that the better (more rational) argument will win approval. This might be the case in an ideal talk situation where no interests are at stake, what Adam Smith and later John Rawls called *behind a veil of ignorance*.

This ideal talk situation (a situation with no dominance, without any formal positions by the participants) is problematic in itself, because people are supposed to be stripped of most of their human characteristics, and to act only reasonable, not strategically. In real life, people are only to some extent rational; when there is a trade-off of individual interests, moral values and rationality, other characteristics might occur. If the better argument is against the interests of one party, he might want to leave the dialogue, *pretend* he disagrees or has a better argument or appeal to authority. In the Foucault-type of discourse these features are expected. However, the breakdown of discourse may not only occur as a result of individual characteristics. There might be issues and tasks characterised by uncertainty, by communicative irresponsibility or by manipulation of dissent, all leading the discourse away from a rational outcome (Kettner, 1993, p. 41).

The communicative process is presupposed to lead to resolutions and mutual understanding which have an increased degree of objectivity. The objectivity results from arguments being put up against each other until the better argument wins. In this, we find an optimistic perspective. The tension that emerges in such a process comes from the respect of the individual, partly taking part in a critical dialogue, being reflexive and taking autonomous stands, and at the same time (or when a decision is made) being loyal towards their social context.

This will be reflected in the structure of the communication. Think of a situation where two people communicate. Person A says the following: 'we should reorganise this department!' The further communication may be characterised through how person B responds. Assume that he answers: 'I hear what you're saying.' Such a response gives no opportunities for further dialogue. B neither identifies himself, expresses agreement or disagreement, comes up with commitment nor invites further conversation with A. Let us assume that B says: 'why?' Through this answer, B at least opens up for further dialogue. Assume that B answers: 'interesting, why?' Now B has, in addition to inviting further dialogue, also identified himself with A. An even more binding statement from B would be to answer: 'I agree. What is your proposal for the reorganisation?'

Subsequently, validity has to be established in this reciprocal relation. By engaging in a communicative relationship, at least four validity claims have to be met:

> The comprehensibility of the utterance, the truths of its propositional components, the correctness and appropriateness of its performatory components, and the authenticity of the speaking subject. (Habermas, 2001, p. 18)

Communication is embedded in a social context; a discourse transcends the particular communicative situation. The example above shows how different communicative practices reveal underlying motives for the communication. A central dimension in the communicative concept of change is to get communicative action in the signification of motives aiming at mutual understanding, rather than looking after strategic interests.

Communicative Rationality and Social Deliberation

Communicative rationality implies a development towards a more sustainable economic and social development, by a better understanding of the relation between the economic and the social processes. Are these processes working equally in different contexts and under different varieties of capitalism?

When it is argued that rules and norms play a rule in discursive processes, it should be emphasised that even these terms are ambiguous. Hayek is arguing that the *type of order* is an essential characteristic of the social realms. Hayek's concepts of *kosmos* and *taxis* (Hayek, 1979) distinguish these two orders – *kosmos* is the evolved, undersigned order of the open, abstract system, while *taxis* is the organisational order characterised by a commonly shared concrete purpose.

Hayek has emphasised the *distinction* between *kosmos* – the open, abstract order – and *taxis* – the closed, designed order. The market order is, according to Hayek, one example of *kosmos* and so are the institutions that govern the market (private property rights and money). *Kosmos* implies that ethics should not serve as a criterion for other forms of spontaneous order. Moreover, there are two forms of ethics: (1) ethics of distributive justice, which spontaneously emerges in small social groups; (2) ethics of free market relations, which also emerges spontaneously, but much later – and this ethics in some aspects contradicts the ethics of distributive justice. However, what is less emphasised in the discussions of Hayek is that he equally argues that *taxis* has a certain internal logic which is as crucial for social development.[3] The close relation of the *taxis* order, therefore, has an important function in the development of the person as a moral individual.

Following the same type of reasoning, Vanberg argues that there are trust rules and solidarity rules, where the former have meaning in the abstract (market) order, while the latter only have meaning in the small relational group. I can expect to be shown solidarity to a higher degree by those who are relationally close to me than by others (Vanberg, 1994, p. 66). Being a free-rider is a type of conduct that, while we only mildly condemn it in the market, we strongly condemn it in the small relational group. At the same time, even in the market there has to be some sort of agreed-upon rules of just conduct (trust rules), but these do not stretch into a particular concern (solidarity) for me as a person. The argument is that the individual and their characteristics have developed within society through an *evolutionary* process. What we count as individual action today is not a reflection of some genuine human nature, rather the response of individuals to their

---

3   Hayek writes: 'What we call mind is not something that the individual is born with, as he is born with his brain, or something that the brain produces, but something that his generic equipment (e.g., brain of a certain size and structure) helps him to acquire, as he grows up, from his family and adult fellows by absorbing the result of tradition that is not generic transmitted. Mind in this sense consists less of testable knowledge about the world, less in interpretations of man surroundings, more in capacity to restrain instincts – a capacity which cannot be tested by individual reason since its effects are on the group. Shaped by the environment in which individuals grow up, mind in turn conditions the preservation, development, richness, and variety of traditions on which individuals draw. By being transmitted largely through families, mind preserves a multitude of concurrent streams into which each newcomer to the community can delve. It may well be asked whether an individual who did not have the opportunity to tap such a cultural tradition could be said to have a mind' (Hayek, 1988, p. 23).

surroundings, including their history.[4] I discuss this further in Chapter 9 'Knowledge, Market and Social Justice'.

According to Hayek, individuals have a mental (cognitive) structure by which they are able to perceive the external world. This cognitive structure works in such a way that external informations are categorised and coupled into meanings. Each individual has a unique configuration of these categories and therefore a unique ability to combine information into meaning.[5]

The ethical content of the natural order has not only interested classical liberals. Even classical socialists were concerned with this, and Karl Marx, based on Hegel, made some comments, although contrary to the liberal point of view. Marx makes the distinction between nature as *first nature* and society as *second nature*. It is the central claim of Hegel and Marx, that we are the masters of our destiny, and if we know the working of the spontaneous processes of nature, we are able to both control and decide over them. This is the Hegelian *herrschaft* position, which is criticised by Hayek (1979) as constructivism.

Vanberg argues that agreement

> ... takes on somewhat different meanings in different contexts and that, accordingly, there exist systematically different interpretations as to what kind of agreement actually carries with it legitimizing force. (Vanberg, 1994, p. 162)

Following this general observation, he argues in favour of an integrated model of agreement forms. Vanberg's *agreement form* notion is close to Habermas's discourse notion. However, Vanberg's perspective emphasises more clearly the instrumental relation between the three notions of agreement (discourses). In Vanberg's perspective we can talk about three processes that are distinct and that correspond with Habermas's discourses: conflict resolution (social choice or pragmatic discourse), development of knowledge and mutual information (dialogue or moral discourse) and rules for regulating behaviour (constitution or ethical-procedural discourse). Vanberg argues that we need to have all three processes in order to establish legitimacy.

What does it mean in practice? Well, in the transition from a strategic to a communicative interaction regime, we must drop the focus on the importance of joint identity, unity, collective action and security through conformity. We must think of discursive arenas, not as negotiation arenas but as arenas for increased mutual

---

4   Hayek writes: 'What then are the essential characteristics of true individualism? The first thing that should be said is that it is primarily a theory of society, an attempt to understand the forces which determine the social life of man, and only in the second instance, a set of political maxims derived from this view of society. This fact should by itself be sufficient to refute the silliest of the common misunderstandings: the belief that individualism postulates (or bases its arguments on the assumption of) the existence of isolated or self-contained individuals' (Hayek, 1976a, p. 6).

5   Hayek (1988) has commented on the relation, tension or interplay between the mental order of the individual and the social order of society. The process by which order develops in society has some of the same tacit elements that characterise the development of the mental order: 'The decisive effect that led to the creation of the order itself, and to certain practices predominating over others, were exceedingly remote results of what earlier individuals had done, results exerting themselves on groups of which earlier individuals could hardly have been aware, and which effects, had earlier individuals been able to know them, may not have appeared at all beneficial to them, whatever later individuals may think. [...] Many of the evolved rules which secured greater co-operation and prosperity for the extended order may have differed utterly from anything that could have been anticipated, [...] Hence, at no moment in the process could individuals have designed, according to their purposes, the functions of the rules that gradually did form the order – and only later, and imperfectly and retrospectively, have we been able to begin to explain these formations in principle' (Hayek, 1988, p. 72).

understanding and learning. Some have criticised Habermas's de-emphasising of the interest aspect as idealised and naive (Honneth, 1982; Outhwaite, 1997, p. 25). Their main argument is that interests are a necessary part of the self-identity and autonomy that Habermas presupposes in the discursive process. Further, these critics of Habermas claim that it is inconceivable to design arenas which are interest-free. Habermas argues that just interests are created in a discursive process.

DEMOCRATIC MIND

An important aspect of Habermas's communicative project has been to derive how cognitive and normative structures being aimed at mutual understanding are communicated through the language and the communication. To establish such connections, Habermas involves development psychology (Dryzek, 1996). Communicative action has a strong development element within. Participation in communicative processes contributes to personal development and growth.

Communication has what others have called a self-transformation effect (Warren, 1992). However, as Habermas himself emphasises (1998, p. 10), psychology is only part of the explanation and his theory is not a social-psychological theory. The self-transformation hypothesis is the idea that over time individuals who take part in communicative processes will increase their likelihood to be involved in such processes by communicative action (Warren, 1992). In the alternative reading, the self is transformed, but still retains autonomy:

> Inner experience, though it may not be formulated in discourse, anchors part of the self that not only 'disturb' language, but also account for happiness, uniqueness, and difference. Taken as a theory of the self, Habermas's approach threatens to sever autonomy and happiness, and produce a tyranny of discourse over needs, something he does not intend. (Warren, 1996, p. 194)

The self-transformation thesis (Warren, 1992; Eccles, 1996) argues that the individual, through participation in the democratic communicative processes, over time develops a *democratic mind*. This implies, in other words, that over time the communicative processes will result in communicative action as opposed to strategic action by the individual. The individual does not internalise set values at the sacrifice of their own reflexivity. The self-transformation applies to the transition from strategic to communicative action, or rather – the transition from a strategic to a communicative mind. To some extent, one could argue that this idea of self-transformation is in conflict with the idea of an autonomous, reflective mind.

The main challenge is to establish common support for sound and constructive arguments and formulated goals, and to avoid unwanted and destructive arguments and behaviour. Communicative processes are supposed to be a filter for selecting good and bad arguments. Communicative change is brought about by a combination of *individual intention* and *institutional design* (Habermas, 1997). Also credibility, trust and legitimacy influence the development and the outcome of the communicative process.

In organisational theory, a tension exists between those who argue that shared values are important for organisational change (Huber and Glick, 1995) and those who emphasise the importance of *dissent* and *critical debate*. Communicative processes, in functional relations such as firms, have a cost and need to balance agreement and shared goals on one hand against critical debate and dissent on the other.

A discourse runs the constant threat of turning into unsolvable disputes. In so far as they do, Habermas (1998, p. 21) argues, they may result in communication breaking down and the actors shifting over to strategic action. What should restrain them from doing so? Language itself provides us with a source of social integration, since even our disagreement must be articulated through (a common) language. However, some discourses make individuals more involved than others.

In the Scandinavian collaboration tradition, the interest aspect and interest negotiations have been central. The communicative development concept challenges this aspect. There are both practical and theoretical approaches to the further development of the Scandinavian collaboration tradition of finding a limit between the communicative processes and interest negotiations.

Pragmatic discourse is about negotiations over interests within a set of formalised rules of cooperation. Although this implies that moral and ethical discourse do not apply, the process of pragmatic discourse has to be made on the basis of moral and ethical discourse. This means that before negotiations over interests can start, there has to be a process of broad participation, engagement and reflection.

Table 3.2 tries to represent the most referred to forms of modes of influence and steering on the one hand and organisational forms on the other. Democratic steering through representation of a public bureaucracy is a classical form (Weber, 1978) as well as the distinction between political system and market. Furthermore, individuals will be able to utilise free choice within a market system ruled by general laws of competition and trade, and they will engage in transactions in the market under the rule of law.

Against this, normally informal, direct and collective mobilisation has been seen as the social force that might influence and informally regulate both the formal political system and individual choice. This *third force* is often portrayed as a counterforce to the other, a third way of organising that opposes both the political forces and national political power, as well as individual, egoistic behaviour (see the discussion in Ennals and Gustavsen, 1999).

Table 3.2   Participation forms in different organisational settings

Modes of participation and influence versus modes of organising	Indirect/ representative decisions	Direct/ collective action	Individual (free agent)
Hierarchy (formal organisation)	Democratic steering of bureaucratic processes	Direct participation as opposed to departmentalism	Rights, rule of law
Network (informal organisation)	Governance systems	Informal participation and social mobilisation	Utilising strong and weak ties
Market (contracts based, transactions)	Classical distinction between the political system and the market	Imperfect contracts, collaborative, communitarian processes	Transactions, free choice, freedom of (perfect) contracts

Conclusion

Can communicative rationality through conditions for dialogue, truth beyond interests, the presence of arguments, ignoring the contextualisation of social structure and based on subjective reflexivity solve the challenge of establishing true knowledge? I try in this book to argue for a social theory of knowledge. That implies that social deliberation plays an important role in developing knowledge in society. I have in this chapter introduced the concept of communicative rationality. In Chapter 11, 'Knowledge and Democracy', I will try to take the discussion forward, and see how this concept materialises as part of a democratic process.

Habermas's theory has two dimensions that are intertwined and at the same time decoupled. On one hand it is a moral theory in the sense that in order for change to happen, individuals ought to reflect on the changes and decide (morally) if they can accept the change. On the other hand, it is a system theory by which individuals have to adhere to a system.

These two dimensions can be intertwined in two different ways. Firstly, they follow in time: those things that are institutionalised have at one time been reflected on. In that case, we should expect to find reflection prior to any social (collective and individual) change. Secondly, the two systems might refer to different levels of aggregation. On small-scale changes in close communal relations, individuals reflect on change, but on the larger trends in social development, individuals adhere to change. Still in this second case, we should expect to find individuals reflecting on change in a medium-sized workplace.

The different discourses represent different types of involvement and participation. Habermas has said something very general about this. Also, Habermas argues that there is an interrelation between the discourses. Legitimacy of the communicative process is related to this interrelation between discourses. The epistemological aspect relates to Habermas's discussion of the relation between knowledge and interest. His perspective on science illustrates this. Habermas recognises the problem of interpretation; he subscribes to the critique of positivism and accepts the subjectivity of the scientist (Skjervheim, 1959). However, as shown in Habermas's critique of Skjervheim, there is not only local knowledge, but also universal knowledge (Habermas, 1997, p. 111).

> There is a systematic relationship between the logical structure of science and the pragmatic structure of the possible applications of the information generated within its framework. (p. 8)

> Therefore the technical and practical interests of knowledge are not regulators of cognition which have to be eliminated for the sake of the objectivity of knowledge; instead they themselves determine the aspects under which reality is objectified, and can thus be made accessible to the experience to begin with. They are the conditions which are necessary in order that subjects capable of speech and action may have experience which may lay a claim of objectivity. (Habermas, 2001, p. 9)

Furthermore:

> The underlying 'interests' establishes the unity between this constitutive context in which knowledge is rooted and the structure of the possible application which this knowledge can have. (Habermas, 2001, p. 9)

Habermas summarises his argument against *objectivism* in three points: the relation between knowledge and interest (which is inadequately stated in the objectivist position), the inadequate understanding of self-reflection (which has no role in the objectivist approach) and the neglect of objectivists to see that there is an organisational aspect of science. By acknowledging this, we may be able to recognise rational, true knowledge. I return to this in the next chapter where I discuss how science makes knowledge.

Knowledge in Social Structures

In this second part of the book I present five studies of knowledge development processes. In Chapter 4, 'How Science Makes Knowledge', I look into methodological processes in science. I apply three perspectives on this: methodological, sociological and discursive. In Chapter 5, 'Economic Thought, Market and Knowledge', I discuss the concept of knowledge in economic theory. In Chapter 6, 'Knowledge Organisations: Developing Knowledge in Practice', I discuss the idea of knowledge organisation and knowledge management. In Chapter 7, 'Cultural Knowledge and Market Development', I discuss the idea that culture has impact on knowledge. Finally in Chapter 8, 'Modernist Criticisms and Development of Social Knowledge', I argue both that and how modernist art has had a substantial impact on knowledge in society.

PART

II Knowledge in
Social Structure

4 *How Science Makes Knowledge*

Introduction

The reason why we call something science is that it differs from everyday activity. If we were to argue that science is able to contribute to development in society, it has to be a certain activity and a certain way of developing knowledge. Science has had a good reputation in society. The Industrial Revolution would probably not have happened without the advances in science. Modern society is, among others, based on scientific progress. However, as I will discuss below, the optimism on behalf of scientific knowledge was strongly questioned after the Second World War. The Holocaust and the atomic bomb are two references to the type of despair that modernism had created. It resulted in a debate on the foundation of scientific knowledge.

What I discuss in this chapter is what is special about the way science make knowledge. If science does not produce some sort of unique knowledge (and true knowledge), it is hard to understand how it contributes to the development of the knowledge society. I will refer to it as three interrelated questions: (a) how science makes knowledge, (b) what knowledge it makes and (c) why that knowledge differs from other knowledge. These main questions can be further specified in the following way. Based on the argument that science is a reflection of the society it is part of: how does it produce valid knowledge? Science is not only a producer of true and valid knowledge. Science is part of a *knowledge system* in society. How does it relate to that? Given the fragmentation among sciences, how can we know that it produces valid knowledge? When society uses science, how do we know that it chooses the right or more valid research?

THE NEW PRODUCTION OF KNOWLEDGE

The background for this discussion is that scientific knowledge to an increasing degree has been integrated into the knowledge system in society, not least in relation to innovation policy. Gibbons et al. (1994), in their now classical work on Mode-2, *The New Production of Knowledge*, write:

> In transdisciplinary contexts, [...] institutional differences between, say, universities and industry, seem to be less and less relevant. [...] performance and excellence judged by the ability of individuals to make a sustained contribution in open, flexible types of organisation in which they may only work temporarily. (Gibbons, Limoges, Nowotny, Schwartzman, Scott and Trow, 1994, p. 30)

Gibbons et al. (1994) and Nowotny et al. (2001) define a new *governance mechanism* for research. That is, science increasingly operates in a blurred field of engaged, applied research, where researchers are involved in industrial development, social improvements and other practical tasks.

The blurring of the relation between research and practice, the situation that Nowotny et al. (2001) describe as the new way of producing knowledge, has made an impact on the general work situation of science. To the extent that they actually give an accurate description of some major tendencies in contemporary Western society, one might try to interpret what it implies. One perspective is to argue that it is the administrative systems that want to direct research into useful areas. It is a form of political steering of science. The new regionalisation and regional governance systems go hand in hand with the third role of the university, one can argue. Innovation policy wants to see that universities are useful to industry and business. One implication of this might be the commoditisation of research.

The blurring of relation between science and practice, and the emphasis of the universities' *third task*, might actually have had other effects on research and social science. Disciplines have become even more isolated, more closed and more *arrogant*, in the sense of being less willing to go into dialogue with other perspectives. The competition for funding between different disciplines, and steering of research through funding programmes and administration of research, may have reinforced this tendency.

When Bourdieu (1990) and Nowotny et al. (2001) argue that the distinction between science and practice (industry) is blurred, they are referring to science as just one out of many practices, or only one among many producers of symbols in society. If we are to argue against this, we will have to answer whether there are specific features of science and the researcher that makes it distinct from other practices. This could be superior knowledge due to procedures, professional standards or distinct forms of knowledge.

What is the particular scientific part of this activity and to what extent is the scientist's and researcher's contribution in these processes different from any other practitioner (Johnsen and Normann, 2004)? *How do we know that we know?* What are the right ways of thinking in order to get a more correct understanding of the social world? What expectations do we have with regard to knowledge: do we want to explain, seek truth or just find something reasonable or common sense (Johnsen, 2013)?

At the core of this bundle of issues about the role of sciences is, as I see it, the issue of what knowledge is and how knowledge is produced. Note that the development in the knowledge society is not only about making science useful, but also about producing knowledge (and science) in a new way. To illustrate the argument with a dualism: on the one hand, one can argue that if knowledge is only local, personal, temporary, contextual and practical, one can hardly see how science can contribute in a way that cannot be provided by others; on the other hand, if knowledge is universal, interpersonal, durable and abstract, theorising gives meaning. The deeper debates on scientific knowledge, particularly during the twentieth century, have implied that the concept of knowledge in general has been reformulated and reinterpreted.

The positivist idea of science has been challenged. The anti-positivist debate plays into a context where the understanding of research and science is under discussion. The anti-positivist positions question positivists' instrumentality by arguing for the primacy of life-world (Husserl), existence/Dasein (Heidegger), tacit knowledge (Polanyi), for knowledge in action (Schön), or in practice (Bourdieu), or the importance of inter-subjective knowledge (Dewey), or contextual knowledge as in communities of practice (Wenger). Also part of this big box of perspectives were democratising science and research (Habermas, Bourdieu), the practical turn (Bourdieu, Nowotny et al.) and the reflective practitioner (Schön).

All these are issues about the quality of research, but also about the social dimension of research. I argue that in order to answer them we need to know more about how sciences produce knowledge, including the governance mechanisms related to research. I further argue for a more self-reflecting discourse within science disciplines, about their limitations, how they produce knowledge across disciplines and how they are part of a knowledge system in society.

In order to achieve that, I have organised the chapter in the following way. First I discuss the methodological perspective in science: science as a quest for the right, true, method. Secondly, I go into the anti-positivist critique and present the sociological perspective on science. I argue that anti-positivism takes many and different forms. Thirdly, I discuss science in the discursive perspective. I argue that these three perspectives give different answers to the three main questions I have asked.

The Methodological Perspective

The methodological perspective implies that we can ask the following question: by what scientific method can we know that something is objectively true? Knowledge in this perspective is about producing truth in the sense of knowledge that corresponds with facts (Popper, 1979, p. 19).

Taking Karl Popper (1979) as a point of departure implies that the term science is defined in a restrictive way. Popper makes two main distinctions: between (pure) science and applied science, and between natural sciences and other (human) sciences. Table 4.1 positions this perspective.

In Table 4.1, it is only the pure, natural sciences that for Popper count as science, and it is based on this that scientific methodology is developed. Popper restricts his discussion to pure, natural sciences. This is also how the field is mainly discussed in what is termed theory of science, and that I will refer to as the methodological perspective on science.

Table 4.1   The positivist perspective on sciences

	Natural sciences	Human sciences
Pure science	Theory of science (science as methodology)	Science is based on human beliefs, interpretations. Truth is a state of mind
Applied sciences	Science as useful, pragmatic adjustment of knowledge	Science is meaningful and helpful, adjusted to human needs and opinions, interaction in society

Source: Based on Popper (1979).

A similar position is held by many scientists and implies that only theories such as Newton's theory of gravity, Maxwell's theory of electromagnetism, Einstein's theory of relativity, Mendeleev's periodic table, the theory of quantum mechanics and Darwin's theory of evolution would count as science (Grundmann and Stehr, 2012). It is within these limitations that we can say that science is about valid truth claims. How did this idea of a pure science evolve?

Karl Popper writes in the introduction to *The Growth of Scientific Knowledge*:

> *The history of science, like the history of all human ideas, is a history of irresponsible dreams, of obstinacy, and of error. But science is one of the few human activities – perhaps the only one – in which errors are systematically criticised and fairly often, in time, corrected. This is why we can say that, in science, we often learn from our mistakes, and why we can speak clearly and sensibly about making progress there. In most other fields of human endeavour there is change, but rarely progress (unless we adopt a very narrow view of our possible aims in life); for almost every gain is balanced, or more than balanced, by some loss. And in most fields we do not even know how to evaluate change. (Popper, 1979, p. 9)*

This optimistic view by Popper on behalf of science (and a gloomy view on behalf of society) was based on his understanding of what science is, and how science advances. In short, Popper had a very restricted opinion of what science is, an opinion we normally refer to as *positivism*, and a specific set of criteria for scientific development. However, not all would accept this position. In fact, there are large controversies on these issues, and I will argue that the recent reference to knowledge economy and knowledge society has influenced the border-setting in this field. This then implies that there has to be criteria for what is and what is *not* science. So I agree with Popper that, by defining this, we can learn about knowledge and knowledge development processes. The methodological refinement of science has developed over time but has also created new controversies, as I will argue below.

THE CLASSICS

The dispute between Plato and Aristotle was to a large extent over methodology. They shared many of the same metaphysical positions, but their methods of advancing knowledge differed. While Plato has written about Socrates' method of dialogical reasoning, Aristotle has given us more empirical-based approaches to knowledge. One can to some extent, by using a modern terminology, argue that Plato used a *deductive* method, while Aristotle used an *inductive* approach. The method of observation and testing can be traced back to Aristotle. Aristotle's project was to find the true essence of things, and he believed that by studying them in detail, one might find it. For example, by dissecting animals he could identify their differences and the core things that made them into what they were. As such, a comprehensive system of classification was to a large extent born with Aristotle. Plato, on the other hand, had tried to reach the right understanding of things through reasoning. One of the arguments we can refer to is related to the myth of the cave, where truth is hidden to us in its pure form, although we can form lots of knowledge based on the indirect access we have from our understanding of how truth has to be in order to make sense.

Aristotle, in his quest for classification, also made classifications that came to define science. Much of what fits within the restriction of science by Popper was defined by

Aristotle as *theoresis*. This perspective on science as only *theoresis* ignores Aristotle's other concepts of knowledge: *theoria*, *tekhnê* and *phrónêsis*. However, Aristotle also argues that *theoria*, *tekhnê* and *phrónêsis* were different things: *theoria* would never be able to deal with (explain) what happened in practice (Eikeland, 2008).

The controversies over types of knowledge would dominate Western thought up to our time. Aristotle's concept of *theoresis* became a main reference to modern empirical science. This happened in different stages. Scholastic theology, that is, Thomas Aquinas (1225–1274), had a fascination for Aristotle's empirical method and his system of classification of the physical world. This opened a further development of this method, mainly through the work of Roger Bacon (1214–1294), who extended Aristotle's methods to *experiments* (not only observation) to disapproval of Aquinas.

Further advances in the methodological development were, for instance, Francis Bacon (1561–1626), who argued for *empiricism* (critique of rationalism and, consequently, of deduction): we can know only what we observe. The advances in science increasingly came into conflict with the church and political order of society, and the issue of how to define scientific ethics arose. Scholars of the renaissance (such as Leonardo da Vinci) broke ground in not only dissecting nature but also human bodies. John Searle (2004) argues that this was the reason why René Descartes (1596–1650) made the strong distinction between human and nature. This Cartesian dualism allowed for giving nature to science, and still keeping the discussion on the human mind, morals and ethics within the domain of the church.

Francis Bacon and Jeremy Bentham (1748–1832), with their discussion of utilitarianism, implied a perspective on why we do science and what science is allowed to do. A distinction between truth or facts on the one hand, and utility on the other, made it possible to discuss science's discoveries of facts independent of its application (assessment). At the same time, with the utilitarian argument, ethical restrictions on experiments with animals and humans might be debated.

This led to a discussion on how to do theory-building or interpret data (induction and deduction): what about deduction? Should that be ruled out (because it was based on speculation)? Was induction possible? Were there different rules for moral science (human science and social science) than for natural science (physics, chemistry and biology)? David Hume (1711–1776), for example, was a strong critic of rationalists like Descartes (and therefore of deduction), and more or less developed the approach that we refer to as *induction*. He thought that moral science could develop methods (induction) that were different from, but still similar to, natural sciences, thereby developing true understanding of human and society (Levison, 1974). He accepted the split between moral science and natural science, but also believed that one can systematically understand human beings. These were ideas that later Mill and Brentano followed up on.

MODERN POSITIVISM

The development of science, from the classical period towards positivism, is a process of removing metaphysical speculation from science. Science developed as an empirical-based search for facts. When social science developed in the nineteenth century, its ambition was to copy natural science. The systematic growth of scientific knowledge that had made engineering and industrial development possible, and thereby had contributed to the Industrial Revolution in Britain, was to be copied in social sciences. Objective science, or positivism, a term used by Auguste Comte (1930–1842 [1988]) and repeated for instance by Emile Durkheim (1893 [2000]), was very explicit on this ambition. There should be sciences of man, as there were sciences of nature.

But if science is to make *valid truth claims*, how is that possible with regards to phenomena that are in constant change, and where the scientist is part of the practice and social processes that unfold? The response from the part of natural sciences is that they try to find the constant aspects of changes (motion), for example the *Boyle–Mariotte law* (published in 1651), which states that the absolute pressure and volume of a given mass of confined gas are inversely proportional if the temperature remains unchanged within a closed system. Analogously, in social sciences we may try to find some constant patterns of social change. For example, Emile Durkheim in his treaties on *Suicide* from 1897 tests the hypothesis that increase in suicide coincide with modern society, urbanisation and individualisation of culture and religion, and finds support for this hypothesis (Durkheim, 2005). In *De La Division Du Travail Social* from 1893 (Durkheim, 2000), Durkheim writes about solidarity:

> But in science we can know the causes only through the effects that they produce. In order to determine the nature of these causes more precisely science selects only those results that are the most objective and the best lend themselves to qualification. Science studies heat through the variations in volume that changes in temperature causes the bodies, electricity through its physical and chemical effects, and force through movement. Why should social solidarity prove an exception? [...] Thus the study of solidarity lies within the domain of sociology. It is a social fact that can only thoroughly known through its social effects. (Durkheim, 1997, pp. 26–7)

Auguste Comte believed, in the mood of the French Revolution, that positive science could make a new foundation for society. He held rather radical thoughts on how a society built on science, rather than religion, could modernise the life of man. Positivism therefore came to be identified with political radicalism. This became a strong position in the science/society debate at the end of the nineteenth century (Mackintosh, 2005).

The work that became known as *logical positivism* in the early twentieth century had a more clearly defined methodological and a less political focus. Logical positivism referred among others to David Hume and his ideas of sensation and pure facts. A key contribution to this position was Ludwig Josef Johann Wittgenstein (1889–1951), who in his *Tractatus Logico-Philosophicus* from 1921 had argued that the world consists of *facts*. But he also argued that science has limits as our knowledge has limits. There is knowledge beyond facts. However, between man and facts there is language. Science has to solve the problem of how we know that the language gives a correct representation of facts (correspondence with facts). To this he wrote:

> What we cannot speak about we must pass over in silence. (Wittgenstein, 1921, p. 75)

For this reason, logical positivists and logical empiricism in the early twentieth century became occupied with the logic of language: is there a scientific language that is so pure that we know that it represents objective facts only, or can we get beyond language?

In his 1951 paper *Two Dogmas of Empiricism*, where he criticised logical empiricism, Willard Van O. Quine discussed two of the dogmas that had been made: that of distinguishing analytical (that are only logical) statements from statements synthetically (that imply meaning or correspondence with facts), and that of reduction of statements to facts. He argued that none of them in fact meet logical criteria. Analytical statements cannot be distinguished from synthetical statements simply because the words we use in analytical statements are developed (give meaning) from our experience. And, all theories are insufficiently supported by empirical data.

POPPER ON OBJECTIVE TRUTH

It is on this background we should read Karl Popper's argument for the growth and objectivity of scientific knowledge. Popper had in earlier works argued that deduction and induction as methodological criteria did not fulfil the ambition of an objective science. Positivists had discussed deduction as a complex concept. Furthermore, we cannot induce, from the fact that all observed swans are white, that all swans are white. Therefore he rejected David Hume's argument, and presented falsification (and later testability) as the criteria for a scientific statement. A scientific statement is a simple one that can be *tested* and that can be *refuted*.

Furthermore, Popper wanted to save positivism from its critics by arguing that there is indeed scientific progress, and that science produces objective knowledge. His argument was that the only reason in science to replace a theory by a new theory is if the new one gives better description of the facts, or covers more facts than the old one. It is as a result of us knowing more that we develop new scientific theories. Also, his argument is that a more complex theory is more exposed to falsification than a simple one. So we can talk about degrees of falsification, in the sense that a higher degree of falsification implies a more advanced theory. Thereby, science makes progress. Popper was also aware that purely speculative or metaphysical statements could in principle be falsifiable. He therefore also had the criteria that a theory had to be testable.

On the issue of truth of a statement, he was aware of the critique of correspondence theory: how can we know that words, concepts and sentences give a meaningful description of the phenomenon we want to observe? First of all, he dismissed the idea that instead of talking of correspondence to facts, we can refer to coherence with beliefs, usefulness or evidence (arguments posed by the epistemological critique that we will return to below and where we find the idea that *truth is justified beliefs*). Building then on Tarski's correspondence theory that states that A is B simply if A in fact is B, Popper argued that falsification and *testability* will meet this criterion. If we can critically test if our theory corresponds with facts, and can critically adjust (falsify) the theory to make it more advanced so that it corresponds better with facts, and if this is an ongoing (scientific) process, we are on the track to truth.

By arguing in the way he does, Popper has omitted as scientific questions most of social and human issues. In practice only very few questions can be empirically tested in the scientific way that Popper refers to. For instance, if I argued that capitalism is better for society than socialism, it is difficult to imagine what sort of test could support or falsify such a problem. Most data for society and humans are contextual in some sense and thereby comparing cases and data in ways that meet the criteria of natural science with its controlled experiments is problematic.

POST-POSITIVISM AND ITS CHALLENGES

Those who refer to themselves as post-positivists have in general taken a more pragmatic approach to method. One sees methodology more as a toolbox which combines approaches in accordance with the topic at hand. Chalmers (2007) refers to a series of methodologies and argues that none of them are universal, but all of them have relevance. Chalmers' list is induction, deduction, abduction, falsification and probability. One could also add other approaches such as retroduction, network analysis or games. Anti-positivists would add the critical method and decomposition, as well as dialogue and action research. This implies a sort of methodological pragmatism. The role of science might therefore consist of:

- *understanding* the importance of general discussion in the context and meaning of various social phenomena;
- *interpreting* in more detail and more methodically, in order to understand things, what is called hermeneutics;
- *explaining* a phenomenon – if something is explained, one must know something about the causes and contexts;
- *helping*, which means that one has an ethical purpose in research;
- *changing and improving*, which is an ambition we have, for example, in what is called action research;
- *predicting* can be an object of research that assumes that one can explain, but also goes further beyond explanation, to say something about what will happen, a form of determinism, or systemic predictability, which forecasts;
- *falsification*, which is the ambition often said to be the safest for science.

In practice, as I see it, this implies that the methodological argument is not sufficient to define science. In order to define what science is, and to understand how knowledge is made, and what knowledge is made, we need to take a different philosophical approach.

If we consider the two pairs of concepts, *science and truth* versus *research and knowledge*, we easily see that the second pair is more open and elusive than the first. I think that if we look at all the things that researchers do today, all the things that happen in universities and in research institutions, very little of that would meet the positivist criteria for science. With the advances of research into the knowledge society, there is a call for scientific knowledge but also for the expansion of research and sciences into new areas.

THE INTERPRETIVE POSITION

One of the first objections to positivism and rationalism in science came in relation to what is called *Methodenstreit* in German social science in the late nineteenth century, in particular between the Austrian School (Carl Menger) and the (German) Historical School (Gustav Schmoller). The German historical/idealist tradition had roots in Hegel and included sociologists and philosophers such as Marx, Dilthey, Simmel and Mannheim. Part of it inspired the *sociology of knowledge*. The core of the controversy was whether historical development is *context and culturally specific*, or whether there are universals, *a priori* dimensions that transcend historical particularities. Menger had argued that although historical development was contextually specific, we could still identify a priori principles guiding for instance economic development. We can understand the logic of the economic system independent of a specific historical situation. Schmoller objected to this.

Wilhelm Dilthey (1833–1911) brought the controversy back to Descartes and Hegel that both had discussed the dualism between subjectivity and objective reality. He developed the two concepts of *explaining* and *understanding*, what is called the *interpretive method*. Levison (1974) argues that the dispute between Weber and Durkheim was very clear on one issue: if social events can only be understood through the idea that people have, that social science is of a different character than natural science. However, the difference between them is due to the fact that Weber argued that this is the case (we can only understand social phenomenon through the beliefs and ideas that people hold), while Durkheim denied this.

How do we observe and interpret? Wittgenstein talked about our pre-understanding as a fundamental element in our reflection. The interpretative position argues that we need, in our orientation towards realty, to combine *understanding* and *explaining*. The position is arguing that society is more than the sum of individuals. It is also arguing against reductionism: that we can understand both individuals as subjects and society, but through the use of multi methods. Furthermore, it argues that we can understand social differentiation as different meaning systems. That implies that knowledge is socially situated (sociology of knowledge) and this again has implications for methodology. For example, Geertz (2000) argued that the way to understand context-sensitive phenomenon is through *thick description*. Goffman (1974) developed his *framework analysis* as a methodology for analysing situation-specific events. The clearest development of this idea came with what we refer to as the hermeneutic position (Gadamer, 2006).

The Sociological Perspective

THE SCIENCE WARS

One can, roughly speaking, say that positivists focused their attention on the ontological issue: the nature of things. What they ignored, or at least claimed they could cope with, was the epistemological question: how do I get to know things? But what I will refer to here as anti-positivists is a large and diverse group, and not all of them are antagonists to positivism, although they reject some of the positivists' arguments.

The anti-positivists argued against a social science that had natural science as its ideal. As lots of positions go into this box, I do not intend to give a comprehensive presentation of these. The point I will make is that the anti-positivist critiques had in common a questioning of the foundation of social science, in particular that social science should copy the success of natural science. However, part of this critique also included, as we shall see, Husserl (1970), who indeed argued for objectivity in science, and Hayek, who argued against the constructivist tendencies in science (false rationalism), but still argued, as does Habermas, that science tries to identify transcendental truth.

C.P. Snow, in his famous speech in 1958, talked about two cultures and argued that natural and humanities would never meet, as they are simply too different (Snow, 1959). So, humanities cannot have as an ambition to copy natural science. Some, such as Jon Elster, have even argued that social science is impossible as a science (Elster, 1989).

However, there are also voices that have questioned the pretence of objective truth in all science, not only in social science. Thomas Kuhn (1970; 2000) makes this argument. In defence of arguing that sciences develop through paradigms, he argues that this historically is the case both for natural sciences and social science. However, he also argues that there is a difference between the two, as the constant development of new paradigms is more apparent in social science than in natural science.

A discipline is often thematically and administratively determined. A paradigm can be defined as a research tradition with consensus on method, empiricism, epistemology or theory. Paradigms, or research traditions, limit the methodological, thematic and/ or epistemological perspectives. Within paradigms there is a *normal* scientific discourse. Thomas Kuhn talked about scientific revolutions, when there is a shift in a paradigm. Discourses can be seen as different language games, that is, linguistic practices within a set of rules, norms, customs, and traditions. A discourse is a constitution of legitimacy of an intersubjective practice. Discourses are not cultures (unit thinking); they are subject to plurality. If what we observe is unified thinking, domination or indoctrination, it means that it is a cult rather than a discourse. In the preface to *The Structure of Scientific Revolutions*, Thomas Kuhn wrote:

> *Particularly, I was stuck by the number and extent of the overt disagreements between social scientists about the nature of legitimate scientific problems and methods. Both history and acquaintance made me doubt that practitioners of the natural sciences possess firmer or more permanent answers to such questions than their colleagues in social science. Yet, somehow the practices of astronomy, physics, chemistry, or biology naturally fail to evoke controversies over fundamentals that today often seem endemic among us, say, psychologists or sociologists. Attempting to discover the source of that difference led me to recognise the role in scientific research of what I have since called 'paradigms'. These I take to be universally recognised scientific achievements that for a time provide model problems and solutions to a community of practitioners. (Kuhn, 1970 [1962], p. viii)*

Science has been atomised into disciplines and research programmes (Lakatos). Research programmes imply that science is moving between observation and reflection within frameworks. These frameworks are not necessarily correct; rather, they reflect the particular choices of that scientific group.

PHENOMENOLOGY

The interpretive and the hermeneutic positions are largely in debt to the work of Edmund Gustav Albrecht Husserl (1859–1938). However, the core of Edmund Husserl's scientific programme was to develop a theory of *transcendental subjectivity*, based on an interpretation of Hume and Brentano. He was close to the positivists in many respects, but criticised them mainly for ignoring the human dimension. Husserl's attack on positivism was explicitly oriented against natural sciences. He said that they 'discovered' the true world of atoms, which is superior to our life-world and determines it; consequently, if man consists of atoms which are causally determined, he/she, too, is causally determined and his/her freedom and conscience are illusions or epiphenomena. According to Husserl, there has been forgotten that the natural sciences serve only as an instrument of predictions, and their predictive function is applied within our life-world;

Husserl, like Kant, denied the existence, or 'true reality', of atoms; he treated them as explanatory-predictive schemes/models. Husserl is mainly known for his proclamation: To the things themselves! What he means is that Decartian philosophy has been preoccupied with discussing the relationship between things as we perceive them and things as they really are (Kant), while Hussler wants to put brackets on this very problem and focus on the thing itself and its phenomenological appearance. In this way, Husserl tries to break free of the classical divide between subject and object.

Whereas sciences study the relations among objects (this is true also for social science in Popper's and Hayek's definition), phenomenology studies the relations between subject and object; but a true phenomenologist (Husserl) wants to find there what is necessarily common to all subject–object relations, that is, their *a priori* formal structure; in other words he is oriented not to the empirical but to the transcendental subject. Thus, unlike hermeneutics (which is contextual), phenomenology is strongly against relativism. Phenomenology conceives understanding on a more subjective level. One tries to transcend the social veil, the psychological veil, search towards the real, the authentic and the transcendental truth.

HERMENEUTICS

Hermeneutics owes much of its current position to Hans-Georg Gadamer (1900–2002) and his main work from 1960, *Truth and Method* (Gadamer, 2006). It is a position that should be grouped under the epistemological label. However, Gardamer criticised Dilthey for subjectivising too much the scientific method. He criticises methods as some sort of reduction of things. Therefore hermeneutics is about coming to a true interpretation of things; it is not a psychology. Hermeneutics also implies interpreting meaning and can therefore be expanded to a larger area of studies (not only texts). The argument, for instance presented by Charles Taylor (1971), holds that all meaning is developed in a local meaning system. The way we see the world is communicated and 'negotiated' in local contexts of meaning.

In this respect, hermeneutics is understanding meaning, and society is a meaning system. There is meaning to oneself and meaning to others. Thus meaning is negotiated in a social context (hermeneutic circle). This thus implies a critique of subjectivism (epistemology) but also a critique of conceptualisations (concept might be logical but not correspond to reality), a critique of methodological individualism and a critique of universalism. Hermeneutics portrays us as participants in a context of 'local' language games. We are reflexive participants in local contexts.

These last arguments formed the background for the criticism of relativism, posted, among others, by Habermas. And they were discussed, among others, by Paul Ricœur (1913–2005), who defined a *critical hermeneutic* position. One of the themes that Ricœur came to deal with is how our self-understanding is interrelated to the metaphors and language we use (Ricoeur, 1976; 1992).

CRITICAL THEORY

One of the main issues and problems addressed by the critical position is how we can *avoid false consciousness*. And the core of the solution to this problem is, in the conception of Habermas, to develop *communicative rationality*. It is unrealistic to assume that all scientific knowledge is true. Rather science makes huge mistakes. So, the focus should be on how science and society correct these mistakes.

Habermas wrote:

> Within a life-reference fixed by everyday language and stamped out in social norms, we experience and judge things as human beings with regard to specific meaning, in which the un-separated, descriptive and normative content states just as much about the human subjects who live in it as it does about the objects experienced themselves. (Habermas, 1963, p. 166)

It is, according to Habermas, a mistake to base our understanding of knowledge on experience alone. Some experiences are beyond our reach, however skilful we are. Not all understandings of speech can be understood within the speech itself. Consequently distorted speeches (false consciousness) cannot be detected 'from within'. It gives us no criteria to detect false consciousness, distorted opinions and misunderstandings. Our explanatory competence can therefore not only rest on skills to understand and comprehend 'the other' but must also be based on communicative competence to detect falseness.

PRAGMATISM

American pragmatism, in general, argues against (large-scale) theory-building and in favour of a science that produces practical, immediate and useful knowledge. 'The practical turn' is found in Bourdieu (1990), Nowotny et al. (2001) and Donald Schön (1983) and emphasises practice over theoretical knowledge. Tacit knowledge (Polanyi, 1966), science in action (Latour, 1987), or in practice (Bourdieu, 1990), or the importance of intersubjective knowledge (Dewey, 1927), or contextual knowledge as in communities of practice (Lave and Wenger, 1991) are examples of arguments in this line.

Pragmatism builds on a theory of sensation. Our whole sense-apparatus is relevant: feelings, sensing in terms of sound, smell, experiences and interpretation. The development of the position includes: C.S. Pierce's rejection of Descartes' dualism, emphasising the sense order and abduction as a method; W. James, the physiologist who argued that 'the good method is one that works'; J. Dewey, who developed a link between 'impressionism', learning and democracy; G.H. Mead (1962), who discussed the discursive self; Richard Rorty's (1982) discussion of pragmatism and the life-world; M. Friedman (1953), with his methodological pragmatism; Karl Weick's (1995) sense-making in organisations; and finally Apel/Habermas arguing for transcendental pragmatics and pragmatism as rationalism.

STRUCTURALSIM/POST-STRUCTURALISM

The post-structuralist position can be understood on the background of the classical discourses on the evolution of society. Post-structuralism is often called 'post-dialectical' since it refuses Hegel's dialectics. In this way they are a reaction to Marx and Hegel. Dialectical theory of evolution had been presented in Hegel's *Philosophy of Right* and Marx's *The Communist Manifesto*. They represent a distinction between idealist dialectics (Hegel), the spirit in historical development and materialist dialectics (Marx): ownership of the means of production as a determinant of development.

Durkheim in his works on the transition from traditional to modern society studied through 'empirical generalisation' and argued for social facts. Durkheim's main work is *De la division du travail social*. It is based on a method of abstraction from observing development, in his case the transition from segmented to division of labour, from collectivism to individualism and the emergence of money and markets. Though, it is important to be aware of his structuralist criticism of Marxism, and his introduction of concepts such as symbolic systems.

Thus structuralism looked at material causes of structures, similarities of structures, the role of values, that religion reflects material conditions (Durkheim), that ideas/beliefs/values form structure (Weber), that value is seen as exchange (Lêvi-Strauss), and structuration of practice (Bourdieu). Post-structuralism represents a reaction to this analysis. Structure is also seen as discourse (Foucault).

However, there are internal differences in this field.

Durkheim saw structure as material and symbolic. Levi-Strauss poses a critique of this structuralism as social relations are shaped by exchange; structure is not progress. Roland Bartes argued that our own society is a tribal society. Bourdieu, in between structuralism and post-structuralism, argued for social recognition forming social structures; social capital (habitus) forming structuration. He saw practice as mediating structure and individuality. Foucault and Derrida saw structures as just historical phenomena, not constant, right or universal. Structures are 'layers of beliefs' that we think are true. Foucault thus develops a discursive theory of structure. Derrida discussed differences in the sense of multi-level of meaning, Lyotard and Baudillard combine Freudianism and post-structuralism; analysis of how we are seduced by what we believe is right (develop false consciousness). This position is reflected in modern critique of the capitalist economy (Boltanski and Chiapello, 2005). However, one could say that the core of post-structuralism is to seek truth beyond the *veil of social structures*.

COMPARING PARADIGMS

We can see the different positions as paradigms (Burrell and Morgan, 1979) in the sense of different research traditions with different procedures. Examples are:

- phenomenology: the phenomenological method (procedure) of testing assumptions;
- hermeneutic: the hermeneutic method, pre-understanding, testing through reflection in hermeneutic circles;
- positivism: falsification;
- pragmatism: procedures related to participating in problem-solving.

Also, the role of theory changes as we go from one position to another:

- critical realism: theory as representation of an underlying real structure (explain);
- interpretive theory (Taylor): theory as meaning systems, internal, intersubjective meaning and relation to social institutions;
- phenomenology: theory as interpretation, a personal account meaning of abstract relations that can be contested by others (in discourse).

As discussed, Aristotle was aware of the fact that there are different kinds of knowledge. *Theoresis* can refer to a conventional concept of science, while *theoria* was reflexive knowledge, *tekhnê* or technology an applied knowledge, and *phrónêsis* or prudence knowledge about what is proper and what it is to be a good human being (Eikeland and Nicolini, 2011).

One can argue that theories are codified knowledge, that is, theories are formulated in a language that allows them to be compared (with other theories). This language is codified, which means that it is available to all who speak the language. However, theorising has limitations. Some knowledge is tacit, outside the reach of theories. An example often used is the knowledge of how to ride a bicycle: most people know how to ride a bike, but do not necessarily have a theory of why and how. It is a skill that is acquired through practice (and not through theory). Even one who reads lots of theory about biking will not necessarily be able to ride or be a good cyclist.

The term theory is not an unambiguous phenomenon. We use it here as a broad term to describe scientific explanations. However, there are many types of theories, and many types of theoretical knowledge. For example, a general theory assumes stable practice, while nomological theories involve a claim that there is no variation in practice. These requirements are rarely met. In social science, theories will often only provide partial explanations for a phenomenon.

All knowledge is not theoretical knowledge; rather, theories are a special kind of knowledge. Theories are simplifications, stylisations and codification of phenomena. One theory might say something about causes and effects, which implies that it is an assumption about a relationship. What, then, is a good theory? A theory's goodness is determined by the underlying assumptions. The more comprehensive and accurate these are, the better the theory. Friedman (1953) argued that the goodness of a theory is determined by its explanatory power and ability to predict. Hayek (1949) argued for theories as simplified frameworks to understand complex phenomenon (that cannot be fully understood).

For example, a theory can say that the low percentage of female senior managers is due to priorities women make between work and family. Such a theory does not have to be either right or wrong, but it can prove to have a certain explanatory power. That is, the theory is part of a complex of statements that together explains why the number of female executives is so low. Most social phenomena we study are complex, where no single theory provides a complete explanation. These and other distinctions between approaches allow different research strategies to be relevant. One can distinguish between causal explanations (physics), intentional explanations (social phenomena), functional explanations (biology) and aesthetic explanations (that something is beautiful, for example art) (Elster, 1989; Ghoshal, 2005).

THE SOCIOLOGY OF SCIENTIFIC KNOWLEDGE

Holzner and Marx (1979) use the framework of *sociology of knowledge* to discuss two structural features of modern society: expert systems and ideologies. Expert systems or professional work group systems exist very much on the basis of controlling information. Their logic of working and prevailing follows the general system of control and reinforcement. Society allows expert systems to develop, because they are regarded as essential to certain areas of knowledge and wealth. Ideologies, likewise, are general norm systems aimed at legitimising a certain power structure in society. They are systems of defining who we are and who they are, who is inside and who is outside. Subsequently ideologies will always exist as long as there are social groups, and these groups (by their nature) have to define some consistent formulations that give the group identity.

Knorr-Cetina has studied epistemic cultures that are the sociology of scientific groups. She defines epistemic cultures as:

> ...cultures that create warrant knowledge, and the premier knowledge institution throughout the world is, still, science. (Knorr-Cetina, 1999, p. 1)

In her article *The Fabrication of Facts* (in Stehr and Meja, 1984), she argues that science does not describe or discover facts, rather it produces knowledge. Subsequently, science is a particular branch of knowledge production, and one that establishes its own internal system of validity (which might not be the same as objective validity). In fact, science has its own system of validation, such as peer review, which judges innovation and selects areas for further investigation.

Knorr-Cetina's model for science thereby resembles Luhmann's self-referential system theory (Luhmann, 1995). The internal process is self-referential, for instance within a scientific group (epistemic community), while this group will have to relate to other groups, and to interpret external pressures to produce and develop knowledge. In her 1999 book, *Epistemic Cultures: How the Sciences Make Knowledge*, Knorr-Cetina argues that epistemic cultures have a specific and contradictory impact on the knowledge society, parallel to the confusing role of expert systems in a modern, knowledge society.

The Discursive Perspective

Some anti-positivists have been antagonists to conventional, positive science, and we should not hide the fact that these debates have been highly conflict-ridden. A general position in anti-positivist controversy is that, over time, grand ideas and systems have developed into discourses. Science as a discursive process could be used as a general description of the theory of science debates that occurred after the Second World War, and not least the debate that followed Thomas Kuhn's concept of *scientific paradigm* (Kuhn, 1970). What Kuhn showed, by making a historical analysis of science, was that, what at one time was regarded as truth, at other times was overthrown. Normal science was the type of scientific activity that happened within a framework of accepted truths; however, scientific revolutions might overthrow these truths. Put differently, any normal scientific activity happens within a paradigm, and as there are paradigms, there are also competing paradigms. Even Karl Popper observed that:

> 'Normal' science exists. It is the activity of the non-revolutionary, or more precisely, the not-too-critical professional: of the science student who accepts the ruling dogma of the day. (Popper, 1979b)

Lakatos (1959) used the term *research programme* to describe how scientific activity happened within frameworks, and Feyerabend (1975) coined the term *anarchy* to describe how different positions within science compete on truth claims. The position that science basically is a discursive process includes Peter Winch's work on science (Winch, 1958), and similar arguments posed by Stephen Toulmin (2001). Social science is a discourse among other discourses and a discourse in society. It is an argument for democratising science and research (Habermas, 1968; Bourdieu, 1990).

Dick Pels (2005) argues that Knorr-Cetina as well as Bruno Latour (1987) and John Law (2004) have shifted their perspective from a Bourdieuian emphasis on material (economic) causes for knowledge creation to a more Foucaultian (symbolic power, politics) perspective. Science is increasingly politics. A compromise between these positions can be identified in the *community of practice* theory. A community of practice (Lave and Wenger, 1991; Amin and Roberts, 2008b) can be seen as social process, however, linked to solving real problems and challenges. What the community does is to engage in common effort to use the best available knowledge to solve a problem that is commonly recognised. It is less of a construction process, but still has elements of it.

How can we bridge paradigms or transcend paradigmatic differences? Richard Rorty, who argued from a pragmatic perspective, argues that philosophy itself has difficulties in defining common truths, and even a common understanding of philosophy (Rorty, 1979). If we firstly accept the division between nature and humans (man), would it not be reasonable to also assume that nature is interpretation and that what we understand as nature is our understanding or interpretation of nature and not a mirror of nature? There are good reasons to stop believing that we can reach a higher understanding through philosophising. But what about the critical theory position, hermeneutics, interpretive sociology or phenomenology? How can these be defended in the vibrant philosophy of science discourse?

William Rehg (2009) argues for a cogent theory. By cogent he refers to the convincing quality of the argument:

> Both in the sciences and in the various contexts in which the sciences meet society, one must examine scientific claims from their strength: is the finding conclusive, probable, or mere possibility based on a limited amount of research? (Rehg, 2009, p. 5)

The cogent theory is supposed to be a more flexible concept than, for instance, validity, which often refers more specifically to a certain scientific procedure. It is an argument that acknowledges the discursive nature of scientific development, but tries to transcend some of the differences that develop.

THE EPISTEMOLOGICAL TURN

As a starting point for presenting the discursive perspective, one can refer both to the epistemological and the linguistic turn in science. The epistemological turn dates back to large philosophical debates started in the nineteenth century. Jürgen Habermas traces the discussion back to Hegel. He argues that Hegel pioneered the understanding of modern society in the tension between *instrumental rationality* and *subjective reflexivity* (Habermas, 1987). Modern society has made technological advances and instrumentalised life under the discipline of modern production systems, but has thereby produced alienation, as subjective reflexivity is suppressed for the sake of instrumentality. In *Knowledge and Human Interest* from 1968, Habermas writes:

Positivism could forget that methodology of science was intertwined with objective self-formative process (Bildungsprozess) of the human species and erect the absolutism of pure methodology on the basis of the forgotten and repressed. (Habermas, 2007 [1968], p. 5)

One philosophical position that tried to address this gap is found in the work of the phenomenologist Edmund Husserl arguing for the primacy of human nature. Further advances in this development were Husserl's development of the concept of life-world, Heidegger's conceptualisation of being (Dasin) and French existentialist exposition of subjectivity. Anti-positivism is in this sense a position that challenges the pretence of objectivity in social sciences. Hans Skjervheim's seminal work from 1958, which was later translated into English under the title *Objectivity and the Study of Man* (Skjervheim, 1959), gives a very accurate name to the whole anti-positivist position. The argument – that the study of man is not one of finding objective truths, rather a question of understanding humans in society and, furthermore, that by objectivising the human being, one will end up in dehumanising man – was not new when Skjervheim wrote his essay. Already William Dilthey had been writing in the 1880s about the distinction between explaining and understanding, arguing that social sciences were primarily about the latter (Dilthey, 1976). Edmund Husserl, in one of his last works, in 1936, made a strong attack on social sciences that he argued was entering a crisis, because it had lost sight of the subject and the human being (Husserl, 1970).

The issue is how we can combine the two insights: that of the *instrumental*, natural world, and that of subjective and *reflexive* existence. Habermas takes the epistemological turn as a point of departure and argues that social science (and all science) is basically a social process, integrated in the social fabric of powered relations and interests. Science is not outside, above, unaffected or independent of society. Science is mirroring structures of the society it is part of, that is, it is embedded in social interests. Science has, as Habermas argued, become *democratised*, which is a concept that must be understood as an abstract description and not a discussion of organisation. Therefore, Habermas argues that this does not imply a rejection of positivism and conventional research's call for truth and objectivity. Habermas talks about a *subjective objectivity* (Habermas, 2007).

Habermas's main point is that in a post-metaphysical society, science, philosophy and theory cannot claim a role in its own right. It is part of societal processes. Furthermore, in a liberal, democratic society, theory and philosophy cannot claim authority over the individual and his or her pursuit of good and bad and own goals in life. However, science still searches for truth. Therefore, Habermas criticises Rorty as well as the idea of paradigms by Kuhn, Feyerabend's defence of anarchy in methods, and the concept of a research programme by Lakatos. He sees all of them as an attempt to defend *relativism* in science and make any discussion of *scientific progress* impossible.

BETWEEN SUBJECTIVISM AND OBJECTIVISM

Habermas takes as a starting point a sociological perspective on science, that is, he regards science as a social practice in its own right. So the value freedom or objectivity of science is defined by the institutional and social process within science. It is a negotiated truth. The value question, Habermas argues, can be termed as the relation between facts and decision, or the dualism of *is* and *ought*. He writes:

> *The dualism of facts and decisions corresponds, in the logic of science, to the separation of cognition and evaluation and, in methodology, to the demand for a restriction of the realm of empirical-scientific analysis to the empirical uniformity of natural and social processes. (Habermas, 1976, p. 145)*

The question, then, is whether we can separate knowledge (facts) from evaluations (decisions). This question highlights a problem (or question) within pragmatism: is there on the one hand a continuum between theoretical (scientific) knowledge and practical processes on the other? Popper's answer is that scientific knowledge is distinct, because it has to have the property to be falsified. Habermas disagrees that this is a universal criteria, because he regards this criteria as in itself a (social) norm.

   This leads us to Habermas's main point that even (social) science is a social activity and performed within the framework of institutions, norms and pre-understandings. There is no such thing as pure theory. The circle of arguments that this leads to is that even criteria of value freedom are socially constructed (a product of social processes). He argues:

> *Within a life-reference fixed by everyday language and stamped out in social norms, we experience and judge things as human beings with regard to specific meaning, in which the un-separated, descriptive and normative content states just as much about the human subjects who live in it as it does about the objects experienced themselves. (Habermas, 1976, p. 166)*

This perspective corresponds with, and supports, the general argument that science is a social practice and has to comply with the same control, critique and social questioning that holds for society as a whole.

   Habermas does not take an extreme anti-positivist standpoint. That is, he recognises different ways of studying society and different types of theorising. He discusses and compares two approaches to society as a system, that is, system as understood by Hegel implying that individuals are part of a comprehensive whole (society), so-called dialectical theory, and system as understood more technically, as a deterministic, functionalistic process. He discusses this relation along four themes:

1. The meta position is that no system can study itself, so all system approaches have to be regarded as some sort of social sense-making, or what he calls an *ordering schemata*. On the other hand, he holds that any such general perspective that the scientist has will influence the research that he or she does; it has an indirect impact on our perspectives. And he proclaims:

> *For we know hardly anything about an ontological correspondence between scientific categories and the structure of reality. (Habermas, 1976, p. 133)*

2. Furthermore, in comparing the functionalist systems theory with a dialectical systems theory, he argues that functionalist systems theory is analytical-empirical based (ref. empirical sociology), while dialectical system theory is experience based.
3. Habermas explains the difference between the two systems approaches as follows: the functionalist system presupposes society as if it was a natural phenomenon that we can observe, where one element is a functional part of the whole, and where

we get the same result independent of how we research it. This implies a direct relation between science and practice. The dialectical approach acknowledges the dependence of individual phenomenon upon the totality, but rejects that this can be perceived in law-like terms. In this perspective, social phenomena are not constants, but particular, concrete events that must be understood in their application (practice). Social laws become a reality in this practice, that is, as a result of individuals' interpretation of the concrete situation. In this sense, social structures and laws are objective in the sense that that they are perceived as real by individuals in a particular situation. This points in the direction of sociology as interpretation (*verstehen*). Following this, the dialectical approach implies that we must distinguish between theory (science) and practice and, not the least, of meaning and interpretation.

4. Given the above points, analytical social theory can only be regarded as partial in the sense that it is restricted to some interpretations. Furthermore, the dialectical approach implies that science must explain (and legitimise) itself and reflect on its own practice.

How can we theorise on social phenomena, how can we get knowledge and what are the constraints of this knowledge? Here Habermas discusses his critical approach against what he calls four competing approaches of positions: (a) objectivism, (b) hermeneutics, (c) systems theory and (d) philosophy of history.

One could argue that this position anticipates that action researchers focus on local practice and local knowledge. However, the fact is that the inherent dialectics of the critical approach imply that one recognises what is criticised, in this case theory. Habermas's point is therefore not one of arguing against theory, rather to argue that theory has to be understood in a special way in social science, as a way of objectivising knowledge, which is in line with Popper (1979a) and Nozick (2001).

Theory has to relate to the general, empirical reality. Habermas (1974) talks about the dual relationship between theory and practice: on the one hand a social practice that makes theorising possible, on the other, political practice that makes theorising meaningful. Stability of social practice is a necessary precondition for social theorising, invariance in Robert Nozick's term (Nozick, 2001). Habermas is not a critique of theory, rather he argues in line with Popper that the social and system world have ontological status (Habermas, 1997; Popper, 1979a).

Based on this general understanding, one has to see social theorising in relation to structural conditions in society. As these change, so does the focus of social theory; that is, in modern (post-modern?) society this has brought issues of legitimacy up in front of societal understanding.

SCIENCE AND INTERESTS

Social theory is not merely an analysis (and observation) of the content of social practice. Social theory also involves social meaning and social engagement. There is a reciprocal relation between theory and practice; they involve a communicative relationship. Habermas argues against a universal systems theory and the idea that *unsolved problems* in social theory can be treated within a self-regulating system. We should not overemphasise the subjective, reflexive capability of man. Habermas (2001) explains some of the pre-studies that lead to his communicative action theory. These are texts written in the mid-1970s, where he spells out the research strategy he intends to use. His starting point is to position himself according to fundamental positions or meta-theory.

The first positioning Habermas does is to contrast his concept of action in relation to the concept of behaviour. For Habermas, it is essential to include meaning in communication in this theory, not only patterns of behaviour. We need to understand social action as meaningful expressions. Behaviour is a sort of adaptation to the environment. Action is an intentional behaviour. It is not causal but can rather be understood as a chain of regularities of intended actions.

This challenges the research on action. While behaviour can be observed, action has to be understood. This further implies some methodological challenges, because intention is hard to observe. Measuring something means presenting data to support a statement. Here Habermas argues that a social theory must be able to explain communicative action:

> Theories that are to explain the phenomenon accessible through the understanding of meaning [Sinnverstehen] – that is, the utterance and expressions of subjects capable of speech and action – must take the form of a systematic explanation of the knowledge of rules based on which competent speakers and actors generate their expressions. (Habermas, 2001, p. 9)

This implies answering questions such as: (1) Who is the subject of this generative process, or is there any? (2) How can this generative process be generalised (cognitive, linguistic, or labour)? (3) Are the underlying systems of rules invariant over social systems, or contextual? This supremacy of theory is no longer in itself valid. Furthermore, theory, such as Marx's historical materialism, often had elements of metaphysics in it. Theory cannot make such claims. Theory has to see itself as one among many different sources of knowledge.

However, having said this, theory still has an independent role as critique. In order to discuss the critical role of philosophy and theory, Habermas refers back to his general framework of discourses in society. That is, he makes a distinction between the subjective, the social and the cultural (institutional) sphere. The role of theory and the role of philosophical critique are different in these spheres. For the cultural/institutional sphere, Habermas refers to the fact that society becomes increasingly complex, and related to that, argues that there is a growing need for expert knowledge. Theory and philosophical discourses can have a role as critical expert knowledge. In the social sphere, philosophy will increasingly have a role as hermeneutics, as trying to find meaning and to guide meaning. The false way to perceive this would be to see theory at an authoritarian voice. The right way to see it would be to see theory and philosophy as an autonomous part in a social discourse.

THE ARGUMENTATIVE THEORY

Anti-positivism has challenged the way we understand science. In fact, science is now increasingly seen as a practice in society, as part of society, more or less as a collaborative and discursive activity. I have presented versions of this argument, and there are of course even more variants of anti-positivism. However, one need not argue strongly in order to see that this position is a great challenge to the role of social science as objectivity, as argued by Auguste Comte and his followers. As social practice we refer to science as meta-perspectives, discipline, paradigm, discourse, model, theory, hypotheses. These may be seen as different levels of arguments.

Meta-perspectives cut across historical lines of thought, and centre on core issues such as truth, validity and relevance. They often represent distinctions between, or reflections on, the universal and the local, explaining (causality and laws) versus understanding, degrees of explanation, simple versus complex phenomenon, and what facts in science are.

As a practice we can argue that science is different from everyday knowledge, in that it is an approach to data characterised by systematic investigation, transparency, verifiability, open communication, codifiable/publishable knowledge, systematic knowledge accumulation and precision. We can also say that science is an institutionalised system for systematic investigation and knowledge. It is a system that relies on legitimacy. Legitimacy is achieved through the conduct and ethics of the researcher: the researcher must define their role in relation to the research question; there must be the possibility of criticism and the possibility of falsification. Research can therefore be seen as a distinct social practice. The point in the discursive position is that we cannot decide the one argument over the other across paradigms. They are simply too different.

One can argue that the researcher can draw more general insights across cases. The argument is that practical, local knowledge can be supplied with more aggregated, general knowledge. Anthony Giddens (1984) makes this argument when he defends social science. Habermas, however, argues that we should not confuse that debate over *method* with the discussion of the *foundation of science*. There might, as argued above, be a plurality (anarchy) of methods, without implying that we cannot discuss the overall truth and objectivity of science.

Science as a discourse might imply that we focus on how different scientific positions have challenged each other: logical positivism as a reaction to historicism; critical theory and pragmatism as a reaction to logical positivism (Apel, Habermas); post-structuralism as a reaction to rational functionalism (Derrida, Foucault); the linguistic turn as a reaction to the practical turn (Rorty), to mention some. It is the argument of Rehg (2009) that we can transcend these differences through an overall social discourse that addresses the truthfulness and trustworthiness of scientific statements.

Conclusion

In this chapter I have investigated and discussed three different perspectives on science – the methodological, the sociological and the discursive – in order to understand how science makes knowledge, and how it can be understood as a particular practice in society. I tried to describe a development from a very pure, positivistic understanding of science to a much broader, integrated concept of research. I have discussed methodological pragmatism, paradigms and the methods, practice and procedures of science.

As science reaches into new areas of social life, which is the expectation in a knowledge society, it also reaches into areas that to a lesser extent meet the criteria of the positivist. For example, a concept such as nation would probably not meet the criteria for being a fact in Wittgenstein's sense. A nation is something we socially choose to call a phenomenon; it is not brute fact as an essential substance of nature, but rather in Emile Durkheim's and Max Weber's sense, a *social fact* which is a much more elusive phenomenon. A similar test would, I assume, reveal that much of what is communicated as science refers to social fact. This alone indicates the interdependence of the social and the scientific realm of knowledge.

I see two related problems that it is important to address: firstly, that research is able to reconcile relations to different research traditions, ending in some unproductive disputes; secondly, how it is able to define the relation to practice. The argument here is that all systems and situations that researchers are involved in produce knowledge, but that the structure of the system, setting or situations has an impact on what and how knowledge is produced. The situation or system has its own logic, rules and meaning construction. The expert system might be a disciplinary system, with its rules, procedures, hierarchies, the community of practice might be a group of researchers and practitioners, involved on solving a problem, again forming its own discourse, rules, meaning construction. How is it that these can become valid truth claims?

I make the claim, in line with Weber (1978) and Schütz (1972), that certain aspects of human existence, meaning our life-world, are and should be beyond the reach of social science, consistent with the early Wittgenstein positivism. That is, science should pretend to understand and report everything about existence and the meaning of life. Furthermore, I argue that by acknowledging this, we can have a better discussion on how to do research that pays respect to individual human beings and at the same time produces robust and valid scientific knowledge.

So what this implies is that there is a relation between how the knowledge development process is organised and what knowledge is produced. Put differently, the type of process that the researcher takes part in defines the type of knowledge that is developed. These are observations in line with the discussion by Jürgen Habermas on expert knowledge and expert systems (Habermas, 1974) and by Anthony Giddens on scientific knowledge versus common sense (Giddens, 1984). The point they make is that there is not one, but many different discourses or knowledge-producing situations. They can be more or less practical, more or less situational, and more or less temporary. This in itself is not the criteria for whether we do research or not. What defines something as research is that it relates to the research discourse that consists of many different arenas. Being research does not imply that what the individual researcher says or claims is true, but it does imply that it can be discussed and contested and criticised by other researchers as valid truth claims. It might also imply that some would call it bad research, and even say it is not research. The boundaries here are not fixed, but are a matter of constant discussion.

CHAPTER

5 *Economic Thought, Market and Knowledge*

Introduction

In this chapter I discuss the development of economic thought in relation to societal issues and politics. In particular I try to address how economics refers to knowledge. What I try to show is that the development of economics as a science on the one hand meant a decoupling from politics, but on the other hand that economics has always been closely related to the prevailing political and societal issues. I then look further into how some important economic theories have approached that question of knowledge. I start with some references to the history of economic thought, in order to show how the economic domain has been conceptualised. After that I discuss theories that address knowledge and market. I will argue that neo-classical economics had the ambition of *logical positivism*, to develop universal, rational and abstract theories about the economy. I will also argue that this attempt was contested by more institutional and evolutionary economists.

The Concept of the Market

In economics, the market is a main reference. Markets are either understood as mechanisms and constructs, or they are understood as processes. This dichotomy is related to more than a static versus a dynamic perspective. It is related to the function of the market and therefore the legitimacy and importance of the market.

The ancient Greeks described the open universe as *cosmos*, while they used the term *taxis* in relations to closed systems. *Cosmos* indicated a system of unendedness, of un-revealed processes, and with unexpected elements. It meant a complex system, not a chaotic system. Complexity meant that a single individual did not have enough knowledge to overview all the processes and individual actions, while at the same time it indicated that some sort of understanding of the system structure was present. *Taxis*, on the other hand, was a closed system with identifiable processes and a totally predictable outcome (Hayek, 1973).

F.A. Hayek has identified two very different concepts of rules and laws related to these two types of system: *nomos* and *thesis*. *Nomos* are rules of the open process. *Thesis* are rules of the closed process. These two types of rule might exist within the same system. There might be enclaves of closed systems within the larger open system. In the political and social system, this might be illustrated with the relation between the administrative processes within the market order. Of course, a closed system within a wider open system might not be totally closed, but only to some degree closed.

One way of thinking of this is to say that the economy is one among many *institutions* in society. For example, we have the education system where we go in order to learn, the religious system where we go to pray, the health system where we go in order to cure diseases and the market system where we go to exchange goods. The problem with such an idea is that there are many market-related and economic elements in the education, church and health system, such as employment contracts, renting buildings or buying services.

Are the economy and the market then special institutions in society? Has it penetrated other institutions? If we take work: is work a result of the market or is market a result of work? Can we have work without an economy or a market? Of course we can. However, today the two are heavily integrated. I think it is difficult to defend an idea of a hierarchy of institutions. So how can we then deal with the fact that the market and economic elements are integrated into other activities which have little in common with the market?

There is a market for goods and services, but the term is also more common and more used with reference to traditionally non-market activities such as politics (the political market) and religion (the market for religion). But do all those who use the word market share the same vision of the market? Do they refer to the same basic conceptions of the market process? Or do they define their concept of the market at all? If so, what is the market and how does it work?

Phrased differently, what type of social institution or social activity are we referring to when we talk about the economy or the market? Is it a distinct social activity, or is it an integrated part of society as such? Is our way of treating it as a separate domain arbitrary, or is it, ontologically speaking, something that clearly demarks what is economic, what is the market and what is not?

On the one hand I want to clarify some of the visions and principles that economists have included in their conception of the market. In other words, the intention here is to try to reveal what sort of social and economic processes economists have had in mind when they refer to the market. On the other hand I will ask whether different concepts of the market can be identified with different paradigms in economic thought. This is a precondition for the economic discussion on how markets make knowledge.

What about the relation between *economics and politics*? Is the market separate from politics? First of all, the theoretical debate about the economy over two centuries has been strongly integrated into political and ideological battles. Referring to the controversies and debates in the 1930s and after the war about the possibility of economic calculation in a socialist society, it is difficult to imagine how all those strong arguments that were offered against the market economy suddenly, over the last 20 years, have faded. It is difficult to see that this would have happened without political changes such as the break-up of the Soviet Union and the GATT talks.

Hard-line free marketeers in the 1970s argued that economic freedom might come before political freedom, because free market economies would eventually rule out dictatorship. This seems to now to be a thesis that is generally accepted in international politics.[1] Although, it is no longer the big controversies over totalitarian ideologies that are debated, in the current debate on the economy, it is the more subtle questions of peaceful social development, the extent of the individual domain, management of the public domain, management of the environment and moral and ethical issues related to the market that are in focus. Of course the threat of leviathan is still there, although not necessarily in the

1   Foremost in arguing this was Milton Friedman (1980, p. 94).

Hegelian, ideological sense (Buchanan, 1977). At the same time, international cooperation and the organisation of international institutions have become even more important issues in the development of the market, as is seen in the current financial crisis.

Can we think of the market and the economy simply as an *activity*, not an institution? For instance: I do some work in my garden. It is not part of the market. However, I offer my gardening service to others for money, although I do the same job as in my own garden, now it is suddenly part of the economy. It is a tempting idea to say that at the moment something becomes a transaction, it is part of the market and the economy.

However, even this is problematic because there are many types of transactions in society that we would not call part of a market. In the social domain, we do transactions constantly. I can sit at UC Berkeley, California, and write this while my colleagues at University of Agder, Norway, handle some of my responsibilities there. They do it because they can rely on me stepping in for them in similar situations. Or take another example: while I am here at UC Berkeley, a friend of mine has said he would look after my house. In both cases there is a transaction, but not a market- or economic-based one.

So, we could argue that what makes something economic or market is that money is involved, that it related to only money-based transactions. No, neither would that work because we could pretty well think of markets without money. Money increases the ability to make economic transactions, but it is no absolute necessity.

One could also try to make the distinction between market and non-market relating to *transactions versus cooperation*. However, cooperation is a central element in a market economy. Literature that addresses cooperation discusses this at different levels. There is a large literature on cooperation within firms. This literature relates to issues such as participation, teamwork and other cooperational forms often in perspective of organisation and leadership. Core dimensions in this literature are organisational efficiency, motivation and power (emancipation). Then there is an increasing literature on cooperation between firms: open innovation, cluster theory, innovation systems, and network forms of organisation, are large areas of research that also get a lot of attention in real life. Finally there is the perspective of cooperation between firms and the administrative and political system. Literature on regional innovation systems, triple helix, network governance are examples of this type of literature.

The collaborative processes at different levels can be explained in different ways. From a rational choice perspective, collaboration can be modelled as a strategic game. The relative strength of partners in a transaction will decide what interaction form to choose. But collaboration can also be explained in terms of culture, institutions or relations (bridging or bonding) among people. Collaboration might also take different forms such as direct collaboration, or more indirect collaboration through discourses, and social networks. A general theory of collaboration relates to issues such as efficiency, effectiveness, fairness, acceptability and sustainable social and economic development. Collaboration is part of the market.

Could we think of the economy or the market as a *mentality*? That is, could we think of it as a way to relate to others? I can relate to others in a social, friendly way. See them as part of my life, as part of a common entity or identity that I regard as involved, inclusive and not based on calculation. However, I, the same person, could go to work and relate to my customers and suppliers as that, as transaction, as someone I calculate in my utility in relation to. Let's say my job is gardening, but that I also am an active member of an art society that runs an art gallery with a large garden. Let's say that in this society there is a lot of voluntary work, what in Norwegian is called *dugnad*, and that I do gardening. Is it work? If not, does this mean that I live two lives? Is it a sort of schizophrenia? How do I keep track of the one and the other? When are my friends no longer friends but based on calculation, or my customers, no longer customers, but friends or fellow members of an association? Is the term business-friend such a mixed-up concept, confusing the two domains?

I think the economy and the market can be defined both in terms of an institution, and activity and a mentality. It may be more based on transaction, than cooperation, but both are present. It might be different from politics; both political decisions and political implications are strongly present when we discuss economics and markets. That is not least important when we try to understand how the economy and the market play a role in knowledge development in society.

The Development of Economic Thought

I find it useful to regard economic thinking as a discourse process that constantly improves theories but that is also strongly integrated with societal development. We could call this contextualisation of economic thinking. Economic thinking can also be seen as a growth of knowledge process and as a process of increased specialisation of thought. It is a fact that classical economists from Adam Smith on had a broader perspective on economics than, for instance, present-day econometricians, that is, economists with a pure mathematical approach. On the other hand, some of the fundamental issues discussed by the classics remain unsolved today; one example is the theory of value (what is the correct value of a product?). Economists have been dealing with such unsolvable issues partly by defining them as outside the scope of economics, and partly to address the issue differently (for instance to focus on relative instead of absolute value).

We can also see the history of economic thought as a *maturing process*. Economics have matured from being elements in theological and historical discussions or theory of law to be a science in its own right. We can see elements of this process in the discussions of early economists about issues such as morals, psychology, sociology, history and political science. Some would say that it is impossible to discuss economic theory isolated from these other issues, while others would say that this is not the problem of economists, but for those who apply economic theories. There are also economists who discuss these other issues, but from an economist point of view. One example is the 1992 winner of the Nobel Prize for Economics, Gary Becker (1996), who has developed an economic theory of human behaviour.[2]

THE CLASSICS AND BEFORE

What are the characteristics of the classical school? Foremost it presented a comprehensive economic theory trying to answer all sorts of questions from problems related to individual transactions to the large issues of public finance and economic policy.

---

2   The term classical was introduced by Karl Marx to describe the theories of Adam Smith and his followers. Smith himself had termed his predecessors as mercantilists and John Maynard Keynes 150 years later called all his predecessors classics. Today one would normally call classical economics, theories from Adam Smith's *Wealth of Nations* (1776) until Karl Marx's *Das Capital* (1867). But within this period we also had other schools of thought, for instance the Historical School in Germany.

This marks a difference to its predecessors, such as the *mercantilists* of the seventeenth and eighteenth century who were almost exclusively focused on public finance. Mercantilists did *not* see any particular function in the market process. The market, if it was ever referred to, was perceived as an exchange mechanism.

Mercantilism was a series of doctrines and theses related to public finance such as the one that surplus in international trade is a measure of the nation's wealth. Mercantilists were focused on the stock of resources rather than the flow of goods. But there were other characteristics as well: they promoted monopolistic trade, protectionism, the balance of trade doctrine and exchange control. Classics, on the other hand, were focused on production, economic growth, the division of labour and the condition of trade. They had a broad debate on the theory of value, often identified (partly incorrectly) as the labour theory of value. These issues were addressed seldom and differently by mercantilists that had a more monetary/public-finance approach to wealth (wealth is measured as the accumulation of public wealth in the form of gold).[3]

Another group of predecessors to the classics where the *physiocrats*. This name was used for some French economists in the eighteenth century who presented ideas on economics in opposition to the mercantilists. The main difference in their ideas was their focus on real activities in the economy, and not just financial aspects of it. Their analysis was, however, static, with a focus on the different levels of economic activity.[4] Although they presented many interesting ideas, and in many ways influenced Adam Smith, the physiocrats did not present a coherent description of the economic process in society. The market was rather understood as a complicated but mathematically logical *coordination mechanism*.

The physiocrats were typical of a tradition that we could call French rationalism (also, for some reason, called Descartian constructivism). The traditions continued in the nineteenth century when, among others, Auguste Comte (1798–1857) developed the *philosophy of positivism*, constructing an ideal model for society. The idea of construction was popular among French philosophers and even economists.[5] Utopian socialists were among these. They wanted to get rid of the inherent egoism and injustice in free market exchange. There are parallels between this and the *moralistic view* of the market and the scholastic tradition and its discussion on value.

A comprehensive description of the economic activity in society as a process was first offered by Adam Smith (1723–1790) in his *An Inquiry into the Nature and Causes of the Wealth of Nations* (1776). Smith started a new paradigm. Through this treatise, he influenced economic thinking for a whole generation and became a point of reference for generations after.[6] Still, some of Smith's insights into the spontaneity and complexity of the market process were later lost. It had been part of the broader philosophical system of

---

3   There is no single economist who represents the mercantilist tradition, but Thomas Mun (1571–1641) is often referred to as its foremost academic. A collection of his articles was published in 1630 under the title *England's Treasure by Forraign Trade: or, The ballance of our Forraign Trade is the Rule of our Treasure.*

4   Two of the most prominent physiocrats were R.J. Turgot (1727–1781) and Francios Quesnay (1694–1774). The latter tried to describe the economic system as a parallel to the biological system.

5   Many economists in France were educated from a technical university, particularly Ecole Politechnique, such as: Marie Charles Fourier (1772–1837) and Comte de Saint-Simon (1760–1825). Both of these economists started their own political/economic movement, later called *utopian socialism*.

6   To some extent, other economists of the classical period came to discuss and elaborate aspects of Smiths treatise. Several of them did so by writing 'Principles of Political Economy', which meant that their treatises were both *practical* and *theoretical*. Among the most famous classics are: Thomas Malthus (1766–1834), known for his theory of population,

David Hume and Adam Furgeson and others to combine an insight into the spontaneous formation of social order with a critical-rational approach to social science as opposed to Descartian constructivism. Already with David Ricardo a new trend was established. After Adam Smith, the classical system became more structured and mathematically logical, less based on a reflection on social and economic development.

The main elements of what is now generally understood as the classical economic system can be described like this:

- Total factor payments received from producing a given output are necessarily sufficient to purchase that output.
- There is no loss of purchasing power anywhere in the economy because people save only to the extent that they desire to invest.
- In real terms, supply equals demand, since people work and produce only because of and to the extent that they demand other goods.
- Disequilibrium in the economy can only exist because the mix of production of different goods is not in accordance with people's preferences for goods.

The classical tradition anticipated many of the subjects later discussed by economists. The problem of *equilibrium* and *disequilibrium* is one. J.S. Mill's distinction between two very different processes in the market – one deciding the *composition* of production, the other deciding *distribution* – is another. Both came to inspire later attempts to dissect the market process. This in turn brought economic thought into a new, more constructivist paradigm.

In Germany an economic theory was developed based not so much on theoretical considerations as on the study and generalisation of historical experience. One of the main influences of this theory came from the philosopher G.F. Hegel (1770–1831) and his theory of the development of history and historical laws, *Elements of the Philosophy of Right* (1821). The German Historical School included a wide range of social scientists with a lot of different theories. But they had in common hostility to universal social laws and a strong focus on the institutional aspects of social development. In short that meant that an economic theory that could be applied in England would not necessarily be appropriate for Germany.[7] The so-called *Younger Historical School* came to a large extent to be identified with Gustav von Smoller (1838–1917). He presented a strong attack on classical economic theory from an institutionalist point of view. Smoller presented his ethical/historical perspective in direct contrast to the natural-law tradition of the rationalistic Wiennese school. And the controversies culminated with the so-called *Metodenstreit* between Smoller and Carl Menger, the Austrian economist. The insight that this debate brought to economic thinking in general and to the concepts of the market especially was the influence of institutional conditions on market order. Austrians shared the insight that law, culture and institutions shape the market order, but disagreed that the capitalist market order was only a historically specific phenomenon.

David Ricardo (1767–1832) and his theory of trade, Jean-Baptiste Say (1767–1832) and his theory of economic equilibrium, and John Stuart Mill (1806–1873) and his theory of distribution.

7   Economists such as Johan Heinrich von Thünen (1783–1950) and, even more so, Friedrich List (1789–1846) developed theories that discussed particular German problems. List is famous for having proposed that the state should protect German industry, contrary to the free trade principles of the classics. In this tradition we could also mention Adolph Wagner (1835–1917), who was the architect of the new social policy in Germany.

Karl Marx (1818–1883) and Marxism was influenced by both the classics and the institutional perspective of the German debate. In Marxism we find both universal theories and institutional mechanisms. Marx the economist is often regarded as the last classical economist: Marx discussed economic problems within the framework laid down by Adam Smith and David Ricardo. This was particularly the case with his discussion on value. By establishing labour as the basis of all value (the labour theory of value), Marx was able to develop his theory of profit, of exploitation and of economic decline. Marx had the same fault as the other classics by focusing too much on the production side of the economy. Too little attention was put to the demand side.[8] By separating the two processes, Marx did not comprehend the complexity and spontaneity of the market order

THE NEO-CLASSICS

The marginal revolution that brought economic thinking into the paradigm that has been called neo-classic theory is identified with three economists: Stanley Jevons (1835–1882) in England, Leon Walras (1839–1910) in Switzerland and Carl Menger (1840–1921) in Austria. At almost the same time (beginning of the 1870s) these three economists published works where they developed the subjective theory of value and made it the cornerstone of this new economic theory. For this they used two principles, later known as the two laws of Gossen (an elaboration of the original theory of the German economist Hermann Heinrich von Gossen (1810–1858)). The first law of Gossen said that the marginal utility of consumption of a single good is declining. This means that the more you consume of one type of good, the less utility the last (marginal) unit will give you. The second law of Gossen said that people will use their resources so that the last unit used gives the same marginal utility for all uses.

If the two laws of Gossen are combined with the equilibrium theory of Say (the theory that supply will always equal demand), we have a set of principles by which the economic system can be defined. This was done by Walras in his general equilibrium theory, which became the basis of the school of thought known as the neo-classical theory.[9]

The neo-classical economic system focused on two things: first, it developed a system of equilibrium and specified all necessary conditions for a logical system of equilibrium. Among these conditions were theories of production and consumption based on the marginal income and utility theory. Second, it specified the conditions of self-regulation towards equilibrium. In doing this, it made assumptions of psychology and individual preferences. Some theories brought these assumptions to a level where one claimed to be able to draw normative conclusions on a scientific level. Some economists made for instance claims of the sort that total welfare in society would increase by a certain redistribution of wealth. The English economist Arthur Pigou was among these.[10]

---

8   In 1871, Stanley Jevons started the first chapter in his new book *The Theory of Political Economy* by saying: 'Repeated reflections and inquiry have led me to the somewhat novel opinion, that *value depends entirely upon utility.*' This came to revolutionise economic theory.

9   Neo-classical economics reintroduced Senior's distinction of positive (descriptive) and normative (prescriptive) economics. John Nevil Keynes, father of the later world-known economist, wrote an essay in 1890, *Scope and Method of Political Economy*, where this distinction was made.

10   Wilfredo Pareto, the Italian economist and follower of Walras in Lausanne, wrote a treatise on economics where these things were specified: *Manual of Political Economy* (1907). Pareto introduced the idea of *indifference*, that is, perspectives on utility where our knowledge of the absolute level of utility is not a precondition for studying individual preferences. This idea of indifference, later built into the equilibrium theory by John Hicks, solved the problem of

However, it should be observed that in the context of the neo-classical system, the market disappears as a process and as a central economic phenomenon. All the features of real markets – uncertainty, limited knowledge, risk, imperfect information, dynamics, change, institutions and contracts – were supposed to be non-existing.[11]

These *other* problems were explored by the Austrian School. Carl Menger had written on the spontaneous formation of order (exemplified with the development of money-economy) in his *Grundsëtze* (1871). Eugen von Bohem-Bawerk (1851–1914) observed the fact that while equilibrium in all parts of the economy seldom is reached, there are periods of temporal equilibrium on the way to a general equilibrium. Friedrich von Hayek (1899–1992) and Ludvig von Mises (1881–1973) emphasised more and more the process of equilibrium: they questioned some of the neo-classical assumptions on how equilibrium is reached. Earlier Alfred Marshall (1842–1924) in England and Knut Wicksell (1851–1926) in Sweden had discussed in their capital theory the problem of intermediate equilibrium and partial equilibrium. All these perspectives represent a paradigmatic difference from the neo-classical system, first of all because intermediate processes presuppose institutions, non-perfect information and firms, that is, real market phenomena.

The neo-classical system was based on some fundamental assumptions that added up to a total system of equilibrium. First of all there is the assumption of individual utility maximisation. Effective demand is created by each individual seeking to obtain the best marginal use of his or her resources. In doing so, the marginal demand is used where it leads to the maximum utility. Secondly, there is a parallel process at work within the firm. Here the profit is supposed to be maximised, indicating that the firm seeks to employ the marginal resources where it leads to maximised productivity. Since difference in profit is a good indicator of what type of production leads to the maximisation of utility for the consumer, that is, an indicator of scarcity, the market equilibrium will be a state or condition with the best possible use of available resources. Thirdly, it is assumed that income from production resources equals demand of the finished products. Equilibrium is thereby obtained.

By the 1930s, economists had questioned many of the elements of the neo-classical general equilibrium theory. The welfare theory had focused on incomplete competition, public goods, monopolism, external effects, and so on. Market imperfections like these were explored and often led to a political conclusion about the function of the state, for example, Joan Robinson's (1903–1983) *The Economics of Imperfect Competition* (1933). The economists' debate again became political; which was the better system, capitalism or socialism, for example Pigou's *Capitalism and Socialism*. Still much of this critique of the neo-classical system was within the paradigm and did not represent a paradigmatic change.

THE BIG CONTROVERSY: CAPITALISM VERSUS SOCIALISM

John Maynard Keynes with his 1936 book *The General Theory of Employment Interest and Money* came to change the course of the economic debate. The core question that Keynes

---

discussing *cardinal utility*. In his book Pareto also introduced a 'weak' normative element that would enable economists to discuss the welfare aspect of society, the so-called Pareto criteria: *an economic change is a welfare improvement if at least **one** person has improved his situation by the change and **no one** has worsened their situation.*

11   Other developments of the neo-classical system came in areas such as capital theory and monetary theory. In America, Irving Fisher (1867–1947) developed the quantitative theory of money and later discussed the relation between interest rate and monetary change.

raised was this: will a free market without any interference by the state be able to produce full employment (that is, general equilibrium) and the best possible use of the resources of society? Keynes said no, it will not; some sort of state action is necessary to correct the market.[12]

Keynes set his discussion in the context of the general equilibrium system of Walras. He started with the assumption of neo-classical equilibrium analysis that the total cost of production (payments of factors of production) equals income by individuals or firms. The value of what is produced equals the income generated in producing it. It all adds up to a circular flow.

Keynes introduced two important qualifications to this model. First he pointed at the function of money. The general equilibrium model presupposes that money is neutral, that it is only a medium of exchange and does not affect the physical production. But what if people did not spend everything they earned. What if they saved a part of their income, so that there was not enough demand to buy the total amount of production? Then there will be unemployment.

To this argument, the neo-classics would reply: the prices would fall until demand again equals supply (in money value). Therefore Keynes introduced his second main argument. There might be cases, as for instance with wages, where price and supply is not elastic, that is, where reduction in price will not lead to increased demand, or where surplus of supply will not lead to increasing of prices. An example of the first is what Keynes called the liquidity trap (a price of money (interest) where a further reduction of the price would not increase demand). An example of the second is employment and wages (to reduce wages is difficult and will normally lead to civil unrest). The market is perceived as a mechanism.

Based on these assumptions, Keynes argued that there might be cases where the economy would stagnate, and that the only way to stimulate it and create growth would be through government spending. Government spending would have an accelerating effect on the economy (the so-called multiplier effect). Although Keynes was a liberal, and even in his general theory expressed wishes for the liberal market economy, he does not seem to have had a positive understanding of the function of the market.

But there was opposition to the Keynesian theory. The Austrians, particularly F.A. Hayek, criticised Keynesianism for lacking a microeconomic foundation. There was no logical connection between what Keynesians claimed would happen under certain conditions on an aggregate level and what any reasonable theory of human action would suppose. Even before Keynes published his *General Theory*, there had been a debate between him and Hayek. In 1930, Keynes published his *Treatise on Money*. At almost the same time, Hayek published his *Price and Production* (1931). Both Keynes and Hayek in these works elaborated Knut Wicksell's theory about business cycles caused by changes in the money supply. Keynes had supposed that the effect of the change in money supply only affected prices and that for instance a depression was caused by the fact that as money supply decreased, prices as well as profit would fall, leading to bankruptcy and unemployment. Hayek introduced a new aspect of this argument, where he said that not only would prices be affected by a change in money supply, but also the composition of

---

12   Economists such as John Hicks and Alvin Hansen in England had developed the Keynesian model and explained it within the framework of neo-classical equilibrium theory. By this, they had been able to make a synthesis between neo-classicalism and Keynesianism: the IS-LN diagram, introduced in John Hicks *Mr Keynes and the 'Classics'; a suggested Interpretation* (1937).

production. For instance, if the money supply increased, leading to reduction in interest rates, there would be a relative increase in the supply of capital goods compared with labour. The capital goods industry would expand relative to labour-intensive industry. In the longer run, this argument indicated that the effect of inflation would be a dramatic change in the structure of production. Depression would subsequently result, since at some point in time there would be a mis-coordination between inflationary production structure and real demand. (On the Hayke/Kayens debate, see Waspshott, 2011.)

Based on this approach, the neo-Austrians had a rather different opinion of the causes of depression and the function of the market than that of the Keynesians.[13] Later, the monetarists with Milton Friedman as the main actor argued that Keynes had overlooked the long-run monetary aspects of the economy and that the problem with unemployment in the 1930s was due to monetary change, and not a matter of lack of fiscal policy.

The debate over macroeconomics in the mid-war period went parallel to another large and important debate that more clearly addressed political and ideological cleavages in society. This was the debate about the possibility of economic calculation under socialism. The debate was started with a provoking article by Ludwig von Mises (*Economic Calculation in the Socialist Commonwealth* (1920)) and developed into a broad economic/political debate in the 1930s. The debate was about the possibility to operate a socialist economy that is an economy without price mechanism (that is, without a market). In the 1930s the debate proceeded alongside the discussion of Keynesian economics. By the mid-1930s, Fred Taylor and Oscar Lange (Lange, 1936) had elaborated the socialist argument and claimed that they were able to demonstrate how central planning could work. One of their main arguments were that price mechanism could be copied by a trial and error bargain process. Based on information of available resources, preferences and production functions, it was possible to allocate the resources to the best uses, even better than the market mechanism, since central planning could take into consideration external effects.

As I will go into below, Hayek contributed to the debate with some very important essays, such as *Economics and Knowledge* (1937), where he demonstrated the epistemological flaws in the socialist argument. According to Hayek, the knowledge needed to coordinate economic activity is not available for central authorities, since that knowledge is created by the market process. Later, Ludwig Lachmann (1994) wrote on the market as a learning process and Israel Kirzner (1992) has elaborated this argument and what he calls the theory of entrepreneurs. Parallel to the economic calculation debate, increased attention was set on real market phenomena, for instance the formation of organisations and firms.[14] These phenomena could not be explained within the neo-classical framework. Information cost, uncertainty and contracts are real market phenomena that a market economy has to observe. Entrepreneurial activity has to be built into economic models.

---

13   Public choice theory – with James M. Buchanan and Gordon Tullock: *The Calculus of Consent* (1960) – criticised the Keynesian assumption that market failure could be corrected by government action. Public choice explored the fact that there are also government failures.

14   Frank Knight wrote an interesting book in 1921, *Risk, Uncertainty and Profit*, which discussed many elements that had been ignored in the neo-classical theory, such as uncertainty and risk. By introducing these elements in the theory he was able to elaborate the theory. At Chicago University, where he worked, this influenced many young economists, such as Milton Friedman, Ronald Coase, George Stigler and Gary Becker, who all received a Nobel Prize in Economics. The Chicago School based their work on methodological individualism but worked within a partial equilibrium theory. This point of reference off the mainstream general equilibrium theory might have inspired them to introduce many new topics, perspectives and elements to economic theory.

Even the legal structure and property rights can be discussed within an economic setting, as did Ronald Coase in *The Problem of Social Cost* (1960). To an increasing degree, these discussions shifted attention to the market process. Perhaps one of the largest challenges facing today's economic theory is how to combine the increasing insights of microeconomics with the working of the market, with macroeconomic thinking.

Controversies over the Nature and Extent of Economic Planning in Norway

Norway, having for 300 years been a part of the Kingdom of Denmark, became an independent country in 1814 in the turmoil after the Napoleon War, but only for a few months. In November 1814, Norway had to accept a union with Sweden which lasted until 1905.

The first Norwegian university was established in 1812. Before that, the political, cultural and intellectual centre of the kingdom was concentrated in Copenhagen. It is therefore difficult to speak about an independent Norwegian intellectual debate before the beginning of the nineteenth century. However, the newly established independence of Norway in 1814 and the period of union with Sweden, which had a rather decentralised structure, started a process of vitalisation of Norwegian intellectual debate.

In spite of this vitalisation, there are very few contributions of theoretical interest by Norwegian economists in the nineteenth century. Economic debate was mainly a practical debate over economic policy. The main influence on this debate came from British and German economists. In this respect, Norwegian economic debate could to some extent be regarded as a melting pot of British and German ideas. In the twentieth century, on the other hand, Norwegians came to give some genuine contributions to the development of economic theory. One could to some extent say that while being a small nation on the outskirts of Europe was a disadvantage in the nineteenth century, it became an advantage in the twentieth century since Norwegians had been used to being open-minded towards different schools and trends of economic thinking. The history of economic thought in Norway is to a large degree a controversy over the nature and extent of economic planning.

ECONOMIC DEBATE IN NORWAY IN THE NINETEENTH CENTURY

When the nineteenth century started, two main streams of economic ideas dominated the debate: firstly, mercantilism had its sympathisers in many political groups. The first professor at Kong Fredriks Universitet (University of Oslo), Niels Treschow (1751–1833), was a mercantilist and his successor, Gregers F. Lundh (178–-1836), was teaching the theory of national housekeeping, which was a main idea within the German school of thought called *cameralism*.

Secondly, economic liberalism of the British classical school had its followers. In the late eighteenth century, the Danish king had introduced a very liberal constitution with free trade and freedom of contract as its main pillars, directly influenced by Adam Smith. *Wealth of Nations* had been translated into Danish in 1783 and a group of influential businessmen and civil servants in Copenhagen had established contact with Smith himself. It has been seen as a paradox that a supreme king introduced liberalism, the same king that the independent Norway wanted to distance itself from. The debate about economic policy right after 1814 became confusing, and *patriotism* came, for the same reason, to be identified with *mercantilism*.

One of Norway's few landlords, Jacob Aall (1773–1844), wrote in favour of the classical doctrines of liberalism. But it was not until the middle of the nineteenth century that Norway adopted a liberal, free trade policy. The man who is credited for this development is the economist Anton Martin Schweigaard (1808–1870).

ANTON MARTIN SCHWEIGAARD

Schweigaard was more of a practical politician than a theoretician. He never wrote a book on economic theory, so we only know his ideas from a few articles he wrote and from the lectures he gave at the University of Christiania (Oslo) in the 1830s, where he held the chair in economics and law. We also know his ideas for the positions he took in the debates in the Parliament, where he was a dominant figure, particularly between 1842 and 1866.

Schweigaard is said to have held conflicting views on economic policy. On the one hand, he was one of the architects of Norway's free trade laws of 1842. These laws ended the area of privileges in trades and in production, for instance the regulations on sawmills and mining. On the other hand he was one of the main architects of Norway's industrial policy in the second half of the nineteenth century. During that era, Norway had a system where the state provided cheap credits in order to help establish industry and infrastructures. It has been called the Norwegian System, although it is well known from other countries from the same period, for instance France; the idea was that private initiatives should be supported by state loans, guarantees or capital. Infrastructure such as railways, telephone and telegraph, and electric power were established through private initiative and were privately run in the first period, but with government loans and guarantees, while later the state took over the operation of these activities.[15]

I think it is only possible to understand this dualism if it is related to a long tradition of dualism in the Norwegian economy: Norway is a country that is dependent on international trade. Norway's natural resources give it a surplus of certain resources, but underproduction and even lack of others. The possibility to trade these resources internationally is necessary for the continuation of life in Norway. Over hundreds of years this has encouraged a free international trade attitude in Norway. But this attitude is contrasted with a long tradition of protection and state interference in the internal commercial life of Norway. Some have called this a *dualistic economy*.

When Schweigaard is to be understood in this context, some have tried to compare him with the British economists Nassau Senior and John Stuart Mill, while others have indicated that he might have held some opinions in theory and others in practice. It has been argued in order to protect the credibility of Schweigaard that even British and continental liberalism became more pragmatic at the middle of the nineteenth century. If so, Schweigaard might be regarded as a mainstream liberal (Sørensen, 1988, p. 58). On the other hand, I think it is difficult to find in Mill or Senior any references to active

---

15   Historians disagree on the question of whether Schweigaard was a liberal or a conservative; whether he was against or in favour of state interference in economic activities (Sørensen, 1988, pp. 55/58; Maurseth, 1990; Seip, 1988, p. 82).

industrial policy by the state. Still, I think it should be admitted that the general attitude of Schweigaard is within the liberal tradition, although he might have been a little pragmatic as regards state involvement in commerce.

This view is confirmed when one reads his essays, *Treatise on the Present State of the Science of Law in Germany* (1834) and *On German Philosophy* (1835). In both essays he rejects the Hegelian philosophy and presents himself as an empiricist and a sympathiser of utilitarian philosophy. He also takes the position of, for instance, Savigny, on the *organic concept of law*, a position later confirmed in his rejection of constitutionalism and the fact that he took a common law attitude to legal development in Norway.

Schweigaard can even be regarded as an exponent of two traditions in Norwegian economic politics. The first is the tradition of a relatively independent Norwegian economic debate. According to this tradition, Norwegian economists, although internationally oriented on the theoretical level, have tended to look for special solutions to specific Norwegian problems. The argument: *we are different, so that generally accepted theories do not apply!* is not unfamiliar in Norwegian debate. The second is the tradition of a strong influence by academic economists in politics. As we will see, particularly after the war, economists came to have a strong influence on government policy.

TORKEL ASCHEHOUG

In the second half of the nineteenth century, the face of Norwegian politics changed. In 1884, Norway introduced parliamentarianism, the system by which the majority in parliament elected the government. This resulted in the formation of parties and in the polarisation and ideologisation of politics. One of the leading figures in the Conservative Party was Torkel Aschehoug, the successor of Schweigaard as professor of economics and law. It could be relevant to call Aschehoug a Norwegian Alfred Marshall, and like Marshall he managed to write a comprehensive treaty on social economics, based on the marginal utility theory and combining everything from price theory to business cycles theory. However, Aschehoug as a politician came to be strongly influenced by the German tradition, and especially the economist Adolf Wagner and his *paternalistic conservatism*, which resembles modern socialism. Many of the ideas of the social state, the predecessor of the welfare state, were introduced in this period, with the support of the Conservative Party. In fact, it was not until the 1920s that the Labour Party had any formal position in the execution of Norwegian politics, probably as a result of this social dimension in conservative politics.

CONTROVERSIES OVER TAXATION AND MONEY

Aschehoug's paternalistic approach to politics came to be one of the two main factions of the Conservative Party. The other faction, free market liberals, were less supported by academic economists. This can be seen in the debate over taxation in Norway in the 1890s. The Norwegian economist Einar Einarson presented in this debate a libertarian approach to taxation, while Aschehoug's successor Bredo Morgenstierne advocated an active social state, although he also defended the idea of private property.

The Liberal Party (the centre-left party) that was in charge of government in most of the period from 1890–1920 had as its leading economist Nicolay Rygg, later chairman of the Bank of Norway. Rygg was a theoretical economist with strong beliefs in the scientific answers to practical economic challenges and had a strong moral belief in individual duty and sacrifice for the common good. He was convinced that marginal utility theory had proved that progressive taxation was a fair tax. He was later (in the 1920s) convinced that contraction of money would bring the Norwegian Kroner back to gold parity (which had been abolished in the inflationary years under and shortly after the First World War) and that this was a matter of national pride. As a consequence of his deflationary parity policy, Norway had a much more severe depression in the 1920s than later in the 1930s. Similarly, the parity policy brought with it political turmoil and social unrest. Although economists were involved in these events, many of the leading academic economists had turned more academic and departed from the public debate.

MARGINALISTS IN NORWAY

The leading academic economist in the period between 1900 and 1920 was Oscar Jæger. He wrote his doctoral thesis on Adam Smith, but should be interpreted more in the context of the Lausanne school. He was a follower of Friedrich von Wieser, who, although he was an Austrian, had more in common with the Lausanne school than with the Austrian school of economics. Jæger developed and extended the general equilibrium theory and marginal utility theory. He wrote an extensive textbook and gave the economic profession of Norway a solid theoretical foundation.

It is interesting to speculate whether the gap between the extent of the economic problems in Norway in the 1920s and the passivity of the economic profession in offering any solutions to these problems encouraged the development of applied economics in the 1930s. It is a fact that Norwegian economists presented ideas of macroeconomics planning and policy years before Keynes, and that the main architect of this approach, Ragnar Frisch (1895–1973), regarded himself as a predecessor of John Maynard Keynes in this respect.

THE FRISCH GENERATION

There is little doubt that Frisch came to dominate economic thinking in Norway between the end of the 1930s until the beginning of the 1970s. He was the first Nobel laureate (together with Jan Timbergen) in economics in 1969. His pupil, Trygve Haavelmo (1911–1999), received a Nobel Prize in Economics in 1989. Other pupils of Frisch came to occupy academic, professional and political positions in Norway to the extent that one could talk about a sort of *coup d'état*. This development ran parallel to the Labour Party's dominance in Norwegian politics. The Labour Party controlled government, with the exception of a two-week period in 1963, for 29 successive years between 1936 and 1965.

The marginalistic approach as it was thought in Norway in the first part of the twentieth century was mainly influenced by the Austrian school, and particularly by the works of Bøhm Bawerk. The dynamic features of Bøhm Bawerk's theory may have influenced Frisch in his approach to economic theory. It was these dynamic features that Frisch tried to understand and to describe in his dynamic models. Also, Wicksell and Marshall, with their analysis of the industrial sector and structural differences within industries, were an important source of inspiration for Frisch.

Frisch started out to model the behaviour of the economy and the possibilities and consequences of government control. *Circulation Planning*, Frisch's work from 1934, is the groundwork of this approach. Here Frisch describes the fluidity and exponential changes in the economy, the same effect that Keynes later called the multiplier. Frisch often used the term *fiction economy* to describe monetary disturbances of inter-sectarian exchange. Fiction economy was opposed to *real* economy, or what Keynes later called *effective demand*, and real economy was what the economic policy should focus on.

Frisch had a normative approach to economic planning, but he at the same time ignored all moral, ethical and political aspects of economic models, except for a few economic goals (stabilisation and equal distribution), and subsequently he proposed a rigid system of intermediate institutions to reduce the spreading of accelerating effects of decline or increase in demand. These and other ideas were proposed without any great political approval, but part of Frisch's system was used in the primary sector. However, there is reason to suppose that the generation-long Norwegian hostility towards monetarism and monetary policy, and its affection for fiscal policy, was inspired by Frisch's strong emphasis on what he had called real economy.

NATIONAL ECONOMIC PLANNING

Frisch had inspired the development of applied economic planning, but it was his pupils who developed and implemented these programmes. One of the main architects of the programmes was Leif Johansen. Economic planning started with a rather ambitious national planning project in 1946, which was modified in 1948–9. In the 1950s an enormous effort to industrialise Norway was made with the help of, among others, American capital. Norwegian shipping started to take off, while the domestic economy was heavily regulated. This dualism had, as we have seen, long traditions in Norway. By 1960, the regulations had to be abolished as Norway entered the EFTA free trade agreement and as political pressure to encourage the consumer goods economy increased. But all through this period, there were few economists that had either the courage or the skills to oppose Frisch and his followers.

Of course, there was some opposition, both political and theoretical. Trygve Hoff had established on a personal basis a relation with the libertarian economists such as Hayek and Mises in the 1930s. He wrote his dissertation on the economic calculation debate in 1936: *Economic Calculation in the Socialist Economy* (with Frisch as his mentor). William Keilhaug strongly opposed the proposed price law, claiming that it was in conflict with private property rights and the rule of law (1952). Similarly in the 1960s there was a tendency among economists to focus on the institutional effect of central planning, among others, on wage bargaining (that tended to lead to wage-driven inflation) and on economic policy. Leif Johansen pioneered the implementation of institutional elements in economic models and he also inspired the implementation of *game theory* into econometric models. This meant that some of the ideals of Frisch were dropped and that normative models used as practical and political tools were more in focus than theoretical economics (Bergh and Hanisch, 1984, p. 223). Johansen's dissertation, *A Multisectoral Study of Economic Growth* (1961), was one of the first attempts to implement institutional elements in econometric models, and later similar models were developed in order to predict the effect of national wage bargaining.

Changes were to come in the beginning of the 1980s. Before that, at the beginning of the 1970s after the oil price increase (which was favourable to Norway as an oil producer) the government and the pupils of Frisch implemented the most rigid economic policy programme ever to be attempted in Norway, with price and wage control, heavy state involvement in banking and industry, and counter-cyclical measures. By the end of the 1970s this policy had gone out of control, with industrial decline, huge public debt, inflation and social tension as a result. By the mid-1980s Norway liberalised almost all of this and adopted a monetarist policy that still prevails.

THE ECONOMICS OF FRISCH

Although Frisch is regarded as the great Norwegian economist in the twentieth century, his production is not impressive. In fact, he worked on many ideas that were never completed, and the only comprehensive treatment of economics *Innledning til produksjonsteorien* was written as a compendium in 1927 and used in lectures at Oslo University, and although revised several times, only in 1962 was published in English, at a time when many of its pioneering ideas were past their time. However, Frisch's ideas where internationally known long before that. In 1930–31 he taught at Yale University and, as he was offered a post as professor there, the Norwegian government established a new chair in economics at Oslo University in order to get Frisch back to Norway.

At that time his main concern had been *business cycle theory*. In was in this field he did his major work between 1925 and 1934. His contribution was both methodological and technical. As he was an excellent mathematician, he brought in sophisticated mathematical tools in the construction of economic models. He was, not surprisingly, one of the founders of The Econometric Society and for 20 years he was editor of the journal *Econometrica*.

Frisch's economic approach was to separate models from reality. He did *not* regard models as representations of reality; neither did he think that results from economic models could explain real problems. On the contrary, he thought that models were constructed according to their uses, as practical tools to serve some particular purpose. For the same reason he was uninterested in whether assumptions made in models would be meaningful as related to individual action or not. This methodological view is parallel to what later was called *instrumentalism* (Caldwell, 1982) and ironically enough had one of its main advocates in Milton Friedman. Although Friedman in his 1953 essay on methodology refers to Haavelmo and indirectly to Frisch, there might be some differences in their views. It is for instance possible that Frisch would be less concerned with empirical verification then Friedman was, and that Haavelmo would be more concerned with the validity of assumptions than Friedman. Friedman did not pay attention to the identification problem (the problem of identifying the correct variables to be measured in the models) that Frisch had been very concerned about. However, their general approach on focusing on model design as something related to *usefulness* and not as some *search for truth* is the same in all three.

Partly as a consequence of his methodological view, Frisch (and not Keynes) pioneered the concept of macroeconomics by treating these aggregates as separate phenomena and not deduct them from microeconomics phenomena. Another consequence of his methodological view was that he found the distinction between *positive* and *normative* economics totally misleading and uninteresting. In his view it was only meaningful to talk about *truth* and *relevance*. A true model or theory was one that was logically consistent (not whether it would fit reality or base itself on assumptions that could be verified in real life). The link to reality was a matter of relevance.

By separating models from reality, Frisch started to investigate business cycle from the opposite perspective of, for instance, Hayek and Keynes. Instead of speculating on how decisions and actions of groups of individuals manifested themselves in business cycles, he started to construct models that would behave in almost the same cyclical way as business cycles did, and then try to find out what underlying process influenced the aggregate result. In doing so, he revealed some dynamic features of the model, which he could then attach to real problems.

Frisch did so when in 1931 he involved himself in the discussion on the economic depression. His business cycle studies had convinced him that government could take counter-cyclical measures in order to get the economy out of the depression. However, he found little understanding of this by Norwegian politicians, although he was engaged by the Labour Party to elaborate an economic programme for recovery. While this programme, which was presented in 1934, was not implemented by the Labour Party when it came to power in 1936, it did form the foundation for the economic policy and Frisch's influence on this policy after the war. *The Norwegian model* that emerged was a three parties planning system (the two social partners and government) where wage level was set at a level reflecting competitiveness in the export industry, and then applied to all other sectors.

From the late 1930s Frisch started to work on his other major economic project, the *økosirk* (economic circulation) system. Frisch had found inspiration for this system in the economic tableaus of the physiocrats. It was this system that formed the basis for his work on the national budget, which became an economic planning tool of the utmost importance and in which Norway was a pioneer. This work had its parallels in Wassili Leontief's input-output model and Richard Stone's work on a national accounting scheme in England.

At the same time, in the period after the war, there was a political effort not only to use economic planning for stabilisation purposes, but also for political purposes as part of a socialist policy. However, the more technical and scientific works by Norwegian economists during this period were not done by Frisch himself, but rather by his pupils, and among them another Nobel laureate, Trygve Haavelmo.

AFTER FRISCH

Haavelmo is perhaps internationally best known for his 1944 study, *A Probability Approach to Economics*, in which he both introduced the concept, and explained the technical implication, of statistical methods in econometrics.

Haavelmo became interested in the theory of growth, and in that respect he was less critical than his mentor Frisch. Haavelmo's approach to the growth theory was to study those cases of successful and less successful experiences of economic growth and to specify determining factors. He also engaged in the environmental debate, proposing relatively early to use duties on pollution. Similarly he engaged in problems such as unemployment, international trade price policy, as well as the formation of preferences, welfare and the theory of investment. In *A Study in the Theory of Economic Evolution* (1954) he discusses the relation between population growth, natural resources and economic growth.

The main contribution to economic theory by Haavelmo was his work on the methodology of econometrics in the 1940s. His *The Probability Approach to Econometrics* (1944) is a major work in this field. Here Haavelmo discussed identification, estimation and testing of variables in econometric models when there are simultaneous equations. This work is very technical and only available to mathematically skilled economists. A non-technical explanation of Haavelmo's main argument would be as follows: economic models seldom fit reality because there are often unexpected changes in some external factors that influence the development. In traditional models, these factors are regarded as constant. In order to overcome this problem, Haavelmo introduced a method by which the probabilities of change in these factors are measured simultaneously. By this method the probability of a predicted outcome can be determined.

It is interesting, however, to note that when Haavelmo returned to Norway in the 1940s after his long stay in America, he did not continue his work in the forefront of econometrics, rather he engaged in a wide spectre of economic topics, and with a critical mind. In fact, if you read his more popular articles from the 1950s onwards, they are very critical of inconsistencies in economic models and statements. This critical approach led him to discover shortcomings, even within econometric models, and in particular when these models were applied and used for practical purposes. It was perhaps then not surprising that Haavelmo got his Nobel Prize in 1989, at a time when the remains of the old dogmas of economic planning fell apart as the Berlin Wall went down in Europe.

Haavelmo agreed with Frisch that the real distinction in economics is between truth and relevance, not between positive and normative economics. For the same reason, his critical approach would focus either on the logical consistency of the arguments or on the relevance of these arguments or assumptions. As an example of the latter, Haavelmo was very concerned about how to formulate variables in order to get the right figures into the models. His reluctance towards the use of econometric models for practical political purposes had to do with the difficulty of choosing the correct facts to be used and measured in the model.

An example of inconsistent use of models is, according to Haavelmo, Keynes' *General Theory*. The purpose of Keynes' discussion is to reveal disequilibrium, but he does so by the use of neo-classical equilibrium models. The feature of these models is to explain what happens in equilibrium, while they are incapable of analysing problems outside equilibrium. Therefore there is a major logical flaw in Keynes' argument.

In all his arguments, Haavelmo followed his own advice as how to approach an economic problem: firstly he defined the problem, choosing the decisive variables, secondly he constructed a model in order to analyse the problem. A very interesting remark he made was that when it comes to constructing a model, there is no standard procedure. It is a creative work, a work of art by the economist, a phrase later used by Milton Friedman.

SOME RECENT TRENDS

It has been said about Scandinavian economic thinking that to some extent it is a melting pot of ideas from different cultures. This might be a strength in certain times, since it might encourage scientific breakthroughs. But it might also be a disadvantage in times when relatively few economists work on rather different subjects. Today, there is no dominant school of thought in Norwegian economics. Neither does Norwegian economic policy draw any particular inspiration from Norwegian economists. Policy in recent years has been focused on harmonising the Norwegian domestic economic system to that of mainstream European trends. The main economic debate has been over the extent of economic liberalisation. Although the belief in some special Norwegian solution to economic problems faded at the beginning of the 1990s, recent years have seen a reintroduction of debates about national models, including the Norwegian model.

Market, Entrepreneurship and Knowledge

Perhaps the most revolutionary overall development in economic thinking over the last two centuries is related to the change from an absolutist to a relativist approach. Instead of searching for the meaning of value in absolute terms, economists have come to be concerned with marginal changes in subjective value. Instead of speculating on causes of demand, economists have come to be concerned with marginal changes in demand. In this way, economists have been able to study partial as well as aggregated problems. The clue is all the time to isolate the factors of interest and suppose everything else constant, and then to look at how marginal changes in one factor influence other factors.

In so doing, the assumption is that the same models can be used to analyse economic problems in quite different societies. The basic economic laws are supposed to operate the same way everywhere. To the extent that there are different institutional settings, these are only introduced as modifications of the general model, but will generally only affect the absolute level, not the marginal changes.

Are there any flaws in this way of thinking? Has the development of economic thinking left anything undone? Are there issues that we should discuss that are expelled by the modern theoretical apparatus? Have economists lost sight of the overall perspectives? Or to put it more specifically, is marginalism the cause of the paradigmatic change away from the market?

Paradigmatic changes have taken place among economists, and that this mere fact illustrates the problem that economists often miss important aspects of reality in their analysis. The conception of the market illustrates this phenomenon. The neo-classical debate, as well as Keynesian economics, misinterpreted or even ignored important aspects of the market, leading them in my view to wrong conclusions on important issues.

According to Hayek, there are at least two basic conflicting concepts of the market process present in contemporary debate (representing two different paradigms in economics): on the one hand there is the rationalist concept of the market as a mechanism, inspired by the rationalist school and neo-classical economics, and on the other hand there is the market-process perspective, including spontaneity and complexity of the market. The first emphasises the neo-classical perfect market as an ideal. Attention is put on whether the market is open, information available to all parties, there is real competition, best of all, many suppliers, there are low barriers to entry and control of fair play. The second views the market not primarily as a distribution mechanism, but rather as a creative, discovery process, a learning process. Attention is put on risk, motivation, organisation, property rights, contract rights and laws that stimulate entrepreneurial spirit. Perfection of the market is not decided by low profit or many suppliers, rather it is the creative activity, development and spontaneous emergence of new products and new services that are in focus. These two concepts of the market illustrate two basic paradigms in the history of economic thought, and might therefore be used as criteria for understanding the basic differences between trends and schools in economic thought.

ALFRED MARSHALL AND INSTITUTIONAL AND SPECIAL EXPLANATIONS

Institutional economics is a branch of economic theory that discusses the relation between economic forces and processes and the institutional and organisational environment that the economic activity plays itself within. It goes far back in the history of economic thought. Von Thünen had (in *Isolated State*) in the early nineteenth century, described the emergence of urban centres. His explanation for why centres emerged, and what pattern of centres that was created, related to the marginal cost of agriculture products with an emphasis on transportation cost. In short, agricultural products would be traded by farmers in the market where the price/cost ratio was most favourable. That is why we have urban centres with countryside around.

Alfred Marshall in the late nineteenth century described industrial districts and reflected on the agglomeration of industries in particular districts. One obvious explanation was natural resources. In *Principles of Economics* (1890) he writes:

> When an industry has thus chosen a locality for itself, it is likely to stay there long: so great are the advantages which people following the same skilled trade get from near neighbourhood to one another. The mysteries of the trade become no mysteries; but are as it were in the air, and children learn many of them unconsciously. Good work is rightly appreciated, inventions and improvements in machinery, in processes and the general organization of the business have their merits promptly discussed: if one man starts a new idea, it is taken up by others and combined with suggestions of their own; and thus it becomes the source of further new ideas. And presently subsidiary trades grow up in the neighbourhood, supplying it with implements and materials, organizing its traffic, and in many ways conducing to the economy of its material. (Marshall, 1890)

Marshall divides between internal and external (to the company) economic forces that determine development and competitiveness (economics of scale). According to Marshall, the further agglomeration process (concentration of an industry in a geographical location) is defined by the skills that develop in that location, supporting industry, and personal skills in the labour force.

Friedrich von Wieser, one of the leading Austrian economists in his time, wrote in his 1914 book on social economics about what he termed the location of industry:

> One craftsman needs another in order to obtain the wherewithal to practice his trade: one and all they need the merchant and trader who facilitates the intercourse with foreign places. Then the fact that they are brought together in one place creates for the artisan as well as for the merchant a local market of mutual exchange. [...] Finally, the concentration of nascent industries in definite locations led to the organization of guilds, which opened the way to a far-seeing and comprehensive policy for the protection of natural interests, while the various governments were induced in their economic administration to take an active interest in these matters. (von Wieser, 1967, p. 315)

von Wieser's argument is similar to Marshall, however he introduced a wider set of social mechanisms in order to explain the development of cities: division of labour, internal markets, networks and politics.

JOSEPH SCHUMPETER ON MARKET AND ENTREPRENEURSHIP

The work of Austrian economist Joseph Alois Schumpeter (1883–1950) illustrates one of the points I like to make, that the theoretical modelling of the agent in neo-classical economic theory has mainly related to a pure logic of choice. The agent is an optimiser, somebody who seeks profits and opportunities, and does so in a rational way. The agent acts rationally (bounded or with full information) within a set of institutional constraints. He or she will always choose what in money terms gives the best outcome. The capitalist system puts a money price on everything. By that, everything can be compared in terms of one standard, money, which is also available. Because of this, we can anticipate that if a price goes down, demand will increase. Market equilibrium is possible and so is the use of economic incentives to motivate action. These are in short some of the fundamental features of the capitalist market economy. It is in a sense functional, instrumental and rational.

It is worth recalling that not even Leon Walras, with his *General Equilibrium Theory*, was able to demonstrate the relation between a theory of human action and that of pure logic of choice. Milton Friedman writes in his treatise on Walras:

> There are two main themes in the Elements: the analysis of marginal utility; and the theory of general equilibrium. Walras regarded the two as fitting together in one harmonious whole, which is certainly tenable; and he also viewed the marginal utility analysis as indispensable for the study of general equilibrium, which seems much more dubious. (Friedman, 1955)

Schumpeter writes in a comment on Walras that he was not sufficiently aware of the fact that the unique solution, where it 'exists', need not be economically meaningful in the sense that an actual system might work with it. On the other hand, Schumpeter says that it was not the intention of Walras to answer the question whether there actually:

> is any tendency [...] to establish these solutions, [...] nor the question whether these solutions or equilibrium values are stable or not. (Schumpeter, 1950, p. 1006)

The problem of equilibrium consists of many related problems, such as:

- Is there a tendency within the market towards equilibrium?
- Is there a unique solution to the equilibrium question?
- Is the solution to the equilibrium problem (if it exists) a stable solution?

By mixing the concepts of rational action, profit maximisation and marginal utility theory, it is possible to demonstrate that a unique and stable equilibrium solution exists. That this argument is static and that it presupposes an uncritical combination of psychology and mathematics is seldom discussed. It is no wonder that Fritz Machlup gave the following characterisation of the concept of equilibrium:

> Perhaps we may say that equilibrium is a Fata Morgana, a mirage that lures people on its track and thus determines the direction in which they are going. Equilibrium is a mental aid in our analysis of decision-making, an indispensable analytic device; it should not be hypostatized into anything observable, or into anything more than a mere vision in somebody's mind,

presumably in the mind of a decisionmaker, but surely in the mind of an outsider who analyzes the essentials of decision-making and of the processes of adjustments to specified changes. (Machlup, 1984, p. 253)

Hayek's contribution to this debate has to be understood in relation to this general debate, and his essay from 1937, *Economics and Knowledge*, is an attempt to define more closely what is in the notion of equilibrium and how it occurs.

To see economic activity and economic behaviour as a special mode of action is not new to the economic discussion. Early discussions on the relation between economics and social development referred to these different modes of behaviour. Joseph Schumpeter had, in *Theorie der wirtschaftlichen Entwicklung* from 1911 (translated as *The Theory of Economic Development: An inquiry into profits, capital, credit, interest and the business cycle*), argued that the entrepreneur plays an important role in economic development, different from economic calculation. Schumpeter developed a dichotomy between the neo-classical understanding of the economy and his more evolutionary approach (see Table 5.1).

On the growth of the economy, Schumpeter writes:

> *The slow and continuous increase in time of the national supply of productive means and savings is obviously an important factor in explaining the course of economic history through the centuries, but it is completely overshadowed by the fact that development consists primarily in employing existing resources in a different way, in doing new things with them, irrespective of whether those resources increase or not. In the treatment of shorter epochs, moreover, this is even true in more tangible sense. Different methods of employment, and not saving and increase in available quantity of labour, have changed the face of the economic world in the last fifty years. (Schumpeter, 1911, p. 68)*

Schumpeter argued against a functionalist understanding of economic development and towards a more evolutionary understanding, where the human factor (the entrepreneur) plays an important role. Also, he introduces the distinction between radical (new combination) and incremental (smaller, organisational innovations) innovation. When it comes to explaining the sources of innovation, Schumpeter applies a much broader perspective than what is found in later (neo-classical) treatments. He argues that *new combinations* imply the ability to break with the common and established, and to see new possibilities. This implies initiative, authority and foresight (1911, p. 75).

Table 5.1   Schumpeter's classification of neo-classical and evolutionary economics

(Neo-)classical	Evolutionary
The economy as circulation	The economy as development
Static, equilibrium	Dynamic, spontaneous change
Capitalists	Industrialists (entrepreneurs)
Management	Entrepreneurial
Optimise, 'best methods'	Develop, innovate

Source: Based on Schumpeter (1911).

Schumpeter acknowledges that there are few people with this entrepreneurial ability; they are rare personalities. Subsequently, he applies a psychological explanation to why there are entrepreneurs. But Schumpeter introduces another group of explanations, namely social factors. These he describes as both mentality – social and legal restrictions and enablers for entrepreneurs – and the economic environment, including private property rights and market arrangements. Schumpeter thereby anticipates much of what later has become the core of innovation and entrepreneurial policy. It is also important to point out that Schumpeter never developed a theory of innovation. He was always very focused on the entrepreneurial role when it came to innovation. It was a theory that for many decades was not taken seriously by economists.

Schumpeter had for a long time been a critic of static equilibrium theory. His interest was the dynamic development of the economy. Business cycles theories had been developed by economists such as the American W.C. Mitchell (1874–1948) (*Business Cycles* (1913)) and were reintroduced in an institutional setting by Schumpeter in the late 1930s in *Business Cycles* (1939) and *Capitalism, Socialism and Democracy* (1942). Schumpeter focused on the dynamic processes of the economy, contrary to the static equilibrium theory of the neo-classical economists.

Schumpeter developed a comprehensive approach to economic, social and political development. In *Capitalism, Socialism and Democracy* he integrated the economic, social and political system and tried to explain the development of the one system with the other. His argument was a combination of economic, social and institutional processes. He talks about the *crumbling walls* of capitalism, when the entrepreneurial role of the bourgeoisie is taken over by technocrats and the intellectuals. With it go bourgeois values. He saw (contrary to Marx) a relation between tendencies of mass production, concentration of capital and the development of socialism (the big capital, big government deal!). This means that capitalism, through its success, destroys the social structure and values which were a precondition for its own existence (Schumpeter, 1976, p. 161).

The classical treatment here is of course Max Weber's analysis of the relation between protestant ethics and the emergence of capitalism in Western Europe (as I will discuss in the chapter on culture and market). Schumpeter used this theory in his crumbling wall story. Parts of his approach were taken up by John Kenneth Galbraith, who in the 1950s and 1960s criticised neo-classical economists for not having any understanding of society, not being related to history and not taking into account political and technological change, as he wrote on this in *The Affluent Society* (1958).

Back, then, to the 1911 book on entrepreneurship: where did these ideas come from and what type of contemporary discourse did it play into? I will try to address this by discussing Schumpeter's arguments in relation to modernist movements at the same period of time. I discuss that movement in Chapter 8. The closing sentences in Schumpeter's 1911 book *The Theory of Economic Development* go like this:

> But no therapy can permanently obscure the great economic and social processes by which businesses, individual positions, forms of life, cultural values and ideals, sink in the social scale and finally disappear. In a society with private property and competition, this process is a necessary complement to the continual emergence of new economic and social forms and of continual rising real incomes of all social strata. The process would be milder if there were no cyclical fluctuations, but it is not wholly due to the latter, and it is completed independently of them. These changes are theoretically and practically, economically and culturally,

much more important than the economic stability upon which all analytical attention has been concentrated for so long. And in their special way both the rise and the fall of families and firms are much more characteristic of the capitalist economic system, of its culture and its results, than any of the things that can be observed in a society which is stationary, in the sense that its processes reproduced themselves at a constant rate. (Schumpeter, [1911] 2008, p. 255)

Why should an economist pay so much attention to issues such as culture and forms of life? Why is it so apparent for Schumpeter to underline these things in his treatment of economic development? My intention is not to give a historical or biographically correct answer to this, rather to place Schumpeter's remarks in relation to other ideological and cultural trends in this time. One such description is found in Janik and Toulmin's 1973 book *Wittgenstein's Vienna*. They describe Vienna and the last decades of the Habsburg reign, the period 1890 until the First World War. It is the area of Kraus, Loos, Schönberg, Mahler and Klimt, to mention some, who all in their field change the direction, be it literature, architecture, music or painting. It was a period of creativity, but also one of radical change in the way of life. The old authoritarian (and feudal) and elite regime was coming to an end, the new, industrial and bourgeois society and the broad masses of people were setting the new stage. In short, one entered modern society.

A story told by Hans-Georg Gadamer:

1919 was a time of confusion and new organization of German awareness, a time in which debating clubs, both large and small, fairly swarmed. I remember a discussion within a young academic circle that I attended as a wide-eyed, curious student. Every possible means of salvation was offered for the sickness and crisis of the time. One person spoke out for a socialist society; another saw the poet Stefan George as the founder of a new human community; a third wanted to build anew on the basis of antiquity and humanism; a fourth saw in Gierke's Genossenschaftsrecht the ideas for the construction of a new state. And then a fifth student came forward and said fervently that the only salvation from our difficulties was phenomenology. (Gadamer, 1977, p. 133)

The fifth student was Edmund Husserl. The main point is the description Gadamer gives of the times. It was the jazz age, symbolised by the Cole Porter song *Anything goes!*[16] Modernism in art, as I argue in Chapter 8, can be seen as a response to, but also an analysis of, and inspiration to, many of the things we associate with the term modern society. Life in modern society gives the individual incredible freedom. It is a freedom for the majority of the population in material terms not formerly seen in society. However, it is also a society that poses anxiety, dissolution and subsequently calls for institutional stability. It is a society that acknowledges subjectivity and change (innovation) but at the same time creates new ways of structuration, instrumentalisation and bureaucratisation.

What is modernism in art? No universal answer exists, but the reference is to the art that came as a reaction to modern society (from 1850 to the Second World War, or from 1890 to 1920). Firstly, modernist artists to a large extent denounced institutions, in particular historical heresy. Futurists, such as Marinetti, formulated manifestos on

---

16   The expression is taken from the interesting and provoking article by D.C. Stove in *Encounter*, June 1985: 'Karl Popper and the Jazz Age'.

destroying museums, yet they were deeply dependent on the new interest in art that followed modernisation (art galleries, museums, private collections, in short the new art market).

Modernists denounced the bourgeoisie class and praised the common, the alternative, at the same time modernist artists were very much a part of bourgeois society. They flourished in places where the new bourgeois class developed, in the large European cities, in particular those cities that were transformed by the new industrial bourgeois class. Modernist art explored the instrumental (to some extent inhuman) modern organisation of production, at the same time had some of the great industrialists as their patrons (Guggenheim supported modernist milieus in Europe, and industrialists such as Sir William Burrell developed an art collection with classical and modernist art; in Norway, the industrialist and ship owner Fred Olsen bought many of Edvard Munch's works, a tradition followed in recent years by Saatchi & Saatchi and their collection of contemporary art, to mention some). In fact, the contemporary interest in art and culture as a part of social and economic development, for example Richard Florida's theses (Florida might be one of the few to regard the extensive impact of innovation and cultural change), builds on assumptions supported by these curious symbioses of modern art and capitalist development (Florida, 2002).

Schumpeter foresaw the role of an entrepreneur as a more radical figure, one that might change the rules of the game. That is inherent in his concept of *creative destruction*, as he was later to describe it. As we celebrate the creative part of this term, we should also discuss the destructive part. Schumpeter saw early on that development would imply changes that were harmful for some. He was aware that economic development influences other aspects of life. When we discuss innovation and entrepreneurship today, we should be more willing to address these changes as well.

F.A. HAYEK ON MARKET AND KNOWLEDGE

F.A. Hayek wrote an important article in 1945 called *The Use of Knowledge in Society*. In the article he demonstrated how society is dependent on a variety and diversity of 'knowledge. In fact, the distribution of individual knowledge is the cornerstone of knowledge in society. It is a strong argument for a liberal society. Evolutionary economics has acknowledged the role of knowledge in development. One exponent of this position, the works of Hayek, can stand as an example. In summarising Hayek's theory of knowledge, Desai writes:

> [...] (1) equilibrium involves compatibility of individual plans ex ante end the congruence (correspondence) of subjective expectations with objective data; (2) there is a causal connection between experience and knowledge and this is the avenue through which congruence helps to make compatibility possible; (3) Knowledge is fragmented among individuals; the content of this specialized partial knowledge is not only prices but also some incomplete knowledge about the alternative use of resources (the opportunity set) owned by the individual concerned; (4) local knowledge may lead to equilibrium but such an equilibrium need not be optimal; (5) one sufficient condition (among others unspecified) for attaining optimality is connectedness of fragments of knowledge; connectedness requires that over all the individuals there is complete knowledge of, say, the opportunity set, though non possesses it individually. (Desai, 1994, p. 42)

Equilibrium, coordination and natural order are central concepts in the philosophy of Hayek. And, as Hayek to a large extent is developing these thoughts along the same lines as classical economists such as Smith and Hume, these concepts are central in the understanding of the classical idea of a liberal society.

Hayek says in the introduction to his 1937 essay on *Economics and Knowledge* that he intends to say something more about equilibrium than the standard formal analysis that he calls the pure logic of choice. His ambition is to say something about how equilibrium comes about in the real-life situation. What does it mean when we say that people in real life are in a state of equilibrium?

> *The first answer which would seem to follow from our approach is that equilibrium in this connection exists if the actions of all members of society over a period are all executions of their respective individual plans on which each decided at the beginning of the period. (Hayek, 1937, p. 51)*

This definition of equilibrium indicates that individuals over a period of time have to be able to realise their expectations. This again means that equilibrium is dependent on the possibility for everybody to have their expectations realised, that their expectations have to be coordinated or based on some sort of common external factors. But:

> *... since some of the data on which any one person will base his plans on will be the expectation that other people will act in a particular way, it is essential for the compatibility of the different plans that the plans of the one contain exactly those actions which form the data for the plans of the other. (Hayek, 1937, p. 38)*

This is how Hayek defines equilibrium. And one can immediately see the problems that this definition raises: how can an individual gain insight into the plans and expectations of others? The answer, of course, is that they can't. There has to be some sort of medium by which the expectations and plans of individuals is transformed into information to others. The question is: how is this process operating?

To put the issue very briefly, one could say that equilibrium is a result of coordination and leads under certain conditions to natural order. The concept of natural order is the opposite of artificial order, the latter meaning an order deliberately made by human beings while the former means an order that results from human action but not from human design. In the classical treatment, and with Hayek, there is an important distinction between these two types of order, because the *artificial order* is regarded as an ethical order, while the *natural order* is regarded as ethically neutral and universal, and in that respect it is fundamental to the realisation of the liberal, open society (Hayek, 1967, p. 102).

There is a long road that leads from the psychological motives of the individual, via the process of equilibrium, into the natural order of the open society. The central element in Hayek's theory is the knowledge of the individual: structures and processes in society have to be seen in relation to the knowledge of the individual. Hayek's later works are elaborations on this basic idea that nothing will happen in society unless it has some sort of relation to individual knowledge. With reference to the debate in the 1930s over the possibility of economic calculation in a socialist society, Hayek argued that as the knowledge in society is scattered among its individuals and can never be centralised, efficiency in the economy is a question of to what extent the economy is able to utilise the knowledge of the individual.

Tacit knowledge, ideal types, institutions and norms might be regarded as ordering devices in the social process. I think that the solution to Hayek's coordination problem lies beyond these ordering devices; that the coordination problem is not primarily a problem of perception. However, I think that individuals' perception of the social process is an important aspect of the efficiency process, and therefore we will find these phenomena discussed by Hayek.

The intersubjective world of structures, roles and functions is important and does have some coordinating effect. And, if that is all there is in the coordination problem, its solution might be sought within the discipline of *hermeneutics* or *institutionalism*. Equilibrium is insight into other people's plans. The utilisation of individualised knowledge through the market order is more efficient than any centralised system of control. Order is a feature of the human mind; we look for order in what we perceive. Natural order is a result of human action but not human design. Without order, there would be no society. Society exists because and to the extent that there is order. Order is a consequence of the fact that people prosper from cooperation with others. The more general and impersonal this order is, the more people will be able to prosper. Tacit knowledge and learned rules that emerge through evolution have the potential to bring prosperity in society. Individuals learn to practise rules and appreciate order before they are able to explain in full detail how they were formed and how they operate. Only later, when we have experienced the advantage of this order, do we start to explain why and how.

Although these are all different types of explanation, I think they throw light on the equilibrium process. First they say that equilibrium exists because it has a function, secondly that this function is important for the development of social cooperation, and thirdly that we are able to appreciate this function without being able to explain how it occurs.

This efficiency argument, which was mainly presented in his 1945 essay, is essential to Hayek's later discussion on the superiority of the market economy and the liberal society. However, this efficiency argument is not the same as the coordination argument that he presents in his 1937 essay. Both have to do with individual knowledge, but how individuals coordinate their actions and how society utilises knowledge are two different questions. Although Hayek uses the notion of equilibrium in his later works, and extends the use of this notion to include social equilibrium (spontaneous order, and evolution) he never returned to the question he discussed in 1937 of how equilibrium comes about.

It has been one of the major arguments of Hayek to point at two different traditions of rationalism in Western thought: on the one hand *constructivism* or deductive rationalism of the Descartian type, and on the other hand the *critical rationalism* that acknowledges complexity, spontaneity and uncertainty. This last kind is what really brought about liberal thinking according to Hayek. Both French constructivism and German idealism is of the first kind, while British empiricism is of the second. It should, however, be added that the tradition of *spontaneous order* thinking has at least two different ancestors: one is the British, which acknowledge the spontaneous growth of social institutions, the other is part of the German idealist system, as found in the writings of both Hegel and Marx.

The central element that explains the efficiency of the natural order is that it contains complex information: that is, more complex information than any single individual could ever control.

... by relying on the spontaneously ordering forces, we can extend the scope or range of the order which we may induce to form, precisely because its particular manifestation will depend on many more circumstances than can be known to us, and in case of social order, such an order will utilize the separate knowledge of all its several members, without this knowledge ever being concentrated in a single mind, or being subject to those processes of deliberate coordination and adaption which a mind performs. (Hayek, 1979, vol. 1; 1973, p. 41)

Hayek's argument has been called a rule-utilitarian argument. It has as a principle that utility is measured, not by the end result of individual action, but by the potential of actualising individual knowledge. It is the *open-endedness* and general nature of the natural order that bears this potential.

ISRAEL KIRZNER ON MARKET AND LEARNING

An approach in the same tradition as Hayek, but with a more rationalistic type of explanation, has been developed by Israel Kirzner (1992). In Kirzner's model, there are two processes: one external process of technological and social change that constantly disturbs the market equilibrium, and one internal process of entrepreneurial activity that constantly helps to restore equilibrium. The reason why entrepreneurial activity leads to market equilibrium is that each disequilibrium situation contains the possibility of entrepreneurial profit, since disequilibrium is defined as a gap between the prices of supply and demand. This gap has a profit potential that the entrepreneur will try to fill, and in that way, he helps to restore equilibrium. But although the entrepreneurial activity of discoveries is a constant corrective to market disturbance, there are a number of qualifications to this market process.

The main one is that entrepreneurs may be wrong; they may make mistakes and in that way increase disequilibrium. To this challenge, Kirzner remarks:

If we maintain, nonetheless, that the market process can fairly be described, in general terms, as equilibrating, this is because of a conviction that in the face of initial ignorance there is a systematic tendency for genuine discoveries, rather than spurious ones, to be made. (Kirzner, 1992, p. 45)

What this leads to is the emphasis on the discovery and learning process. The central question that is addressed is: how do we learn to correct mistakes and make the right discoveries (that will restore equilibrium)? And the answer to this question might lie within the theory of learning.

Kirzner's approach does not answer the question of why there is equilibrium. It does answer the question of how equilibrium is restored when it has been disturbed (which means that there already is a tendency towards equilibrium) and it even throws light on the efficiency question of the market economy.

There are three partial problems in relation to equilibrium: (1) Is there a tendency towards equilibrium? (Both Hayek and Kirzner answer yes to this question.) (2) Is there a unique solution to the equilibrium problem? (Hayek and Kirzner seem to think so, although this is only a hypothetical situation.) (3) And is this solution stable? (Hayek and Kirzner seem to indicate that the process towards equilibrium is stable.)

The definition Hayek gave of the equilibrium problem did not bring us closer to the understanding of the first question. Hayek regards tendencies towards equilibrium as an empirical fact. Although he does try to explain how this tendency comes about, his primary concern in his 1937 essay and his later works in psychology is related to how we are able to perceive equilibrium and how we are able to restore equilibrium when it is disturbed. It is a paradox that we know so little about something so important as the answer to how equilibrium is achieved within the market economy.

To accept the idea of division of knowledge, and to explore methods to utilise different types of knowledge on different levels, has been called by Kirzner 'knowledge problem A' (Kirzner, 1992, p. 169). The central aspect of knowledge problem A is coordination of knowledge.

But there is also a knowledge problem B. Knowledge problem B is related to developing new knowledge, inventing new ideas or building new theories. Knowledge problem B cannot be solved through coordination; it cannot even be comprehended as a coordination problem. Knowledge problem B is related to how genuine creation or learning takes place.

Hayek has addressed the question of how it is possible to act in a complicated world when it is impossible for each individual to know every piece of information that might be relevant for his decision. The Hayekian answer to this coordination problem (knowledge problem A) is that people relate their actions to common norms (Kirzner, 1992, p. 173). The constitution of society with its general structures and norms is a common point of reference for the social process. In Kirzner's words, that is:

> For us the existence of systematic market forces means the existence of a spontaneous process of learning. (Kirzner, 1992, p. 201)

What are the driving forces behind the learning process in the market? According to Kirzner:

> ... they are driven by alertness of individual's intent on achieving their purposes. (Kirzner, 1992, p. 204)

Alertness and purpose drive individuals to explore possibilities, learn from mistakes or try new alternatives. Purpose means that one constantly looks for something, that is, looks in a specific direction.

Purpose and alertness are, according to Kirzner, sufficient elements to explain how the spontaneous coordination of the market process emerges. It is sufficient to explain how knowledge problem A is solved: it is solved because unless the seller is able to agree with the buyer on a price, there will be no exchange. As long as both seller and buyer have a purpose, and therefore involve in exchange, they have to generate enough knowledge about each other to agree on a price. In a service encounter, this might also be a norm, or a quality standard.

Knowledge problem B, however, is not solved in this way. Knowledge problem B is not a coordination problem; it is the problem of how genuinely new knowledge is created. Knowledge problem B is related to genuine creation and discoveries. One might ask: why is it that some people go on expeditions of discovery and what are the qualities of the discoverer? Take the story (metaphor) of Columbus: what was it that led him to travel, and what were the qualities needed for him to complete the project? Note that these might have been two different sorts of qualities. It is also important to acknowledge the distinction between production, discovery and luck (Kirzner, 1992, p. 221): when Columbus invested resources in his travels, he did not know the outcome, so it was not a production process. However, what eventually was the outcome was not a result of blind luck. Columbus did have a plan; he did search in a particular direction, so he was a discoverer. This phenomenon cannot be explained by the market process (Kirzner, 1992, p. 178). It is a deliberate quality of the individual that makes him a discoverer, such as courage, curiosity, sense of mission or sense of crisis. But there are some qualities of the learning environment that might encourage discoveries.

The market encounter can be understood as the moment when the customer meets the supplier, usually a company or an organisation. This meeting involves many different processes that can be analysed in different ways; there is the customer reaction to the product, to the artefacts or to the behaviour of the employee. There are the different types of production processes that are activated by customer demands. There is also the reaction of the employee to customer behaviour, that is, the interaction processes. The market encounter may also involve reflections both by members of the organisation and its customers. Some of these can be analysed and implemented by administrative procedures. We can call these the analytical elements of the encounter: analysing customer expectations, improving technical quality or improving delivery systems.

Knowledge of system structure and the need for generative knowledge is important in complex situations. But generative knowledge might involve two kinds of knowledge related to two kinds of complexity: complexity due to a large number of cues (which is an analytical problem) and complexity due to the fact that there are no logical solutions (what we call intuitive situations). In intuitive situations, where there are no ready solutions, judgement has to be made on the basis of generative knowledge. Learning means knowing both the special and the general structure of the situation. The challenge is to be able to combine the intimate knowledge of the market encounter with the more general knowledge of the larger economic system.

The market encounter is the organisation's encounter with the market. This encounter forms the basis for the organisation's learning and decision-making. The market process is in itself a learning process. Learning in the market process is related to knowledge problems A and B. Problem A is a coordination problem. Learning means gaining insight in the customer's preferences and needs in order to establish exchange. Norms play an important role in this coordination. Knowledge problem B, however, is not a coordination problem and requires a different kind of learning.

This indicates that there are two separate learning processes related to the market process. In Kirzner's words, the problem can be formulated like this:

To be sure, the spontaneous emergence of any institution indeed relies on the very same process through which Knowledge Problem A is solved in markets. [...] On the other hand, however, it has been our aim to point out [...] that these earlier economic insights into the spontaneously co-operative properties of markets do not, in themselves, provide any reassurance concerning the benign quality of the long run tendencies of institutional development. [...] The explanation for such benign tendencies, if indeed they exist, must be sought elsewhere. (Kirzner, 1992, p. 179)

Since learning is going on in the market process constantly, the organisation must constantly adapt to new realities. The ability to learn, or to learn how to learn, is important when one is facing changing environments (Agyris, 1982). Organisations that are very dependent on the market have to be alert to market changes. One important way in which the organisation learns is through the service encounter, since that is when the customer steps on to the discourse arena of the organisation. The service encounter is a voice situation, that is, a situation where the customer expresses his opinion. Note that the activation of voice by the customer is a function of loyalty, that is, that the customer is entering a discourse arena (Hirschman, 1970, p. 77). The alternative situation is exit, when customers leave, or do not enter the arena of the organisation at all. But in both situations, it is important for the organisation to gain knowledge about the market. This knowledge is not about each individual customer, but about the norms that customers refer to. In order to understand the market, it is important to understand the process of emergence of norms.

In spite of this insight, Geoffrey M. Hodgson (2001), in my mind rightly, observes that within the economic discipline, the integration of an economic and an institutional perspective on socio-economic development has never really happened. The two more or less still live in their separate discourses.

Conclusion

In this chapter I have discussed two things: firstly, how economics has developed as a science (neo-classical economics) with more and more elaborate and rigorous theoretical approaches, and secondly, how there is a deep split in economics between those who take a more institutional perspective and neo-classics. At the same time I have tried to show that both types of economic theory have developed in relation to society and integrated with economic policy. I have also tried to argue that the market is a special kind of social domain.

What does this tell us in relation to knowledge? It tells us that it is difficult to say something general about economics and knowledge, since economics is not a unified entity. It also says that if one should say something in general, it has to be that economic processes (and theorising on them) are integrated into social and political processes. Furthermore, I have tried to show that there are economic theories that are able to discuss more in detail the leaning and knowledge creation processes that go on in the market. This perhaps becomes clearer when, in the next two chapters, I turn to the knowledge organisation and the relation between culture and market.

Knowledge Organisations: Developing Knowledge in Practice

Introduction

The term knowledge is being used more and more to describe the challenges today's organisations and businesses face. Knowledge is seen as a major resource for organisations and firms. The concepts of the *knowledge organisation* and *knowledge management* have become popular references in organisational studies and practice. Peter Drucker, one of the pioneers in developing these concepts (also including the concept of knowledge workers), argues that the concepts were developed in a sort of response to the Tayloristic tradition (Drucker, 1999). While the traditional (Tayloristic) workplace was concerned with utilising natural resources, increasing efficiency in production (productivity) and achieving economics of scale through mass production, the modern knowledge organisation is much more concerned with utilising human resources (knowledge), increasing innovation and creativity, and customising production. Prusak and Matson (2006) talk about a *knowledge movement* with an increased emphasis on organisational learning and knowledge development. However, Foss (2005) warns against having too ambitious a conception of these changes. At the same time he points out the effect that more distributed knowledge and information flow will have on firms' internal organisation and boundaries.

Of course, the main question for an organisation, if we accept this general description of a change in perspective towards a knowledge society and knowledge economy, is how to utilise knowledge in the organisation: what does this perspective require in the way of structures, routines, management, culture and strategy? In order to answer that, we need to have a conception of what this knowledge is, what it does and how we can influence it.

In discussing this I will refer to the work of my colleague Harald Knudsen. In his four books on strategy and organisational development, published in the period 1998 to 2001, *Traveling for the Sake of Theoriea, Theory Building in Practice, Mentor* and *Sirens*, Harald Knudsen develops a concept that he calls *theory-building in practice*. This core concept is argued from both a philosophical and a practical perspective, draws on insights from business studies, strategy, organisational theory and psychology, to mention a few, and integrates these other theories (Knudsen, 1998–2001). What I will discuss here is whether the concept of theory-building in practice helps us to understand how knowledge is developed in organisations, and how it might lead to better decisions.

Knudsen (1998–2001) writes about Solon (638BC–558BC), the great leader of Athens, who, in order to broaden his perspective on political leadership, made a journey in the

Mediterranean 'for the sake of theory'. It resulted in a new constitution of Athens that lasted for more than a hundred years. What is the real content of this theory-building in practice that Solon exemplified? Knudsen argues that it involves both understanding the social system as well as developing a variety of experiences, intimacy of communication and increased competencies. The *action-learning model* that Knudsen refers to, inspired among others by *pragmatism* and the work of William James (James, 1978), establishes a relation between action, response and reflection. One develops competencies (practical skills and *phronesis*) through learning from action in practice. However, this is not a mere mechanical or instrumental form of learning. *Phronesis*, or practical knowledge, is also about being a good person, that is, being ethical and honest. How does this link up with organisational, management and strategic theory?

To investigate this, *theory-building in practice* must be understood along at least two dimensions: firstly, it is about how we understand organisations as researchers. We understand them in the way that we develop knowledge about them from practice. I will below refer to this as an *anti-positivist* perspective on research, and argue that it has implications for how we study and understand organisations (Johnsen, 2013). Secondly, the concept of theory-building in practice is about how organisations come to understand their own practices and conceptualise the environment within which they are situated. This implies that the knowledge organisation faces an *epistemological* challenge.

This chapter is intended as a tour to explore the issue of how organisations *develop knowledge in practice*. Many textbooks (e.g., Amin and Cohendet, 2004; Fuller, 2002; Newell et al., 2009; Devenport and Prusak, 2000; Hislop, 2005; Tsoukas, 2005; Choo, 2006; Amin and Roberts, 2008a; Jashapara, 2011) on the theme would argue that there are different dimensions related to these questions. I argue that what I will call the *constitution of the organisation*, which is its particular configuration of routines, norms, values and structure, is a core issue. The perspective of this chapter is to try to reconcile some conflicting positions in organisational theory. In order to do that, I have organised the chapter around eight questions about knowledge in organisations.

What are Knowledge and the Knowledge Organisation?

Most textbooks will argue that knowledge is not the same as facts or data, and not the same as mere beliefs or fantasies. There are theories from those who argue that knowledge is something personal and epistemic (Tsoukas, 2005) and from those who argue that knowledge is something structural and inherent in routines and rules (Jashapara, 2011). Many argue that knowledge is something in between these two poles. Some look for a relation between information, constructed meaning and the creation of knowledge (Choo, 2006). There is also an epistemic issue related to the discussion of knowledge (Fuller, 2002). Not surprisingly, the field of organisational epistemology has many examples of attempts to structure the epistemological process (Cook and Brown, 1999; Jashapara, 2011; Seirafi, 2012). There are exceptions (e.g., Fuller, 2002; Tsoukas, 2005), but there is logic in the fact that organisational theory looks for structural solutions to epistemological questions. Organisations are inherently about organising.

Another dimension in understanding knowledge in organisations relates to different phases in the production process. Many textbooks will argue that different knowledge is needed in different phases of the production process, and for different kinds of products or tasks (Amin and Roberts, 2008b). More scientific knowledge may be relevant in a developmental stage or in a research and development department; more practice-based knowledge might be relevant in relation to contracting and marketing; more knowledge of a communicative and human kind is perhaps needed in a service situation. Furthermore, many textbooks will argue that knowledge is related to organisational form. Team-based organisations use different ways of communicating and sharing knowledge than hierarchical organisations.

The focus on knowledge opens up many different discussions and can be used to analyse different aspects of an organisation. One of these aspects is the epistemological question. Tsoukas (2005) argues, with reference to Daniel Bell (1973):

> Put simply, data require minimal human judgement, knowledge maximum judgement. Knowledge is the capacity to exercise judgement on the part of the individual, which is either based on an appreciation of context or derived from theory, or both. (Tsoukas, 2005, p. 120)

This is in line with the main literature on strategy. For example, Mintzberg (1994) discusses the calculative versus the commitment styles of management and argues that strategy-making processes should be:

> ... capturing what the manager learns from sources (both soft insights from his or her personal experiences and experiences of others throughout the organisation and hard data from market research and the like) and ... synthesising that learning into a vision of the direction that the business should pursue. (Mintzberg, 1994)

Foss and Klein recently discussed and:

> ... outlined an entrepreneurial theory of the firm built upon Knightian uncertainty and Austrian capital theory. The theory regards entrepreneurship as an active, owing, controlling agency, the function of the assembling, configuration, and reconfiguration of bundles of heterogeneous resources under conditions of 'true' uncertainty, with strong implications for our understanding of the nature, emergence and boundaries of the firm. It also shows how entrepreneurial judgement about resources is distributed throughout that multi-person firm, as the owner's original judgement is shared with employees who experience derived judgement on the owner's behalf. (Foss and Klein, 2012, p. 221)

How can we develop strategies that utilise knowledge resources and judgement throughout the organisation? Theory-building in practice is about ways of handling this challenge. It is about the perceptual capability to cope with the complex (intuitive) situations many knowledge organisations are facing. There are three perceptual levels to be addressed: markets, organisational processes and individual motivation.

A knowledge organisation could be defined as an organisation that holds knowledge resources that are essential to its existence (Drucker, 1993). In order to provide a competitive advantage, these resources must of course be rare and valuable (Barney, 1991; Foss and Klein, 2012). We can imagine that knowledge organisations must also have other resources than knowledge, so we might talk about degrees of knowledge in the resource base of an organisation. For example, a mining company might have access to mines (physical property rights) as their main resource, but will still need knowledge in order to utilise it. Knowledge is something often linked to other resources. However, here I focus on knowledge (including intellectual property rights) as a resource.

We can therefore argue that the core of knowledge organisations is to develop and utilise resources in ways that are competitive in the market. Further, this implies some sort of formal organisational structure, which will not only be instrumental in governing the knowledge resources of the organisation but also enable adjustments to be made to market/customer needs and demands and to societal regulations and norms. Organisations therefore need to define their borders and remain open and alert to societal and market information and change.

How is it that the Organisations, or Individuals such as Employees or Managers, Come to have Specific Knowledge?

A key word in understanding knowledge development is learning. Learning can take many forms and can happen at different levels. There can be individual learning, but organisations can also 'learn', and markets (structures) can learn. These latter forms of learning are of a different kind than individual learning. They are structural and often involve adjustments (new routines, norms, structural borders and relations) as a result of new experiences or structural changes (Johnsen, 2013).

Chris Argyris, who developed an action learning theory close to that later used by Harald Knudsen, takes a human perspective on learning, and defines learning in this way:

> Learning may be described as a process in which people discover a problem, invent a solution to the problem, produce the solution, and evaluate the outcome, leading to the discovery of new problems. (Argyris, 1982, p. 38)

This means that learning at an individual level is a creative process leading towards a change in the status quo. Learning means development. At the same time, it is assumed that learning is not an accidental action. Learning is a deliberate action, reflecting the intention of the learning individual (Argyris, 1982, p. 41). However, although people are focused on causal relations between their actions and those of others, they frequently tend to produce consequences that formed no part of their original intentions. To some extent, they are unaware of these unintended consequences. This is partly due to incorrect premises for their conclusions, partly due to being inaccurate in their reflections, and partly due to the fact that people at work do not reveal all of their feelings, motives and eventual plans but admit them to themselves.

In order to overcome these problems, Argyris and his colleagues have been able to identify two very different learning processes, which he calls model I and model II learning (Argyris, 1965; 1982; 2004; Argyris and Schön, 1996). Model I learning presupposes that the actor has clear intentions, is striving to achieve his goals, suppresses negative feelings and emphasises rationality. These three characteristics have profound consequences for interaction with others and for the environment in which the actor operates. In order to achieve control, the acting individual will try to control information and the meaning of information. In the end, this strategy will tend to be defensive and, because of unilateral control, will not produce valid feedback. Learning will, in other words, be a self-sealing process, with little public testing of theories, leading, in the end, to decreased effectiveness.

This learning strategy tends to be defensive, with a strong emphasis on control. When this individual strategy is brought into the organisation, the organisation tends to overlook valid information. The ability to master unexpected situations is reduced. This might be good for developing effective routines, but with the likelihood that creativity, adaptiveness and willingness to change is reduced. Problems arise on two levels: inside the organisation and in the relation between the organisation and the market. Information of the unsystematic kind, namely vague, inconsistent and inaccessible information, tends to be overlooked. To the extent that such information flows into the organisation, a process of camouflage and defensiveness occurs, leading to less trust, conformity and eventually a breakdown of communication and cooperation.

Model II learning is not presented as the opposite of model I learning. Rather, it is an extension of some of the features of model I learning, with significant consequences for interactions between the actor and the environment and therefore also for the learning that takes place during the process. In model II it is assumed that individuals have intentions and articulate them but it is not assumed that they unilaterally control the environment and the meaning of information, rather that others are invited to express their meaning in order to obtain the most valid information present. People are inspired to seek out and share valid information in order to solve problems. Therefore, model II will lead to shared power in decision-making. On the other hand, the actor will not be the only one responsible for his actions. There will be some sort of shared responsibility. In an organisation this means that, in comparison with model I, more information is brought into the decision process, other types of information will be used and more alternative interpretations will be part of the decision process. Furthermore, the assumption is that errors will be avoided, that new possibilities will be revealed, and that energy within the organisation will, to a larger extent, be used to produce better performance in the market. There are many parallels between this and communicative rationality (see Chapter 3).

There is a large literature on workgroups and practice-based communities, communities of practice (Lave and Wenger, 1991; Brown and Dugrid, 1991; Wenger, 1998) and epistemic communities (Merton, 1951; Holzner, 1968; Holzner and Marx, 1979; Knorr-Cetina, 1984; 1999), as well as research arguing for local knowledge (Geertz, 2000), personal knowledge (Polanyi, 1958; 1966; Polanyi and Prosch, 1975) and how to make personal, tacit knowledge explicit so that it supports organisational learning (Nonaka, 1988; Nonaka and Takeuchi, 1995). These workgroups are meaning systems. One of the challenges for knowledge organisations is to align different meaning systems.

What implications can such learning models have for organisational design? A basic problem with learning from experience is the distance between action and outcome. This distance causes time-, space- and complexity-related distortions. The linkage between action and outcome becomes causally weak. What management can do, primarily, is introduce cybernetic elements. In service management, where the linkage between action and customer response is weak, the systematic use of detectors can be introduced. Where communication between detector elements in the organisation and decision-making elements is weak, systematic feedback can be implemented. Goals and standards of performance are thereby refined. Implementation control is overhauled. Beyond the basic control elements of cybernetics, however, the organisation may engage in more advanced systems analysis and control mechanisms, such as archetypal identification (Senge, 1990), soft modelling and the like. Another general recommendation found in the learning literature is to reduce organisational complexity through the reduction of organisational interdependence, through the simplification of strategies (fewer product areas and markets) and through relying on simpler signal systems in the organisation, such as price-quantity-quality signals and normative standards of decision-making (Knudsen, 1998–2001).

How Can Organisations Develop Strategies that Fit the Type of Knowledge Development They are Seeking?

The market encounter can be understood as the moment when the customer meets the supplier, usually a company or an organisation. This meeting involves many different processes that can be analysed in different ways: there is the customer's reaction to the product, to the artefacts or to the behaviour of the employee. There are the different types of production processes that are activated by customer requirements. There is also the reaction of the employee to customer behaviour, that is, the interaction processes. The market encounter may also involve reflection, both by members of the organisation and by its customers. Some of this reflection can be analysed and implemented using administrative procedures. We can call these the analytical elements of the encounter, comprising analysing customer expectations, improving technical quality and improving delivery systems. When an organisation has found the best formula, it might be able to copy it and make it into a routine.

The market encounter can also take other forms, however. These are situations that cannot easily be copied because they do not follow any particular pattern. Such situations could be critical incidents such as when a customer has a special need, when the delivery system does not function or when an employee behaves in an unforeseen manner. They could equally well be everyday situations, though, involving the employees showing interest in the customer. They could also be situations involving ethical dilemmas.

The Austrian and the evolutionary theories of the market process emphasise creativity and learning. F.A. Hayek and Israel Kirzner have been strong exponents of this approach to the market process and in their theories the dichotomy of open and closed processes can be found, as discussed in Chapter 5. According to Hayek (1937), the economic problem as it has been identified within the neo-classical economics approach is a coordination problem. However, coordination in itself cannot give any insight into the dynamic features of the market economy: economic growth and creativity. According to Hayek (1937), what is central within the market is the knowledge problem. The assumption of Kirzner (1992) is that the market process contains not only the need for the coordination of the knowledge of individuals, but also the need to overcome the participants' mutual ignorance that is waiting to be discovered. The market is an open system since constant changes are taking place in it. Participants adapt to these changes but, by doing so, they tend to bring about equilibrium. The underlying assumption is that dis-equilibrium contains market opportunities that are yet to be revealed. The discovery of these opportunities is part of the corrective process of the market, while avoiding error in the market is not the same as genuine correction, since constant change is a feature of the market process (Kirzner, 1992, p. 45).

Kirzner has identified this knowledge problem as comprising two distinct problems: knowledge problem A and knowledge problem B (Kirzner, 1992, p. 163). Knowledge problem A is a coordination problem. Knowledge problem B is related to developing new knowledge, inventing new ideas or building new theories. Knowledge problem B cannot be solved through coordination; it cannot even be comprehended as a coordination problem, since it is about how genuine creation or learning takes place. Part of this process lies in finding new solutions to new problems, which implies establishing new understanding and a new *praxis*. Hayek's model contains not only the entrepreneurial learning of how to exploit market possibilities but at the same time an institutional learning of rules, norms, values and institutions related to the social process.

One should expect democratic values, critical discourse and human flourishing to be more essential for a knowledge organisation than hierarchical organisations (Johnsen, 2002). The reason for this is that the individual employee and his or her knowledge are more important to such organisations. Is it possible to combine the authoritarian needs of the organisation with the positive processes of discourse and individual learning? Organisations represent some sort of stability, some sort of formalisation and some sort of consistency. We move outside of the organisational realm if we talk about completely idiosyncratic choices, completely random decisions and completely open systems. In this last case, we might rather talk about a network or a social process.

Organisations cannot expect to purchase persistent competitiveness on open markets. Such advantages must have their origin in or be controlled by the organisation, and must be resources that cannot be imitated or substituted. An organisation's culture may represent such a strategic resource (Barney, 1991). For example, organisations that develop a change-oriented culture will probably be more capable of constantly meeting new challenges and adjusting to new terms and conditions.

Some management problems related to developing these strategic resources are easily solved by means of *analytical tools*, which are predefined recipes, concepts and manuals that can be used in cases where there is a causal relation between action and outcome, and where past experience is relevant or the process is cyclical. Under these conditions it is possible to establish full information and there are no discussions about ends or priorities. There is a means–end rationality. However, there might be other situations that are perhaps up-front, that are open-ended, where cause and effect are difficult to perceive, and where there is no past experience or where relevant information is not available. For example, James G. March (1988) emphasises the problems of ambiguity in decision-making (i.e., unclear tasks and unclear means in decision-making). This might also include situations where the organisation is involved in creative work, new experiences or a changing environment, or it could relate to the problem of how to cope with ambiguity. Tsoukas (2005) talks of complexity, referring to the fact that organisational rules and routines will never fit the challenges in the market.

We can therefore classify some managerial challenges as *intuitive tasks*. *Theory-building in practice* concerns the development of new major concepts and solutions, and intuitive problem-solving at all levels in the organisation; creative new behaviours, new ideas for customer assistance and other additions to tacit knowledge may be included. These are tasks that cannot be accomplished by means of analytical tools alone. Past experience is only partially relevant, so that the individual has to find his or her way by creating new theories: he or she has to become, according to Harald Knudsen, a *theory-builder in practice*. These are challenges that are common to knowledge organisations.

Knowledge organisations can be argued to exist in the border landscape between subjectivity and the individual mind on the one hand and the social structure and market on the other. The core task of organisations, a planned, closed order in Hayek's sense, is to utilise the resources they possess (Hayek, 1945; Tsoukas, 2005). As such, organisations have more limited objectives than society. Ronald Coase (1937) used the notion that organisations embody conscious power within an ocean of unconscious coordination. Increasingly, though, organisation and strategy literature has emphasised how organisations belong to networks and are integrated in structures and social relations (Powell, 1990; Porter, 1990; 1998; Porter and Kramer, 2011). This double obligation, comprising formalisation and openness, also applies when it comes to the human resources in a company.

Strategies are concerned with the direction in which one chooses to go. Organisations have many directions to choose from and can develop in different ways. There are ideological and paradigmatic differences in how organisations are perceived by the owners and leaders, by the employees and from the outside. Employees are both resources for the organisation and, at the same time, sovereign individuals. The organisation has to balance the need to give the individual some space for its individual demands, forms of expression and character, with the alignment of the employee's resources so that it supports the objectives of the organisation.

I argued in an earlier article that one way of managing knowledge organisations is through its values and norms and that organisational strategy is primarily a question of value choices (Johnsen, 2009). Values will to a large extent determine the *raison d'être* of an organisation. Often these will be the values of the owners or the management. Employees have to accept these values to some extent, and they do so de facto by agreeing to work in the organisation. The values change only very slowly. The constitutional structure of the organisation might be a written code, but it might also be the informal, unwritten codes of acceptable and unacceptable activity in the organisation. Norms are established in order to simplify communication within an organisation and between the organisation and the outside world. They are those more practical rules that legitimise everyday activity.

Can We Identify What Structural and Organisational Form is Best for Utilising Knowledge and Encouraging Learning and Development?

There are a number of different ways in which individuals create knowledge. Firstly, we can discuss this through the *pure logic of choice*, where the main idea is that individuals optimise the outcome of a situation with reference to preferences or agency theory. Secondly, we can discuss it as *pragmatic socialisation*, where the core idea is that individuals are part of a social meaning system, and that they form preferences in relation to that. Group pressure might support this type of mechanism. Thirdly, we can discuss this topic as *subjective reflexivity*, and argue that knowledge formation in this case has to be seen as a subjective, reflexive process, with autonomy and personal judgement.

If we are linking these concepts to organisational theory and organisational psychology, we can refer to the theory of *motivation*. In the motivation literature, it is common to distinguish between intrinsic and extrinsic motivation. We can to some extent argue that the three perspectives on individual knowledge development represent three different variations of extrinsic/intrinsic motivation. The pure logic of choice model is perhaps more responsive to extrinsic motivation, the subjective reflexivity model to intrinsic motivation, and the pragmatic socialisation model to a combination of the two. Individuals are complex; they are subjective and make judgements. Alchian and Demsetz (1988) write:

> Corporations and business firms try to install a spirit of loyalty. This should not be viewed simply as a device to increase profits by overworking or misleading the employees, nor as an adolescent urge for belonging. It promotes a closer approximation to the employees' potentially available true rates of substitution between production and leisure and enables each team member to achieve a more preferred situation. The difficulty, of course is to create economically that team spirit and loyalty. (Alchian and Demsetz, 1988, p. 145)

How, then, given this complexity, do we align individual motivation with organisational goals? The *pure logic of choice* assumption implies that we can direct individual preferences through external incentives. Let us say there are conformity mechanisms at work in an organisation that produce low performance. What can the management do in order to increase effort? First of all, they might try to reorganise, in order to change the social structure that has led to this conformity. Individualising the work could be a way to do this. If they cannot change the conformism as such, however, their (the managers') only option is to increase the collective effort level. Leibenstein (1987) assumes that this can be done through peer pressure, which is a function of management pressure. He assumes that management pressure is highest at the top, and that it decreases with each hierarchical layer. One management option to increase effort is therefore to reduce the number of hierarchical levels (Leibenstein, 1987, p. 226).

In order for hierarchy to be able to apply pressure, there should be clearly defined goals. Multiple goals, competing goals or ambiguous tasks are obstacles for the effectiveness of management pressure. However, this pressure will only be effective if there is a committed workforce and transparency of communication. If employees in the organisation have private goals, sub-units are autonomous or motivation is fragmented, this pressure theory will not hold.

Effort could also be increased by means of a contract according to which employees receive extra rewards (e.g., a higher general salary) in exchange for greater effort. In making such a bargain, managers should have an idea of the increase in revenue that will be achieved as a result of greater effort. This should be the basis for any bargain with the employees regarding effort level and rewards. This would probably lead to some sort of internal bargaining process before an effort/reward level is found, during which the employees will have to present some supply options. Thereby, a norm for what is expected in terms of effort can be established.

Of course, the management can choose to overlook these norms; they can choose to make choices and take actions contrary to these norms. These alternatives cannot easily be evaluated in advance, since it is part of the quality of management to take action and surmount obstacles when needed. It is the visions of the management that the organisation relies on in order to survive. This might explain why successful companies do not always go by the book, and why also democratically run companies can lack success. On the other hand, there are limits to what the management of an organisation can do without there being consequences for the rest of the organisation. If the management is too authoritarian, it will lose the utility and advantages of the democratic process within the organisation:

> *The psychological literature on attribution and social perception suggests that we form attachments to courses of action through a cognitive process of reconciling our behaviours with our beliefs and making attributions about the causes of our behaviour. The key point of this discussion is to emphasise how an organisation's HR practices (and the processes by which those practices are implemented) can affect commitment and motivation, sometimes in ways that those who design and implement those practices did not anticipate. (Baron and Kreps, 1999, p. 102)*

This more limited use of individual participation at work has at least two shortcomings: firstly, it presupposes some fixed idea of how individuals relate to their work processes, and to what extent they can be manipulated. Secondly, it runs contrary to a trend towards autonomy and teamworking in the workplace.

One can argue that motivation is not an individual response to stimuli, but is related to social relations and interactions between individuals. This would be in line with the perspective on individual learning and development that we called pragmatic socialisation earlier.

Participation in general, and teamwork specifically, is claimed to have such a social motivational effect. Firstly, teamwork is regarded as a better and more flexible way to organise and utilise resources. Secondly, through peer pressure workers are more motivated and put more effort into their work. One might regard these as two distinct and different effects. However, an increasing literature, especially on teamworking and organisational learning, argues that they are interdependent.

Culture can be defined in different ways. Schein (1985) refers to six different meanings of culture, ranging from common beliefs and values, to rules and norms. I refer here to a rather narrow definition, where:

> *Culture is made up of intangible things that are shared by the people in the organisation – values, beliefs that guide action, understandings, even ways of thinking. (Mintzberg et al., 1998, p. 168)*

Studies on corporate culture emphasise the positive relation between culture and performance (Kotter, 1996; Kotter and Heskett, 1992; Kunda, 1992). However, this literature also emphasises the heterogeneity and complexity of the concept of culture (Powell and DiMaggio, 1991). A few core elements seem to be important in the development of company culture, such as management commitment, a clear vision, information, involvement and participation (Kotter and Heskett, 1992, p. 57).

The literature on teamwork has acknowledged the importance of individual participation and involvement at work. This literature has put specific emphasis on the relation between individual involvement and organisational structure. In transaction cost terms (Williamson, 1985), one might say that organisations choose teams when the cost of organising in traditional hierarchical ways is too high. Teams allow individuals to use their individual knowledge in problem-solving and so as to have local learning. Teams are also supposed to increase motivation and participation through involvement. This last assumption has made it relevant to integrate organisational psychology into the discussion of organisational structure.

The more empirically based studies underline this conceptual position. Brown and Dugrid (1991) studied *communities of practice* or learning entities at work.

They argue that an important type of learning that takes place at work is very different from what is found in transfer models, models that view learning as a transfer of information between individuals. Rather, they argue for a socially constructed type of learning that takes place during practice:

> *The central issue in learning is becoming a practitioner, not learning about practice. This approach draws attention away from abstract knowledge and cranial processes and situates it in the practice and communities in which knowledge takes on significance. (Brown and Dugrid, 1991)*

When studying this type of learning, Brown and Dugrid (1991) found that, in successful communities of practice, much of the knowledge-sharing took the form of *storytelling*. The community developed its own narrative culture as an essential part of communication. Being part of this culture, being involved in it, was essential for understanding the knowledge.

Put differently, this type of knowledge is embedded in the situational context. What people do when communicating with the external world is to re-contextualise this knowledge. Studies have also shown that the idyllic ideas of organisational openness, flexibility, local autonomy and other structural means do not in themselves avoid non-involvement and learning errors such as competence traps and superstitious learning (March and Levitt, 1988; Argyris and Schön, 1996, pp. xxiv, 282). Avoiding this problem requires involvement (Argyris and Schön, 1996, p. 283).

The challenge that Alchian and Demsetz (1988) refer to as 'creating economically that team spirit and loyalty' is one of the key issues in theory-building in practice. Common knowledge tells us that well-functioning teams make people work harder, and make them more committed and more involved. Teamworking is therefore being used more and more to organise work. According to Cohen and Bailey (1997), a team is a:

> *[...] collection of individuals who are independent in their tasks, who share responsibility for [the] outcome, who see themselves and who are seen by others as an intact social entity embedded in one or more large social relationships across organizational boundaries.*

Kunda's (1992) study of the high-tech firm underlines this conclusion. However, the more general picture, he argues, must be a little different. Kunda finds that the high-tech firm has the features of a club with different groups: an inner circle of full members of the organisation and various circles of less involved members. The management of this culture, he observes, is, in spite of the rhetoric produced, a very practical matter, engineered and monitored carefully and deliberately. As for the members' commitment, he finds it to vary among groups. The full members are more committed, while those aspiring to full membership suffer from ambivalence. The full members (employees) are found to be under strong normative control. He concludes:

> *The race to meet corporate standards of accomplishment, get corporate approval, and procure the pecuniary and personal rewards the culture promises becomes the only way to find stable meanings and compensate for a sense of confusion, lost authenticity, and inner emptiness; but it is a self-defeating exercise, one that recreates and reinforces the very circumstances it seeks to correct. (Kunda, 1992, p. 222)*

Culture has a framing function, as I discuss in Chapter 7. There are two reasons why a strong culture in an organisation is valuable: firstly, a strong culture may support strategy goals, and secondly, it may increase employees' commitment to the organisation (O'Reilly, 1991). However, if there are fuzzy concepts in organisation theory, culture is probably one of them. If anything, the closest we will get to culture as a generic form might be to call it a normative order (O'Reilly, 1991). Culture is a set of values and norms. These norms may have different features. For instance, as O'Reilly argues, there may be norms that promote creativity (openness and commitment to change) and there may be norms that promote implementation (common goals and beliefs in action).

Culture, as such, is a neutral concept in relation to the contents of the norms. However, there may be some common features of organisational culture. For instance, a cultural system needs symbols, it is dependent on participation, there has to be communication and the provision of information, and it probably must be related to some kind of comprehensive structure (e.g., a reward system and rankings). In short, a culture will sort perceived-as-appropriate from perceived-as-inappropriate action within an organisation.

There still might be unexpected critical incidents in which the employee must rely on his or her own judgement, however. Reflexive subjectivity implies such a judgement. How does he or she act and how does he or she learn from such situations? In the Hayekian theory, individuals will search for very simple structures to which they can relate their actions. This might be norms (I do this but not that!), prices (I choose the cheapest alternative!) or rules (I do this because it seems to be right!). In order to act, one has to simplify the decision problem.

The learning process will, as referred to in Harald Knudsen's argument, be a function of variety of experience, intimacy of communication and imagination. For people to use their knowledge qualities to the advantage of the organisation, they have to be committed to the task and identify with the needs of the organisation. People can bring new experience into the organisation or stimulate the development of experience by learning from other organisations. They will have responsibility for establishing intimacy of communication. The sort of sensitivity and intimacy that exists within an organisation will affect the extent to which the organisation is sensitive to its customers. Commitment is a function of trust and dialogue, and will be encouraged by the same process. In the same way: if customers feel they are taken seriously, they will be more loyal to the organisation.

How Can We Develop an Understanding of How Organisations Create Knowledge, Beyond Dualisms?

In an early discussion of management and innovation, Burns and Stalker, in their 1961 book *The Management of Innovation*, made the distinction between mechanistic management and organic management. With *mechanistic management*, they implied that there are differentiations of functions according to tasks, defined as abstract categories, differentiations between hierarchies in the organisation, a precise definition of rights and obligations, and rights and obligations translated into methods and responsibilities in functional positions. They argued that this implies a hierarchical structure of control, and the localisation of specific knowledge in the hierarchy, with interaction being mainly vertical. Accordingly, work behaviours are governed by instructions, and there is a strong insistence on loyalty. This management and organisational form implies that greater importance and prestige are accorded to specific and local knowledge, as compared with general knowledge. This resembles many aspects of Max Weber's ideal type of bureaucracy (Weber, 1947; 1978).

With *organic management*, Burns and Stalker (1961) implied, special knowledge relates to the common task of concern, the overall situation defines the individual task, and individuals are task-adjusted and redefined in their interactions with others. This implies limited definition of rights, obligations and methods. Reasonability is expected of everyone and commitment stretches beyond one's individual task. The system of control, authority and communication is seen as a network. This organisation is omnipotent in the distribution of tasks. Tasks are located where they are most relevant. Communication is lateral (both horizontal and vertical) and tends to take the form of consulting more than commanding. There is a strong commitment to progress and values, and to prestige related to the whole organisational milieu.

This description of two approaches to organisation and management has many parallels in the organisational discourse. In 1911, two different works were published on two different continents. In the USA, Frederick Winslow Taylor (1856–1915) published his *Principles of Scientific Management* (Taylor, 1911). This book has become a reference, partly because large organisations such as Ford used it as a reference for their mass production plants in the auto industry, utilising economics of scale. Taylor, an engineer, argued that one could, through scientific methods, identify the optimal and most resource-efficient work routines. His argument resembles that of Auguste Comte (1798–1857), two generations earlier, who had made similar arguments in favour of the philosophy of *positivism* (Comte, 1988). Henri Fayol also developed a similar conception of management in the early 1900s. His major work, *Administration industrielle et générale; prévoyance, organisation, commandement, coordination, controle*, was published in 1916. One of the methods that Taylor proposed was to identify best practices and make them into standards and routines.

That same year, 1911, the Austrian economist Joseph Alois Schumpeter (1883–1950) published *Theorie der wirtschaftlichen Entwicklung* in Austria (translated in 1934 as *The Theory of Economic Development: An inquiry into profits, capital, credit, interest and the business cycle*). In this book, Schumpeter discusses how we can explain the dynamics of the market. He developed two categories of economic actors: on the one hand the capitalist or industrialist, who utilises economies of scale, on the other the entrepreneur, who is an inventor, somebody who sees new, innovative ways to use resources and explores market opportunities.

This dualism between exploitation and exploration, production and innovation, bureaucratisation and formalisation versus learning, development and creativity was thereby established. We can talk about two ideal types. Max Weber developed the ideal type of bureaucracy in a discussion of modernisation and differentiation in society. He saw the development of bureaucracy as a natural response to the emergence of modern society. At the same time, there developed, both academically and in society, hostility to some of the features of modern society. The dualism therefore also became political and ideological.

One of the references to this debate is the Hawthorne experiments of the 1920s and 1930s. Starting out as a scientific management project, the experiments soon became an ideological battleground. Gillespie's (1991) analysis of the Hawthorne experiments shows how they manufactured knowledge in the sense that (a) the theoretical perspectives of the researchers influenced what they emphasised, and (b) the same experiments were interpreted in very different directions. The ideological shift, from *scientific management* to *human relations*, was not so much an outcome of the experiments as a shift among those who managed the experiments. However, the project established the reference point for the divide between scientific management and human resources that has existed ever since.

Another reference to the dualism between the formalised, structured and routinised organisation and the more dynamic, innovative and creative one is found in Philip Selznick's 1957 book, *Leadership in Administration: A Sociological Interpretation*. In it, Selznick argues that there is a distinction between being an administrator and being a leader. Leadership goes beyond supervising procedures and rule-following. Leadership implies looking forward, motivating new possibilities and making adjustments in the organisation. Administration is authoritarian, top-down, and hierarchical; leadership is communicative, bottom-up and vertical.

Other examples could be presented but the main point here is to argue that this dualism that roughly distinguishes between a static, hierarchical and bureaucratic vision of the organisation on the one hand and a more flexible, dialogical, open and innovative organisational vision on the other is a well-established dualism in organisational and management theory. We can see them as two ideal types; we have at one extreme the analytical tools related to model I learning, implemented through the use of authority, and at the other, intuitive tasks, related to creative learning and theory-building in practice by means of dialogue. These two extremes presuppose two very different kinds of personal qualities in other respects as well: analytical problems presuppose loyalty, predictability, the obeying of, and non-individuality, while intuitive tasks presuppose creativity, individuality, vision, commitment and other qualities such as variety of experience, intimacy of communication and responsiveness.

These two kinds of tasks and approaches to knowledge have parallels in two types of approaches to the market encounter. The analytical knowledge situation resembles market situations in which the following of routines and fixed standard products are essential to the customer. Deviations from these standards have a negative effect. In intuitive situations, however, in order to find some common ground so as to solve a common problem with the customer, it will be necessary to enter into a *dialogue*.

Knudsen (1998–2001) in line with Isaacs (1999) identifies the genealogy of the word dialogue as consisting of two Greek words, *dia* and *logos*, meaning shared knowledge. Dialogue is a non-reversible process whereby one shares knowledge with others in order to find new solutions to a common problem. This concept can be contrasted with the concept of authority. Authority might imply that one is implementing a meaning without a dialogue, that is, without sharing knowledge, but it might also take other forms, for instance ideological, charismatic or procedural and institutionalised. However, there are reasons to question some of these dualisms (Johnsen et al., 2009).

One can find this dualism in the perception of the market and the organisation and in the perception of the individual in the organisation. We can also identify two different traditions in approaching these challenges that have been inherent in our discussion: the hermeneutic tradition (Schön, 1983; Lave and Wenger, 1991; Brown and Dugrid, 1991; Knudsen, 1998–2001; Tsoukas, 2005; Amin and Roberts, 2008b) and the analytical tradition (Williamson, 1985; Barney, 1991; Barney and Ouchi, 1988; Foss, 2005; Foss and Klein, 2012). Can we reconcile this divide?

One example of this is the broad perspectives and cross-disciplinary approach to innovation (Zaltman et al., 1973; Holbek, 1988). Also, Mintzberg (1994) talked about the formalisation edge in strategy. It is a concept aimed at indicating that organisations need to find a balance between the dualisms I have discussed in this chapter. Organisations are formalisation in the form of structures, rules, procedures and formal power, but they are also human societies. Organisations are communicative communities (Habermas, 1997). They require some structure, but also personal engagement. Knowledge is developed within this balance.

How Can Organisations Organise in order to Make Good Judgements?

In order to illustrate the arguments I will try to develop here, I will present a case: on 23 April 2013, the Norwegian newspaper *Aftenposten* contained the following:

> On March 22, 2013 Ivar Petter Røeggen won his case against DNB in the Supreme Court. DNB must pay Røeggen compensation of 235,000 NOK. In addition, they must pay court costs of 4.8 million NOK.
>
> In autumn 2000 Røeggen borrowed 520,500 NOK from DNB. He put the money into two structured products. After six years, Røeggen had lost 230,000 NOK in fees and interest charges.
>
> Røeggen complained and won against the DNB Financial Appeals (then the Complaints Board) and the Oslo District Court but lost in the Court of Appeal. The case was heard by the Supreme Court in the autumn of 2012. The court then asked for clarification of the bank's calculations.
>
> The case was therefore sent for new consideration by the Supreme Court's Grand Chamber.
>
> The Consumer Council believed the matter to be of fundamental importance and to have consequences for 2,000 similar cases pending the Røeggen judgment. The Council took on legal costs on behalf of Røeggen.
>
> 'Guaranteed products' are also called 'structured products'. Other names for them include 'bank deposits with stock returns (BMA)', 'bond index (IO)', 'equity-linked bond (AIO)' and 'bank deposits with property return (BME)'. On the Friday before Easter, DNB was sentenced by the Supreme Court in the so-called Røeggen case. This has consequences. DNB CEO Rune Bjerke confirmed a few weeks ago that they are ready to pay out hundreds of millions in compensation to customers who purchased leveraged structured products for more than ten years. (Aftenposten, *23 April 2013, author's own translation*)

The following also appeared a few days earlier:

> Rune Bjerke has made it clear that the bank will settle and cover the losses of other bank customers:
>
> 'Now we'll make up for our mistake. We will clean up this mess following the defeat in the Supreme Court, and compensate all those who have purchased similar products and complained to the Complaints Board,' Bjerke said after the verdict was made. He admitted that the structured products DNB offered through debt financing in the early 2000s were not good enough. (Aftenposten, *19 April 2013, author's translation*)

This is a case related to the financial crisis that started in 2008. It involves many banks and many small, private investors. DNB is the biggest Norwegian bank, and its majority owner is the Norwegian state. The media in Norway has calculated that the total amount to be compensated by the banks exceeds 1 billion NOK. Thousands of customers are affected, and the whole affair must have involved hundreds of bank employees, who have now had to admit that they sold poor products and tried to get away with it. It is a case of *poor judgement*. The core of the argument that Harald Knudsen tried to develop in his four books was about how to avoid poor judgement.

Foss and Klein (2012), as referred to above, emphasise the importance of entrepreneurial judgement, not least employees' judgement on the owner's behalf. The concept of judgement puts the focus on the individual and how he or she perceives a situation, as we referred to in the introduction, based on Aristotle's concept of prudence (*phronesis*). It is therefore a central part of understanding theory-building in practice. However, it is not in itself a concept that solves all questions related to understanding what happens in decision-making. Basically, the problem of understanding judgement in organisations involves two main dimensions: one element concerns the content of the decisions you make: how clever are they? The other concerns the governance problem: how can you be sure that the employees, when using their judgement, will behave in the interests of the organisation (or owner)?

To take the issue of judgement first, if we look at the work of Franz Brentano (1838–1917), who was one of those who initiated the debate about intentionality and also subjectivity in the social sciences, we find that his concept of judgement is very idiosyncratic. Johannes Brandl (2010) makes the following remarks about Brentano's conception of judgement:

> *… he holds that judgements do not require the existence of complete thoughts or propositions which have to be grasped before a judgement can be made. It is the mental act of judging, not its object or content, which is the bearer of truth-values. In view of these differences Brentano's theory of judgement has been called existential (non-predicative), idiogenetic (non-reductionist), and reistic (non-propositional). (Brandl, 2010)*

We can speak of two traditions: the Aristotelian, which sees this as cognitive processes (logic), and the psychological perspective, which sees this as social/psychological (contextual) processes. Meaning has to do with same, as well as truth/non-truth. Brentano, who was in the Aristotelian tradition, saw judgement as a logical system (internal logic). If you hold one thing to be true, it affects how you look at other, related things. This opens for judgement to be formal logic.

We could say that Brentano gives us a concept of judgement that positions it in the subjectivity of man. On the other hand, we can refer to Immanuel Kant (1724–1804), who, to a larger extent than Brentano would do later, saw judgement as related to the social structure. There is in Kant's conception an element of communicative rationality, in the sense that judgement also refers to universal principles. Robert Hanna (2009) summarises Kant's concept of judgement in this way:

> *… a judgment is a complex conscious cognition which refers to objects either directly (via the essentially indexical content of intuitions) or indirectly (via the essentially attributive or descriptive content of concepts); in which concepts are predicated either of those objects or*

of other constituent concepts; in which concepts are intrinsically related to one another and to intuitional representations by pure logical concepts expressing various modifications and truth-functional compounds of the predicative copula; which enters into inferences according to pure laws of logic; which essentially involve both the following of rules and the application of rules to the perceptual objects picked out by intuition; and in which a composite objective representation is generated and unified by the higher-order executive mental processing of a single self-conscious rational subject. (Hanna, 2009)

One main difference between the two conceptions concerns the subjectivity of the assessment. We could think of extremes: on the one hand, judgement could be thought of as completely idiosyncratic. Such a judgement could easily be regarded by others as random, irrational or incomprehensible. On the other hand, another conception of judgement could prescribe criteria for evaluation, for instance to maximise utility. This therefore has to do with the degree of predictability and the degree to which one can model judgement.

Gadamer (2006) discusses judgement from the perspective of good sense and intellectual virtue. For him, it is a matter of enlightenment and of having a wider understanding of what context our actions play into. A sense of community and responsibility is part of this. Thereby, judgement has to do with education in a wider sense than formal education. He talks about *reflexive judgement.*

Can we use these conceptions and perceptions of the market, the organisation and the individual to analyse the case I introduced above? One way to do so would be to look at what the case might look like under different perceptions. One could argue that by seeing the market as a development problem we are implying that the firm can be opportunistic and explore imbalances in the market. Selling poor products can be a way of exploiting the lack of competence of the customers. However, knowledge problem B also implies that the firm is responsible. It does not only follow routines (as in knowledge problem A). It should be fairly alert towards misconduct.

At an organisational level, one might discuss whether such misconduct would have taken place if individual work groups had been in charge. At least one would expect that, in a decentralised structure, different work groups would have had different interpretations of the quality of the product they were selling. There would most likely have been some questioning of the content of what they were selling. One could argue that misconduct at a liability level of NOK 1 billon was only possible because of the hierarchical structure of the banking sector.

At an individual level, one has to question whether the hundreds of bank employees involved were acting opportunistically, following rules and culture, or were being reflexive in the sense of making their own moral judgement of the situation. Obviously, this misconduct was supported by the internal culture of the banking system and of DNB, since the bank justified its behaviour in the court system all the way to the High Court.

Are Knowledge Organisations Concerned with Theory-building in Practice?

Knudsen argues that theories on business development and organisational development are not primarily areas in which academic knowledge represents any sort of superiority. Rather, he advocates removing or at least reducing the barrier between business theory and business practice, and not least showing how the practitioner can become (and in fact is) a theoretician.

Sumantra Ghoshal (1948–2004), in an article published in 2005, just after he died, argued that bad management theory drives out good management practice. He would probably argue today that what led the bankers to their bad behaviour was that they could legitimise their decisions through bad theory and thus ignore their natural, decent judgement.

This discussion on theory (*techne, theoria*) and practice has a long ancestry. Even Aristotle made a distinction between *techne* and *phronesis*. They are, he argued, different epistemological categories (Eikeland, 2008). *Techne* is a 'productive state that is truly reasoned', while *phronesis* is 'the type of knowledge and reasoning that forms the basis for praxis' (Flyvbjerg, 1993, p. 14). These two concepts presuppose two very different ways of using knowledge. *Analytical* knowledge is related to model I learning, that is, the ability to identify a specific problem and to apply tools to solve it (*techne*). *Intuitive* knowledge presupposes individual judgement, but also creative learning, which is the ability to see new possibilities in a situation where only part of the problem can be identified (*phronesis*). Practice (*praxis*) is often context-dependent and concrete. Universal truth does not apply to all aspects of practical challenges; it is rather the case that particular knowledge is necessary in order to meet particular tasks. If we go back to Aristotle, it is important to recall that his concept of *phronesis* was developed as a response to the fact that not all knowledge could be phrased as theories. *Phronesis* is outside *theoria*. Knudsen's *theory-building in practice* tries to make a link between theory and practice, beyond Aristotle's conceptualisation.

There are many predecessors to Knudsen's argument that sound, practical knowledge should be better acknowledged and also made into a basis for theoretical reasoning. Michael Polanyi makes similar arguments in his *Personal Knowledge: Towards a post-critical philosophy* of 1958. Polanyi also develops an argument that is critical of positivism in science, and argues that individual reflection forms the basis of knowledge (Polanyi, 1958; Polanyi and Prosch, 1975). Similar arguments and conceptualisations have also featured in the debate on business studies and business education. For example, Henry Mintzberg wrote:

> When strategic planning arrived on the scene in the mid-1960s, corporate leaders embraced it as 'the one best way' to devise and implement strategies that would enhance the competitiveness of each business unit. True to scientific management pioneered by Frederick Taylor, this one best way involved separating thinking from doing, and creating a new function staffed by specialists: strategic planners. (Mintzberg, 1994)

Donald Schön, in his 1983 book *The Reflective Practitioner: How professionals think in action*, had previously argued that the skills needed to make the right decisions in organisations should and can be developed by practitioners. Pettigrew (2001) discusses what he calls the relevance gap between management research and management practice. Van der Ven and Johnson argue in their article from 2006, *Knowledge for Theory and Practice*, that there is a division between theory and practice, but also that it can be overcome.

This discussion that Harald Knudsen's work plays into is both a larger debate on perspectives on social science (the debate on the relation between theory and practice, and the separation of theory from practice) and is to do with how businesses are organised and managed. *Theory-building in practice* is a concept that tries to re-establish a balance between theory and practice in management science, and to place this balanced concept within practice.

How do Organisations Learn to Handle Intuitive Situations?

I have identified two ideal types of markets and organisational and management forms. I have also argued that over time there has been a trend/development moving away from seeing markets as driven by *economies of scale*, organisations as *mechanistic and bureaucratic*, management as *authoritarian* and *controlling*, and employees as single-task and (*extrinsically*) incentive-motivated, towards seeing markets as *dynamic* and changing, organisations as *organic* and flexible, management as communicative and *dialogical*, and employees as *intrinsically* motivated, and multi-tasking. Some facts support such a perspective. For example, the development of information and communication technology (ICT) has made it possible to industrialise and mechanise what used to be routine work, for example in banking where cash withdrawals have been replaced by ATMs, removing these jobs from the work scheme, and allowing employees to do more developmental work.

However, the argument I will try to develop here goes beyond this dualism. As I see it, organisations face both structural and developmental tasks, the need to both formalise and utilise resources efficiently within known technologies, and at the same time the need to be alert to change, to be innovative and to be creative. In order to discuss this strategic challenge, I have identified three perception levels: the market, the organisation and the individual. My core point is that the strategic challenge is to align understanding and decisions within and between these three levels.

Strategic choice to a large extent defines how the organisation is perceived both internally and externally. If action means systematically taking new directions, it will eventually influence norms and values and thereby the constitution of the organisation. It will be difficult for an organisation to maintain a particular impression over a longer period of time if it continues to change how it operates in the market. To give an example, a company might have environmental concern as one of its values and still be able to cause some pollution, but if it was revealed that, in situations where it had a choice, the organisation was systematically emphasising other values over the environment, the general impression of the organisation's values would change. The bank case presented above is a clear example of a divide between intended and exposed values. The CEO had to take action in order to align practice with intended values.

How then do we align individuals in organisations and their subjective reflection to organisational goals and market development? One way forward is to create a common understanding, a *communicative community* and deliberative organisation. The key to the communicative organisation is to make a connection between on the one hand critical incidents in market encounters, and on the other hand a personally felt sense of importance. We can call this the principle of identity. Unless someone identifies with the problem, nothing will result; no learning will take place. Company goals need to be aligned with personal values, personal objectives and imagination. Company feedback systems need to involve a personal sense of crisis and stimulate a personal interest in the project. Company decision-making needs, at some point, to be aligned with personal interpretation.

The organisational and managerial structure most in line with the learning perspective we have called subjective reflexivity would create a place that allowed for discussion and deliberation. Michael Polanyi (1891–1976) argued in his book, *Personal Knowledge: Towards a post-critical philosophy* (1958), that all knowledge contains an element of judgement:

> ... *I shall not try to repudiate strict objectivity as an ideal without offering a substitute, which I believe to be more worthy of intelligent allegiance; this I have called 'personal knowledge'. (p. 18)*

> *Even the most strictly mechanised procedures leave something to personal skills in the exercise of which an individual bias may enter. (p. 19)*

The main point to consider when we are trying to understand the deliberative organisation is the fact that individual subjectivity is acknowledged. There simply is no one right answer to the questions facing the organisation.

In relation to this learning problem, we might conclude that involvement means the process by which individual willingness to learn is linked to the particular structure of the learning situation. Modern learning theories have a more integrated view of learning than is found in Argyris's works. Weick's term *sense-making* refers to the mental process of developing cognitive scripts (Weick, 1995, p. 17). Sense-making is only linked to action indirectly. If we convert it into Argyris's terms, we might say that sense-making is the mental adoption process. However, learning in the terminology of sense-making is at once an ongoing, social and personal identity formation process.

This process is included in the Weber/Habermas term *communicative* action (Weber, 1978; Habermas, 1997). Following Argyris's (1982) dichotomy between model I and model II learning organisations, we might argue that certain organisational tasks have greater potential than others for the utilisation of model II learning. Some tasks are of a rule-following type, while others are more intuitive in nature, less structured and more dependent on the individual. If we could divide organisational tasks into these two groups, we might be able to retain what DiMaggio and Powell (1991) has called the *iron cage*, in some parts of the organisation, and leave room for model II learning in other, more limited parts.

It is not only individuals in the organisation that develop their own knowledge; work groups and expert systems also develop particular forms of knowledge. It is the responsibility of the manager to utilise knowledge in the organisation by creating a learning arena. This should not be done by the use of authority but by establishing criteria for the growth of knowledge. Thus, one of the main challenges in an organisation is not only aligning individual knowledge with organisational goals but also developing sufficient communication between sub-groups of knowledge (Johnsen, 2002; 2011; Johnsen et al., 2009). However, this requires a constitutional structure. As Hanna (2009) writes, it will '...involve both the following of rules and the application of rules to the perceptual objects picked out by intuition'.

There are different layers of processes and structures that support the structuring of the organisation, such as values and norms, and these allow for a myriad of combinations (what I have called constitution of the organisation) and approaches to internal discussion and decision-making. The development of and emphasis on values might be encouraged by what we have called the division of knowledge and the variety of experience. An organisation is not an open arena for discourse. It has a purpose, a structure and a system of authority (that is, of decision-making). In that respect, it can never live up to the purified version of post-conventional discourse (an ideal-talking situation). On the other hand, it is generally acknowledged that in organisations there are processes of an informal nature that their management have to take into consideration.

Discourse processes might be encouraged or suppressed. If an extensive internal debate were desired, one would choose different forms of management and activities than if such a debate were not required. In a knowledge organisation it is important to create a place where dialogue, both within the organisation and with the customer, can take place. In an earlier study, I found that an internal discourse process depends on three principles: that individuals are equal partners in the discourse, that the discourse is useful in itself, and that each individual regards the discourse as useful (Johnsen, 2002; 2011). The alternative to discourse could be exit, conflict or some sort of use of authority. The constitution of the organisation should establish rules for dialogue. The organisation's purpose and strategy will be an important basis for the discourse. Over time, patterns will emerge that might lead to a change in the company's strategy.

Conclusion

I argued in the introduction that this would be a tour exploring the issue of how organisations develop knowledge in practice. I have discussed eight questions related to understanding knowledge development in organisations. The first two were about the term knowledge itself:

- What are knowledge and the knowledge organisation?
- How is it that the organisations, or individuals such as employees or managers, come to have specific knowledge?

The next two questions were about the organisation as a context for understanding knowledge development:

- How can organisations develop strategies that fit the type of knowledge development they are seeking?
- Can we identify what structural and organisational form is best for utilising knowledge and encouraging learning and development?

The next question related to how theorising often conceptualises the organisational challenges, namely through dualisms:

- How can we develop an understanding of how organisations create knowledge, beyond dualisms?

Finally, I asked three questions based on a specific approach to the questions above, namely Knudsen's approach of theory-building in practice:

- How can organisations organise in order to make good judgements?
- Are knowledge organisations concerned wish theory-building in practice?
- How do organisations learn to handle intuitive situations?

Most of these questions are how and what questions, that is, explorative questions. The first two are of an epistemological kind. I have argued that the challenge relates to two main levels of perceptions: perceptions of the market and perceptions of the organisational processes. These perceptions are again linked to how one perceives the individual in the organisation, what motivates the individual employee, and what helps him or her learn and develop knowledge.

I have discussed the conceptualisation of the strategic challenge of the organisation as *theory-building in practice*, in relation to what we can call a knowledge organisation: to what extent are knowledge organisations concerned with theory-building in practice?

I have pointed at two discussions in strategy and organisational theory: the relation between theory and practice, and how organisations have been conceptualised through dualism. I have discussed the dualism of formalisation versus process, individuality versus routines, intuitive versus analytical, planning versus learning by doing, top-down versus bottom-up, explorative versus exploitative, and open versus closed innovation. What do these two discussions have in common?

One argument that can be made is that the conceptualisation of the organisation is based on philosophy of science perspectives. Positivism or the analytical approach, for example, holds that there are general truths about the organisation to be revealed by social science, thereby creating a dualism between theory and practice. Anti-positivists, for example, in the form of hermeneutics, have argued that the two should be integrated because theories on organisations are not superior to practice. They might even be completely wrong about practice.

My position is to link this discussion to the type of organisational situation in question. In knowledge organisations, knowledge is what is perceived by the individuals. It is subjective and to some extent idiosyncratic. The individual is an essential contributor to organisational knowledge, both in terms of competencies and skills and in terms of critical thought, learning, cognition and interaction. There are also other structures that support knowledge development and learning, though, such as work groups that contribute to sense-making, meaning, dialogue, tacit/explicit knowledge (communities of practice) and hermeneutical circles. The organisation as such is a bundle of routines, absorptive capacity, capability, political processes, decision rules and rules of participation.

Theory-building in practice, as I see it, is primarily a concept that refers to the process of internal dialogue, discussion and deliberation in the organisation. It happens within a constitution (understood as the organisation's configuration of values, norms, structure, goals), so that there is always a degree of formalisation in an organisation. This again implies that theory-building in practice is not a completely idiosyncratic process. It also implies, however, that it is not a completely formalised and predictable process. There are strategic choices to be made and organisations expose their values through the choices they make. Therefore I argue that strategy is a choice of values.

7 *Cultural Knowledge and Market Development*

Introduction

In this chapter I discuss knowledge development in the relation between culture and market. The thought that triggered me to look into this was Florida's critique of Weber. Two main issues are discussed here. The one issue is what type of cultural (moral, ethical, religious) values are most favourable to economic development. The other is the discussion of the relation between economy and culture as such. How integrated and differentiated are or should they be?

Discussions on knowledge, innovation and development will always have the characteristics of being cross-disciplinary because there are so many factors that influence social development. The theme of this chapter is about the broader, contextual, cultural and institutional conditions for the development of the market. I argue that the relation between culture and market is a continuous issue for dispute and discussion. This is in line with contemporary debates within the innovation literature that increasingly emphasises the relation between social innovations and product innovation, as I have discussed in Chapter 5.

Culture and market is a complicated relation, but probably also one that holds the key to understanding some of the dynamics of the market and how it stimulates innovation and social change. I therefore believe that it is important to conceptualise this relation. The chapter argues for a structuring of this relationship in order to identify two dimensions: on the one hand the degree of integration between culture and market, on the other hand the issue of how the two influence each other and make knowledge. This, I believe, can help us understand the relation better.

WEBER AND FLORIDA

When Max Weber argued for the rise of capitalism being supported by protestant ethics, he really pointed at a rationalisation and functional differentiation that implies a dualism between market and culture. Your religious life is (in Protestantism) decoupled from or separated from your economic activity, even though your religion gives some restraints on how you do your business. This separation of culture and market was probably an important reason why the market became so rational. It allowed the market to in some sense develop separately from religious, cultural and political disputes. On the other hand, there is an element in Weber's argument that also points out that protestant ethics have given inputs to the foundation of the capitalist market economy. By accepting and supporting profit-making, investments and accumulation of capital, Protestantism freed the market economy from moral constraints on these issues. At the same time, protestant ethics implied constraints in other areas relevant for the market.

However, this is not all there is to be said about the cultural foundation of the market economy. The dualism and dialectics of market and culture have prevailed and become an ever returning area of dispute. What is the relation? How much of civic culture is needed for the market to function? Should the market be constrained by ethical standards? Are some attitudes and social practices more favourable to the market economy than others?

The structure of the argument in this chapter is to take as a point of departure the recent discussion about innovation, where Richard Florida, among others, argues that innovation, creativity, knowledge development and economic growth will be encouraged by more tolerance and less compliance with conservative moral norms. These are ideas that have inspired innovation thinking. In one of his latest books, Florida (2005) contrasts his perspective directly with that of Max Weber and his *Protestant Ethics and the Spirit of Capitalism*. He argues that Weber (in a modern interpretation) is wrong. The disciplinary effect of protestant ethics is not the cause of economic growth in the creative economy, he claims. However, even Florida argues that there is a cultural foundation for the market.

I will use Florida's critique of Weber as a platform for addressing the larger issue of the relation between culture and market. I will argue firstly that Florida has got Weber wrong. Secondly I will show that there are at least two issues involved in his critique: the relation (degree of integration) between market and culture and the type of influence the one has on the other.

The chapter is organised as follows. First, I present Weber's theory of protestant ethics and the market. Second, I bring in Habermas in order to bridge Weber's discussion with contemporary social theory. Third, I present Florida's argument for a new creative economy and how that influences the relation between culture and market. I argue that Florida is wrong in his critique of Weber. Florida confuses Weber with conservative, religious arguments like the ones found in Daniel Bell. But I also argue that the debate he has started is interesting and relevant in order to discuss and understand the relation between culture and market. Finally, I discuss how contemporary innovation discourses approach these questions.

Weber's Argument on How Market and Religion Became Differentiated and Still Interdependent

Max Weber's argument in his book from 1904 *Protestant Ethics and the Spirit of Capitalism* (Weber, 1972) is that there is something distinct with the capitalist production system that developed in Europe from the seventeenth century onward. His argument is not that there is not (was not) capitalist production in other parts of the world at that time, or that rational economic calculation is something specific for Western cultures. Rather his argument is that the specific form of capitalism in Western countries is different in this respect. It is the Western *form of capitalism* with the bourgeois type of capitalist and the rational organisation of free labour that is unique in world history and which Weber would like to explain.

This capitalism is dependent also on the development of other institutions and features of society, such as the development of natural and rational sciences, and the system of rule of law and a rational system of justice. These institutions helped a rational capitalism to develop, but are not to be explained by protestant ethics; however, it is curious that the development of these institutions also happened in Western societies after the seventeenth century, and not in Africa, China or other parts of Asia or the world.

It is the specific formation of this *rationalism* in Western society that Weber wants to explain. He argues that this specific rationalism in the social culture is defined by a special *practical-rational* way of life, which again can be explained by a specific rational mentality that is found in mysticism and religion and a certain understanding of ethics as *duty*. It is this *mentality* that Weber wants to explain. To explain such a phenomenon is not a matter of looking for one cause, rather to assemble a picture from many pieces and many sources, he argues.

Part one of Weber's book tries to elaborate the issue of how, historically, certain religious perceptions developed and how this influenced ideas on social organisation. Furthermore, he seeks to demonstrate how this development corresponded with the specific historical development of capitalism in Western societies from the seventeenth century onward.[1] Weber's first argument is that Protestantism and its different forms, such as Calvinism, pietism, Methodism and Quakerism, as it developed in northern Europe, had in common a critique of Catholicism as aestheticism, and instead turned its attention to the material, practical world.[2]

If we turn the argument around and look at how we can explain the specific capitalism of the West, Weber uses Benjamin Franklin in order to show that the feature of capitalism he wants to explain is its element of an *ethically informed way of life*. To behave honestly, modestly, trustworthily, deliver on time, and so on, are not only things that will help your business, but are also the ethical norm you should live by. The two have merged or created a symbiosis. Capitalism in this sense is to be understood as a norm-obedient behaviour. And this behaviour by that new capitalist class came, from the seventeenth century onward, more and more into conflict with traditionalism (Catholicism) as an emotional phenomenon.[3]

Weber argues that the particular form that this capitalist behaviour took, cannot, as Werner Sombart had argued,[4] be explained rationally, because rational behaviour might lead for instance to a situation where you work less if you earn more (as was often the case in Catholic countries). Why did (only) northern European, protestant areas develop the ethics of disciplined labour that would continue to do their duty independent of their income? And how could a system of social division and economic differences prevail in these countries with less totalitarian and more liberal regimes and based on (more or less!)

---

1   It is interesting to observe that Weber takes a very different approach to sociology of religion than that of, for instance, Emile Durkheim. Durkheim saw religion as a symbolic system that to some extent mirrored material conditions. Durkheim observed and tried among others to explain why there were parallels between the hierarchical structures of religion and the characters in the godly universe on the one hand, and the structure of the secular society on the other. He tried to examine this relation across cultures.

2   It is important to have in mind that Weber made his analysis in a context. The issue of capitalism was highly debated in the German historical school. Weber's argument was contested by many, among them Sombart (see Sombart, 2001). Sombart wanted to trace the sources of capitalism in the mentality and culture of different nationalities (not in religion). He also argued that any nationality could adopt the spirit of capitalism.

3   It should be mentioned that Weber did not argue that there is only one form of rationalism and that non-economic behavior is irrational. On the contrary, he tries to develop a theory of different forms of rationalism. The point he developed was that different spheres of society have different types of rationality. One way of seeing this is to say that it is rational in economic life (markets) to optimise profit, but it is likewise rational in your personal life (private sphere) to be altruistic.

4   Werner Sombart had used the term *capitalism* in his book *Der moderne Kapitalismus* (1902).

free labour? It is this disciplined, rational labour that makes a calculating, rational capitalism possible. The only way to explain this discipline is by the predominant spirit that informed people. It is the *ethics of practical duty* that corresponds with the needs of a calculative, rational and modest way of life, which makes this social phenomenon possible. And this ethics of duty came from the predominant *protestant ethics*.

If this thesis is correct, it implies that we are able to deliver reasonable arguments that it was the protestant ethics that in fact created, or at least delivered strong support for, this mentality of a materialism, with rational, calculating behaviours and a disciplined, modest way of life, that in short can be termed *ethics of duty*: did the ethics of duty emerge out of the protestant movement? Weber's argument, therefore, has to answer three questions: (1) is there an ethical code that historically was only developed within the protestant movement, (2) is the same ethical code a unique and important feature of a certain type of capitalism, and finally (3) does this religious movement and the specific form of capitalism emerge at a corresponding time and place?

In order to understand the particular development of an ethics of duty, Weber discusses four protestant movements – Calvinism, pietism, Methodism and Baptist – and their religious theses. And he explains that his treatise will to some extent develop ideal types that transcend many of the differences and similarities between the movements to be considered.

Common to the protestant movements was their *'innerweltliche Askese'* (worldly application). That is, the prime focus in religious action is shifted from the eternal to the practical world. Calvinism managed to transfer the focus of mercy (*'nåde'*) from God and the eternal to the practical world. To be a servant for practical purposes in the world would count as a praise of God. One assumed that one was *a chosen* and that one would reach salvation. The key to both was ascetic action – not mystical sensation.

By this way of reasoning, practical work to the praise of God become decoupled from speculations about God and from the religious practice of trying to reach God. Furthermore, Calvinism put this ascetic action into a system; it wasn't necessarily the individual ascetic action that counted, but each individual's participation in an *ascetic community*. That is, each individual participated in an ascetic system. It was the method of living, the systematic ascetic way of life that was the key to salvation. This led to a system that was throughout rational; each individual was integrated into a system of modest and ascetic behaviour to the praise of God and this led in turn to a *rational community*. It can, in my words, be regarded as a form of *voluntary collectivism*. It implied the formation of groups (sects) and of social structures.

Pietism developed further the idea of a worldly ethics and of an ascetic way of life, but problematised the individual, emotional call for mercy. They developed the ascetic system of life to a higher degree, but they also looked for signs of mercy from God. Their eagerness to be ascetic made them more committed to secular tasks such as commerce. They even to a large degree argued for secular activities in the name of a *call for mercy*. Their strong commitment to duty and their sense of rules meant that they, in Weber's opinion, developed an attitude closer to that of bureaucrats than capitalists.

With the Methodists, the more emotional relation between man and God was reintroduced. In that sense it was a critique of Calvinism. However, the Methodists developed a systematic 'method' and control in order to reach mercy, and in practice it was rather close to Calvinism. With the Baptists, the emotional impact became stronger. However, in spite of this, the worldly activities and the communal ties became even stronger than with Calvinists, as did their commercial activity. To serve God and to do commerce was argued along the same lines.

Common to all these protestant movements is that the internal, moral policing was stronger than any force in civil society. The voluntary obedience and the communal forces created a form of voluntary collectivism with a worldly call. The rational, collective organisation of society became the immediate response to the call for God's mercy. The rationalised everyday life in the duty of commerce was at the same time the realisation of the ascetic behaviour in the name of God.

The Rationalisation of the Social

How, then, can we see these religious ideas in relation to the ascent of capitalism in the Western world? The Protestants rejected the individual striving for pleasure and replaced it with transactions in praise of God. To seek profit was to serve God – not to seek individual, material wealth. Ascetic behaviour and the duty to work were all done for the praise of God, not for individual utility: 'God blesseth his trade'. However, the purpose was not to collect goods, but to trade goods, keep them in circulation; be their guardian ('*forvalter*') – not their owner and user. Thereby, savings (in line with ascetic behaviour) and the formation of capital for investment were made possible. This furthermore led away from the patriarch and aristocratic social order (that collected goods) to the modern work organisation (that produced and circulated goods). Obedient labourers had a personal duty to serve and work; the capitalists served the Lord. They all were part of a rational system; they all were part of a collective that served the formation of the modern capitalist system. The voluntary collectivism and the voluntary obedience made modern work organisations possible because of the self-discipline that came from the idea of *work as a call*. It created the structured, rational forms of life that made a developed, capitalist and industrialist economy possible.

Jürgen Habermas (1997) uses Weber as an important reference and source for his own social (and critical) theory, the *theory of communicative action*. The common structure in his and Weber's theorising is the interaction between three *formal-pragmatic relations*; the subjective/expressive, the social/conformative and the objective (institutional)/ objectifying. Habermas basically agrees with Weber that the Western world has over some centuries been going through a process of *rationalising* social relations; they have over the last hundred years become more and more based on rational, countable parameters (such as economics, production, and materialisation). This is, in short, a significant feature of *modernity*.[5]

Furthermore, Habermas complies with Weber's general scheme that says that some religions were more adaptable to this development than others, and that the protestant movement is outstanding in this sense. Habermas sees in Weber a structure for analysing the modern, rational and to some extent *disintegrated* state. That is, modernity exists alongside a series of dilemmas or tensions between different parts of society: in short the subjective, the social and the objective (institutional) sphere. These parts have inner

---

5   There were discussions within the German historical school about this issue. Tönnies (1979), writing on the distinction between *Gemeinschaft* and *Gesellschaft*, exemplified a broader discussion on modernisation and differentiation of different spheres of society. See for instance Sombart (2001).

tensions, but there are also relations between them. The objective (institutional) sphere is in the modern state a constant threat to invade the subjective, personal sphere. Likewise, the social sphere supposes a public discourse that challenges both the institutionalised (objective) system as well as the private sphere. The one sphere creates rational conditions for the other.

As Habermas argues, Weber was, with his protestant ethics analysis, pioneering this theorisation of the relation between the inner, private and subjective world of beliefs on the one hand and the logical and rational concerns of the social and structural world on the other. His critique of Weber (1997, vol. 2, p. 378) is based on an interpretation of this theory that he sees as leading to some sort of *reductionism*. That is, if we understand Weber in a way that he in his theory tries to structure society along one dimension by which subjective, social and structural conditions are more or less integrated as one and the same (which is a possible way to read Weber), it represents a limited perspective on society. But this is not really Habermas's view. Rather, Habermas argues that Weber might as well be read as a discourse on how different parts of a society interact, and how the social, structural and institutional levels of modern society are challenged and criticised. Society is subjected to attempts by subjective (religious) beliefs to control it. In Habermas's own secular view, it is important that this does not happen.

Does the New Creative Economy Mark a Difference?

The point of departure for Richard Florida's theory is the assumption that the (post-) modern economy, in contrast to the traditional (modern) economy, has a new growth dynamics. In the new, (post-) modern economy, growth is less dependent on exogenous factors (natural resources) and more on endogenous factors (human resources). More specifically, Florida introduces the three Ts: technology, talent and tolerance. These three factors, he argues, are the main drivers in the new economy; technology is developed by talent and talent flourishes where there is tolerance. Subsequently, his theory assumes that location (such as a region) means something in the sense that it represents a cultural area where people live and that this cultural area can be more or less tolerant. Based on statistics from mainly the US, he shows in his book, *The Rise of the Creative Class* (2002), that economic growth indeed has happened in areas with tolerant and pluralist cultures (such as San Francisco) rather than in more traditional, less tolerant areas (such as Pittsburgh).

In his book, *The Flight of the Creative Class* (2005), Florida elaborates his argument and directly contrasts it with Weber's analysis. Here he argues, firstly, that the creative class represents somewhere between 30 and 40 per cent of the workforce in Western countries. By this he includes all types of professions and work where the employee can use his or her own judgement in performing the work. This might be artists, architects and designers, but it might also be engineers, technicians, lawyers and so-called free professions. They are the talents that drive innovation and subsequently economic development. He terms this *creative capital*, as a parallel to physical capital (machines), human capital (educated people) and social capital (the resources you can utilise in a group). Creative capital is a sort of innovative capacity within the population in a certain area (city, region). This creative capital increases with tolerance because a tolerant, pluralistic society attracts creative people and stimulates new thinking and new combinations for competence.

In a chapter called 'The Open Society' (inspired by Karl Popper, 1945), Florida argues that we must rethink how culture affects the economy. Culture as understood by Weber, he argues, motivates economic growth by focusing energy and effort on work, and away from the pull of non-work activities. 'Human beings are seen as undisciplined agents in need of rules and constraint' (Florida, 2005, p. 68). This is at best a reductionism in the reading of Weber (refer to Habermas's argument above). Also Daniel Bell argues:

> In the United States, one could say that the status discontents of small-town Protestant moralising (and moralising is distinct from morality), was the resentment (and fear) of free life-styles of the cosmopolitan urban class. (Bell, 2001, p. 447)

Bell took this argument further, according to Florida, and argued that the more open, expressive and hedonistic culture during the 1960s had the effect of undermining the social discipline that was essential for innovation and economic growth.

THE ROCK 'N ROLL ECONOMY?

Against this view Florida holds the argument that it is pluralism, tolerance, even the creativity of the hippie and rock 'n roll generation, which has driven the new, innovative economy; Steve Jobs' invention of the personal computer (Apple Computer) could stand as a symbol. The road from Woodstock to Silicon Valley is shorter than one should imagine. Florida also argues that these new rock 'n roll entrepreneurs are not primarily greedy. It is not greed that drives the new, creative economy; rather it is creativity and the possibility for each individual to realise ideas and to be creative that's the main drive for their actions. Furthermore, it is *bridging* rather than *bonding* (that is, relations between diverse social groups, rather than strong ethical norms within social groups) that increases creative capital and drives innovation.

This last argument had, by the way, been developed by, among others, Mark Granovetter (1985) and his discussion of embeddedness and of *the strength of weak ties*. In relation to this, it is interesting to notice the discussion around Robert Putnam's work *Bowling Alone* (2001). Robert Putnam argues that social capital is in decline in the US. This argument has been picked up by neo-conservatives as supporting their view, while Putnam himself is rather a liberal.

Florida's empirical analyses are intended to show that liberal and tolerant cities and regions (in terms of culture, laws, attitudes to gay marriage, abortion, and so on) do better because they attract creative people (immigration, foreign students, percentage of population with foreign family background, and so on). He argues that cities do better than rural areas and that liberal cities do better than conservative ones.

This argumentation, based on statistics, is of course not unproblematic: for instance, Dublin will score high on tolerance and innovation in these statistics, in spite of the fact that Ireland is a very conservative country in many religious matters. We also know that the Irish economic miracle in the period up to the financial crisis (2008) was to a large extent fuelled by EU support (subsidies, exemptions from taxation, and so on). In more technical terms one can argue that cross-country surveys are problematic because we do not know if evaluations of constructs in one country are comparable with another. Furthermore, indexing concepts such as tolerance implies the complicated and questionable task of comparing and evaluating different tolerance indicators.

So Florida's statistics are not of the sort that proves anything, although they do indicate that there are certain relations. For example, we know that big cities in the West (and also in the world generally) have grown over the last decades, that their percentage of GNP has increased, that they have more immigrants (logically, since they grow so fast) and that they are more liberal and market-driven than rural areas (again logical since their scale and growth implies that communitarian principles have less possibility to succeed in this type of environment).

Jane Jacobs (1984) identified this urban phenomenon many years ago: urban areas (cities) seem to have an endogenous growth dynamics related to their heterogeneity, complexity, multiculturalism and diversity. In fact, it was an observation already among the mercantilists in the eighteenth century that cities had their own development dynamics. Cantillon wrote about the political economy of the city in 1755, when he in particular was fascinated by the development of Amsterdam. And urban development has been a particular theme in innovation theory (Buck, Gordon, Harding, and Turok, 2005). So, any statistical comparison between rural and urban areas will probably comply with these general trends. Florida adds some interesting elements to this general knowledge of urban development.[6]

Beyond the discussion on statistics, it is interesting to look at the more theoretical part of Florida's argument and see to what extent he presents a counter thesis to that of Weber. Florida gives some support for arguing that conservative (moral majority and family values) regions are doing worse in terms of the new innovative economy than more liberal, democratic areas and regions.

WEBER AND FLORIDA COMPARED

I do not think, as already commented, that Florida in his critique does justice to Weber. His reading of Weber implies, at best, an extreme reduction of Weber's argument. Furthermore, Florida seems to identify Weber's historical analysis of protestant ethics with today's debate in America on the positions on family values and conservative religious thought. However, it must be a contradiction, even for Florida, that the Scandinavian countries, the place where Protestantism and even a form of Calvinism had its greatest impact, is the area that comes out at the top of indexes on tolerance, talent and innovation.

In fact, over the last few years the Scandinavian countries have come out on top on almost all social statistics, because in a global comparative perspective they are both liberal and conservative, both market-driven and have a large public sector, both advanced in areas such as equality between sexes, high educational level, liberal law on issues such as equal sex relations, and at the same time they have a high percentage of people who are religious. In addition they are on top in innovation and low unemployment, low on social unrest and crime, and on top in the world in GNP per capita. That means that conservatives as well as liberals and socialists can argue that Scandinavia proves their case.

---

6   However, the issue of why some urban areas grows faster than others is rather complex. London had grown tremendously the last years before the financial crisis in areas that are in line with Florida's description of the creative economy; however, it is also one of the places where the financial crisis has hit hardest because it has become so dependent on the financial service sector. Growth can be explained by agglomeration processes and decline by lock-in processes (such as sunk capital or redundant technologies), to mention some of the alternative explanations. The rust belt in the US probably has suffered from this.

Table 7.1   Comparing the arguments of Weber and Florida

	Weber	Florida
The phenomenon they describe	The development of a certain form of capitalism in western Europe (rational, bourgeois trade and industrialisation with its modern work ethics)	Innovation in the modern, knowledge economy is a function of technology, talent and tolerance. A liberal, open, tolerant ethics will attract talents and lead to technological innovation
The factors that are considered in the theory	Ethical mentality, religious movements, emergence of capitalism	Ethical norms in society, innovation, economic development, regional demographical changes
The theoretical foundation: philosophical position, underlying theories	Historical analyses, ideal types, hermeneutics (related to religious texts)	Empirical analysis, comparative cross-country data, social statistics
Their underlying assumptions	Society develops as a result of cultural values as well as material causes	Society develops as a result of creativity that comes from talented people

However, I do not think that these types of argument bring much insight into the controversy of the relation between culture and market or protestant ethics and the ascent of capitalism. In fact, I do not think Weber and Florida address the same issue, as indicated by Table 7.1.

My argument here is that Florida does not present an alternative to Weber's comprehensive sociological theory. He does not discuss how inner, subjective beliefs are interrelated with social and institutional characteristics of society. In short, he does not present a sociological theory.

Such a theory could be found in Berger and Luckmann (1966). In their *The Social Construction or Reality: A treatise in the sociology of knowledge*, they argue that our immediate understanding of social order (rules, norms, routines, structures) are objectivised through, among others, social practice and language. Furthermore, some of these structures are institutionalised and legitimised, and society invests a lot in maintaining some of these structures (refer, for instance, to religious rituals). Furthermore, these structures have a socialising effect and are internalised in people's self-understanding and identity. Berger and Luckmann subsequently described a social mechanism on the macro level by which societies internalise beliefs and through them create structures and how these become interlocked and self-concealing. They are challenged when immediate everyday practice and experience contradicts these structures and norms. Subsequently, Berger and Luckmann's theory is very well able to explain how more traditional and religious societies are challenged by modernism and more plural ways of life. However, it is unclear if this is what Florida has in mind.

The main argument by Florida relates then to a series of dichotomies that are further discussed in other disciplines, such as individualist and collectivist cultures, *gemeinschaft* and *gesellschaft*, communitarianism versus liberalism, the city versus rural areas, service industry versus industrial society, family values versus women's rights or gay rights, and so on. These dualisms are indications and labels for important controversies in contemporary society. Their underlying causes, their concrete appearances and the possibility for reconciliation is a very complex, and partly a local and contextual issue. However, having said this, I will close this discussion by restating the argument by Weber and by Florida in a form that makes them comparable in the contemporary debate, although this implies that we deviate from their original meaning. I turn now to this discussion.

The Liberal/Conservative Debate and the Issue of Secularisation

Florida's arguments go, as I have shown, directly into the liberal/conservative debate in the US on the role of values in society. Daniel Bell (1978) argued that economics, politics and culture are three realms that stand in a relation and tension to each other in society. While economic life is commoditised, bureaucratised and specialised, aiming at efficiency, and the political realm is guided by participation and collective engagement, the cultural realm is basically a realm of self-expression and self-gratification. In the cultural realm, individuals seek to avoid institutionalisation, standardisation and repetition in order to commercialise. Bell argued that this implies a contradiction. What is necessary in economic life is *contradictory* to the meaning of cultural expression. This definition of the cultural realm does not see culture as a precondition for social behaviour and values in the economic or political realm.

Another observation Bell is making is that culture becomes co-opted in the modern society and that modern culture itself, in particular modernism, is, paradoxically in its rejection of the cultural tradition, less likely to stand as a counterforce against capitalism. Culture has become co-opted by the economic system, Bell argues, an argument which is in line with, for instance, Theodore Adorno's critique of what he called *cultural industry* (Adorno, 2001).

Critical positions in line with this warning about the reduction of art and culture to economic activity and instrumentalisation include Hanna Arendt (1958) and Jürgen Habermas (1997). Seen in relation to Florida's argument, this position of Bell (and paradoxically also Adorno, Arndt and Habermas, to mention some in the critical tradition) is less optimistic in relation to the harmonic interaction between culture and economy.

Florida argues that the one supports the other because he sees the creative economy as a result of human, cultural flourishing, so that for him culture supports economic development. Bell points at the contradiction between them because he sees culture as something different from economic activity. At the same time Bell argues that the market is where culture and production (economic activity) meet. That implies that this meeting implies a transformation that influences both the economic life and culture. In short, Bell argues (and here he departs from Adorno, Arendt and Habermas) that the modernist cultural movement has undermined the cultural foundation of capitalism.

One interesting aspect of Bell's argument is that he distinguishes between different forms of culture and how they influence economic activity. It is not any one religion or any one cultural activity that is favourable to capitalism. One could interpret Bell as saying that religion and art, where both are understood as activities that cultivate attitudes that civilise man, will create the cultural foundation for a well-running economy. At the same time, the wrong cultural values will have the opposite effect. A culture based on greed, hedonism, self-expression without a feeling of responsibility for others, criticism without a contribution to a good society, and so on, things and attitudes that Bell connects with *modernist culture*, will undermine the economy, not support it. And modernist culture is – if we take Florida's reasoning where he points at San Francisco as the prime example of a combination of modernist art and creative economy – the key to economic development. So here they disagree strongly. I develop this argument more in the next chapter.

One could also say that Bell argues in line with Weber's approach in the sense that Weber also argues that some religious practice was more favourable to capitalism than others, particularly those practices that restrained some actions (such as greed) but at the same time allowed for others (such as accumulation of capital, investment, trade). Similar arguments are found in Gray (2009). Although John Gray is more a liberal than a conservative, he still argues that culture is eroded (in modern society) and that this undermines the market (mainly because governments subscribe to globalism). His argument is that the global economy (globalisation) and the wrong idea of separating the market from its cultural base are to blame.

Florida, on the other hand, does not make such a distinction when it comes to art. When it comes to religion, he more or less makes such a distinction as he argues (contrary to Bell and Gray) that conservative religion conflicts with the new, creative economy. To him, religion has a coercive dimension that undermines or restricts creativity.

Bell argues in favour of a set of conservative values, found in Christianity, that he – in line with what Weber did in his historical analysis – sees as being in support of economic development. The core of these values are the Christian values of duty and (self-) disciplines in combination with the norm of maximising profit. It gives us a (self-) constrained, ethically bound capitalism that is different from a hedonistic, egoistic and consumption-based capitalist system.

Similar arguments, that Christianity has provided us with the necessary foundation for a free society, are found in Cardinal Ratzinger's (later Pope Benedict the IX) discussion with Habermas (Habermas and Ratzinger, 2005). In this discussion, Habermas argues that on the one hand a free, civilised society needs a normative, legal foundation. On the other hand he rejects the assumption that this necessarily implies that religion or religious beliefs have to be that foundation. Rather he argues that these norms follow from any reasonable reflection on the necessary foundation for free exchange and dialogue in society. They are the logical (and ontological) preconditions that free men will acknowledge when they want to live in a free and civilised society, and when they acknowledge the similar freedom of others.

The Market/Culture Relation and Varieties of Capitalism

In an attempt to use the Calvinist argument of Weber to understand the particular capitalist development in the United States up to the present, Ditz (1980) finds that the relation between individual constraint and collective action gives meaning. Ditz adds another dimension, namely to look at structural changes in the economy over time, not least the development towards what he calls *consumer economy*.[7] Along this dimension he

---

7   It is interesting to link this to Sombart's article *Why is there no Socialism in the United States?* (reprinted in Sombart 2001). Sombart argued in this article from 1906 (about two generations before Putnam wrote *Bowling Alone*), that the

argues that Calvinist ethics comes in a dilemma. This type of reasoning and arguing is also found in analysis on the political right (neo-conservatism) in US politics that argue for the need for a more constrained ethical code in society to counter the erosion of society, morality and market (Bell, 2001).

Sanchez-Burks (2005) argues that the separation between the work sphere (market) and the social sphere (culture) when it comes to the view of the role of relations is significantly more present in the American society compared with Asia and southern Europe. He relates this difference to the Calvinist influence in the United States, claiming that this dualism is and was a central part of the Calvinist understanding: what you do in the economy is separated from the worship and relations of your private life.

DO DIFFERENCES IN INSTITUTIONAL CONFIGURATION MATTER?

Economists disagree on whether specific configuration of institutions within a certain area gives a specific comparative advantage. Things that create endogenous properties of a specific area (nation, region) include: oligopoly position, economics of scope (reflecting varieties of and related knowledge), network externalities and the nature of property rights.

This is supported by analyses of what is called *varieties of capitalism* (Hall and Soskice, 2001; Amble, 2003). These and other studies find a striking difference in economic and institutional structure between the Anglo-American world and the North European and Nordic countries. They indicate that there are many different ways of organising the economy. Cultural and historical conditions are mirrored in the structures we observe.[8] One can argue that centralism in France, the cooperative system in Germany and communitarianism in the Nordic countries are replicated in the overall institutional structure, in spite of the fact that the general trend over the last century has gone in direction of more market-based solutions (privatisation, corporatism and globalism).

Hall and Soskice (2001) contrast this with theories that emphasise non-economic factors of explanation; for instance innovation system theories that look at relations to public institutions. They also argue that this literature emphasises absolute advantage and not comparative advantage.

It is assumed that there are systematic differences in how economies are organised and how they perform and innovate (Hall and Soskice, 2001; Lorenz and Lundvall, 2006). However, it has also been argued that economies have different configurations that are seen to stand in some sort of logical relation to each other (Whitley, 2006). For example, if the economy is more market-driven, the companies are more likely to take responsibility for vocational training (Amable, 2003). The more central question is how we can model these systemic effects of how institutions compensate or complement each other.

Amin and Cohendet (2004) discuss different knowledge forms and the relation between governance of firms and governance of communities. They make the distinction between interaction (which can be weak and strong) and communication

United States never adopted a *Gemainschaft* way of thinking. The whole society is based on capitalism. This is because those who came there, came to work to get away from Europe. There was always a market, always new land, always need for labour in the US. The main issue was not that of distribution (*Gesellschaft*) but that of production. Therefore even workers subscribed to the capitalist system.

8   Similar variations can be found in the study of religion, refer for instance to Berger et al. (2008).

(which can be weak and strong) in relations between forms, and argue that there is a distinction between what they call hard and soft architecture of learning both in and between forms. Whitley (2006) outlines six types of innovation systems: autarkic, artisanal, technology teams, state-led, group-based and highly collaborative. They have different ways of developing knowledge, sharing knowledge and using knowledge. This relates to both internal organisational structures and external network configuration. It also relates to the type of knowledge that is shared and is needed to share. Main factors: steering and organisational structure can be more or less hierarchical and more or less expert driven. Networks can be loose, mobilising or more structured, managed. Knowledge can be more or less technological, more or less codified and more or less contextual.

It has been argued that the sort of collective participation that we find in the Scandinavian model gives high commitment, motivation and positive attitudes to workplace reforms. The Scandinavian corporate collaboration model got its theoretic basis developed through what is called the collaboration experiments in the 1960s and the 1970s. The theoretic anchorage and understanding from these experiments was made in a framework, which was marked by a belief in scientific approach to the work processes, in the direction of finding better adaptations between the efficiency demand and the individual employee's needs. The perspective was, in addition, politically in the way of more corporate democracy. One wished to outweigh the asymmetry in the power structure between employees and owners/management, by making arenas based on balance and symmetrical power between the parties.

The economic differences of spaces can easily be explained by functional processes such as agglomeration, economics of scale and monopoly competition. This was also the argument given by Paul Krugman, when he in 1991 reinvented the economics of space (Krugman, 1991). If we look at this historically, general neo-classical economics in the mid-war period, disregarded the economics of space. The nation state economics appeared and was strengthened after the First World War and again after the Second World War. Keynesianism and national economic planning led, in Western Europe in particular, to national industrial policy, public ownership of capital, control of investments and exploiting natural resources (as a source of wealth). In Norway, fiscal policy and state control of the economy through industrial investments was a main policy area after the Second World War. It was a policy that collapsed with the collapse of world economic order in the beginning of the 1970s.

Hall and Soskice (2001) argue that institutional economic thinking has gone through different ages after the Second World War. In the first period up to the 1970s there was what they call the modernisation period. During this period, there was a strong belief in national industrial policy, technology and capital-driven investments and state planning. The second period came in the 1970s under the inflation period, and they call it the neo-corporatist period. A key thing in this period was how large organisations such as labour unions were brought into economic and industrial policy. Their role gave them the possibility to influence development but it also implied that they were disciplining their members and had a stabilising role in the economy. The third period, which Hall and Soskice (2001) call social systems of production, came in the 1980s and 1990s. In this period, the social and sociological characteristics of organisations and networks were highlighted. Production regimes were understood (as in Piore and Sabel, 1984) as social systems of interaction, learning and trust relations.

Table 7.2   Forms of innovation

	Individual/ micro: Innovation as invention	Organisation: Innovation as organisational change	Inter-organisational: New patterns of interactions between organisations	Societal, institutions, macro: Cultural change, institutional change
Radical	New product, totally new perspectives, attitudes	New organisational forms	Total re-conception of interaction forms	Large cultural and institutional change
Incremental	Improved products, attitudes	Improved organisational forms, changed value chains	Changes in cooperative patterns	Small changes in cultural and institutional patterns

As a further development in this thinking on the institutional economy, Hall and Soskice (2001) call for an approach that is more linked up with strategic perspectives by companies (and less related to understanding relations as sociological). The new focus is not on what the region or space is, but on what it can be, how it can develop and how it can produce factors of production. This leads Krugman to ask if the new institutional economies and economics of space is not about comparative advantages, but about developing absolute advantages (Krugman, 1991). Regional and spatial differences in economic structure can probably be easily explained by the traditional functional terms such as agglomeration, comparative advantage, monopolistic competition and economics of scale. Collaboration can also be seen along these dimensions, as functional organising of local activity. However, it is also likely that there are local/regional forms of development that cannot be explained with these theoretical concepts.

Innovation can be of many forms: it can refer to market-driven versus technology or science-driven innovation, to complex products (like airplanes) versus simple and singular products (like improving the razor). It can be the result of single processes or relations between changes at different levels. In the last case, innovation theory needs to explain what mechanisms transform changes from one level to the other. Often we divide between radical and incremental. Furthermore, I argue here for a multi-level perspective. This gives us a whole range of possible interpretations of innovation (see Table 7.2).

Following Whitley (2006), one can classify innovation systems in different types. He has identified six types, from autarkic to highly collaborative. His point is that the collaborative model is sharing authority, has a highly involved public sector, has lots of non-market coordination, is strong in incremental innovation but is limited in radical innovation. The autarkic model is less authority sharing, less involved with public policy, less based on market coordination but with a high degree of radical, firm-specific innovations.

Can the pure logic of choice explain all these collaborative and innovative forms? I have tried in Chapter 5 to argue that the market encounter involves exchange and learning. When people meet in a market encounter, they try to learn enough about each other to make an exchange. The market encounter might result in an improvement of norms. In order to reach a level of exchange in the market encounter, three elements have to be present: the utility of the process, purpose and alertness. This argument is in line with what we would regard as the underlying logic of the communicative process. The communicative approach is about the creation of a situation where individuals will take the risk of revealing private information. The commitment to non-opportunistic behaviour is one important element in this strategy.

Miller (1992) argues that economic incentives might work in certain situations, but not in all:

> But in the presence of marked information asymmetries and team interdependence, there is no such ideal incentive system. Individuals in hierarchies inevitably find themselves in situations in which their own self-interest is clearly in conflict with organizational efficiency. These situations seem to be increasingly the norm in contemporary society. Vertical dilemmas in hierarchy create an environment for politics and political leadership. Rather than relying only on a mechanical incentive system to align individual interests and group efficiency, hierarchical leaders must create appropriate psychological expectations, pay the 'startup costs' for appropriate cooperation norms, kick-start the secondary norms, and create institutions that will credibly commit the leader to the nonexploitation of employee 'ownership rights' in the organization. (Miller, 1992, p. 232)

If there are social dilemmas, multi Nash-equilibrium and non-repeated game coordination, what is needed in order to secure the best solutions are commitment, trust and shared beliefs, which implies a milieu where individuals reveal private information and coordinate preferences. This, according to Miller, can be achieved through participation, training and gain-sharing.

The field of innovation goes beyond a narrow interpretation of economics as a pure logic of choice. The core of economic behaviour is adaption to possibilities in the market and choice of the optimal form of organisation. Concepts and theories such as comparative advantage, economics of scale, agglomeration and monopolistic competition are adequate to explain regional differences. Concepts such as incentives, monitoring, cultural pressure and games can explain collaboration forms at organisational level. Institutional theory can identify national differences in institutional configurations and subsequently what forms of collaboration that will dominate in a national setting.

Subsequently, I argue that it is absolutely feasible to claim that what we can call economic arguments are able to explain some of these forms of innovation and change. That does not imply that the explanation is correct, or that the explanation covers all that is implied in these innovations and changes. As Hayek writes:

> The belief that the market order ought to be made to behave as if it were an economy proper, and that this performance can and ought to be judged by the same criteria, has become a source of so many errors and fallacies that it seems necessary to adopt a new technical term to describe the order of the market which spontaneously forms itself. (Hayek, 1978, p. 90)

This indicates that the discussion of the relation between market and culture is relevant, but it also indicates that we have to have a certain degree of context sensitivity when we discuss this. The role of culture and institutions still differs between national and local contexts, in spite of globalisation. If we are to understand how the one influences the other, we have to look into these specific contexts.

Table 7.3   Different conceptualisations of the market/culture relation

	Market and culture as integrated realms	Market and culture as differentiated realms
Culture influences market	Norms and attitudes in the social culture are embedded in economic action.	Culture and norms are used as arguments to modify or to argue against market solutions.
Market influences culture	Social culture and norms have to comply with market rationality.	Market logic invades the cultural and normative social realm.

TRYING TO CONCEPTUALISE THE RELATION BETWEEN CULTURE AND MARKET

The idea of this chapter has been to open up the large and complicated discussion of the relation between culture and market. The thought that triggered me to look into this was Florida's critique of Weber. My first reflection was that Florida had not looked deeply enough into Weber's argument. My second observation was that as we open this discussion, the number of relevant issues and positions are so large that it soon becomes complicated to follow the debate. My purpose has been to structure this discussion. In concluding, I will try to summarise my point.

Two main issues have been discussed here. The one issue is what type of cultural (moral, ethical, religious) values are most favourable to economic development. The core theme here is whether or not moral and ethical contrarians of the type we find in protestant ethics, and which Weber argued were favourable for the early capitalist development, are still the values that should guide the new, creative economy. But parallel to this, there is the discussion of the relation between economy and culture as such. How integrated and differentiated should they be? One can think of the following ideal positions: the market is part of the social and cultural realm. There is no difference between the two. Alternatively, the two realms (market and culture) are completely differentiated.

The logic and modus of operation in the one is different from the other. In these two models or positions, one can think that the relation between culture and market takes different forms. Table 7.3 tries to illustrate this.

Table 7.3 is supposed to illustrate what might be at stake when we discuss the relation between market and culture. It is actually a little confusing to try to place Florida's argument in this model. He is on the one hand a proponent for a liberal position, encouraging innovation and creativity and liberal cultural values and an open market economy. On the other hand, his argument can be read as an argument for integration of the cultural sphere and the market sphere.

Conclusion

The point I should like to make is that although the differentiation between market and culture might be criticised, since the market does not then comply with social norms, it does not follow that we will prefer an integration of the social realm and the market realm.

In a differentiated society, the relation between market and culture (the social realm) is one of a *discursive kind*. That implies that there is and should be a constant discussion between them. The social is to correct the market through criticism. The market will of course influence (and *try to* intrude and invade) the cultural and social realm. However, even if that happens, it is important in a differentiated society that the different spheres maintain independence.

The alternative might be a market that is integrated in the cultural and social realm. It would imply that only certain social norms are guiding economic action. It would also probably imply that the cultural realm had to compromise with market logic. Even if we call for ethical considerations into the market logic, for example that we ask corporations to be socially responsible, we might not mean that social norms and politics should take over from the market.

The important thing, I think, that Weber made us aware of the possibilities that were opened up as the religious realm (culture) and the economic realm (market) disintegrated and how that allowed for both the market and culture to flourish. Also, at least at one period of time there was a good fit between the two. This we can acknowledge, although they have had a turbulent relationship ever since, and still should.

8 *Modernist Criticisms and Development of Social Knowledge*

Introduction

This chapter is about the complex relationship between art, culture and politics. The example I discuss is *modernist art*, which appeared in the early 1900s, and the criticism it made of modern society. I have chosen modernist art because it represents an extreme position in the discussion between art and society. Modernist art, I argue, has an unclear relationship with modern society, partly because it provoked and challenged society itself. The purpose of the chapter is to emphasise various dilemmas with modernist criticism and how it has been interpreted. The thesis is that the criticism presented by modernist art exposes dilemmas and internal contradictions that have had an impact on knowledge development and that still have some relevance in contemporary society. I argue that this is part of the discourse and understanding of modern society, that the core of this dilemma is the autonomy of art and that art is an integrated part of society. My question is: based on what we can learn from the history and debates of modernist art, how can the balance between art as autonomous and art as influencing and criticising society be understood?

The structure of the chapter is as follows. First I try to define modernism and modernist art. Secondly, I link the discourse in art to the discourse on society. I define *subjectivity* and *resolution* as the main characteristics of modernist art criticism. Furthermore, I argue that there is a relation between modernist art and postmodernism in social thought and through that the critical positions in modernist art are absorbed and developed within postmodernism. I then present five cases to illustrate the dilemmas and contradictions in the criticism of modernist art. *Case A: Aesthetics and politics* shows how modernist art became politicised and a dimension in the large ideological battles in society in the early twentieth century. *Case B: Hamsun and Ibsen: criticism's different forms* tries to show how differently modernist artists exposed their criticism. *Case C: Art and consumerist society* presents the debate after the Second Wold War on what modernist art had contributed to and how the social conditions for criticism had changed. *Case D: Art and market* addresses the larger debate on art and market in contemporary society. *Case E: Modernism, pluralism and the autonomy of art in contemporary society* presents the political discussion about modernist art after the Second World War. I then summarise and discuss why the criticism of modernist art has been so problematic. Finally, I conclude by arguing for a pluralist perspective. I argue that modernist art criticism must be seen as part of knowledge development in society. I discuss what that implies.

The Ambiguous Concept of Modernism

What is *modernism*, how does it challenge us and why is it difficult to comprehend? *Modern* refers to many different classifications (Attali, 2013). Often we argue that Hobbes and Machiavelli were modern social thinkers, or that Cervantes and Melville were early modern novelists. Others will think of modern times as characterised by the Industrial Revolution and the emergence of capitalism and individualism (and urbanisation if we relate it to Durkheim's classical discussion from 1887 (Durkheim, 2005)). One can also argue that the proper art form related to modern, capitalist society is realism, distinguishing it from in particular romanticism.[1]

So, *modern* and *modernism* are not the same. Anthony Giddens (1995) and Jürgen Habermas (1987) use the word *modernity* as a term to describe life in modern society. Discontinuity is the label used. Martin Humpal makes the following distinction:

> *Modernism is an aesthetic usually in opposition to the cultural-historical phenomenon of bourgeois modernity which has 'produced the notion of realism'. (Humpal, 1998, p. 18)*

Modernism is something other than *the modern*. Nevertheless, I argue that the two are tightly integrated. I choose to see modernist art as *art's discourse on modernity*,[2] that is, a discussion of the various (problematic) aspects of modern society and life in modern society.

How should we approach modernist art? Jeff Wallace (2007) argues that:

> *[...] the discourse on modernist fiction is fundamentally Janus-faced, looking simultaneously inwards, towards form and language, and outwards, towards the changing material circumstances in which fiction was being produced and consumed. (Wallace, 2007, p. 15)*

My primary gaze is focused on the external conditions: modernist art in relation to society. Modernist art can be defined in different ways. Time is a possible scale. Some will say that modernist art had its breakthrough in the period 1890–1930 (Bradbury and McFarlane, 1991; Hughes, 1979; Williams, 1989); others that it began around 1850 and lasted until the Second World War.[3] What most agree on is that modernist art converges with the rise of industrial society, urbanisation, technological breakthroughs (such as cars, airplanes) and democratisation and universal suffrage. In total, this and other modern inventions

---

1   Habermas (1987) attributes the classification of ancient, pre-modern and modern era to Hegel. The modern era starts with the rationalisation and individualisation of thought in the renaissance that gets its full-blown form in the nineteenth century. I follow the classifications of modern and postmodern (post-capitalism), like that found in Bell (1973) and Cooper and Burrell (1988). For a critique of these classifications, see Bruno Latour (1993) *We Were Never Modern*. The argument is that classifications such as that, and the idea of society developing through accumulating stages, are wrong. Some of the positions I present defy such classifications. However, my position, with reference to the philosophical discussion (Frege, Kripke) is that classifications are necessary aspects of our capacity to communicate.

2   Habermas (1987), *Discourse on Modernity*. However, my discussion is more narrow and different, although I build on Habermas. Habermas's primary objective is to investigate to what extent art became a structurative principle in modern society, and the problem that implies. He does not treat modernism as a separate phenomenon, although he refers to avant-garde art as a certain form of modern art. I here treat art as only one (among many) activity in society. Habermas does not distinguish modern and modernist art. Habermas sees Hegel as the first philosopher to identify subjectivity, and the subjective reflection as a separate force in forming modern society. This is among others seen in Hegel's concept of alienation, where the subject and the rationality, differentiation and temporality of modern society contradict. Thus Habermas's modernism concept includes both the understanding of the modern and its subjectivist antagonism.

3   See Bradbury and McFarlane (1991). Gay (2009) argues that it is almost impossible to identify precisely modernism in time and place.

gave us a new form of community, or new conditions of society. A period of change, some would call it, and among them you have writers such as E.M. Forster, who reflects on the lost time,[4] as much as James Joyce, as his way of embracing the new era.[5] I will refer to this by the two terms *subjectivity* and *resolution*.

Modernist art can be seen as a collective term for some general ideas that developed in the late 1800s and came to influence thinking in society in large parts of the 1900s, at least in the Western, industrialised world. Bradbury and McFarlane (1991, p. 49) argue that it should include: impressionism, post-impressionism, cubism, vorticism, futuristic, expressionism, Dada, and surrealism. I will use modernist art as a reference to these particular groups, and modernism or modernists as a wider term of others that were in line with these groups. What should be observed was that these groups were conflicting and to some extent opposing each other. However, my perspective is to concentrate on what they had in common.

What, then, makes this or these groups' ideas current? In short: they highlighted the changing, the ground-breaking, the opportunity-seeking, they criticised the traditional standard-based, hierarchical and fixed, and they brought out the individual, the subject, the senses and the existential.

The *modernist* influence stretches beyond the core period around the First World War. Later trends such as Beat art in the United States in the 1950s had clear anchors in European modernism,[6] and this again was the forerunner of the hippy era (student uprising) in the 1960s.[7] The common denominator is liberation, subjective emancipation, rebellion against the existing social structures and patterns, and rejection of authority. It also inspired more anarchist movements.[8] The foundations of social structures are questioned. In other words, scepticism and relativism were a reference to their critical approach. The further road leads into consumerist society that created new conditions for art (Baudrillard, 2005).

Modernism: Subjectivism, Liberation and Resolution

Subjectivism had gained momentum in late nineteenth-century European thinking. Wilhelm Dilthey comprehended culture as a subjective phenomenon, hence his

---

4   See for example *A Handful of Dust*. It can be read as a gloomy doomsday portrayal where society falls apart towards primitiveness, in line with Eugene O'Neill's *Long Day's Journey into the Night*, or as an early version of Coppola's film drama *Apocalypse Now*. Richard Ennals has commented that Forster had a very strong political and personal project, and only dared display some of it in his novels published in his lifetime.

5   It is interesting to reflect on the fact that Joyce was so eager to introduce cinema to Ireland. He had a strong belief in new technology and new media.

6   Marjorie Perloff criticises in an article in TLS (*Times Literary Supplement*) on 18 February 2011 the film about Allen Ginsberg, *Howl*, because it has not communicated the absurdity that was an important part of the poem 'Howl'. The poem's absurdity will be easier to understand if one views it as part of the modernist tradition, she argues. Landauer (1996) argues that the experimentalist and expressionist movement in the USA during and after the Second World War was an American adaption of European modernism.

7   One example is Herman Hesse's modernist novel *Steppenwolf* from 1927, which inspired not only the rock band Steppenwolf (with their hit 'Born to be Wild' in 1967), but also the movie *Easy Rider*. In Denmark, the modernist group of writers and poets, *Arena*, appeared in the 1960s (Rasmussen, 2012).

8   For example, during the Spanish Civil War this conflict line was visible between artists and authors on the Republican side, anarchists (*anarcho syndicalist*) against the communists, that is, those who perceived rebellion and resistance as a liberation process (George Orwell illustrates this position), and those who saw it as the match for a new order (communism) that was to replace another (fascism). Ernest Hemingway may represent this position.

discussion of the difference between understanding and explaining in social sciences. Emile Durkheim analysed suicide and its social causes, Max Weber criticised positivism. Edmund Husserl discovered the life-world. They all spoke in the direction of what later in the 1900s was to be designated as social constructivism.[9] The discovery of the subjective and the significance of the symbolic, including analysis of religion as a symbolic field, are also part of this picture.[10] Hughes (1979) and Thyssen (1998) attribute to Nietzsche and Schopenhauer an important role in this development, and the *constructivist* and *epistemological* turn in European thinking.

Critique plays a crucial role in this development. The established norms or patterns of society are exposed to criticism. Marriage and standards related to it prevent Nora, in Ibsen's play *A Doll's House*, from experiencing love, 'the most wonderful!'. In Henry James's novel, Isabel is caught in the social game around her. The *Grand Tour* of the enlightenment area has in James's novel become a dark descent into doom. In Hamsun, many of the main characters are already 'out of the world'. One might say that it is the subject against society.

Paul Johnson (1991) sees much of the modern art's emergence as an illustration of Freud's theory of man, our neuroses created by the enclosed norms that we comply with. Impressionism in art had already, earlier in the 1800s, showed us that things are not objective, but appear as we perceive them. Husserl was inspired by these ideas. Intuition and the impression were referred to by Henri Bergson (1912) as cornerstones of our consciousness. The objective world is falling apart. Marcel Proust worked out the same thoughts in his great novel work on *Remembering the Time Lost* in the early 1900s: the construction of a subjective world (Proust, 1997).

One could refer to it as individual liberation, or emancipation of the subject. In time it runs parallel with the fight for workers' rights and emancipation of workers in industry, and the struggle for women's suffrage. However, there is an important aspect of this liberation as expressed in modernist art, that it was not related to social realism, but rather explored the knowledge that the objective world does not exist. Brooker (2007) refers to the 'art for art's sake' movement that around 1890 had the non-moralising novel as a goal. Art should not deal with injustice of society, enlightenment, the social conditions, nor be subject to them.[11] Georg Lukács wrote in 1914: 'The novel is the epic of a world that has been abandoned by God' (Lukács, 1971, p. 88). Man without a sound foundation on which to ground its beliefs and convictions – a vacuum? Lévinas and Sartre spoke later of *discomfort* (nausea), Milan Kundera even later of *The Unbearable Lightness of Being*, a discomfort that the liberation of the modern poses, hence Giddens' *discontinuity*. Philipp Blom calls the period 1900–14 *the vertigo years* (Blom, 2008). It is important to note, however, that the discomfort is something that we have inside us; it is not out there! Modernism highlights us as subjects that make each of us visible, also in the sense (of both Sartre (1946) and Lévinas (1993), see Critchley (2009)) that we all have a personal,

---

9   See Weber (1978), Dilthey (1976), Durkheim (2005), and Husserl (1970). Of course, constructivism is an interpretation from these philosophies, but also rationalist interpretations are possible.

10   Jürgen Habermas (1987) sees Hegel as an early exponent of this modernist approach. Michel Foucault (1986) argues that Kant can be interpreted as an early exponent of the understanding of conceptuality of knowledge.

11   As Gay (2009) observes, although avant-guardist artists argued for *l'art pour l'art*, they were at the same time very political (T.S. Eliot, F.T. Marinetti, W. Kandinsky, etc.). The liberation of art from society has nonetheless become a strong idea in contemporary society, which in example is seen in the discussion of the Free Speech Act (*Ytringsfrihet*) in Norway.

ethical responsibility. Their thoughts were revolutionary at their time, some would say innovative.[12]

Stuart Hughes (1979), in a classical analysis, has described the changes in European social thought in the period 1900 to 1930 with the words *Consciousness and Society*. The terms consciousness and society link the individual to the social, or we could say subjectivity breakthrough in thinking. Enlightenment (Hume/Kant) had been keen to harness emotions and passion in order to celebrate rationality.[13] Modernist art (perhaps especially expressionism) would release the innovative and creative in mankind; bring us back to the primitive, the real that lies hidden behind the veil of civilisation; as when Nora walks out of the bourgeois home. The rational individual and the epistemological turn had received their place far earlier in philosophy, but subjectivity was something else. It covers everything from Freud and Jung's discovery of the unconscious, of Bergson (1912) and Croce's (1909) intuition, to Pareto's analysis of the irrational in politics (Pareto, 1923).

The subjective perspective meant that the early Lukács, later Sartre, Merleau-Ponty, the Frankfurt School, to mention some, developed a Marxism more focused on the micro-sociological understanding of the individual in society. A good and later exponent of this perspective is Hannah Arendt's *The Human Condition* (Arendt, 1958). As much as this affected their ideological view, the subjective perspective also affected the understanding of knowledge, by questioning the rational basis for thinking (Hughes, [1958] 1979). It is in this field that the early Hamsun can be viewed as a pioneer, as I argue below.

From Modernist Art to Postmodernism in Social Discourse

Two main concepts capture some of the key aspects of modernist art: subjectivity (understood as an elaboration of the epistemological turn) and resolution (understood as differentiation or fragmentation), but from that point the roads virtually lead in all directions. The point I am making is that, in the many faces of modernist art and the ideologies that took nourishment from it, there were many different and conflicting positions. At the same time I think most with an insight into the topic will argue that modernist art has had an impact on society. We might need to talk about modernist art in plural form, since it takes many forms that move in different directions. On the other hand, few can point at exactly how some particular piece of art has influenced society.[14]

---

12   Both inspired by Søren Kierkegaard that made this existentialistic reflection, like '*dette Spil med Livet, denne Svimmelhed, idet Døden viser sig snart som noget uendeligt betydningsfuldt, snart som Intet*' ('this Play with Life, this Vertigo, as Death appears soon as something infinitely meaningful, sometimes as Nothing') [*my translation*]. Also: anticipating the theme of Milan Kundere, Søren Kierkegaard wrote: '*Naar nemlig Alle forene sig om paa alle Maader at gjøre Alt lettere, saa bliver der kun een Fare mulig, den nemlig, at Letheden blev saa stor, at den blev altfor let; saa bliver der kun eet Savn tilbage, om end endnu ikke følt, naar man vil savne Vanskeligheden.*' ('For when All unite in every Way to make Everything easier, then there is only one possible Danger, that the Lightness is so great that it is too easy; then there is only one Longing back, though not yet felt, when one will miss Difficulty [*my translation*]') Citations taken from http://www.sk.ku.dk/.

13   However, Foucault (1986) argues in the essay *Kant on Enlightenment and Revolution* that Kant really pioneered 'philosophy as a discourse of and upon modernity'. The argument is that Kant in the essay 'What is Enlightenment?' problematises the present and subsequently the foundation for thinking on philosophical questions.

14   As an example of how knowledge is developed and transformed between art and society: an artist (i.e., Marcel Duchamp) puts a non-functioning toilet in the middle of a room (Morris, 2006). An architect will never place the toilet in the middle of a room. That does not imply that art hasn't influenced architecture in order to think on new functional

So, referring to Duchamp's urinal and Robbe-Grillet's absurd film, what sense can we make out of their art? How does art relate to real life or to society? Is it Robbe-Grillet's comment that investigations are absurd, or of truth is non-existing or that Duchamp's urinal could be placed anywhere? And secondly, does it have any bearing on real life, societal activity? For instance, that we should rethink what is a crime, or what is a toilet? To say that art is only fantasy and has no relation to the rest of society, that it is a play within the artistic community, is not fully convincing, because it has references to real-life things. It provokes. It makes us reflect.

In an attempt to create a very simplified summary of these, I would use a distinction that Thomas Sowell has made, between what he called a limited (constrained) and an unlimited (unconstrained) vision. Sowell (1987) uses this distinction to identify the various positions within liberalism, but I choose to see it as a distinction that runs across different ideological positions. Modernism can be (mis-) interpreted and (mis-) understood from both perspectives, as liberating and liberal or totalitarian.

The distinction between the constrained and unconstrained is of course not new. In one of the works of the Austrian economist Joseph Schumpeter from 1911, in what we have called the modernist period, he talked about two perspectives on economic development: on the one hand the rational agent as the manager that optimises and streamlines production (developed by Frederick Taylor as a management philosophy, implemented by Henry Ford in the automobile industry, described as Taylorism and portrayed by Charlie Chaplin in the film *Modern Times*), on the other hand the entrepreneur, inventor and even rebellious actor who was to be creative and come up with new ideas (Schumpeter, 2008). In recent years, this work has been highlighted as a reference to the new, creative and entrepreneurial economy as I have already discussed in Chapter 5 and in Chapter 7.

Schumpeter himself saw this dualism in a larger social context and talked later about *creative destruction*, a concept that is futurist in style, meaning a form of development that is ground-breaking and unpredictable (Schumpeter, 2008). Schumpeter had captured the dilemma of modernism and saw how it played out in the economy. In other words, social visions, even if they are change- and modernisation-oriented, can take various forms, which I highlight in relation to (unlimited/unconstrained) goals on one side, and the change in the form of restrictions and the constrained on the other.

I choose to see modernist art as the inspiration for a series of unconstrained tendencies in Western society by the early 1900s. As the strongest expression of how this came to influence society, I choose to see postmodernism (Lyotard, 1984; Jameson, 1991).[15] The postmodern position has many other elements, not least when it comes to the idea that language is central to understanding the basis of our thinking. Society is, in postmodern thinking, often interpreted as language games and a discursive practice,

---

and non-functional relations. A similar example: Alan Robbe-Grillet in his novels and films portrays situations in which objects appear seemingly randomly and the person in the story tries to behave to 'make meaning' out of this encounter with 'meaningless' objects. The project can be seen as an existentialist, phenomenological exercise. In the film *La Belle Captive*, based on the novel of the same name by Alain Robbe-Grillet and René Magritte, there is a crime that is never solved, a Kafkaesque, absurd inspector that appears without giving us as viewers an understanding of what his project is, rooms that transform in contradiction to everything we know about the physical world and a timeframe that has been made totally illogical and chaotic. The story is referring to absurd paintings of René Magritte, and also references paintings such as Francisco Goya's *The Third of May 1808: The Execution of the Defenders of Madrid*. This is knowledge, but what relevance and relation does it have to other knowledge?

15 For example Gay (2009) and Bradbury and McFarlane (1991) argue that postmodernism is the social science and political parallel to modernist art.

but it is also inspired by modernist art.[16] And postmodernism has also become a trend in art (Adamson and Pavitt, 2011).

Foucault (2011), in the preface to *Anti-Oedipus* (the work by Gilles Deleuze and Félix Guattari), argues that surrealism is an important prerequisite for innovation in philosophy after the Second World War. Modernism, in the form of a 'meeting' between Freud and Marx, created a new prerequisite for social understanding. It allows for a claim of free political action, for freedom from the totalitarian, from a development that subverts to hierarchies, rejection of the traditional social categories, and general rejection of categories such as right and true. This is what we in practice today would call postmodernism.[17] For example, Lyotard writes:

> *A postmodern artist or writer is in the position of a philosopher: the text he writes, the work he produces are not in principle governed by pre-existing rules, they cannot be judged according to a predetermined judgment, by applying familiar categories to the text or to the work. Those rules and categories are what the work of art itself is looking for. (Lyotard, 1984)*

Resolution, one could call it, a resolution based on the argument that good and true must constitute itself. The community must find the categories it must assess their community after.[18] This process appears to be authentic, because you can explain and expose the choice you make.[19] I see modernist art as an early exponent of this thinking. This also represents a logical link to existentialism, understood as the existentialist perspective on the one hand, the dissolution of relationships and connection to the objective world on the other hand, which implies the reconstruction of the human being from its inner qualifications.[20]

Michel Foucault (1983) describes two main features that characterise art until the twentieth century and that refer to the relationship between art and the object in the world:[21] on the one hand, that there is the desire to represent the object, on the other the desire that art should be playing back to the object, that is, say something about it. In both cases, the work is subject to an object, standing in a hierarchical relationship to it. What happens in the surrealist art is that this link is abandoned. Avant-garde art had already launched this project, through seeing the work of art as something separate, not as a representative of something outside itself. In other words, it can be seen as a development of the aesthetic, as something floating, something unique in itself, as its own language.

Merleau-Ponty in his 1945 essay *Cézanne's Doubt* had argued that politics and philosophy could learn from what had been developed within art (Merleau-Ponty, 1989; Johnson, 1993). Derrida later developed his philosophy to a large degree based on literary

---

16 Rancière (2011) argues that postmodernism represents the surrender of modernist art. By adopting ideas from the aesthetics of art, postmodernism destroys the conditions for the independence of art.

17 Jameson (1977) makes a similar argument. He uses the phrase 'aesthetic populism' about postmodern culture.

18 According to Habermas (1987), this is actually the core of modernist, analysed already by Hegel.

19 This is a point that Critchley (2009) makes with reference to Derrida, that deconstruction actually is a very ethical imperative and links it to Levinas's theory on ethics.

20 I do not argue that this relation is causal, that avant-garde art leads to postmodernism. I merely point at the fact that some postmodern thinkers directly refer to the inspiration from modernist art.

21 Foucault in an article in *The Times Literary Supplement* (6 October 1961) argued that surrealism is art, and inspired Alain Robbe-Gillets' new novel (Robbe-Gillets, 1965; 1989), thereby making the link from painting to literature to philosophy.

or art criticism (Derrida, 1987; Thomassen, 1988). Subsequently, in postmodernist thinking, art is separated from society, but society copies what has been revealed by art, and art became at the centre of understanding the condition for social life. What are the dilemmas that this poses? In the following I discuss five cases.

CASE A: AESTHETICS AND POLITICS

Let us assume that the points I have made above are some of the features of modernist art in the early 1900s. What about the relation to society, and its norm, and where is the way forward? How do we end in an absurd approach to totalitarian ideologies? How is it that a liberating, subjective and individual approach leads to praise of totalitarian regimes? Is there a line from liberation to violence? Paul Johnson (1991, p. 306) refers to the fact that many modernists in art were admirers of fascism (such as Cocteau, Yeats, Eliot and Marinetti) and many also pro-fascists (such as Celine, Pound and Spengler). Many futurists were admirers of fascism and, according to Marjorie Perloff (2003), there were also many Italian futurists who sympathised with communism. The new ideologies were viewed as innovative. Paul Virilio argues that modern art between the wars such as Dadaism, German expressionism, Italian futurism, French surrealism and American abstract expressionism had developed, on the one hand, a response to alienation and, on the other, what he calls 'a taste of anti-human cruelty' (Virilio, 2003).[22]

Paradoxically it is liberation that stands as the benchmark here. The almost endless series of manifestos that were made (futuristic, Dadaists, vorticists, surrealists (Breton, 1924), to name a few) had a reference to the manifesto idea, that is, the *Communist Manifesto* of 1848.[23] They should be liberating, rejuvenating. For example, Marjorie Perloff notes that the futurists made: 'a short-lived but remarkable rapprochement between avant-garde aesthetic, radical politics, and popular culture' (Perloff, 2003).

Futurists were among those who called themselves avant-garde during the early 1900s. They were crossing the old borders (in society) but they also opened up new opportunities. What gave art and artists that role? What had liberated them and made it legitimate for them to change the existing boundaries? The roots are probably, as I have argued, back to the earlier part of the 1800s, to Nietzsche and Schopenhauer. The differentiation of the various social spheres is a key. Aesthetics as liberated from ethics, art for art's sake, or the full liberalisation of the aesthetic, is the key.[24]

It is a historical fact that Italian futurism became linked to fascism, French surrealism to communism, and German expressionism to Nazism. Based on the subjectivist foundation of modernist art, how was that possible? One way of explaining it is to say that, as modernists defied the existing order of society, they were looking for an alternative order. Ideologies in the early 1900s provided these alternatives. Also, it is a fact that fascists, communists and Nazis saw in modernist art that it exposed the decadence and desolation of capitalist, bourgeois society, and in their view this was supporting a call for revolution.

---

22   See the discussion related to Pasolini's film *Salto*.

23   See Danchev (2011), who has identified 100 artists' manifestos.

24   Still Andre Gide in *The Immoralist* argues on the one hand that 'the problems of art should find it solutions in art', on the other hand write a novel about a homosexual relationship that provokes society. Furthermore, it is interesting to note the impact Gide's work had on the young Jacque Derrida (see Peeters, 2010).

The futurists used aesthetics devolution as one of their arguments. A call for a new aesthetics was developed and supported, as well as the aesthetics of war and violence. They also presented visions for a new future. In retrospect, we may choose to see some of this as innovation. Art at the beginning of the 1900s, in the modernist period, inspired innovations in other fields. Architecture, design and technical solutions were important parts of this future project.[25] They had a dream of creating a new social reality.[26] Aesthetics was the centre of attention; however, also in the form of violence and brutality that came naturally with social change, and which was admired aesthetically. This theme has tracks into fascism. This is parallel to what by Schumpeter referred to as *creative destruction*.

We can consider Benedetto Croce and Giovanni Gentile's analysis of the interface between politics, aesthetics and ethics, an analysis that in different ways inspired fascism, as a recognition of the symbolic and irrational. Both Croce and Gentile argued in favour of recreating the relationship between ethics, aesthetics (culture) and state (the ethical state), even if Croce gradually distanced himself from fascism, while Gentile became a fascist ideologist (Harris, 1960).[27]

Goebbels had some admiration for German expressionist art.[28] As also some of the artists had Nazi sympathies, it became rather incomprehensible for them when Hitler in 1937 exposed them as *Entartete Kunst*.[29] Likewise, Lenin seemingly had some interest and supported modernist theatre, art and music, and artists saw communist Russia as a playground for modernist art[30] until the Moscow processes.

This should seemingly imply contradictions, not only between art and totalitarian ideologies, but also between different ideologies. How can we explain that? One key is Lukács article on German expressionism from 1934 that inspired a debate between him and, among others, Benjamin, Brecht, Block and Adorno (see Adorno et al., 1977). Lukács' argument was that expressionism implied a revolt against reason, and some type of mysticism that went hand in hand with the irrational politics of Nazism. On the other hand, he argues that modernist art is not really a revolt against rationalism, rather an attempt to reach a more realistic understanding of society.[31] Thereby he revealed one of

---

25   Jameson (1991) argues that modern architecture (in the spirit of futurism) led to: 'destruction of the fabric of the traditional city and of its old neighbourhood culture.' This architectural form has even got its own name: brutalist architecture. See article in *San Francisco Chronicle* (3 March 2013) 'Brutalism looks better with age'. In Godard's *2 or 3 Things I Know About Her* (1967), one of the classic new wave films, Juliette living in a modern suburban landscape of concrete buildings is portrayed by her daily routines that include taking her daughter to kindergarten, going to the hairdresser, chatting with a friend at a café, selling sex, doing some shopping, and going home to cook dinner, all done with the same lack of passion. It is modernity without limitations, without passion and, one would say, without meaning. The apathy of people in the urban landscape resembles the pictures of Edward Hopper.

26   In the exhibition *Bauhaus – Art as living*, Barbican Art Gallery 2012, the argument is that there was a strong link between German expressionist art, and later cubism and abstractionism on the one hand, and Bauhaus social constructivism (Marxism) in designing a new social reality. It is a paradox that some of the architectural environments made by the Bauhaus-inspired architecture become rather gloomy contexts for Italian and new wave films in the 1950 and 1960s, such as the films by Antonioni and Godard.

27   In the January/February 2012 issue of *Foreign Affairs*, articles by both Gentile and Croce are presented in a large retrospective section called *The Clash of Ideas*.

28   See Ernest Block's essay *Discussing Expressionism* from 1938, reprinted in Adorno et al. (1977).

29   For example, it is said about Paul Klee that he did not understand that the exhibition in 1937 was an insult.

30   In the 1930s artists such as Picasso and Breton as well as Nordahl Grieg hailed the Soviet Union.

31   Some of the debate on this related to abstractionism in art in relation to the objective. Historically, abstractionism was a reaction to the subjective, and a search of the rational and the objective. This is in contrast and partly in dilemma with what has been previously said about subjectivity. Lukács' argument was that abstraction was an analysis of the real and a way to get rid of mysticism; his communist opponents argued that it was elitist and against the building of a communist culture. See Adorno (1994) for discussion on Dmitri Shostakovich in relation to the Soviet state: the criticism

modernism's internal contradictions. Lukács thought he could defend modernist art in relation to communism.

It is this attempt that Adorno finds extremely apologetic. Adorno's argument is that art and politics are not the same and should not be the same, although art is part of society. The confusion of art and ideology is, for Adorno, the great fault that led Lukács from his early sharp analysis of modern art to become a petty apologist for communism (Adorno et al., 1977). What became more and more apparent after the Second World War was that totalitarian ideologies could hardly be in accordance with the subjective and devolutionary aspect of modernism.[32]

Adorno and Horkheimer (2010) had tried to develop arguments that would demark the right and the wrong kind on modernism. Their argument was to show the Janus face of enlightenment and more particularly how modernist art could decay into fascism. They tried to rescue modernist art from fascism.[33] Postmodernism, one could say, provided a way out, presenting an unconstrained vision.

CASE B: HAMSUN AND IBSEN: CRITICISM'S DIFFERENT FORMS

Ibsen and Hamsun were early exponents of modernist art (Gay, 2009). They both brought forward new ideas, and thereby also acted as critics of the prevailing ideas of their contemporaries. Through their writing, the two addressed different aspects of current standards in the Western world (mainly by using Norway as a case of the modernisation process in society at the end of the 1800s), and where they focus attention on what would later become the new conflict lines in modern society. Their criticism went along various dimensions, and Hamsun emerged as a strong critic of Ibsen, but common to them was that they asked important questions about aspects of modern society as it was starting to take shape from the middle of the 1800s. The tension between Ibsen and Hamsun tells us something about the inherent contradiction of modernism, and hence its difficulty.

Hamsun's early works and Ibsen's later works are both modern and constructivist, in the sense that they change not only the content but also the rules for the arts (the text) they create: the modern drama (Joyce, 2000); the modern novel (Lunden, 2008). Without in any way going in depth in the analysis of their literature, one can detect a difference in the way social issues are addressed by the two. Paul Auster (1997) writes about Hamsun's *Hunger*:

> *Hamsun's character systematically unburdens himself of every belief in every system, and in the end, by means of hunger he has inflicted upon himself, he arrives at nothing. There is nothing to keep him going – and yet he keeps on going. He walks straight into the twentieth century. (Auster, 1997, p. 20)*

---

of his formalism counter claim (which he to some extent bent down) on the social-realistic (normative) art. This demand that art should be edifying is a difficult and dangerous exercise. Thomas Mann in *Der Tod in Venedig* had portrayed a gloomy vision for modernist art. In Luchino Visconti's filming of the novel in 1971, there is a deliberate reference to Gustav Mahler as the role model for the main character in the novel Gustav von Aschenbach, who was liberated from his depression in the meeting with the frivolous Venice, but that this also leads to his death.

32   Similar reflections to Adorno's are made by George Orwell in the essay 'Inside the Wale' (1940), which deals with Henry Miller's controversial book *Tropic of Cancer*. See Orwell (1957).

33   Polanyi and Prosch (1975) make a similar comment on modernist art: that it decayed into fascism. One further example is Adorno's discussion of Schönberg, who he argued had gone from modernism to fascism in his music. This became a role figure for Thomas Mann in his *Doctor Faustus* (Fetzer, 1996).

Hamsun's early works inspired Beckett and his modernist, minimalist, existential novels (Marcus, 2007), and created a reference for other existentialist literature, such as Sartre or Miller.[34] It is an art that explores the inner, existential universe.

As many have pointed out, there is no direct political message to read out of Hamsun's literature. Hamsun, as a political debater, often took positions that were contrary to his fictional characters. Heroes' stances and opinions in his novels went against Hamsun's own. I suppose one way to interpret it is that his literature did not intend to argue against society, but to explore it; another is to see it as modernist in the sense that the aesthetics and ethics are separated. A third is to argue that Hamsun's aesthetic denunciation of contemporary society might have its parallel in Hamsun's aesthetics of politics.

Social relevance is more direct and visible in Ibsen's work. When Ibsen's *Ghosts* was played for the first time in London in 1891, it was met with denunciations and was dismissed and ridiculed (Gay, 2009). What was the point in exposing this poor and tragic soul? Today, it is not very controversial to see *A Doll's House* as an analysis of the individual in relation to society's norms,[35] *An Enemy of the People* as an analysis of democracy, and *Ghosts* as an existential drama. Ibsen lets his characters play out their personal dilemmas and moral conflicts in direct contrast to society's norms and structures. He makes a direct link between the two and provokes this relation.

Ibsen's modernist art period relates primarily to his late symbolic pieces such as *The Master Builder* (Bygmester Solness) and *John Gabriel Borkman*. *A Doll's House* (Et Dukkehjem) can be ranked here, too, because Ibsen shows how strong women individually break the rules and conventions, and Nora behaves in a non-human way by abandoning her children. It is an attack against the institution of family. *Hedda Gabler* breaks the norms, too, but she punishes herself. Nora, on the other hand, is not punished. Somebody could say that the norms and rules (against which Nora's revolt is oriented) are obsolete and outmoded, and therefore unjust, but they did not. The same relates to *Rosmersholm*.[36] Also, *The Lady from the Sea* (Fruen fra Havet) deals with the problem of individual freedom, but Ellida wants only to know that she is not coerced, in order that she could decide genuinely and freely. But she does not misuse this freedom; she stays with her husband.[37]

But, as was discussed by James Joyce (Joyce, 2000), what was important and new in Ibsen's drama was not just content, but the shape and use of drama, and the ground rules for the drama. In this sense it is natural to see both Hamsun and Ibsen as modernists, although they play different roles in this field. Two concepts can characterise the main subject of modernist art: *subjectivity* and *resolution*,[38] implying fragmentation of social structure.

---

34   Henry Miller in *A Tropic of Cancer* has many references to Hamsun and his main character wanders around in Paris, hungry, as a pendant to Hamsun's *Hunger*.

35   In *Ragtime*, Doctorov let the anarchist Emma Goldman say: '[...] Ibsen in whose work lay all the instruments for the radical dissection of society.'

36   A play that Alain Resnais uses as a reference in his 1960 film, *Last Year in Marienbad*, a film that introduced the existential New Wave.

37   These are points adapted from Jan Pavlik. See also Williams (1989). Pinkney (1989) argues that Ibsen's *When We Dead Awaken* is his most expressionist play.

38   Gay (2009) uses other but similar terms. He talks about the two dimensions: *the lure of heresy* (which parallels my term resolution) and *self-scrutiny* (which parallels my term subjectivity). Williams (1989) sees the revolt against conformity as a theme of modernist art. Again I see this as parallel to my terms subjectivity and resolution.

CASE C: ART AND CONSUMERIST SOCIETY

Postmodernism implied a new perspective on the art–society relation.[39] Art had become absorbed into consumerist society (Adorno et al., 1977; Jameson, 1977; Baudrillard, 2005; Boltanski and Chiapello, 2005; Bauman, 2007). Already *Dialectic of Enlightenment* (German: Dialektik der Aufklärung) by Max Horkheimer and Theodor W. Adorno (first appearance in 1944) had argued that modern, mass production and consumerist society had created new conditions for art (Adorno and Horkheimer, 2010).

Art had become consumerist production, or as Adorno later wrote, art is '... decaying into cultural commodities' (Adorno et al., 1977, p. 177). Modernist art had defied society's celebration of art (futurists planned to bomb the Louvre!) but paradoxically co-develops with the emergence and expansion of the art market (Gay, 2009).

Baudrillard (2005) argued that the new, borderless capitalism posed a new form of illusion. He argued, for example, that the term illusion is meaningless when you do not have anything to dream about, or desire, when you have nothing to conceal. For example, pornography deteriorates the erotic. When art is not in a relationship to something else, is taken out of context, it is all or nothing. The boundaryless becomes meaningless. By not going to be a representative of something in the world, art has given away the opportunity to be critical of society, argues Baudrillard.[40]

In his provocative essay from 1996, Baudrillard attacks contemporary art on its own grounds. He claimed that art had failed or abandoned its own grounds (Baudrillard, 2005). Andy Warhol may stand as representative of this: his art has *become* products, consumer goods, not only about products and consumer goods. The boundaries between them are subsequently blurred. The problem is not Disneyland as a contrast to the society, a sort of society, the problem is that society has become Disneyland; the problem is not art as critical, unattached, making its own rules; the problem is that society as such is this,[41] and thereby has washed out borders of art.

Baudrillard accuses Warhol (and pop art) for just complying with this consumerist development (as they expose fakes of a fake society, like the Campbell Soup box), and do not use the opportunity to develop a new role of art in going beyond this. Art has become nil, nothing, just absorbed into the rest of consumerist society.

---

39   It is the argument of Rancière (2011) that the way modernist art influences society, in spite of its call to independence, was through the aesthetics. Postmodern society has adopted an aesthetic dimension that has blurred the relation between art and society.

40   Badiou (2005) observes that one of the main battlegrounds for modernist art has been the area of sexuality. To use it as an example: while Norman Mailer (2004) writes that he will support pornography (and boxing!) because it (at least) is honest, Baudrillard sees this kind of liberation as meaningless, as a prevention of the authentic, as coercion. Two interpretations of the same phenomenon, in other words: liberation and coercion. It is e relevant debate. For example Julie Burchill in an article in the *International Independent* (12 May 2011) on boxing as pornography writes '... I still have more respect for someone who pays money to watch pay-per-view porn or a live sex show than I do for someone who pays to watch one man injure another ...' How do we compare these expositions and where is the limit between artistic expression, innovative exploration and obscenity? For example Tinto Brass's film *Lady of the Night* plays with the same dualism between boxing and eroticism, thereby provoking the topic of the relationship between sexuality and violence. As a side note: if you go into a *Narvesen* newsstand today and see what they offer during the vignette erotica (a picture of how the borders between acceptability and obscurity is regarded in today's society) you will find that it's nudity in all possible forms, of all sexes and at almost all ages. In truth, diversity! Again, is it liberating, innovative? Probably the category pornography is too broad if you want to discuss the content, quality, etc. The diversity suggests that there are many forms, many different quality levels, and many versions, and perhaps that pornography has become 'democratic'.

41   A similar analysis of contemporary society is found in the recent work by Leo Tandrup (*Det oppreiset mennesket I-III*, Århus Universitetsforlag 2012); life as lonely and superficial (see: Kai Sølander, *Weekendavisen* 29 July 2012).

Identity in modernist society is self-constituted (Giddens, 1995); consumption is part of a new, inauthentic self-understanding (Baumann, 2007). Aesthetics in politics is no longer restricted to fascism; it applies to the entire political life. The human liberation and deconstruction has become pornography (Baudrillard, 2005; Boltanski and Chiapello, 2005). This argument provokes some of the liberating ideas of modernist art.

As liberation had been an important element in modernist art, crossing borders to artificial restriction such as sexuality and definitions of what is classified as pornography had also been part of this art movement (Badiou, 2005). Recall trials on accusation of pornography or obscenity against for instance James Joyce's *Ulysses* (1922), Henry Miller's *Tropic of Cancer* (1934), and later Alan Ginsburg's *Howl* (1955). As art had crossed some of these barriers, it had political implications, as supporting the *sexual revolution*, but also inspired philosophical discussion exploring the body. Merleau-Ponty's (1945) study of the body had tried to develop a link between the existential and the physical.[42] George Bataille,[43] who was a member of the surrealist group of Brenton, in his 1957 book *Eroticism* (Bataille, 2006) calls nakedness discontinuity. Discontinuity, because it strips the human naked, in the sense that all the things we possess and use to form our person, is taken away. The naked I is then an image of the existential I, one could say.[44] He furthermore links eroticism to death and to the call for the divide, the myth of Orpheus being a reference here. But there is also a link towards violence through (religious) obsession and sacrifice.[45] Deleuze (1991) sees the works of Sade and Sacher-Masoch as important analysis of cruelty and dehumanisation.[46] These are themes that have been explored back into art. Subsequently, one can see in modernist art that the border between nakedness, eroticism and pornography is exposed and analysed (Solana, 2009). The unrestricting of societies' moralising on sexuality and pornography is a precondition for this exploration.[47]

CASE D: ART AND MARKET

The relation between art and market is, as argued above, complex. Adorno (1994) discusses, among other things, the innovative in Stravinsky and Schönberg, in relation to impressionism, intuition, phenomenology and further how it has inspired and been adopted by modern marketing and popular culture. Therefore Adorno's project was to rescue art both from fascism and from the market.

Cubism in art and decomposition in philosophy have undoubtedly affected how we currently think about organisations (Cooke, 2002). Modern (postmodern) organisations

---

42   See Merleau-Ponty (1945) about the body's 'permanence' (based on Proust), was a response to the temporal and fragmented in modern society, or in Husserl's terminology, 'epoché', the existential moment.

43   Habermas (1987) sees Bataille as a continuation of Nietzsche. As Nietzsche, he explores the limits to aesthetics.

44   Some have seen Lucian Freud's portraits as exemplification of this. Lucian Freud, who was the grandson of Sigmund Freud, is also seen in relation to Merleau-Ponty. This relation also had a personal side, as Sonia Mary Brownell (1918–1980), the second and last wife of George Orwell, later had relationships with both Lucian Freud and Maurice Merleau-Ponty (source: Wikipedia).

45   Bataille's analysis can be seen in the perspective of exploring the limits to subjectivity in society. Drawing on surrealism and its expository of the artificial limitations to human existence in contemporary society, Bataille takes this further in a scientific investigation into how the limits to exposing the person (their emotions, sentiments, sexuality) is constructed in society (Habermas, 1987).

46   Similar arguments are given by Knausgård (2013). He argues on the one hand that a discussion of limits to cruelty in literature and art should be debated, on the other hand that society is on the wrong track if it should ban such art.

47   Badiou (2012) argues that sensuality was an important dimension in the argument developed by French philosophy after the Second World War.

could probably not be understood without the development in art between the World Wars (Cooper and Burrell, 1988). Phenomenology in social science (Merleau-Ponty, 1989) would probably not exist without the precursor of existential philosophy, and impressionism in art. This in turn has affected how we think around themes such as social services, and treatment of people who need help or care.

Also, development in areas such as fashion trends, marketing and knowledge economy (Cooke, 2002) can be attributed to modernist art and the understanding of the postmodern. Some of the arguments in Croce, in his vision for a cultural community, can be seen again in what is called the cultural economy. What one was not able to create through the political system is reinterpreted and realised by the capitalist market system (Boltanski and Chiapello, 2005).

Fragmentation and decomposition have inspired new links of phenomena that have created innovative solutions and understanding of organisations (Cooper and Burrell, 1988). Apple Corporation may be seen as an exponent of this; where lifestyle and technology and new forms of behaviour have been engineered in a way that probably would have impressed even the most dedicated futurists. Criticism of capitalism also refers to the transaction economy as fragmented and incoherent. That is, capitalism allows for the temporary. However, the temporary is also used as a reference to the authentic – *the moment of truth*.

Marxist analysis argues that the instrumental use of art, art as experience, art as entertainment or as community development can easily get to misappropriate the unresolved and important ideological, conceptual and value-based discussions that modernism highlights. Boltanski and Chiapello (2005) criticise capitalism for its duplicity and inauthenticity, in line with Baudrillard (2005), who criticises the market where art becomes instrumental, rather than meaningful. Boltanski and Chiapello (2005) go further to argue that the market does not offer liberation, but in and through its fabrication, a new form of oppression. We are victims of the oppression of market forces, they argue. The new type of artistic criticism, which we see as part of this market economy, or culture economy, teams up with this oppression. Only when art realises this will it be open to a truly artistic criticism, they argue.[48]

Bourdieu (1993), on the other hand, rejects this type of analysis. Bourdieu looks at Andy Warhol as much as an avant-garde of his time as were the impressionists in their time. For Bourdieu, art is a field that plays in relation to other social fields. It is a social phenomenon that must be understood historically and structurally.[49] However, the complex relation between art and market is acknowledged. Habermas's discussion of the

---

48   This view is not unlike the kind of criticism that many intellectuals have launched against Western civil society. Hannah Arendt's *The Human Condition* from 1958 addresses this. Film art in the post-War period, from Luis Buñuel's *Discreet Charm of the Bourgeoisie* to Fassbinder's *BDR Trilogy* stand for me as images of this: simply put: disclosure of the bourgeois deception. Ibsen's *A Doll's House* and *An Enemy of the People* are not far away in mind when watching these movies or reading Hannah Arendt.

49   However, this implies some sort of structuring of the art field. For example, Bjarne Melgaard's provocative art has made headlines as: 'Collectors in line for "pedo art". Suggestions of paedophilia and sexual assault do not scare Norwegian art collectors' (*Dagbladet*, 21 December 2009). Is there a free zone for art or is this something our community should have an opinion about? Another example: *The Independent* (23 February 2011) writes under the headline 'The artist who crossed the line', about the Russian art collective Voina. They refer to themselves as futurists and have conducted a series of stunts that the authorities described as pure vandalism. What is crossing the line, where is the line, who sets the line? Similarly, a debate started in Denmark when a theatre group wanted to make a play based on Breivik's manifesto. Among commentators, Ole Thyssen defended the play because it is aesthetics and outside the realm of politics (*Berlingske Tidende*, 20 January 2012). It is at the intersection of politics and art that these lines are drawn (Knausgård, 2013). That's what makes this a difficult relation in the modern.

life-world versus the system world provides an image that associates art as threatened by the market, but still distinguishes the two.

A more positive approach is found in Richard Florida's theories about the use of culture as a vital part of the creative economy, and to create an attractive community (Florida, 2002; 2005), as discussed in Chapter 7. One would have expected Florida to reflect on Adorno's perspective on the cultural industry (Adorno, 1991). However, he does not acknowledge the challenge Adorno had described. Also Bourdieu (1993) rejects Adorno's static image. He chooses to see art as a social activity and as a social field. Moreover, he sees that this field stands in relation to other fields: market and politics. The field is changing over time; what once was the avant-garde is now regarded as conventional; the new move in contrast to and in dialogue with the old. Bourdieu's perspective allows for a differentiation of various social spheres, including the various social levels. The artistic sphere is not threatened, because it differentiates itself (at least in a liberal society) by highlighting its autonomy.

The conservative Daniel Bell (1973; 1978) looked at the avant-garde art as destructive in terms of society's culture. Bell argued for a differentiation between culture and market. That is, the cultural life is a sphere outside the market. We can live a cultural life that is not directly related to doing work. Culture's values are precisely those that contribute to giving meaning to life (such as religion), and that is something we develop and enjoy outside of work and the market. He described the argument of the avant-garde culture, namely criticism and challenging of society and economy as pointless and destructive.[50] It is this view of culture as a distinct, separate domain that Florida (2005) criticises.[51] Florida's point is that culture has, and will have, a creative impact on the economy, both directly (as a contribution to innovation) and indirectly, as a contribution to making attractive homes and cities. Thus, he does not reflect on art as a discourse of modern society; rather he sees it as an activity and an attraction in society. In other words: perspectives from both right and left sides of the political spectrum use various aspects of modernist art in their arguments. Opponents and fans are on both sides.

CASE E: MODERNISM, PLURALISM AND THE AUTONOMY OF ART IN CONTEMPORARY SOCIETY

Following the discussion so far, a core issue becomes the autonomy of art. Autonomy of art can be understood in different ways. I would like to highlight two: autonomy, understood as an inner dialogue, and autonomy, understood as the (lack of) relationship to other social spheres. The discussion of autonomy has often been about the latter. I will therefore comment on it first.

Autonomy of art in this understanding is about the liberation of art from the artist. Art for art's sake is about art as it stands on its own, not as an expression of the artist's mind or feelings, not as a manifestation of a psychology, not as a representation of something else, but as something separate, something for themselves in dialogue with other artworks, as a separate call. The artwork as the artist's own voice in society gives a different understanding of art than that the work of art is something completely

---

50   See Landauer (1996), who refers to the debate in the USA after the Second World War where politicians, led by President Truman, attracted modern art.

51   I have discussed this further in Johnsen (2010).

autonomous. It also provides different understandings of the question about art and art's role in society (Goldsmith, 1999).

Autonomy as inner dialogue can be understood as a discursive perspective on art. Pålshaugen (2010) refers to Husserl and Derrida in the discussion of images that refer to images, which refers to images. Derrida (1987) elaborates on this, arguing that art develops its own internal language that is based on references to references. My example is taken from painting, where you can see an infinite number of images from Titan's *Venus* via Goya's *Maja* to Manet's *Olympia* and beyond, that develops an internal dialogue, and a language that stretches out in new symbolic directions.[52] Another example: Picasso was in a near dialogue with Diego Velázquez. When one sees his images, one can see them as political comments, while they may in fact be part of a historic dialogue.[53]

Art's devolution implies that art is its own discourse: within what limits? How free-standing is art in relation to provocations? German expressionism, called by the Nazis *Entartete art*, and which was ridiculed, persecuted and criminalised by Nazism, was to a large degree focused on brutality. Heavily influenced by impressions from the First World War's monstrosity, its aim was to show brutality. Where is the limit when it comes to admire or be obsessed with brutality?[54]

If we think of art in society in a postmodernist perspective, we will just consider it as inner dialogues that structure the field itself. On the other hand, both impressionism in art and philosophy of pragmatism (see for example John Dewey (1980)) are legitimate children of modernism. Both emphasise the individual, the immediate experience; it corresponds to that foundation of understanding. Both repeal the link to metaphysics, to the Cartesian ontology, or the Hegelian ideology. The challenge lies in the art as an expert system in relation to the democratisation of art.

This is a major point in Jameson's (1991) analysis. Decomposition of aesthetics, ethics and politics have led to new structures and new variants of the ethical state lifted out of the social/historical context and perhaps explains why it is so difficult to structure the art field through cultural policy.

Richard Rorty, in a strong attack on postmodernist (especially Derrida's) reading of modernist art, makes a dualism between the private and the public (Rorty, 1989).[55]

---

52   For example, the Moroccan photo artist Ella Essaydi presented a photo at the exhibition Paris Photo in Carrrousel Louvre, Paris in 2009 called *les Femmes au Maroc*, posing as Venus. *Aftenposten* on 12 February published a photo by Brent Stirton awarded the best photo in the world in 2011, showing the Ukrainian drug user and prostitute Maria posing in the position of Venus/Olympia. Sacher-Masoch (1991 [1870]) used Titan's painting as reference to his *Venus in Furs*, thereby contributing to the ambiguity of this character.

53   The question of how political Picasso 'really' was is discussed by John Richardson, in an article in the *New York Review*, 25 November 2010, titled: 'How Political Was Picasso?' His thesis is that Picasso was not particularly political, and among others negotiated with the Franco regime on a celebration of his 75th birthday.

54   Today, this art is given great interest in the major art venues around the world, collecting large amounts of visitors without any apparent provocation. There is certainly no one who shows up to protest as far as I have registered, the expression of disgust, although it appears that is shocking. I was able to visit MoMA's comprehensive exhibition on German Expressionism in April 2011. Even on an ordinary weekday the show was visited by large crowds. In any case, I did not register any strong reaction when I visited the MoMA. The idea lives still in your head when you walk around on this show: what does this art say to me? Why do I (and thousands of others) want to see it, and even pay to see it? Perhaps this particular art, as a result of the years, has been transformed from politics to aesthetics. Or maybe what makes it art is that it is part of a dialogue with other art.

55   This is not a direct parallel to Habermas's distinction between life-world and system world. In Habermas the system world and life-world are both part of the same 'form'. There is also a relationship between them. The 'system' around us affects our life-world, and even invades our life-world. The discussion between Habermas, Derrida and Rorty is presented in Thomassen (1988).

The private sphere and public sphere are two completely independent discourses. The validity of the one has nothing to do with the validity of the other, he argues. What is right for me does not need to have any significance or relevance to what should be valid norms in society (although through the principle of freedom that I enjoy, it does). Rorty's argument is to distinguish what he calls *the private ironist* and *the public liberal* (Rorty, 1989).

Rorty furthermore argues that the entire postmodern project belongs to what he calls a private scepticism perspective. It addresses the existential questions and discusses the individual and his circumstances. It has relevance to understanding the self in the world. In that sense it is liberating. It answers the more personal issues that art has helped to shed light on, and which denies that there is one (personal) opinion, one (personal) truth and one (personal) form to live one's life. The right, truth, as something universal and true for all individuals on a subjective level, has been thoroughly analysed and rejected, he argues.

According to Rorty, although this private perspective is correct, it is not true that this perspective is valid when we ask the question: how should we organise society? The public liberal is the critical questioner who tries to find the answer to what is needed to ensure a free, liberal society. It is a question that must be addressed in other discourses than those presented by deconstruction and the postmodern.

The Difficulty with Modernist Criticism

In this chapter I have tried to show with examples how the relation between modernist art and philosophy and politics has developed over the last decades. I have tried to argue that modernist art represents inner contradictions and different strategies towards society (illustrated in cases A and B). I have also tried to discuss how modernist art both criticises society but also influences the development and is integrated into society (cases C and D). Modernist art calls for the autonomy of art, but is also challenging society (case E).

Modernist art creates conflicts and dilemmas in relation to society, both on a personal, subjective level, and related to social structure and politics. The reason is that the principles of modernist art, and the provocations that it represents in relation to the traditional, imply that one sees conflicting interpretations when it is transferred to the practical and political spheres. The difficulty with modernist art, in other words, is that it plays into the social field a variety of topics and perspectives that are both open to innovation and creativity, but also create new tensions and dilemmas.

The relation between art and society represents a dilemma – between the autonomy of art on the one hand, and the integrated relation between art and society on the other. How can we make sense of this dilemma, and argue for an unconstrained social vision? I have argued that modernist art has been of importance for social development in Western societies in the twentieth century, although I have also pointed at its destructive elements. It has inspired philosophy and political thinking that has questioned the foundation of modern society. I have defined modernist art's criticism from two main concepts: subjectivity (a new epistemology) and resolution (questioning about ontology). I have tried to show that different understandings and misunderstandings of them, and discussions about them, have given different interpretations of the modernist perspective.

I have chosen to distinguish between a limited (totalitarian) understanding and an unrestricted (liberal) understanding, and between a private (life-world) and political (system world) perspective. I have argued for a decoupling of the systemic from the private. Key in what I have argued is that modernist art is still a source of important conceptual issues in society, and that a discussion about this will be enriched by readdressing those who helped bring forth this perspective. One of the great social innovations that modernist art contributed with was the separation (liberation) of art from society, in line with the liberation of institutions such as the press and the university.[56] It is, as I have argued, a difficult issue, but important.

I think an important factor in all social thinking is to avoid a form of reductionism where everything is reduced to the categories of the same guiding principle. Pluralism and liberality in society requires a polyphonic basis, i.e., we have different ontologies.[57] Issues related to our existential basis are of a different character than issues related to social structure. On the other hand, I would not argue that there should be no interest or relevance to society of what happens in art. In that case, art is reduced to entertainment or personal reflection. So, how do we solve this dilemma?

Given a differentiation in society, the cultural debate would be about how the differentiated spheres discursively challenge and influence each other. They will all refer to meta discourses on what we consider to be good and correct. It is a perspective that implies that the debate on social values is not a finished project, it is something that has to be readdressed and discussed continuously. Modernist art's breakthrough has undoubtedly influenced the development of society, but we are not finished with the questions about the structure of society, or what should be the prevailing values. An important line of conflict runs between the constrained and the unconstrained vision.

Modernist art challenges us in today's modern society. A further discussion of the difficult modernist criticism can be based on two important tensions in the modern project: the tension between the instrumental and the existential; and between the ethical and the aesthetic. We find these tensions in several disciplines even today. We can now see the tension in discussions about technology (tension between science and culture), economics (a field of tension between community and self-interest, between ethics and benefits), social (tension between culture as economic development and social criticism), and philosophy (e.g. the interaction between philosophy and literature).[58]

---

56   My argument is close to Karl Ove Knausgård (2013), who in a recent article argues for the autonomy of art. His argument is that society should debate issues of morality and ethics, but not thereby restrict art in its exploration of these themes.

57   I am well aware of the criticisms postmodernism would pose against such a perspective: on what ground do you define different ontologies? The perspective I develop here has a lot in common with Burrell and Morgan (1979); in a now classic analysis, they defined different paradigms in order to understand organisations. The tension is between a rational functionalism (the more rationalistic perspective associated with the modern) and what they call radical humanism. These paradigms are based on different basic understandings and cannot in principle be 'combined', yet they live side by side in organisational understanding. In a pluralistic understanding of society, different paradigms (visions) exist in parallel. That does not mean they are not problematic and create tension. Bauman (1989) discusses the individual as independent-minded and reflective, subjective and, not the least, fully human, responsible for the systems and structures that govern the individual's life, often in a cruel manner. Tensions are also to some extent parallel to Habermas's discussion about the tension between life-world and system world, although Habermas's project is to integrate these perspectives, and not discussing them as different paradigms. Burrell and Morgan's perspective allows us to see this, not only as opposites, but as parallel perspectives (paradigms). Organisations can be thought of as functional systems, but also as a human community. The diversity of shapes can be attributed to the development of knowledge as the conflict between different systems of thought.

58   Adorno wrote just after the Second World War: 'The autonomy of works of art, which of course rarely ever predominated in a pure form, and was always permeated by a constellation of effects, is tendentially eliminated by

I take a position that is based on Max Weber (1978) and that the sociologists and political thinkers such as Habermas (1997), Bourdieu (1993), Luhmann (1995) and Giddens (1984) have as a reference, where art and culture are their own structures or spheres of society; that there is basically a differentiation between different social spheres. The arguments vary: Habermas argues for a distinction between life-world, the social world and the world system, and these have different validity standards, but they are still part of the same whole. Bourdieu looks at various social domains as structures that establish the legitimacy of different forms. Giddens differentiates between the intimate and the world of structures and social systems. In modernity, he argues, the individual has been set freer, but also gained greater uncertainty in relation to structures and systems. Luhmann looks at the social subsystems such as autonomous systems. They relate to others, but are not necessarily dependent on other systems. One example is the art system, which can live independent of changing political systems and other systems in the community, but that can also be influenced by them without communicating with them directly. The common denominator for all four is a form of differentiation of various social spheres.

Conclusion

Modernist art is and has been criticised for its provocations, its immorality and for its sympathies with totalitarian ideologies. My discussion has tried to demonstrate that modernist art covers a complex and inconsistent field of positions. There are certain things they have in common, where as I have highlighted subjectivity and resolution. However, artists and groups of artists have interpreted these things very differently.

Some modernist art provoked society and challenges both moral and legal border. I choose to see modernist art as a discourse on modernity, and as a voice in society. I therefore reject the idea that art only belongs to personal reflection. It implies that I see art as part of a social knowledge development process. This of course is not unproblematic, not least in the discussion of the autonomy of art and arts independence. How can we deal with that?

Modernism's ambiguity means, in my view, that the art–society relationship must be understood as a discursive field. Important questions are then: how can different discursive spheres communicate with each other? What binds them together? How do they affect each other? What are their internal governance mechanisms? These are central issues in the cultural/social debate. Giddens (1984) talks about concepts that have transformed: a good example is the concept of trust which has different meanings in different systems. Habermas (1997) talks about different validity claims. Bourdieu (1993) speaks of varying legitimacy, habitus and social capital in different spheres. Social capital from one sphere cannot simply be transferred to another sphere (field). Luhmann (1995) looks at social systems as knowledge systems: they have borders to others but consist of inner interpretations.

From this we see that the arguments in these discourses intersect. The point here is not to argue either for or against *modernists' art criticism* of modern rationality and realism. Liberation, autonomy of art, and the economy and society discourse in general

---

cultural industry, with or without the conscious will of those in control' (Adorno, 1991, p. 99). Perspectives that draw on Adorno put authentic art in contrast to mass culture, culture industry and market.

(culture differentiation) are all elements and debates that are connected in various ways. In each of these areas we can point out the relevance of how representatives of modernist art address the challenges and difficulties.

I will maintain a pluralist perspective: art cannot be reduced to market and instrumentality. We can also argue that the impact of art on society is indirect. It means that there is a discursive relationship between art and society, which implies that there needs to be a *translation* from the one to the other. Art produces its own knowledge and its own language. But, art and the criticism inherent in art is also part of the process in society that *produces knowledge*. Such a sociological perspective on the production of knowledge implies that we cannot look at the history of art in a one-dimensional way, or how it affects the rest of society. This is not an argument for relativism, but it is an attempt to understand the social and political processes and discourses in a plural (unconstrained vision) and liberal society. Arts discourse contains unresolved and *difficult questions* that come up again, and become subject to new interpretations, and new controversies and inputs to social debates.

PART III

Knowledge Development in a Liberal Society

In this third and final part of the book, 'Knowledge Development in a Liberal Society', I take a more normative position to this issue of knowledge development. Having argued earlier in the book that knowledge development is inherently integrated with social processes, we need to discuss what are good and bad social processes. This makes issues related to how to organise a liberal society apparent. I discuss this with reference to classical political philosophers such as Hobbes, Locke, Hume, Rousseau, Kant, Paine, Burke, to mention some, and try to bring their arguments into dialogue with contemporary discourses.

I present three chapters. In Chapter 9: 'Knowledge, Market and Social Justice', I argue that for knowledge development to happen there has to be some form of social justice. In Chapter 10: 'Knowledge, Social Systems and Legal Order', I look at what type of legal and institutional system will support knowledge development and reason. In Chapter 11: 'Knowledge and Democracy', I point at the role of democracy in knowledge development and the question of developing true and valid knowledge. I close the book with some concluding reflections.

9 *Knowledge, Market and Social Justice*

Introduction

In this chapter I will discuss the issues of ethics, morality and justice in the perspective of knowledge; I will see the discourse on what is ethical, moral and just as a discourse on what is valid in the sense of socially and personally acceptable knowledge. This implies that I see these as normative restrictions on knowledge or the normative evaluation of knowledge. This also implies a perspective where these normative elements are seen as linking knowledge with action; we might have knowledge of something, but restrain ourselves from acting on this knowledge, because it is morally or ethically unacceptable to do so, or it would be seen as unjust.

I here see knowledge as primarily a social process, naturally linked to social conditions. These are the conditions under which people can express opinions and take part in deliberation. What is acceptable to say and express limits the amount of information that goes into the deliberation. It might also have a material side, since being an active participant in deliberation also implies the ability to participate.

So, I try to relate the issue of knowledge to the discussion of ethics, morality and justice, including perspectives on the market in terms of freedom, rights and common good. Knowledge is a precondition for giving meaning to these concepts, and the themes that these concepts raise have impact on knowledge, not least the discussion on restrictions on knowledge. They represent an integrated set of terms, which all have in common that we want to value and legitimise our actions or structures or institutions in the sense of being right and acceptable with reference to ethics, morality or justice theories. All these concepts have in common that they help to distinguish and differentiate kinds of knowledge.

I will refer to the social impact of these concepts as *social justice*. By social justice I mean the particular perspective one has on ethics, morality and justice related to issues of freedom, rights and common good. These perspectives are not merely opinions, for as Alain Badiou (2001) argues, ethics cannot be an opinion. In order for something to be ethical, it must be true, and truth can never be an opinion; it has to go beyond that. When we discuss ethics, morality and justice, we discuss these principles that guide individual knowledge, but are beyond individual knowledge.

One might argue that in society we have individual decisions and actions on the one hand, and the law that regulates when the individual does something that the law regulates as forbidden. So, do we need ethics and morality? Is it meaningful to say that something is just? Is it not sufficient to say it is lawful or not, and then leave it to the individual to decide what he or she wants to do? What do we need ethics and morality for? The argument I make here is that ethics, justice and morality regulate what is acceptable knowledge and action. They have different references to this issue and different consequences of the perspective one takes.

As a point of departure, I will refer to John Locke's discussion of ethics, rights and common good. The reason for this is that I will present four main perspectives on social justice: *natural ethics, rational ethics, humanist ethics* and *discursive ethics*. Locke, I argue, can help us understand the relations and differences between the four. Locke wrote his *Two Treatises* in 1690, partly in response to Thomas Hobbes. Hobbes can be seen as an early exponent of the natural ethics position. He argued against the republican idea that we need a state in order to help the development of justice in society. Rather, he saw the state as a threat to man's natural freedom and justice (Skinner, 2008). This came to be discussed as the *libertarian paradox*: is the collective power of the state a precondition for liberty or a threat to liberty? Locke takes a position closer to the republican idea: that society needs to protect the individual so that he or she can experience freedom and justice. As I will argue below, Locke also comes close to indicating the rational, humanistic and discursive perspective.

The political discussion on rights and social justice relates to fundamental discussions in economics and an important distinction in welfare theory: social justice derives its meaning from its context and use. The term *social* can also be seen as ambiguous. In the EU, social refers to employment and social policy. Is Amartya Sen (2009) right when he argues that social justice is more a common sense aspect of human nature, more a practice, than an academic exercise? One main divide is the distinction between just distribution of wealth and just distribution of rights: distributive justice versus natural rights relates to a long discourse within liberal political theory. John Locke discussed *justice* in the context of just distribution of rights. More communitarian liberals have argued in favour of distributive justice. However, often the argument relates to how people develop mutual responsibility in small groups or communities. Note also the problem of balancing human rights and property rights, a challenge exposed, among others, by slavery and the slave trade.

The large debate over the contractarian versus utilitarian view of justice played out in the nineteenth century. The debate over cardinal utility, and the possibility for *interpersonal comparison of utility*, was a main reason for the development of neo-classical economics (that thereby with its marginal utility concept rejected such comparison). Different perspectives on ethics have led to conflicting theories on social justice and, as I will argue, to how ethical debates have impact on knowledge.

John Locke's Theory of Justice

Locke's *Two Treatises* (1690) contains two parts, where the first treats 'the false principles' of the king's divine power. It is in this part that Locke develops his theory of individual natural rights. Individual natural rights dethrone the legitimacy of the established totalitarian order. Natural rights is a negative argument, against authority outside the individual.[1] This natural rights argument is much focused on in the Locke's discussion.[2]

---

1   While the *First Treatise* was a discussion about Robert Filmer and his theory of the divine right of the King, the *Second Treatise* was mainly a reply to Hobbes and his theory that a free society without a strong centralised power would be everybody's struggle against each other.

2   Chipman (1988, p. 59).

Undoubtedly, this is the Lockean argument that has had the greatest influence.[3] Locke gives his presentation of a political theory in *The Second Treatise of Government*. The three principles that Locke bases the political system on are natural rights, consent and common good. The discussion in the first part of Locke's book leads to the distribution of rights in the natural condition that means a situation before a political unit has been established. As a critique of a totalitarian regime, this first part is still relevant. But it is in *The Second Treatise* that Locke discusses the challenges the civil political society is facing. On the other hand, it is not possible to understand his political theory independent of his ethical and moral reflections. That is why tacit consent, some sort of conservatism, was part of his theory. That is also why he had a moral theory that forms a part of his political theory. His natural rights argument is:

> To understand Political Power right, and derive it from its Original, we must consider what State all Men are naturally in, and that is, a State of perfect Freedom to order their Actions, and dispose of their Possessions, and Persons as they think fit, within the bounds of the Law of Nature, without asking leave, or depending upon the Will of any other Man. (Locke, 1690, p. 309)

There is an important change in the meaning of the word *rights* when we move from the natural condition to the political society. While rights in the natural condition are given to all individuals independent of each other, those rights that individuals have in the civil society are given by the civil society. These two situations are linked together by the concept of consent:

> The Liberty of Man, in Society, is to be under no other Legislative Power, but that established, by consent … (Locke, 1690, p. 324)

But, there is an important limit to what sort of rights one can trade away through consent and, on the other hand, what rights one can obtain by consent. Nobody can obtain rights through consent that one was prohibited from obtaining in the natural condition, that is, rights over other people's rights. This means that one cannot by consent make oneself a slave. One can, however, through consent agree to establish:

> … a standing Rule to live by, common to every one of that society … (Locke, 1690, p. 324)

It is on this background, and from the limits these principles indicate, that one can better understand Locke's next argument about the political system:

> When any number of Men have so consented to make one Community or Government, they are thereby presently incorporated, and make one Body Politic, wherein the Majority have a Right to act and conclude the rest. (Locke, 1690, p. 375)

The practical consequences of these principles can be many, although they establish some absolute limits on political power. The debate on natural rights and social consent

---

3   Posner (1983, p. 18). In Denmark/Norway, however, Locke's theories were used by J.S. Sneedorffs in an attempt to reconstruct the 'opinion-led monarchy'. It is, however, quite obvious that this use of Locke by Sneedorffs was not correct.

has shown this tension. Consent is in itself a problematic concept for legitimacy. How should it be measured? Few of us were ever asked whether we liked society or not. On the other hand, by living peacefully in society, we give it some sort of tacit consent. But even if Locke thought that many institutions in society are founded on tacit consent, he did not accept tacit consent as a sufficient legitimation for the political order (Rawls, 1971, p. 112). Locke's idea of consent should imply that the social situation is an argumentation situation.

If so, Locke's natural rights theory should also be in harmony with this view. For Locke, a primary condition was that natural rights were rights which individuals had before they entered into society. These rights cannot be traded in the argumentation situation. Neither can one develop social rights directly from these natural rights. Social rights, the division of the social surplus, are a matter of consent, which implies also some sort of tacit consent.[4] The natural rights remain negative rights in the social process.

The same is the case with Locke's third principle, the common good. Locke did not have any distributive justice in mind when he talked about the common good. Instead, the common good should be regarded as the social condition that enables individuals to work for their own individual ends. As Locke writes:

> ... the power of the Society, or Legislative constituted by them, can never be suppos'd to extend farther than the common good; but is obliged to secure every ones Property by providing against those three defects above-mentioned, that made the State of Nature so unsafe and uneasy. And so whoever has the Legislative or Supreme Power of any Common-wealth, is bound to govern by establish'd standing laws, promulgated and known to the People, and not by Extemporary Decrees; by indifferent and upright Judges who are to decide Controversies by those Laws; And to employ the force of the Community at Home, only in the Execution of such Laws, or abroad to prevent or redress Foreign Injuries, and secure the Community from Inroads and Invasion. And all this to be directed to no other end, but the Peace, Safety, and public good of the people. (Locke, 1690, p. 398)

The discussion about Locke has been very much focused on the tension between natural rights and consent: which one should be dominant? Many see this as an unsolved dilemma in Locke's theory.[5] Natural rights and consent are only two of Locke's principles for a free society. Locke also has a third principle:

> ... the power of the Society, or Legislative constituted by them, can never be suppos'd to extend farther than the common good; ... (Locke, 1690, p. 398)

This common good principle forms a third limit to the political power. Not only should this power be exercised within the limits of natural rights, not only should it be based on consent, it should also as its sole objective promote the common good. This means that common good is not the society's end, but that the activity of a civil society should be within what common good is, and only that.

---

4   David Bloor calls this conservatism, and at the same time he uses this as an argument against Habermas's discourse theory that he gives the label 'Enlightenment fantasy' because it overlooks the impact that traditions, authority and power has on forming social consensus. See Bloor (1983, p.79).

5   See Vaughn (1980).

It is natural to see the common good principle as a sort of *Pareto condition*: a political action should at least make one person better off, without worsening the condition of all others. In Locke's theory, individuals entered society to be better off.[6] By *better off*, Locke did not have in mind social welfare. Better off, in relation to the natural condition, meant a better protection of rights:

> *The only way whereby any one divests himself of his Natural Liberty, and puts on the bonds of Civil Society is by agreeing with other Men to join and unite into a Community, for their comfortable, safe, and peaceable living one amongst another, in a secure Enjoyment of their Properties, and a greater Security against any that are not of it. (Locke, 1690, p. 375)*

Locke also says:

> *Every one as he is bound to preserve himself, [...] so by the like reason when his own Preservation comes not in competition, ought he, as much as he can, to preserve the rest of Mankind ... (Locke, 1690, p. 311)*

So, what kind of moral responsibility does Locke have in mind, and how can it be institutionalised in society? It is in this context that one can better understand the much discussed *Lockean proviso*. Since natural resources were there before civil society was established, nobody can claim rights over these resources any more than they could in the natural condition (where everybody had the same right). Only what was created by civil society can be distributed by the civil society.[7]

From this point of view, the legitimacy of the state is based on whether the state is a common good, which means whether or not it protects individual rights. Protecting rights means establishing laws that are equal for everybody, and not to the advantage of somebody. It means establishing laws that cannot be manipulated. Locke does not specify which laws should be established, but makes it explicit that they should be established by consent (Locke, 1690, p. 374/316).

Locke, in his theory of rights, makes a distinction between natural rights, which are rights in the natural condition, and civil rights, which are rights in the civil society. You cannot develop positive civil rights directly from the natural rights; you can only specify the conditions that civil rights have to obey. Natural rights are negative rights.[8] Locke's notion of consent is different from the later rationalistic social contract theories from Rousseau to Rawls. Among other things, Locke takes into account tacit consent.[9] Locke's theory is ahistorical, although his arguments have historical references. The problem whether *will* is prior to historical development, or a result of historical development,

---

6   This is a cognitive precondition in the Kantian sense and implies the individual's autonomy in a consent situation. See Posner, op. cit. p. 89. About the Pareto principles and its relevance for public choice, see James Buchanan (1977), Chapter 2, 'Law and the Invisible Hand', pp. 34–5. For a critic of Buchanan, see Coleman (1975).

7   Locke, op. cit. p. 329 For a discussion of this, see Nozick, op.cit. pp. 174–82.

8   See V.M. Hope (1989, p. 20). When Jules Coleman objects to the justice involved in taking the natural condition as the starting point for distribution of rights since that may freeze unjust distribution of pre-constitutional holdings, he seems to forget that on that constitutional level, it is *not* holdings, but rights that are distributed. See Coleman, op. cit, s.111.

9   Stuart D. Warner (1989) and Posner op. cit. p. 102. Locke is misunderstood even by David Hume with regard to tacit consent. Locke did not think tacit consent was a sufficient legitimacy. See David Hume (1989). See also John Rawls, op. cit. p. 112

is not addressed by Locke, neither is the controversy of nature versus construction, evolution versus rationalism.[10]

John Locke wrote his *Two Treatises* both to show that the totalitarian power was illegitimate and to explain what principles a free society has to be based on. The later discussion of Locke has seen him either as inconsistent, or has focused only on some part of his argument, such as tacit consent, natural rights or his common good argument. I will try to argue that Locke exemplifies an attempt to integrate different perspectives on social justice. These different perspectives have later been developed as antagonistic positions. However, my argument is that they all give some important insight into social justice and on knowledge.

Natural Ethics

Natural justice is one of these positions. It is a position that can be traced back to Thomas Hobbes (Binmore, 2005). It was predominant in the Scottish enlightenment, and David Hume is a central thinker in developing this position. It inspired Charles Darwin and was encouraged by the discoveries of evolution and, later on, the discoveries of genes. Thomas Huxley brought this position into the discussion of ethics in the mid-nineteenth century.[11] In the contemporary debate we find Richard Dawkins' (1976) work on genes, Hayek (1988) and Karl Popper (1979b) have referred to this positioning in their work on knowledge development, and Ken Binmore has developed the position further with reference to game theory (Binmore, 2005).

There are mainly two sets of arguments that form this position: firstly, there is a divide between what the individual does and the total structure and pattern of what everybody does. Secondly, ethics is basically something that exists and not something one ought to follow; that is, it is inherent in our action and our exchange with other persons. It is a position that can be related to the debate on positive and negative liberty.

NEGATIVE AND POSITIVE LIBERTY

In his Inaugural Lecture at Oxford University in 1958, Isaiah Berlin made the distinction between the negative and the positive concept of liberty.[12] Berlin understands negative liberty in this way:

I am normally said to be free to the degree to which no man or body of men interferes with my activity. Political liberty in this sense is simply the area within which man can act un-obscured by others. (Berlin, 1989, p. 122)

While positive liberty is defined this way:

---

10 For a discussion, see Isaiah Berlin's discussion of Vico and Herder (Berlin, 1976).

11 Robert Mackintosh wrote a book in 1899, *From Comte to Benjamin Kidd: The appeal to biology or evolution for human guidance*, where he summarises this development (Mackintosh, 2005).

12 The words freedom and liberty are used as synonyms. The distinction between positive and negative freedom is said to have its origin in Benjamin Constante.

The 'Positive' sense of the word liberty derives from the wish on the part of the individual to be his own master. I wish my life and decisions to depend myself, not on external forces of whatever kind. (Berlin, 1989, p. 131)

Expressed in other words, it might be said that negative liberty is the same as being un-coerced, while positive liberty is defined by the power you have to realise your own plans. The same distinction is later expressed in other words, for instance as freedom *from* and freedom *to*, or, in relation to law, as negative and positive rights. In this latter sense, freedom *from* interference would equal negative rights such as the right to express yourself, while freedom *to* might equal positive rights, such as welfare rights, right to public benefits, etc.

Isaiah Berlin identified the negative concept of liberty with extreme individualism, the protection of the individual sphere and non-interference in the activities of individuals, while the positive concept of liberty was identified as self-realisation. Not surprisingly, then, Berlin addressed much of his critique of the positive concept of liberty to the pragmatists (such as William James) and the idealists (such as T.H. Green) and their self-realisation perspective on social development. Isaiah Berlin even argues that the positive conception of liberty can lead to despotism.

The negative conception of liberty can be found within the Scottish school that reduced the ethical discussion to the theory of interests. Mandeville's, and more particularly Adam Smith's, theory of conflicting but mutually controlling interests that lead to an overall equilibrating structure seemed to remove the individual responsibility for the overall structure of society.[13] The same is true with the theory of spontaneous order that we find in David Hume's work. Certain things are natural. However, sentiments like rights are elaborations of virtues. There are some natural virtues that are virtues shared by everybody. However, these might be local and contextual. Only on a very general level can we talk about universal rights and truths. In this tradition, practical rights are contextual, although they observe the natural feature of human virtue. Social order should be based on tacit and rational knowledge, as understood by its citizens. The extent of politics might vary, but in order to remain liberal, a regime has to respect individuality.

In his book *A Theory of Moral Sentiments*, Adam Smith develops a specification of how sound and natural moral sentiments emerge in a society. Smith says:

The man who acts according to the rules of perfect prudence, of strict justice, and of proper benevolence, may be said to be perfectly virtuous. (Smith, 1759, p. 155)

However, in his *Wealth of Nations*, which he published 17 years later, he says:

It is not from the benevolence of the butcher, the brewer, or the baker, that we expect our dinner, but from their regard to their own interest. We address ourselves, not to their humanity but to their self-love ... (Smith, 1776, p. 27)

Karl Popper in his *The Open Society and its Enemies* (Popper, 1945) challenges the dichotomy of self-love and benevolence. Popper says that if people act according to their

---

13   See M.M. Goldsmith (1985). Adam Smith strongly opposed Mandeville's obscure idea that immorality leads to common good. However, like the rest of the Scottish enlightenment, he was looking for ways to construct social institutions so that they would take advantage even of people's 'bad' sides and become useful. See Skinner (1990). See also Hope (1989, p. 100ff).

own judgement, this judgement might involve both self-love and benevolence. We do not know exactly the motives behind the actions, and we cannot know whether even a benevolent act might be motivated by self-interest.

One is the idea presented by Mandeville in the eighteenth century called *private vices – public benefits* (Mandeville, 1716; Goldsmith, 1985). This idea was to show that society might benefit from actions that did not have this benefit as part of its motive. In the 'baker' alternative, this would mean that although he baked the bread for only selfish reasons, he might contribute to the well-being of society by supplying cheap and good bread. Herbert Spencer argued in the nineteenth century that *individualism is the ultimate human virtue*, and that no other considerations will ever legitimise a disregard of individualism (Hoy, 1984, p. 16).

INDIVIDUAL LIBERTY VERSUS PUBLIC INTERESTS

The problem of reconciling public interests with individual liberty is familiar to economists. In the theory of *public goods*, game theory has been able to demonstrate that rational individual actions leaves everybody worse off than what would have been the case with collective action (Binmore, 2005). However, individual action can also lead to a situation where everybody is better off (that is, the utilitarian justification of the market).

According to Smith, man has no natural moral sense. Every man learns about the world through his own sensation. When he develops feelings towards his fellow citizens, it is mainly because he is able to identify his own feeling in the behaviour of others. But, individuals are dependent on each other and have to develop some sort of mutual understanding. Therefore, Smith says, morality develops through exchange: morality is a result of social learning. Morality is a consequence of the fact that we have to adapt to each other, to find some mutual ground of cooperation. My reward in social relations is a result of my contribution. Other people's sympathy has to be earned. It is an *exchange of virtues*.

An interesting discussion on this issue developed after the publication of Hayek's book *The Constitution of Liberty* (1960). Hayek had in this book defined liberty negatively as absence of coercion (where coercion was defined as following the will of others contrary to one's own will). In most cases this would be a sufficient principle for negative freedom. However, one case was debated where a person is the sole owner of a water hole in the dessert. If he rejects all offers to buy water, he does not coerce his fellow citizens, neither does he violate their liberty as defined by Hayek; however, the effect of such a rejection would be that the other citizens eventually die.[14] As I argue below, the *Lockean proviso* would overrule negative rights in this situation.

RIGHTS

Rights are not *a priori* an absolute; they are social constructions and part of a liberal regime that involves many factors. As Hayek says in a David Hume-like manner, the challenge is not to realise some ideal human liberty, rather to secure the most possible liberty for men in society by reducing coercion. This more empirical perspective on liberty opens the way

---

14   Another example that Hayek gave of the same type of situation was a doctor that knew how to cure a fatal disease. Even here, Hayek argued that the doctor had a duty to help.

to a more complex understanding of liberty than what is suggested by the dichotomy of positive and negative liberty.

As the example of Hayek shows, negative rights exist in a social setting. Rights are meaningless outside society, because you only need rights in order to organise the relation between people in society. Freedom is likewise a meaningless concept outside society. This means the same as that freedom and other rights only exist when observed by others. Whether these rights are negative or positive, they still have a social dimension. The social dimension is different in positive and negative rights. In positive rights, other people (or the state) are obliged to provide you with some benefits, while in negative rights they only have to leave you alone. But in both cases other people are actively involved in realising the rights.

The same point of view can be used with regard to market exchange (the social structure under which individuals most actively express their negative rights). Max Weber argued:

> *Within the market community every act of exchange, especially monetary exchange, is not directed in isolation, by the action of the individual partner to the particular transaction, but the more rationally it is considered, the more it is directed by the actions of all parties potentially interested in the exchange. (Weber, 1978, vol. 1, p. 636)*

Consider a situation where I bargain for a commodity on the market. My expectations are formed by my social knowledge, and the seller has in mind what others are willing to pay. As we bargain and eventually make an exchange, we observe a lot of tacit and clearly defined norms and rules that none of us were in a position to invent ourselves. So even in such a solitary state of two-party exchange, the whole of society is in a sense present.

There is an exchange level of morality in society (a minimum moral regime) created by the exchange process and the market as a learning arena. There is also a system of justice that regulates the social interactions in society.

CAPITALIST JUSTICE

Israel Kirzner talked about *the standard defence of capitalist justice*. One of the most comprehensive defences of this system was offered by the American economist John Bates Clark (1899); people are rewarded according to their marginal contribution to the wealth of society (Kirzner, 1992, p. 212). Clark had supposed that the economy was in a static equilibrium. The problem of how private ownership was originally acquired, or how later transactions could be regarded to be just, was not debated.

Robert Nozick offered, some 75 years after Bates Clark, a defence of the justice of the capitalist system, by stating that the present distribution of goods is just if the original acquisition of the goods was just, and all later transactions were just (Nozick, 1974). As a principle of justice for acquisition of private property, Nozick refers to John Locke. Locke had stated that man is entitled to the fruit of his labour, including the resources of nature in the case that he uses his labour to acquire it. However, there is a proviso on this last principle (the Lockean proviso) – *that there is enough and as good left to others*. What this means is that one could not acquire property rights to limited resources. And, since resources generally are limited, there is, according to Kirzner, very little left for a defence of capitalist justice.

Kirzner's contribution to this debate is to introduce the distinction between *production* and *creation*. If acquisition of resources is regarded as a zero-sum game (if I don't have it you will have it), the Lockean proviso will be violated by such an acquisition. If, on the other hand, my acquisition represents genuine creativity (if I don't have it, you will have no chance of having it neither), the proviso will not be violated. This is the discovery or creativity argument that, according to Kirzner, is an important supplement to the standard justification of the capitalist system. Kirzner refers to this as 'finders, keepers' ethics (Kirzner, 1992).

Both Nozick and Kirzner seem to agree that if people engage in a voluntary exchange, they do so because they expect to be better off after the exchange than they were before. To the extent that voluntary exchanges are made, everybody involved should be better off, and this should indicate the utility and justice of voluntary exchange, as we have in the capitalist system.

Hayek, however, commented on the situation as described by saying that:

> ... *in such instances the unlimited control of the owner over his property has to give way* ...
> *(Hayek, 1961/1976, p. 350)*

In other words, Hayek indicates that his principle of property rights, and rights in general, are subordinated to some other, prior principle.

IMPLICATIONS FOR SOCIAL JUSTICE

According to Hayek, what made civilisation possible was that individuals learned to accept and utilise general structures, institutions and rules, the background of which they did not know, and which they could not attempt to overview (Hayek, 1988, p. 19). This is the same as saying that civilisation is more than the close community where everybody can overview everything. In this perspective, liberalism is strongly associated with the modern project.

Hayek talks about the *mirage of social justice* (Hayek, 1973). By this he means that the idea of justice that we all share (*Nomos*), and that we apply to people and situations that form our immediate surroundings, cannot be applied in the great complex whole that forms society (*Thesis*). We can know of the effects of our actions in our immediate environment, but very little about the effect on the total complex social order. That is why we in our immediate surroundings care for each other, while we for society, as such, rely on rules and norms that we regard as fair. But what do we mean by fair? I cannot say what will be the best benefit for somebody to receive, say, in another country. But I could have an opinion about fair rules and fair norms in that country.

The challenge to the individuals is to be able to live both in the small tribal world of families and close social relations, and on the other hand to live with the extensive division of labour, and observe all the abstract learned rules that make civilisation and the open society possible.

Justice within a *Nomos* order can never relate to the final *outcome* of the process, only to the *fairness* of the process itself. The reason for this rests on two phenomena: first, that ethics can only relate to the deliberate actions of individuals, and since the outcome of the *Nomos*-order is beyond the control of any individual, ethics cannot relate to its result. Secondly, the only thing we can control with *Nomos*-order is the processes by which the order is made. Justice will for this reason have to be related to the *fairness of the rules of the process*. The opposite is the case with *Thesis*: *Thesis* is an order where the process is subordinate to the result. In *Thesis* it is meaningful to talk about justice in relation to result.

We can relate this distinction to the concept of *social justice*. One might agree with Hayek that the overall social order in any society will tend to be so complicated and complex that *Nomos* is a better description of these processes than *Thesis* (Hayek, 1976). For the same reason, the concept of social justice, meaning some specific distribution of social wealth, has little relevance to the overall social order. Within the large system that we call society, no comprehensive conception of just distribution is meaningful: one should rather be concerned with the fairness of norms and rules.

The concept of social justice is for this reason *a mirage* that draws its inspiration from the smaller social order of tribe or organisation, where *Thesis* is a correct description of the order. The market is an institution or a process, while morality is a human virtue. Ken Binmore's defence of what he calls natural justice rests on three principles that such justice must rest on: stability, efficiency and fairness. These are very crude principles that allow for large local variation in the execution of justice.

Rational Ethics

We can attribute the idea of a rational ethics to Immanuel Kant. Kant was looking for the universal and transcendent in human life, and developed a system of thought that would guide us to principles for inter-human understanding of society. Kant has become a key reference for the idea of the rule of law. His most recognised principle is that of the categorical imperative: that you should act in a way so that the principles of your action could equally guide others' action, which means according to a universal law. Kant reached this position through discussion where he rejected both David Hume's scepticism and the metaphysical foundations for ethics. Furthermore, he reached these positions through a complex theorising that included a particular theory of the mind. Kant's argument was that we have mental categories and so we are cognitively capable of distinguishing the universal from the particular and idiosyncratic.

JUSTICE AS FAIRNESS

These Kantian principles form the background to John Rawls' theorising.[15] John Rawls tried to develop a contract theory where justice is not only seen as protection of rights. In Rawls' theory, rights involves material ability. From that point of view, the social contract should not only decide the establishment of just laws; it should also involve the distribution of the social surplus. The idea of a social contract like that of rights has had its predecessors in ancient Greek philosophy, but the modern concept was introduced by Jean Jacques Rousseau. As we have seen, Locke does not discuss the distribution of wealth, only the fairness of rules.[16] Some aspects of the idea of a social contract have

---

15   Rawls' main book is *A Theory of Justice* (1971).

16   Locke and interpersonal comparisons of utility, see Locke, op. cit. p. 311: Locke says that nobody can take from anyone what is rightfully his. On the other hand, everybody have a moral obligation to help others. Locke also limits property rights with reference to God, who is the 'real' owner of everything. Ref. 'the Lockean proviso'.

been restated in contemporary debate by public choice theory and in particular by James Buchanan (1977). Also discourse theory has used the consent principle; an ideal-talk situation presupposes that everybody is an equal partner. During the Enlightenment, at the time Rousseau elaborated the contract idea, Jeremy Bentham introduced utility as a philosophical discipline and as a social principle. John Stuart Mill later used it as the founding principle when he developed the most comprehensive liberal philosophy of the nineteenth century.

In its modern form, John Rawls has used the utilitarian concept to restate a theory of justice. In Rawls' formulation, equal distribution of the social surplus is the best, unless unequal distribution is to the advantage of the most needed in society.[17]

What Rawls tried to do was to create a link between the natural right theory and the utilitarian argument through what he called 'justice as fairness'. Many of his critics have argued that fairness (each individual's right to choose) and justice (some particular norm) are not necessarily linked together. Fairness does not necessarily produce one particular type of justice. Although Rawls introduces a utilitarian element in his contract theory, he rejects utilitarianism as a sufficient theory of justice (Rawls, 1971, p. 27).

COMMON GOOD

The idea of public goods came from the idea of *common good*. The idea of common good, which has followed social science through all times, indicates a belief in something that is common and good for everybody. Behind this belief there is the idea that we as human beings are basically equal in at least some respects and that on this basis there is something that we share and will all have an equal benefit from.

There is a certain tension in economic literature between this common good perspective on the one hand and the utilitarian concept of maximising individual happiness on the other. This tension was already present in John Locke's writing. While Locke was pioneering the theory of utility by linking it to the individual experience of pleasure and pain, he quite clearly stated that the purpose of the political society was no other than the promotion of the common good.

So, while Locke is generally regarded as introducing the hedonistic concept of utility, he at the same time was influenced by the Aristotelian eudaemonian concept. For Locke, this doesn't seem to create any problems. The individualised concept of happiness is related to the idea of utility as an end outside the individual, through two basic assumptions.

The first of these is the basic concept of human nature. As humans, we share some common characteristics, at least at a very fundamental level. The existence of an unalterable nature of things forms the basis for utilitarian thinking. The extent of the utilitarian principle rests on the extent of the uniformity of human nature (Berlin, 1969, p. 182). The second assumption that links the hedonistic and the eudaemonian level of utility is the idea of a general tendency to equilibrium in social and economic processes. The equilibrating process means that human action will lead to some sort of overall social order (Parsons, 1937).

Both of these assumptions were elaborated upon in the literature that followed Locke, especially within the Empiricist tradition. Francis Hutcheson elaborated the theory of natural human good. Adam Smith developed both the theory of equilibrium and the

---

17   Rawls, op. cit. p. 76. Rawls calls this 'the difference principle'.

theory of evolved, natural benevolence. Even John Stuart Mill made use of both theories when he argued for a basic harmony between individual pleasure-seeking and the common good. This indicates that during the classical tradition it was gradually more common to identify intersubjective good with objective good.

The harmony was destroyed by Arthur Pigou when in 1912 he published *Wealth and Welfare*. His modified version, *The Economics of Welfare* (1924), came to be the founding work in welfare theory. Here Pigou argued that welfare could be increased if wealth was taken from the rich and given to the poor (Pigou, 1932, p. 90). He also pointed at inefficiency in the market economy, monopolistic supply, externalities and incomplete use of resources. All in all, his argument was, contrary to Locke and Smith, that individual pleasure-seeking through the market economy did not maximise the public good. Some sort of state action was necessary to fill the gap.

Table 9.1 is intended to show how Pigou only considered two of four possible combinations of choice and goods (state and free market). It was in the discussion following Pigou`s book that the modern economic theory of public good was developed; the first period of this debate was strongly influenced by the dichotomy of free market and state, while other perspectives, such as how individual action leads to public good and how voluntary collective action emerges, were hardly discussed at all.

There were reactions to cardinal utility theory: one of the first objections to Pigou came from Lionel Robbins, who argued against the interpersonal comparison of utility that was involved in Pigou's reasoning (Robbins, 1932). Robbins' argument was part of a broader theory in favour of scientific neutrality towards ethical issues, and against normative statements in economics. Although Robbins accepted normative statements, he did not regard them as scientific.

Robbins' classical statement about economics is that:

(Economics) is incapable of deciding as between the desirability of different ends. It is fundamentally distinct from ethics. Wherein, then, does its unquestionable significance consist? Surely it consists in just this, that, when we are faced with choice between ultimates, it enables us to choose with full awareness of the implications of what we are choosing. (Robbins, 1932, p. 152)

In a way, the neo-classical solution to Pigou's problems is within Robbins' programme. By focusing on the relative change in utility involved in transactions, and introducing *indifference curves* and *social welfare function*, one could demonstrate that the total utility could be increased by a system of taxes and compensations. If everybody would be better off by a change in demand or supply of certain goods, those who suffered from the change could be compensated and those who gained could be taxed.

Table 9.1   Private/public good combinations

	Private good	**Public good**
Individual choice	Free market	Pioneers, entrepreneurs, forerunners
Collective choice	Volunteer sector, social cooperation	State

To this solution, Robbins objected that he would only accept it if actual compensation took place. This means that the neo-classical solution presupposes the market, since transactions can only take place in a market. Again this had the implication that the argument of public goods could not be used as an argument for a general redistribution of wealth. And on the other hand, it implies that there is a relation between the solution to the problem and the social structure. So common good means, to use Douglas Rasmussen's words:

> *Accordingly, the common good of the political community is not a determinate end – it is not the object of a human purpose with identifiable characteristics which can be used to help specify appropriate and inappropriate courses of action for the realisation of that end. Instead, the common good of political community is a procedural end – it is the object of a human purpose the function of which is to define the conditions under which the pursuit of other (determinate) ends will occur. (Rasmussen, 1987, p. 74)*

The important distinction is between the basic social structure, the common good, that enables individuals to reach for their own ends, and what individuals do within this structure to achieve their ends, their pursuit of happiness (Rasmussen, 1990).

MORAL ORDER

John Rawls (1971) presents three laws of moral development that represent three stages of moral activity – the first law says that we are morally attached to ourselves and our family, since that is to be regarded as part of our own dominion. The second law says that given the condition of the first law and that the social arrangements around us is just and generally known to be just, people will extend this moral attachment to their fellow citizens. The third law says that if the first and second law are in place – that is, that one has the capacity to love one's own family and that the social arrangements around us are regarded as just, so that our moral attachment is extended to friendly feelings and trust towards others – one will develop a corresponding sense of justice and be able to recognise that oneself and the people one loves are beneficiaries of these social arrangements (Rawls, 1971, p. 490).

The essence of this theory is that there is a correlation between the institutions of exchange and the development of morals.[18] If the institutions are just, morality will be improved. If they are unjust, morality will be brutalised. Justice is more important than morality.[19]

Nozick, on the other hand, rejects Rawls' theory. According to Nozick, a choice must be made between just procedures or just end results. You cannot have both. So, if you base your theory on natural rights, protection of rights is the furthest you can get:

---

18   There is another aspect of Rawls' theory that I do not discuss here: his emphasis on the close relations as essential for moral behaviour could be interpreted as a critique of civilisation and the complex (in Popper's words: open-) society. It might be that Rawls should be interpreted in the Hegelian, romantic tradition of concern for the primitive society, emphasising the alienation and amorality of civilisation.

19   This view indicates that there is a dichotomy between moral and ethics (justice) – moral is an absolute imperative, while ethics is the practical rules by which this moral imperative is implemented. An ethical rule might be just without being moral in the absolute meaning of the word. Let me take one example: I might be morally committed to help everyone that is suffering, but it would not be just if I was the only one to help them – or if I were to sacrifice everything in order to help others.

The minimal state is the most extensive state that can be justified. Any state more extensive violates people's rights. (Nozick, 1974, p. 129)

Social justice is thereby seen as a tribal phenomenon, or a term used to describe tribal phenomena, taken from a situation where people are collectively concerned with each other because they know each other and each other's needs. However, social justice cannot mean the same in the large, extended order where only general rules apply, since we do not know each individual and his or her need. Natural rights, utilitarianism and contract theory are generally discussed as conflicting theories of justice.

It is in this context one can better understand the *Lockean proviso*: since natural resources were there before civil society was established, nobody can claim rights over these resources any more than they could in the natural condition (where everybody had the same right). Only what was created by civil society can be distributed by the civil society.[20] The legitimacy of the state is therefore based on whether the state is a common good, which means whether or not it protects individual rights. Protecting rights means establishing laws that are equal for everybody and not to the advantage of somebody. It means establishing laws that cannot be manipulated. Locke does not specify which laws should be established, but makes it explicit that they should be established by consent (Locke, 1690, p. 374/316). Rawls is interested in combining the idea of *justice and fairness* and that of *individual moral development*.

John Rawls tried to develop a contract theory where justice is not only seen as protection of rights. In Rawls' theory, rights involve material ability: 'Ought implies can.' From that point of view, the social contract should not only decide the establishment of just laws; it should also involve the distribution of the social surplus. In Rawls' formulation, equal distribution of the social surplus is the best, unless unequal distribution is to the advantage of the most needed in society. Rawls introduces an ethical approach to the collective choice theory. His principle, justice as fairness, is a discussion about a fair way to distribute the social surplus.

The essence of this theory is that there is a correlation between the *institutions of exchange* and the *development of morals*. If the institutions are just, morality will be improved. If they are unjust, morality will be brutalised. For the same reason Smith concluded that *justice is more important than morality*.

IS THE UNIVERSAL NORM SOCIALLY JUST?

There is a comparison between Rawls and the natural justice argument; both positions refer to what is universal truth (Binmore, 2005). Even Hayek made the claim that the natural order of human action, but not human design, is superior to any artificially made ethical order. If we compare only these two kinds of order, we will find that the claim of superiority of the natural order rests on the fact that it is more universal than the artificially made ethical order (Hayek, 1976, p. 26).

A treatment of the relation between morals and degree of universality has been made by Wlodzimierz Rabinowicz (1979). His argument is that it is reasonable to claim that an order that only involves one person (e.g., individual priorities of taste) has less ethical claim than one that appeals to all people (as, e.g., the value of liberty).

---

20 Locke, op. cit. p. 329. For a discussion of this, see Nozick, op. cit. pp. 174–82.

The more universally applicable an order is, the more ethical it is. Also, one will see from this definition, that a universal order will probably be very general in character (since it will apply to all sorts of people).

Whether one can deduce from this common sense principle of universality that the natural order is necessarily more universal and general than the artificial order is not an obvious question. Its claim rests on some assumptions about how this natural order is developed and adopted. Based on the assumptions that Hayek makes about this process of development and adoptions, this claim seems reasonable. But that does not mean that any practical example of traditions and evolved order fulfils these conditions.

When we say that a universal norm is more ethical than one that is deliberately chosen by a single person, this is not the same as sacrificing the one for the others. The starting point here would be a situation with no norm at all. In such a situation we ask what norm will be more binding to others – a purely individual, idiosyncratic norm, or a universal adopted norm?

Then one could ask: what if the idiosyncratic norm is chosen? What if people prefer an ethical norm to that of an ethical neutral norm? If our argument is consistent, the process of choosing a norm will not have any influence on their ethical content. On the other hand, if our choice of norms reflects their relative utility, there is a dilemma. This dilemma comes from the fact that Hayek presupposes that general norms, formed through an evolutionary process, imply such a high degree of knowledge (since so many people have used so much time during its development) that no deliberately designed norm can do better. At the heart of this argument there is an assumption that two processes converge or correlate: that of complexity of knowledge and that of growth of knowledge through evolutionary selection. Hayek also seems to suppose that complexity of knowledge is equivalent with quality of knowledge.

If we take a common sense perspective, it is reasonable to assume that norms are formed in an open social environment (open market), through some process of mutual adjustment, in order to establish some common standards of behaviour. If you want to take part in mutual activities (make an exchange), you have to observe and eventually accept these norms (the market price). This is not the same as to say that norms are good, that they are morally acceptable or in accordance with individual wants (neither is this the case with market prices). However, it is an argument in support of the view that norms are formed through the same process as that of the market order.

IMPLICATIONS FOR SOCIAL JUSTICE

Rational ethics presupposes our cognitive capacity to distinguish the reasonable and universal in our subjective understanding of the world and to live by it. We, so to speak, consent to the common good. However, both consent and utility have been shown to have limitations as ultimate principles of a liberal society. It is relatively easy to demonstrate that utility might come into conflict with rights. In fact, this is one of the most common controversies in modern societies. Consent and social contract is likewise problematic. Civil authority would probably not exist if everybody was to agree on everything, and therefore if a departure from the rule of unanimity is to be made, some other principle has to be introduced to legitimate that departure.

This is the reason why rational individuals would, and actually did, end up with certain agreements on the principles of a civil society. It is, however, difficult to prove the correctness of such a rational agreement. As has been seen in the recent controversies within discourse theory, it is difficult to perceive the content of the *ideal-talk situation* since individuals are supposed to be rational in the sense that they are stripped of all natural human features such as passion, values, dominance, power or fear. In a normal consent situation there is a social process involving all these features and it is difficult to argue that any consent achieved is rational, in the absolute sense of the word.

Humanist Ethics

We may attribute the humanist perspective on ethics to a long tradition, starting from Descartes and finding its modern form in the theory of Emmanuel Lévinas (1993). The core of this position is our moral and ethical sense and understanding, originating from our immediate encounter with other humans (Craig, 2010). We develop our understanding of the world as we identify with others. Humanism and empathy develop in our recognition that the other is a human being as myself. Without this recognition, human society is impossible. Sharing values and respecting values is the fabric that keeps our society together. This is a position that contradicts, among others, Oliver Williamson's theory of capitalist economy (Williamson, 1985). Williamson argues that opportunism is a key mechanism in economic transactions and that its challenges can be solved through contracts that fit the type of principal-agent situation in question.

The British Cardinal Basil Hume said years ago (*The Independent*, 8 March 1993):

> *There are, in fact, basic moral values such as personal integrity, self-discipline, generosity, compassion, fidelity in relationships and respect for human life that we should be able to share. These are founded on the fundamental dignity of being human and are not a matter of arbitrary selection. They are essential to societies' survival. Without such shared values, society loses its way and starts to disintegrate. This is what is happening now and the process must be reversed.*

Paul Johnson, in his reply to Hume in *The Independent* (8 March 1993), called this doom-mongering. Is it correct, what Hume says later in the same article, that there is a tension, or even conflict, between the idea of individualism and that of morality, in the sense that moral means *commitment, shared values, love and stability*? In that case, what should be more up for trial than the market economy, since that is one of the most individualistic institutions we have in society?

MORAL BRUTALISATION AND LIMITS TO THE MARKET

The problem I will discuss is known as the *tragedy of the commons* (Binmore, 2005). It simply states that there are situations in which when people optimise their gain, everybody will be worse off. Furthermore, it shows that people will continue to behave in this way in spite of then ruining their own foundation. Being a fisherman and fishing a lake empty of fish and thus destroying ones source of income could be an example.

Elenor Ostrom has argued that there is a social solution to this problem: people will come together and create a regime that optimises fishing (to follow this example) without destroying it (Ostrom, 1990). I will, however, discuss another aspect of this situation: the sort of moral brutalisation that the tragedy of the commons implies.

Why are people morally brutalised in a free market? The market exchange leaves a lot of freedom to those involved. It does not say anything about how they use this freedom, unless of course they want to make an exchange: in that case we know that they have to make mutual adjustments of actions. How the final result of this coordination process happens depends among other things on the moral quality of the individuals. These are arguments in favour of the market. The problem that the tragedy of the commons discusses is when there is no exchange but exploitation of a common good. However, it can be argued that many situations of exchange imply the utilisation of common goods, so the problem might be larger than expected at first sight.

It can be argued that not all moral values can emerge from exchange or be practised in an exchange situation. Michael Sandel discusses this in his book *What Money Can't Buy: The moral limits of markets* (Sandel, 2012). To put it another way, in the case that all transactions in society are based on the principles of exchange, the society would be morally brutalised.

Israel Kirzner argues:

> The 'finders, keepers' ethic provides a plausible basis for defending the justice of the capitalist system. Such an ethic offers a fresh basis for original private acquisition from nature. Such an ethic offers, in addition, a solid theory supporting the possible justice of pure profit. To the extent that capitalist resource incomes involve a discovery element, they, too, may be held justified, at least in part by 'finders, keepers' ethic. Together these insights significantly supplement the standard defence of capitalist justice. They certainly do not declare capitalism to be free of all moral blemishes (since, in any event, strict justice is not the sole criterion for morality between human beings). They certainly do not pronounce all actions taken under historical capitalism to have been moral, or even just. They do, however, suggest that the capitalist system need not be rejected out of hand as being inherently unfair. Moral improvement may be sought within the framework of private property and free exchange, without the conviction that to participate in capitalism is to participate in an inevitably flawed human institution. (Kirzner, 1992, p. 225)

Does this mean that in spite of all efforts, it is impossible to defend the market from a moral point of view, or that there are some moral criteria that are superior to the market as an institution? If that is the case, we should like to know what these criteria are, since these criteria will be decisive for what part of the market economy can be justified as moral and which cannot.

Moral brutalisation takes many different forms. I have myself been interested in two phenomena known from literature: I should like to call them the *throwing the first stone* effect and the *Raskolnikov* effect. The first effect, known from the Bible, shows how much easier it is to throw the second and third stone than the first. If one person behaves immorally, others will more easily follow, although they would never throw the first stone (and this in spite of the fact that for the person that is hit, the second or third might be more fatal than the first). The other effect, from Dostoyevsky's novel, shows how people who have committed one crime more easily commit a second (Raskolnikov never bothered about his second murder, although from an outside point of view it was much more brutal than the first (since it was a meaningless, blind murder)).

In some situations, people might be unaware and uninterested about the effect of their actions, even though these effects are totally meaningless (in the sense that nobody gains and somebody loses heavily from these effects), and that the acting people themselves would admit that they are totally meaningless if they were confronted with them. For this reason, there is the argument that we need moral principles to guide our action and that morality and ethics are, prior to the actions and exchange we do in society. In the perspective of Lévinas, we might talk about an ontological foundation for ethics (Lévinas, 1972).

CRITIC OF LACK OF MORAL COHESION IN SOCIETY

Some would see this as a critique of the modern, liberal project. The Enlightenment believed in a non-mythical universal truth and this belief (or scepticism) bore the liberal crusade against feudalism, mysticism and conservatism. However, as John Gray has argued:

> ... I shall consider what comes after we accept that liberal society cannot be justified by appeal to universal human nature or reason, but has only a local authority. What does this recognition portend for the liberal institutions and practices we have inherited? I shall submit that, as heirs to the modern experience of individuality and variety in forms of life and thought, we cannot pretend to roll back the heritage of liberal identity (as some recent communitarian thinkers have supposed we might) in the interest of an earlier, and largely imaginary pre-liberal form of non-individualist moral life. For us, at least, individualism is a historical fate, which we can seek to moderate but not to evade. Our circumstance, then, is the paradoxical one of post-moderns, whose self-understanding is shaped by the liberal form of life, but without its legitimating myths, which philosophic inquiry has dispelled. A question arises as to whether this circumstance is likely to be confronted by most or all contemporary cultures, as they struggle towards modernity only to discover the foundationlessness of the modern project. A larger and deeper question arises as to what can be the task of modern philosophical inquiry, when not only the project of the Enlightenment, but also the Socratic founders of the very subject are seen to be misconceived. The ruination of the project of a liberal ideology will then be seen as encompassing the end of an intellectual tradition central to our self-understanding in the west, and this suggests a final question. What might replace the traditional conception of political philosophy (whose last instance is found in liberalism) when that has been subverted by philosophical inquiry? (Gray, 1989, p. 240)

For many, including John Gray, this new way is found in the small community, in the relationship society where human activity and moral responsibility become important and visible. The problem of modern society can only be overcome if people have the quality to understand and engage in other people's feelings. Erich Fromm wrote a book about *The Sane Society*, where he said that brutality is a result of a society where people have lost contact with the emotions of their fellow citizens (Fromm, 1991). My well-being cannot be indifferent to the well-being of others. Brutalisation can only be understood if one feels hurt; involvement in other people's misery is the only way we can perceive misery; to feel hurt is the only way to perceive evil:

> ... even if the common good of the political community can be shown to consist of something more than protection of the right to liberty, it cannot be claimed to be something supra-ordinate to this right; for this right, as already stated, determines whether a political community preserves that condition that is absolutely essential to the possibility that a human being might flourish when he lives with others. (Rasmussen, 1991, p. 143)

The distinction between public and private benefits is, by most economists, taken for granted. According to economic theory, public benefits are goods that nobody will supply in a free market because its consumption cannot be restricted and therefore the goods cannot be sold. The economic theory of public goods indicates that individual action and choice will not give a sufficient supply of goods of this sort. Some sort of collective choice and collective action has to be introduced to correct individual action.

IMPLICATIONS FOR SOCIAL JUSTICE

Basically, this position relates justice to a human sense. It appeals to human beings' consciousness and humanity (empathy) in the evaluation of what is good or not. It contradicts arguments of an opportunistic kind that I can seek to optimise my position independent of what happens to others. It puts the alertness of others' sufferings from my own action on myself. In a way, this is the most individualistic position of the four presented here, as the burden of justice relates directly back to the individual's moral consciousness.

Discursive Ethics

Hilary Putnam (2004) is among those who have argued strongly against an ontological basis for ethics. In his pragmatic understanding, ethics is something developed in practice, in concrete problem-solving. He sees John Dewey as a key philosopher for this position. Dewey's argument is that morality and ethics are part of ongoing learning processes in society. Putnam's argument parallels those who object to the idea of fixed, universal truths about morality and ethics. It actually includes Ken Binmore (2005) when he argues that although justice is a natural process, its local, specific content is contextual. How is it that ethics evolves in a dialogical or discursive process?

A key reference here will be Habermas and his communicative theory. Habermas (1981) has laid down the foundation for dialogue and ideal-talk situations. It implies both structures of a Kantian kind, but also a pragmatic attitude to understand how dialogue means solving problems in practice (Göranzon et al., 2006). I suggest that Locke's theory should be interpreted within something I have called the *liberal argumentation theory* (Johnsen, 1991). A liberal argumentation theory is slightly different from Habermas's ideal-talk theory. The liberal argumentation theory is action oriented and its intention is not to try to develop universal, binding norms. Neither does it take some sort of rational individual action as its premises. When we say that the liberal argumentation theory is action oriented, we mean that when an argumentation situation is established, real people with social knowledge take part in the process (and not, as with Habermas/Rawls, ideal agents who operate behind a 'veil of ignorance').[21]

The individuals are free to participate in the argumentation, but they are at the same time part of a social system of informal norms, authorities, traditions (that can be seen as some sort of tacit consent). The liberal argumentation has, in other words, its parallel in the transformation from the natural condition to the civil society in

---

21   See Jürgen Habermas (1983, pp. 135, 177). For a critique of Habermas's universalisation process to establish norms, see Douglas Rasmussen (1989).

Locke's theory. This means that when the argumentation starts, some fundamental conditions have already been established: as an individual, you are regarded as an equal partner in the argumentation (natural rights), and it is better to have an argumentation than not have one (consent), and the reason why the argumentation is started is that the individuals that participate regard it as better to participate than to stay outside (the common good).

These three preconditions must be taken into account prior to any argumentation. The first of these conditions establishes the autonomy of the individual (natural rights). The second condition is a harmony assumption (it is better to solve social conflicts through argumentation than through violence). We can call this condition consent. The third condition is an equilibrium condition (it is the individual's anticipation that argumentation will lead to a better condition that forces the argumentation to take place). This third condition is the common good condition.

Together, these three conditions make a complete system for a pareto-optimal social structure.[22] I choose to see them as three basic conditions prior to the argumentation, and I regard them as a minimum condition for a free society. Hoppe writes:

> First, that argumentation is not only a cognitive but also a practical affair. Second, that argumentation, as a form of action, implies the use of scarce resource of one's body. And third, that argumentation is a conflict-free way of interaction. Not in the sense that there is always agreement on the things said, but in the sense that as long as argumentation is in progress it is always possible to agree at least on the fact that there is disagreement about the validity of what has been said. And this is to say nothing else than that a mutual recognition of each person's exclusive control over his own body must be presupposed as long as there is argumentation (note again, that it is impossible to deny this and claim this denial to be true without implicitly having to admit its truth). (Hoppe, 1989, p. 132)

Hoppe's discussion throws light on another aspect of the argumentation situation. The argumentation can be seen as a process that emerges because knowledge is a limited resource. This perspective on the argumentation situation forms a bridge to Hayek's theory of limited knowledge and of use of knowledge in society. Hayek notes:

> The classical argument for tolerance formulated by John Milton and John Locke and restated by John Stuart Mill and Walter Bagehot rests, of course, on the recognition of this ignorance of ours. (Hayek, 1960, p. 30)

Division of knowledge is the cement of social interaction and it assumes that nobody has superior knowledge.[23] This implies that condition three presupposes the individual's autonomy, the value of sharing labour and knowledge, and tolerance in the meaning that no one's knowledge is superior to others'. There is no conflict between natural rights and consent because natural rights cannot be consented or rejected. Neither is there a conflict between natural rights and common good because common good is

---

22   These three conditions are sufficient to form a Pareto-optimal political order. Since we are only talking about negative rights (what Sen calls 'direct liberties'), we avoid what he calls 'the impossibility of the Paretian liberal'. See Amartya Sen (1983). However, Locke's three principles do not necessarily create pareto efficiency from an 'objective' point of view; Coleman therefore calls this 'the subjectivist's criterion of efficiency'. op. cit. s. 106.

23   Hayek (1976, p. 77) and Hayek, *The Constitution of Liberty*, op. cit. p. 60. See also Hope (1989, p. 12ff).

not some positive social good that would involve social redistribution in conflict with natural rights.

THE IMPOSSIBILITY OF CONSTRUCTING A SOCIAL DECISION FUNCTION

Ronald Coase was to argue in his famous essay *Problem of Social Cost* (Coase, 1960) that there are at least two distinct solutions to externalities: on the one hand a *transaction solution* within the market, the practical implication of which is dependent on the legal structure of society, and on the other hand a *political solution*, the implication of which is a matter of political priority. Coase's argument is that these two solutions are distinct and based on two different approaches. They are not comparable as principles since their practical implications will differ from one situation to another.

Economists have been too naive about the possibility of constructing a social welfare function. If such a function involves ethical considerations, or if measures necessary to increase social utility have to be decided by political bodies and that in itself involves decision-making processes, we need more insight into these processes before we can choose between different systems.

A similar criticism of the idea of constructing a social decision function came from Kenneth Arrow and Amartya Sen. What Arrow called the *Impossibility Theorem* and Sen called *The Liberal Paradox* both show that it is impossible to construct a social decision function. As Sen remarks:

> ... all Pareto-inclusive, nondictatorial, irrelevant-alternative-independent rules of going from individual welfare functions to a social ordering will fail to generate a social ordering if cardinality is combined with noncomparability. (Sen, 1970, p. 124)

To complicate the matter, Kenneth Arrow, with his *impossibility theorem*, and Amartya Sen have argued that liberal values will never lead to a social decision function. There is no possibility of simply combining collective decisions and liberal values. Amartya Sen has argued that liberal values will never lead to a social decision function. There is no possibility of combining collective decisions and liberal values. In Sen's context, some sort of dictatorship (in abstract sense, meaning majority rule, or limited choice) has to be introduced.[24]

Amartya Sen's *The Idea of Justice* (2009) or Michael J. Sandel's *Justice* (Sandel, 2010), you find inter-relations between terms such as justice, social contract and justice as fairness. For Sen, justice and freedom are closely linked to development. If you look at John Rawls' classical *A Theory of Justice*, he mainly uses the term *social contract*. The term social contract is culturally situated and partly defined in terms of the contracting parties.

Amartya Sen (2009) repeats his critique of a theory of justice. He does not think any single principle can provide us with arguments that solve all justice problems. Thereby he criticises his teacher John Rawls. Sen rather proposes a different avenue to discuss social justice, not as an ultimate principle, but more as a practical comparison. His argument is somewhat discursive: what we need is to have a high level of attention to justice issues

---

24   See Amartya Sen (1970). Even Sen seems to forget that social consensus emerges only if and because individuals are better off, which really is the reason we made society in the first place.

and to discuss them, and also to bring into the discussion factual knowledge. Sen wants to avoid a justice debate that is only normative and political because it might imply somebody's value over another. He also, as mentioned, would avoid theorising the belief in a *logical solution* to justice issues because he does not think it exists. So the middle ground between these two is to have an open, informed debate in society on justice. Note that Sen's arguments are in line with Toulmin (2001).

Sen's conclusion is not surprising. Although the discussion about the liberal paradox has continued for over 20 years, some implications from Sen's argument are very obvious. What Sen is pointing at is basically the nature of the questions that can be decided by collective choice. The types of choice that can be made collectively are typically choices where it makes a difference whether we make it collectively or we make it privately, as is the case with the establishing of laws and norms.

In Sen's model, this difference is not apparent. In Sen's model, individuals decide between pairs of goods. If an individual can decide between any pair of goods, purely by individual (hedonistic) choice without any reference to how other people choose, what we are talking about is typically private goods (since this is how we define private goods) and there is no need for collective choice.

IMPLICATIONS FOR SOCIAL JUSTICE

The argument of Sen and Arrow really does not alter the conclusions of John Locke, since what Locke called the common good was something very different from private goods. A different perspective on the same critique of Sen and Arrow has been presented by James Buchanan (1977, p. 241). Buchanan argues that it was wrong in the first place to assume that individual welfare functions would add up to some sort of social welfare. Social welfare is *not* the sum of individual welfare, but rather the result of a social *process* by which social goals are *chosen*. The nature of the constitution under which this choice is made will have a decisive effect on the result. The neo-classical definition of public goods is something that should be decided by collective choice because it is something that cannot be consumed or chosen independently of other people's choices, and at the same time, its supply will make everybody better off. Badiou (2001) argues that the market as such is not ethical. It is simply an exchange mechanism. According to Lomasky, people who act in a market do so because they have a plan. A plan cannot exist unless there is some value that is pursued. In order to pursue a plan to achieve something valuable, there must be some sort of impersonal value (Lomasky, 1987, p. 234). Therefore, plan-pursuing activities in the market presuppose impersonal values.

Nozick argues that negative rights are not a matter of collective choice in the way Amartya Sen uses it. Sen later admits this (Sen, 1976). However, Nozick's argument is very dependent on the existence of two distinct types of rights, so-called negative and positive rights. And even if this distinction is correct, I do not think that Nozick has solved the basic dilemma between individual action and collective choice.

Nozick argues for a basic harmony between individual choice and a minimal state. The minimal state of Nozick is a state that only protects what Nozick calls negative rights. That is, the state does not interfere with the individual's choice, but rather protects and creates an environment where individuals are free to make choices. Security and protection of negative rights are the basic objectives of such a state.

Table 9.2   A brief overview of the four positions on social justice

	Natural ethics	Rational ethics	Humanist ethics	Discursive ethics
Basic reference	Nature	Universality	Empathy	Social deliberation
Social justice understood as	Just distribution of rights	Universal justice	Justice as positive experiences	Justice as social acceptability
Individual/ society relation	Two independent dimensions: the whole different from individual decisions	The whole defines the part (individual behaviour)	The part defines the whole: individual behaviour as basis for social justice	Interrelation or dialogical relation between individual and society
Limitations for knowledge	Social knowledge as evolution and through exchange	The law defines acceptable and not acceptable knowledge	Subjective knowledge	Socially acceptable knowledge
The role of knowledge	Through exchange	Universal ethics is regarded as true. However in implementation, local, contextual positions should be observed	Debating subjective interpretations	Knowledge a core dimension in deliberation

Summarising the Four Perspectives

Table 9.2 gives a brief summary of the discussion in this chapter. The main point has been to show that there are different perspectives on how to understand social justice.

It has also been an intention of this discussion to argue for some integration of the four perspectives. That was why John Locke was used as a catalyser for the debate. Locke had, as I see it, in his theorising implied arguments from all four perspectives.

To recapitulate the main controversies and dualisms I have discussed:

- positive versus negatives liberty
- is or ought
- the local and the abstract order
- selfishness versus empathy
- universal principles versus discursive solutions.

Hayek argues strongly for the divide between abstract order and the local, constructed just society: through the concept of closed and open order. However, the divide is not that clear

- it is likely that many of the institutions that we celebrate in society are results of design;
- the market order depends on a justice system that can solve disputes and create stability for private contracts;

- it is also likely that these laws and regulations have impact on the overall order: it is likely for instance that inheritance laws had great impact on ownership structure in society.

Ethics is prior to our normative interpretation of just order in society. However, justice and rights are our applications of the ethical principles. I have tried to show four different interpretations of this application. Theorists such as Amartya Sen and Ken Binmore, although arguing from different positions, would probably agree on issues such as the discursiveness of local, just solutions, the adaptation of just principles to local contexts, or the need to have some fairness principles to guide order in society.

Conclusion

The argument in this chapter is that ideas we have on morals, ethics and justice and how they influence our view on social justice have implications for our theory of knowledge. I see three different types of implications: (1) our knowledge about human nature and about social development guide our position of social justice and the market, (2) our perspective on social justice defines what is acceptable and unacceptable knowledge, and (3) the perspective we have on social justice implies a sort of social process in which knowledge is developed. There is also a fourth perspective that is relevant, and that relates to the difference between knowledge and physical resources as main drivers in the economy. There are two issues related to this distinction: firstly, much of the ethics and distribution debates, including the Lockean proviso, relate to a situation with scarce physical resources. With knowledge, the point is that sharing does not imply less to others. Knowledge can be shared infinitely. Justice issues related to sharing knowledge refer to both what is the social need for transparency and information, but also the individual need to protect itself from exposing personal knowledge. Protection of private knowledge is perhaps becoming a bigger issue than securing common information. The second point relates to the value of one's own knowledge in social situations. As Pettit (2010) argues, one argument for sharing resources is that the utility of my resources is very dependent on the wealth of others. This relates to the quality of what is produced in the market, but also on my interaction with others in the market. The wealthier everybody is, the more value will be given to products and services that maintain wealth. With knowledge, this argument can be made very specific; in a communicative situation, the value of my arguments is highly dependent on the competence and knowledge that others have. Others' ignorance is a threat to social deliberation. Sharing competence and increasing knowledge is in the interest of everybody.

Regarding (1), basic philosophical positions have implications for how we reason around justice issues. If we believe in biological evolution as a main force in society, it will have implications for how we think about social engineering. If we believe in the freedom of will, and of subjective consciousness, it has implications for our view on moral development.

Regarding (2), this is perhaps the most serious issue related to knowledge, because it is about how we legitimise restrictions on knowledge development. Issues of free speech, issues of public surveillance in the name of fighting terrorism and issues of discussing religious issues without being constrained by claims of blasphemy are related to this issue.

Regarding (3), this is an important aspect of knowledge development as it relates to how we organise knowledge development processes in society. It relates to who participates, who has a voice or how decisions are made.

10 *Knowledge, Social Systems and Legal Order*

Introduction

John Rawls has asked one of the pending questions about contemporary society:

> *How is it possible that deeply opposed though reasonably comprehensive doctrines may live together and all affirm the political conception of a constitutional regime? What is the structure and content of the political conception that can gain the support of such an overlapping consensus? (Rawls, 1996, p. xx)*

The question both relates to order and to system. The order part refers to the legal structure that attempts to create some coherence in society. The system part is about how to combine dynamic development with structure. Liberal society has to balance pluralism with order and structure. As Jürgen Habermas argues:

> *The social structures of early modernity are dominated by a process in which an economic system steered through the medium of money differentiates itself from an order of political domination, which for its part takes the shape of a system steered through administrative power. At the same time, the formation of these two subsystems stimulates the separation of civil society from economy and state. Traditional forms of community are modernized into a 'civil society' that, under the banner of religious pluralism, also differentiates itself from cultural systems. The need for integration arises in a new way with these processes of differentiation, a need to which positivized law responds in three ways. The steering media of money and administrative power are anchored in the lifeworld through the legal institutionalization of markets and bureaucratic organizations. Simultaneously, interaction contexts are juridically structured – that is, formally reorganised in such a way that the participants can refer to legal claims in the case of conflict – where previously the conflicts arising in them had been managed on the basis of habits, loyalty, or trust. Finally, as the necessary complement to judification of potentially all social relationships, democratic citizenship is universalised. (Habermas, 1998, p. 75)*

Following Habermas's reasoning, there is a close relation between social structure and social law. Law takes a new meaning in modern society as a response to structural changes. Understanding the constitution of society is therefore a question of the relation between *social structure*, of *social system* and of the *constitution* and the *administrative system* of society. Reference to social system implies a holistic perspective on society. Systems theory was an attempt to disclose the natural order of things, forces and processes that operate independently of our individual actions: one should avoid metaphysics and making value judgements. In social science this inspired different theories, some of them close to systems theory, such as functionalism and structuralism.

Social Systems

Systems theory is referred to in many disciplines as different as social systems, biological systems and computer science. Systems theory is used to explain complex wholes, that is, entities where we know the individual elements but not their interrelations, or entities where we are not able to overview the total number of elements, or entities that change over time according to processes we can only explain on an aggregate level.

One can see systems as alternatives to hierarchy. Systems are networks with boundaries and relations. What then is a system? When a concept such as clusters is applied, it often indicates relations, closeness and social capital. Normally we would argue that we either have to be able to identify mutual connectedness (which elements impact each other?) and/or be able to draw a border around the elements that impact each other. However, neither networks nor systems necessarily imply relations.

We might talk about closed systems that are stable and controllable and self-regulating and open systems that are unstable and uncontrollable, with causal relationships, dynamic and change oriented. Systems might also be cybernetic, with input, process, output and feedback (regulator) mechanisms. Learning systems have been understood this way as feedback loops: its theory relates to social dynamics thinking (Jay Forester, Senge) and mental models on shared learning. Soft systems, on the other hand, focus on the relation between technical and the human sub-system. Humans always impact technology and humans are driven by values and meanings construction in their application of technology.

So-called socio-technical systems are open systems in theory, closed systems in reality (because they ignore the impact of the environment). They are systems of optimisation (of the social, the administrative and technology sub-systems). The theory on this argues that in order to optimise, you need a system of preferences. Power is normally excluded in the description on how preferences are developed. Socio-technical systems are thereby often presented as something instrumental and managerial (see Emery and Trist, 1960).

While Parsons discussed closed systems and ended in functionalistic argumentation, Luhmann has tried to develop a comprehensive theory of social system thinking as autopoietic systems. Autopoietic systems are not connected to the world directly or in any material sense, rather they are systems of interpretation. The key to Luhmann's theory is communication; different communication forms within a system are based on the differences between one system and the other. Social systems occur because they constantly have to reconstruct meaning and function, in relation to outside changes.

Different types of system can thereby be identified, such as: open, closed or autopoietic. To the extent that they are different, this should be identifiable along some dimensions, such as: social cohesion, boundaries, environment's impact, relations, connections and influences. Also, we should see differences between systems and system elements regarding dependencies, regularity of interaction, power/relations, nature of hierarchy, learning/impact. Systems and sub-systems might relate to strong and weak ties, have different levels of trust, values, common goals, common language, culture, stability and relations to other framings, such as: organisations, society, networks and communities of practice. A systems theory should also be able to specify its level of analysis, such as: individual versus group, different groups, group versus organisation, organisation versus society and organisation versus institutions.

An important breakthrough in understanding systems came with von Bertalanffy's discussion in the 1960s on the relevance of biological systems in social science. The main feature of systems theory is that it looks at wholes. It is focused on disclosing the processes by which the whole structure develops and operates (von Bertalanffy, 1968, p. xx). It tries to find out the general mechanisms behind the processes in the system, such as: information-, feedback-, control-, stability- or circuit-mechanisms. It looks at interactions, transactions, organisations and teleology within the system. In short, it focuses on what actually happens within the system and how the system operates, whether it is a hydro-dynamic system, a biological system or an economic or social system.

Von Bertalanffy defines systems as:

> complex of interacting components, concepts characteristic of organized wholes such as interaction, sum, mechanization, centralization, competition, finality, etc. (von Bertalanffy, 1968, p. 91)

Systems must have borders, a centre or something that binds it together. It must have a motion, teleology, a tendency or a pattern on an aggregate level that one can observe. This parallels for instance the findings of Ernst Mach of the physical process of entropy, which inspired social scientists to look for similar processes.

Hayek (1967) argued that the system of society contains different systems on different levels operating on different time schedules. There are long-term processes and short-term, everyday processes. The social process generates order on an individual level (rational norms), on a group level (invisible hand processes) and on the overall survival and success of groups (social evolution). The interrelation between these processes is not fixed but is very decisive for social development. It can be understood like this:

1. *A particular order of action can be observed and described without knowledge of the rules of conduct of the individuals which bring it about: and it is at least conceivable that the same overall order of action may be produced by different sets of rules of individual conduct.*
2. *The same set of rules of individual conduct may in some circumstances bring about a certain order of actions, but do not do so in different external circumstances.*
3. *It is the resulting overall order of actions, but not the regularity of the actions of the separate individuals as such which is important for the preservation of the group; and a certain kind of overall order may in the same manner contribute to the survival of the members of the group whatever the particular rules of individual conduct which bring it about.*
4. *The evolutionary selection of different rules of individual conduct operates through the viability of the order it will produce, and any given rules of individual conduct may prove beneficial as part of one set of such rules, or in one set of external circumstances, and harmful as part of another set of rules or in another set of circumstances.*

> 5. *Although the overall order of action arises in appropriate circumstances as joint product of the actions of many individuals who are governed by certain rules, the production of the overall order is of course not the conscious aim of individual action since the individual will not have any knowledge of the overall order, so that it will not be an awareness of what is needed to preserve or restore the overall order at a particular moment but an abstract rule which will guide the actions of the individual.*[1] *(Hayek, 1967, p. 68)*

Hayek's argument is that it is, to a certain extent, possible to identify the utility of social norms. It is also possible at a certain point in time to identify gainers and losers in society. However, it is relatively difficult to be certain about how particular norms emerged, why they developed and changed, and why and how they were adopted by others.

The phenomenon was addressed as early as the seventeenth century by British philosophers. They had observed that orders emerge in society that are a result of human action, but not necessarily a result of human design. Adam Smith talked about an *invisible hand*. He observed that the market process provided good and steady deliveries of bread. It did so, even if the baker had no other intention than his own self-interest. In other words, the market order emerged as if it was led by an invisible hand. He did not talk about a hidden hand; there was no hidden design behind the market order.[2]

How is it that this market order emerges? There had to be a baker who saw his interests in baking bread (a market opportunity). There had to be consumers that appreciated good bread (a quality demand). And there had to be a process by which good and bad bakers were selected (free competition). In other words, there had to be some institutional conditions for the market order to emerge. In this particular case, the institutional elements (the free market order) are able to converge the self-interests of individuals to an overall structure that is in the interest of everybody.

The formation of order in this case is an *open-ended process*. As in the market order, *no one* can say exactly what products will be offered and at what price in the future. However, we can say something about how the market order operates. What we can say something about is the structure of the order, elements that have a stimulating or a reactive effect, and stages of development. But the result of this process is not intentional. The utility of the process cannot be measured by the individual results, but by the *utility of its rules*.

The designed order means a deliberately made order, an order with a *purpose*. To be able to design a social order, you must have specific ideas of what you want to achieve: *means* are chosen according to *goals*; the process is only a road to results. The focus is on *results*. Politicians design a public administration to take care of specific tasks, laws are made to achieve social equality, a specific distribution of wealth, promote specific values, or realise specific projects. However, the problem is that some tasks are so *complex*, some ends rely on so many *processes* and the knowledge needed to achieve some specific goal is sometimes *dispersed*. Politicians may make laws to achieve some specific income distribution, but do not have control of some of the *unintended consequences* of such a policy. Or they may want to promote specific values, but cannot control the fact that people themselves choose different values.

---

1   Hayek: Notes on the Evolution of Systems of Rules of Conduct, in Hayek (1967) p. 68. Hayek is talking about different systems operating on different levels. He is also indicating that these systems represent degrees of rationality, complexity, stability and predictability.

2   See Ullmann-Margalit (1978), Hayek (1967, p. 96ff).

The Constitution

I will refer to different perspectives on law. In the philosophy of law there are different positions (Nobles and Schiff, 2004; Habermas, 1998), such as natural law (Cunningham, 1979), positivist law (Hart, 1961) and economic perspectives on law (Buchanan, 1977). Constitutions are often treated as some sort of extra-legal law. Olivencrona has identified a development from the early constitutions that were concerned with this meta-legal structure to the modern constitutions that are more modestly concerned with organising government (Olivencrona, 1971, p. 96). In Scandinavia there has developed a tradition called *realism*, where one does not search for metaphysical legalising of constitutional law. Rather, legal realism is discussed as a development of legal positivism. While positivism starts by the will of the sovereign, realism is not tracing the origin of law, rather it is investigating which laws are actually practised, obeyed and accepted. According to Ross (1946), there is a whole range of processes that influence the conception of law.

It might be agreed that one of the main purposes of the constitution is to put some sort of *constraint* on political power. However, some constitutions reach far beyond that. Therefore one might say that the visions of the constitution reflect different visions of *social development*. And in that respect, they reach into the political debate of the formation of social order; in the evolutionary vision, social order develops through *natural* and *undesigned* processes. Olivencrona (1971, p. 106) refers to this process as common law.

THE CASE OF NORWAY

Our idea of the legal process is related to how we perceive the constitutions. There normally is a national *momentum* that gives legitimacy to the creation of legal structure. In the Norwegian case, this momentum was not strong enough to allow for a complete change of the legal structure. The Constitution of Norway is, along with the American Constitution, the only one that remains from the revolutionary period at the end of the eighteenth and beginning of the nineteenth century. There was also such momentum in Norway in 1884, 1905 and 1945. However, during all of these upheavals, much of the existing legal structure has been retained. In 1884, a large constitutional change was introduced, namely parliamentarianism, without any change in the constitutional text, only through establishment of new legal practice, while in 1945 one signed a new constitutional document, called the Co-operation Act, which was intended to change the course of social development, and to some extent did, but which today has little practical meaning. In the 1970s and 1990s, a constitutional battle was fought about the possibility of Norwegian entry into the EU. Politicians intend to let this issue be decided by the *will of the people*. In recent years the constitution of Norway has been adjusted to adapt to a more secular social model.

The Norwegian example shows that the process of developing constitutions might involve a mixture of national momentum, legal practice and historical legal traditions. In a revolutionary vision, this process is more formal and the battle over political power more important since those in power have the right to change the constitution. In an evolutionary vision, the struggle of political power is less important, since social practice is an important part of the law-making process.

A Norwegian discussion of the rule of law started after the Second World War as the government was expanding its activities. It was discovered that there was a growing need to see the rule of law in relation to the total effect of government administration. The idea of rule of law was interpreted as the protection of the individual from the state, not by the state.

As the state expanded, it became in the 1950s and 1960s more and more obvious that there had to be some constraining structures within the administration itself. Related to the classical idea of the hierarchy, what was called procedural rights was implemented to protect individuals in their encounter with the public bureaucracy. These procedural rights were of the sort: rules, equal treatment and foresight. As these measures turned out to be insufficient as the public sector expanded, new instruments of rule of law were introduced, such as: openness, participation, political control, administrative control such as ombudsmen, division of power and quality standards. Even the representativeness of the bureaucracy (the question of whether the demographic characteristics of bureaucrats are relevant to the population they serve) was debated.

With all these instruments and with the myriad of organisational forms, the question was raised whether it really had been possible to achieve the level of rule of law that was intended. In fact, no one knew exactly what the total result of government activities in relation to rule of law was. For instance, when the norm of equal treatment was exchanged for the possibility of participating, what was the total effect on the rule of law for each individual (Rokkan, 1966)? The belief in instrumental rationalism faded. It also turned out that the model of participation and cooperation was difficult to manage, was resource-consuming and not very efficient and flexible. In the 1980s measures were implemented to increase efficiency, and the consequences for the rule of law were less in focus. But at the same time, a normative request of individual rights was promoted by increasingly larger groups. The pressure came as part of a political movement that raised the question of whether the welfare state had any future.

DIFFERENT VISIONS

We might identify different visions for the social order. Sowell (1987) identified two visions: *constrained* and *unconstrained*. A *constrained vision* regards human knowledge as limited, social processes as open-ended and human activity as complex. In such a world, the constrained vision has a limited perspective on what the constitution is supposed to achieve. Constrained vision means that there are limits to constitutional design and the prospects of the constitution's role in social development. By the same reason, constrained vision tends to focus on *social structure*, on *fairness of rules* and *limitation of power*.

As opposed to this, we have the *unconstrained vision*, by which there are almost no limits to what the constitution can achieve. The unconstrained vision regards the social process as a blank sheet that can be deliberately designed in almost any way. The constitution is a means in the formation of society and very often this idea is related to some utopian perception of the future. Is law an expression of will or is it based on some moral or ethical principles? This is one of the classical discussions in legal theory (Olivencrona, 1971). It should be observed that, when I used these concepts in the discussion in Chapter 8, I argued for an unconstrained vision of social and cultural development. The argument here is that a constrained constitution allows for an unconstrained social and cultural process, while an unconstrained constitution will lead to a constrained social process.

The visions of the constitution imply different ideas of the law-making process reflecting different ideologies in the tradition of law. In the evolutionary tradition, you find the concept of *common law*, meaning that law is something that develops and emerges as a result of social processes rather than as a result of law-making. *Evolution* and *common law* means that the legal system draws legitimacy from two different processes: *rules of just conduct* are developed through legal practice, while *administrative law*, regulating the public sector, is designed through law-making.

The opposite ideology, which we can call legal positivism, has in its extreme form been expressed by Hans Kelsen (1967). His system of law, by which a lower-level law draws its legitimacy from a higher-level law, ends up in a hierarchical structure. At the top of this structure there is the constitution, which has no other legitimacy than that of the power of the ruling regime. In this system, legality is derived from within the system and cannot, as with the common law, be corrected by the social process. In the common law ideology, there is a lot of law-making going on in society; in legal positivism, only the legally defined laws have any authority.

A Scandinavian tradition of law called *legal realism* has been expressed by, among others, Alf Ross. This tradition is to some extent bridging the gap between the two extremes: positivism and common law. Legal realism means that one is more concerned by what law is actually in function than by the formal structure of law-making. Realism means that a law is *legal* as long as it is *respected*, which again opens for an evolutionary process in the development of law. In the realist perspective, it is more important to secure respect and obedience for the law than to follow any particular procedure in law-making. Legal realism may be regarded as some sort of compromise between the two. Realism indicates that there are many sources of law. One of these may be the original intention of the law-giver; another may be the present interpretation of law, ethical norms inherent in the priorities of the people or in the culture (Ross, 1946, p. 141).

As we will see from this discussion: (1) there is different knowledge about social order and legal systems, and (2) different social orders and legal systems have impacted on knowledge formation in society. In order to approach it, I will refer to the four positions on the dynamics between social order and the legal structure: naturalist, rationalist, humanist and discursive. I will argue that the four give somewhat different answers to the question. However, my discussion will attempt to reconcile the four.

The Naturalist Perspective

The naturalist conception of order has long traditions and is observed in many forms. The idea of seeing society as a system with goals, means and processes has both religious and secular roots. With the emergence of modern (non-metaphysical) social science, the main effort was to explain causal relations in society. Inspired by natural science, social science tried to reveal the social laws. However, parallel to this influence, which mainly came from Newtonian physics, society was by many social scientists regarded as a system, an organism, and so on. For instance, Baron De Montesquieu wrote in 1748 in his famous book *The Spirit of the Law*:

> It is with this kind of government (monarchy) as with the system of the universe, in which there is a power that constantly repels all bodies from the centre, and a power of gravitation

that attracts them to it. Honour sets all the parts of the body politic in motion, and by its very action connects them; thus each individual advances the public good, while he only thinks of promoting his own interest. (Montesquieu, 1975, p. 25)

The above, cited from Montesquieu, is relatively representative of eighteenth-century social thinking. One will for instance note the similarity with Adam Smith's *invisible hand* explanation. Hayek has discussed these theories under the term of *natural order* and *organic theories*. These were theories that tried to explain social development over a long period of time, for instance the development of law, economic order and social institutions. To a large extent they could be classified as evolutionary theories, and again according to Hayek, they later inspired Darwin to formulate his *natural selection* theory of biological evolution (Hayek, 1967, p. 101).

SPONTANEOUS ORDER

The invisible hand is not the particular market order that emerges, but rather the emergence of the institutions that made the market order possible (Hayek, 1967, p. 100). These institutions were not designed; they developed over time. With reference to Carl Menger, Hayek explains the origin of these institutions as this:

The institutions did develop in a particular way because the co-ordination of the actions of the part which they secured proved more effective than the alternative institutions with which they had competed and which they had displaced. The theory of evolution of traditions and habits which made the formation of spontaneous orders possible stands therefore in close relation to the theory of evolution of the particular kinds of spontaneous orders which we call organisms, and has in fact provided the essential concepts on which the latter was built. (Hayek, 1967, p. 101)

The assumption is that spontaneous order emerges without any design, but there is a sort of coordination. There is the process of selection: more successful institutions are replacing less successful ones. Hayek says little about the criteria of selection. Survival is of course the main feature of the evolutionary system. The selection mechanism operates because there is a constant struggle for survival and there are limited resources. Or there might be changes in the environment that stimulate new habits, new species, new institutions. The important thing about evolution is that there is an underlying natural process that forces change.

When the system of evolution is used to explain the economic process, the features of evolution have to be incorporated in economic theory. An attempt to do this was made by Alchian (1977) in 1950 and has recently been restated by Nelson and Winter (1982). Their idea is that the main feature of the market system is the way it selects successes and failures. The system must be imagined as one with more suppliers than there is room for. Among the over-numbered organisations there is the need to adapt in order to survive. The consumers are uncoordinated, but their choice will leave some winners and some losers. Alchian is concerned with the criteria by which an organisation can survive in such an environment. He is especially focusing on how the organisation handles information. Organisations create their own stable environment. Their formal and informal network and structures form relatively stable and predictable environments. Organisations have a tendency to want to create this kind of *stability*.

Values are both rationally defined values and spontaneously evolved values. As a restatement of the ideas of the Italian seventeenth-century philosopher Giambattiste Vico (Berlin, 1976), Hayek writes in his essay *Three Sources of Human Values*:

> *Culture is neither natural nor artificial, neither generically transmitted nor rationally designed. It is a tradition of learnt rules of conduct which have never been 'invented' and whose functions the acting individuals usually do not understand. (Hayek, 1979, p. 155)*

He then writes:

> *There was then probably much more 'intelligence' incorporated in the system of rules of conduct than in man's thoughts about its surroundings. (Hayek, 1979, p. 157)*

And his negative argument is indicated by this statement:

> *Freedom is an artifact of civilization that releases man from the trammels of the small group, the momentary moods of which even the leader had to obey. Freedom was made possible by the gradual evolution of the discipline of civilization which is at the same time the discipline of freedom. It protects him by impersonal abstract rules against arbitrary violence of others and enables each individual to try to build for himself a protected domain with which nobody else is allowed to interfere and within which he can use his own knowledge for his own purposes. (Hayek, 1979, p. 163)*

Although he later says that the evolution of rules is not identical with progress in society, he claims that natural evolved order of general rules is a necessary, if not sufficient, condition for civilisation and progress.

According to David Hume, virtue is prior to sentiment. We approach the social domain with some natural virtues, including sympathy. In the social domain, we find some tacit knowledge and cultural elements as well as engage in rational discourses. This social domain is characterised by some basic structures, regulating the interaction process. Among these are sentiments such as rights, morals and ethics. They are not necessarily a result of a rational discourse process, but they are accepted since they have some utilitarian function.

In the Humean perspective, the most important function of these sentiments is to build a disciplinary structure for the discourse. There is no rational truth in this structure, since it is an artefact and a result of cultural evolution. On the other hand, it does not imply a completely relativistic view of human nature, since its main function is to lay down fair rules for social activity.

We are close to Rawls' theory of justice in this perspective, but the difference is still there, since we do not take the same starting point as Rawls (the natural condition) and so we do not extend this disciplinary structure as far as Rawls does. A structure is needed in order to guarantee fairness in the democratic process. Fairness means that the democratic process is acceptable and reasonable to those who participate and that their mutual influence on the process is taken into account. This means that the actual outcome of the process might vary from time to time, and from culture to culture. In this rather practical sense one might say that there is some relativity in the Humean concept since it will to some extent reflect cultural differences.

Do these considerations bring us close to an understanding of knowledge development in a democracy? The Humean perspective gives democracy a function within the liberal order, a function that other parts of the liberal theory (the Kantian natural rights perspective) have had problems in perceiving. The Humean perspective also represents an understanding of some of the most interesting aspects of the romantic tradition, namely the learning process. However, the Humean understanding of the social learning process is less constructivist than the romantic version. Some of the elements are:

- Self-realisation without positive rights. To be individualised and to enjoy freedom of choice is the most central factor in a self-realisation process. This one element cannot be replaced by any social construct of positive rights. It has also been argued that so-called negative rights are not only negative but are part of a moral regime.
- Sympathy is part of the exchange process. The exchange process cannot be conceived as a purely atomistic transaction.
- The extent of the political is a central question, since individuality will be a meaningless concept if everything is politics. So there has to be some individual domain.
- A disciplinary element is needed in order to secure the good functioning of the democratic process. Principles of fairness are a central part of this disciplinary structure and should reflect both virtues and sentiments as perceived within a culture as well as rational conceptions of justice.
- Social learning is activated through involvement and participation in the social process. Only very little of human nature is natural in a philosophical sense. Only virtues are natural. Most of our sentiments are artefacts. They are learned rules. In this sense, democracy (meaning learning through involvement and participation) is a central element in the liberal (Humean) conception of the social process.

Hayek is concerned with the complicated interrelation between the different orders on different levels. In addition to this, there is the system of perception: *rational norms are a result of active learning.* There is also the process of tacit learning of inhabited rules and norms. And there is the process of patterning: history has shown instances of successful patterns, such as the institution of the family, the institution of the market system, the institution of private property. Individuals are able to recognise successful patterns in the same way as they are able to speak a language. In both cases, one is not necessarily able to describe the underlying arguments or structures. In other words, by bringing in learning and action in this way, Hayek manages to answer one of Habermas's main objections to systems theory: the individual is both an actor and a reactor in systems development. People adjust their plans to each other and form rational expectations, which is a precondition for equilibrium in economic theory. The question is how we can develop learning institutions and learning organisations:

> *The decisive effect that led to the creation of the order itself, and to certain practices predominating over others, were exceedingly remote results of what earlier individuals had done, results exerting themselves on groups of which earlier individuals could hardly have been aware, and which effects, had earlier individuals been able to know them, may not have appeared at all beneficial to them, whatever later individuals may think. [...] Many of the evolved rules which secured greater cooperation and prosperity for the extended order may have differed utterly from anything that could have been anticipated...Hence, at no moment in the*

process could individuals have designed, according to their purposes, the functions of the rules that gradually did form the order; and only later, and imperfectly and retrospectively, have we been able to begin to explain these formations in principle. (Hayek, 1988, p. 72)

There is in this description a process of tacit learning of orders and rules. And there is a distinction between how these orders and rules are developed (by evolution) and how we perceive them. The equilibrating process is a result of human action but not of human design. The main function of the individual is not related to the formation of the order, but to the ability to understand and utilise the order.

Division of knowledge and individual *ignorance* means that no individual has the potential of creating an overall order in society. However, the knowledge in society is there, although it is divided between its individuals. So the challenge of the social order is to be able to *utilise the dispersed individual knowledge*. The *Nomos* perspective of this task is to look at the structure of social development and to see whether the social institutions that operate have the effect of utilising disperse knowledge. The *Thesis* perspective is to deliberately design some order according to priorities and values of those of the designer.

In the evolutionary vision, the constitutional effect of all types of action must be taken into account. Government cannot choose to respect the law on one issue and disregard it on another. People cannot claim the enforcement of law and at the same time try to avoid the use of law in their own domain. In the evolutionary vision, the constitution should be the concern of everybody.

Organisations are *Thesis* within *Nomos*. This opens for interplay between two types of order: the deliberate designed order *within* the spontaneous undesigned order. The largest *Thesis* in society is of course government administration. And as a deliberately designed order, public administration is something different from the social system. Government administration is ruled by *administrative laws*. These are *laws of legislation*, and they are very different from those *rules of just conduct* that operate within the larger social order. Politicians design laws of the administrative type and expect them to function within the open social system in the same way as they do within the administrative system.

The Rationalist Perspective

Social structure and social systems can in the rationalist perspective be linked to functionalism and positivism. Auguste Comte had with his *positivism* tried to disclose the law that governs human behaviour. Spencer used social statistics to make empirical generalisations. Structuralism forms the background for Durkheim's structuralism sociology. In his main work *De la division du travail social*, he analyses the transition from traditional to modern society, from segmented to division of labour, from collectivism to individualism, the emergence of money, and markets, studied through empirical generalisation, and argues for *social facts*. He made abstraction from observing development. It is important to be aware of his structuralism criticism of Marxism and his introduction of concepts such as symbolic systems.

The American sociologist Talcott Parsons was influenced among others by the French philosopher Emile Durkheim and his *functionalism* and by the Italian economist Wilfredo Pareto. The latter had in his great work *Trattao di Sociologia generale* (1916) (translated to: The Mind and Society) made an attempt to disclose the *system of society*.

Parsons used both ideas to make a comprehensive theory of individual action and social development, published under the title *The Social System* in 1951. Later, Parsons extended his analysis to evolutionary theories and developed some megatrend theories on historical evolution (Parsons, 1971).

In Parsons' perspective, society is built by hierarchy of systems, from the psychological system on the individual level, to the great system of social development. Each system defines the boundaries and functions of its subordinated system. There is also a process over time where the system goes through different stages (Parsons, 1971). Individuals are socialised to behave according to the functioning of the overall social system. This interrelation leaves room for individual action and choice and the process is not deterministic; however, the social structure will balance the individual action and keep it within an overall order.

Talcott Parsons' *The Structure of Social Action* presents structural functionalism: society contains invariant structures that emerge according to a development scheme to produce systems and sub-systems according to a process that implies the following phases (AGIL – system or model): adaptation (define boundaries); goal attainment (define instrumentality); integration (establish a power structure); latency (develop values).

Vilfredo Pareto in his great work *The Mind and Society* explains the main constructs in this reasoning: logical and non-logical behaviour, and residuals and derivations. Pareto establishes a theory or model of development: non-logical behaviour produces residues (structures) and derivations (values) that locked in a social group. The group thereby reproduces the arguments for its own existence, i.e., the labour class or farming class.

Actions and beliefs are divided into two: residues and derivations. The residues are the contestant elements that legitimise the variable element (derivations). The contestants are the arguments (validity justifications) that are persistent in an argument (underlying justification of a specific act). Such residues could be when killing is justified (i.e., killing is wrong but in war and self-defence it is just). Any concrete action would have to refer to this underlying norm: was this killing part of a war or self-defence (then justified) or was it not (and cannot be justified)?

Joseph Schumpeter, in the book he wrote in the 1940s, *Capitalism, Socialism and Democracy*, integrated the economic, social and political system in an attempt to explain the development of the one system with the other. His argument is a combination of economic, social and institutional processes. Schumpeter's talks about the crumbling walls of capitalism when the entrepreneurial role of the bourgeoisie is taken over by technocrats and the intellectuals. With it go the bourgeois values. Schumpeter saw (contrary to Marx) a relation between tendencies of mass production, concentration of capital and the development of socialism (the big capital, big government deal!). This means that capitalism through its success destroys the social structure and values which were a precondition for its own existence (Schumpeter, 1976, p. 161).

FUNCTIONALISM

By *rationalist* we mean that the result is a causal and explainable result of deliberate, individual action. We also in these theories anticipate that individuals act rationally and take care of their own interests (Ullman-Margalit, 1977, p. 1). What we are interested in is the relation between individual action and the overall order of society described by norms.

We find this perspective in a lot of predominant theories and works, such as James Buchanan's *Public Choice*, Robert Nozick's *Anarchy State and Utopia* and Olson's *The Logic of Collective Action*. Common to them is that they use *game theory* to describe how people act (or rather interact) in relation to the social structure (norms). The two systems-related components of game theory are on the one hand the social utility of norms (everybody is better off when they take advantage of the division of labour within society) and on the other hand the individual utility of strategic action. In short, individuals have interests in upholding the social structure and at the same time in breaking out of the structure provided it exists.

The public choice school has in the recent years given considerable contribution to the understanding of the effect of voting rules on decision-making and justice. Their analysis has indicated the importance to construct voting rules related to the nature of the issue that is to be decided. What is a just rule for the voting on taxation? What issues can be decided by simple majority vote? These are issues discussed in the constitution and they were central themes in the early days of democracy. In that early period, as we see from Burke, Madison and later De Tocqueville, one was concerned about majority rule and majority tyranny.

There are good examples that show that issues with strong minority interests are not suited for simple majority voting, neither are issues of great general importance or of little general importance; democracies might be under-democratic or over-democratic. But although some rational norms and reasoning can show us how fair decisions can be obtained, it is hard to see that one can avoid the normative questions about what is fairness, and what it is that gives legitimacy to the legal system.

Ullmann-Margalit has identified three groups of norms of this kind: PD norms (prisoner's dilemma type of norms), coordination norms and norms of partiality. *The norms of coordination* are perhaps the easiest to explain. These are norms that emerge as a result of the fact that individuals are better off by coordinating their actions than by acting independently. There does not necessarily have to be any direct communication between the individuals; what sort of norm is chosen is not important. The important thing is that there is coordination: for instance, that all telephones are linked to the same system, that we drive on the same side of the street and that we use a language that other people can understand.

By definition, coordination norms are norms where each and everyone have the same interests in preserving and obeying the norms. They are an example of ideal social equilibrium (Ullmann-Margalit, 1977, p. 1). They provide a natural conformity in society. Coordination norms produce universal institutions, open to everybody. The utility of these norms are given to everybody. On the other hand, coordination norms do not serve anybody's particular interest. Historically, we can see that the extension of the free market has brought forward open, universal institutions such as common language and common standards.[3] At the same time, groups of people, nations and individuals have speculated on being better off by not adapting to these common norms and institutions.

This brings us over to *PD norms*. PD norms are norms where it is in the interest of all to act in a certain way, and at the same time, individuals can be better off by breaking out of the consensus, provided that the others don't do it. PD norms are often exemplified by

---

3   Nozick argues that the *state* is rational to handle certain tasks in society (such as protection, defence, enforcement of law) and thereby can be seen as a result of coordinating norms. Nozick (1974), p. 118.

public goods and the free raider problem (Ullmann-Margalit, 1977, p. 101). It might be in my interest to have a national defence; however, even if I don't pay my taxes (provided that enough people do), I will still be defended. But if everybody acts like I do, there will be no defence. This is a dilemma: by acting rationally, I am about to act against my own interest. A PD norm will help me out of this dilemma; it will prevent me from hurting my own interest.

PD norms are fragile. Ullmann-Margalit suggests that a PD norm will only prevail provided a coercive force is put behind it (Ullmann-Margalit, 1977, p. 73). This brings us over to the third category of norms: *norms of partiality*. These are also coercive norms in the sense that they uphold a certain structure in society, a certain structure that implies inequality (for instance a certain distribution of wealth). In Parsons' analysis, these norms would be termed *structural functionalism*, and Parsons would argue that they both are a result of social development, and at the same time are decisive for social development. Since norms of partiality are protecting inequality in society, it is natural to see them as based on group interests or rather class interests: that they are used by one class to coerce another class even if they are informal and, in principle, voluntary norms. Defenders of social status quo (conservatives) would on the other hand argue that these social norms create harmony in society and make peaceful social change possible. However, Ullmann-Margalit argues that these norms are neither necessarily coercive nor are they necessarily creating harmony (Ullmann-Margalit, 1977, p. 197). Her argument is that society will contain a mixture of norms and interests, both coercive and coordinating ones.

Niklas Luhmann, in his *Social Systems*, tries to avoid the rigidity and determinism of a functional theory. Luhmann's system is thereby dynamic (open), but self-referential (autopoietic) in the sense that a system constitutes and reproduces itself. A system exists as a result of an ability to identify ourselves and the others. A system, such as a firm or an organisation, frames and interprets external and changes in order to sustain as a system. Even the system of law can be interpreted as a self-referential system (Luhmann, 2004). Major processes of reproduction are: communication, integration, interpretation and reformulation of identity. He is dealing with the epistemological problem of how to define a system and be part of it (self-referential).

This idea of constitutional change that we find within the revolutionary tradition, and which is reflected in the school of thought called constitutionalism (Buchanan, 1977), rests on the idea of a two-stage process to social change. First we change the rules of the game (the constitution), then the game itself changes form. This constitutionalist idea might well be criticised (Gray, 1989). *One* critique would be that it is a wrong description of what is actually happening, *another* that it lures people to think that constitutional issues are something we only have to consider at special moments, and that the everyday operation of society has no specific effect on the constitutional issues. The opposite view would be to see the constitution as some sort of abstract of individual action, as something that is formed by the social process and as the underlying guidance of individual action.

The Humanist Perspective

James Buchanan was in his later days increasingly concerned with this evolutionary approach to constitutional development. He acknowledged that constitutional change, for instance in Europe, might depend on a form of European momentum, and if the momentum was not there, constitutional change would not work (Buchanan, 1990).

I use the former Czech president Václav Havel as a representative of the humanist perspective. The humanist perspective is genuinely sceptical to social structures and social systems. Their focus is on the individual and individual moral responsibility.

The political discussion after the fall of the Berlin Wall, particularly in Czechoslovakia, seems to have focused more on rights than on social justice. In East Germany there was a strong debate over the trade-off between rights and justice before the decision to join West Germany. This discussion has actualised a little-noticed aspect of the welfare theory: the distinction between *just distribution of wealth* and *just distribution of rights*. Locke discussed justice in the context of *just distribution of rights*.

Havel argues:

> *My scepticism towards alternative political models and the ability of systematic reforms or changes to redeem us does not, of course, mean that I am sceptical of political thought altogether. [...] Above all, any existential revolution should provide hope of a moral reconstitution of society, which means a radical renewal of the relationship of human beings to what I have called the 'Human order', which no political order can replace. (Havel, 1986, p. 118)*

There is a natural reason for Havel's scepticism:

> *Ich habe die Französische Revolution erwähnt und die schöne Deklaration, die sie begleitete. Diese Deklaration hat ein Herr unterschrieben, der einer der ersten war, die im Namen dieses herrlichen, humanen Textes hingerichtet wurden. (Havel, 1989, p. 63)*[4]

The totalitarian regime has even destroyed the meaning of words. This is part of the reason why Havel is more concerned by content than by formal structures:

> *And the political consequences? Most probably they could be reflected in the constitution of structures that will derive from this 'new spirit', from human factors rather than from a particular formalization of political relationships and guarantees. In other words, the issue is the rehabilitation of values like trust, openness, responsibility, solidarity, love. I believe in structures that are not aimed at the 'technical' aspect of the execution of power, but at the significance of that execution in structures held together more by a commonly shared feeling of the importance of certain communities than by commonly shared expansionist ambitions directed 'outward'. (Havel, 1986, p. 118)*

Havel's conclusion turns out to be similar to the one I try to present in this part of the chapter:

> *It is only with the full existential backing of every member of the community that a permanent bulwark against 'creeping totalitarianism' can be established. These structures should naturally arise from below as a consequence of authentic social 'self-organization'; they should derive vital energy from a living dialogue with the genuine needs from which they arise,*

---

4   'I mentioned the French Revolution and the beautiful declaration that accompanied it. This declaration has signed a gentleman who was one of the first to be executed on behalf of this wonderful, humane text.'

and when these needs are gone, the structures should disappear. The principles of their internal organization should be very diverse, with a minimum of external regulation. The decisive criterion of this 'self-constitution' should be the structure's actual significance, and not just a mere abstract norm. (Havel, 1986, p. 119)

CONSTITUTIONAL CONSTRAINTS

Humanists are sceptical about constitutions. The constitution puts some sort of *constraint* on the social process and the political power. These constraints can be of different types: there might be *procedural* constraint, which lays down rules for how decisions could be achieved, and there might be *substantial* constraints by which certain areas of social activity are protected against all types of intrusion, including legislation itself.

I would argue that Philip Pettit's *Republicanism* belongs here (Pettit, 2010). The core of his perception of social and legal order is to develop non-domination as a core principle. Republican government should attribute as much freedom as possible within the constraints of non-domination, which would allow individuals to utilise their personal freedom.

It is interesting to note that substantial constraints are less relevant within the evolutionary approach than within the revolutionary approach to constitutions. This is the reason why James Madison and the Federalists did not want to include the Bill of Rights within the American Constitution. This is also the reason why the British do not accept the idea of a Bill of Rights, while the French have proposed it as a founding element of the Common Market. The discussion about the Social Charter within the Maastricht Treaty runs along these lines. Let me explain this a little further:

Madison did not want to include natural rights in the constitution because he thought that would imply that natural rights were *established* by the constitution (Hayek, 1960, p. 184). In his opinion, natural rights are *prior* to the constitution. If it was established by the constitution, it might even be removed by the same constitution, while in his opinion the constitution had *no right* to interfere with individual natural right.

The example shows some of the features of the evolutionary constrained vision of the constitution and its contrast to the revolutionary unconstrained vision, for instance of the French Revolution, where rights were the founding idea of the constitution. When that is said, I should like to repeat that these are *ideal type* visions and do not reflect in their pure form any actually working constitution. It would be more correct to use expressions such as that the British constitution has a tendency towards the evolutionary, constrained vision, while the French and Continental tradition has a tendency towards the revolutionary, unconstrained vision.

Questions such as what should be decided by the political system, what is the extent of the individual integrity, what is the public domain are questions with very different answers, even within the two traditions. If we look at some extremes, we can find on the one hand a conservative thinker such as Carl Schmitt who introduces an omnipotent conception of the state, but within a constitutional setting, while radical and revolutionary thinkers such as Franz Oppenheimer (1975) opposed the extension of the political realm.

The constitution is *not* the expression of the sum of individual interests. It is something *very different* from private interests; it is a *common good*. It lays down rules for how individuals can pursue their own interests. It also defines the public domain.

The constitution makes constraints both on public and government activities and on individual activities. These constraints can be divided into two groups: substantive constraints and procedural constraints (Gwartney and Wagner, 1988, p. 37), that is, constraints on *what* is done and constraints on *how* things are done.

A strict formal concept of the rule of law, like the one we find with Carl Schmitt and the positivists, might not be sufficient to grip the essence of the rule of law: *the security that each individual enjoys under the rule of law* (Wolin, 1992). Formal instruments might be important, but they are not the only conditions that matter and they ought to be altered according to the situations that occur. Our discussion has particularly focused on the importance of altering these instruments according to the organisation of public administration.

An important condition for the security of individual integrity and protection under the rule of law is to be able to give priority to the right values under conflicting conditions. Constitutions legitimise certain actions and restrict others. This might sometimes lead to conflict. The purpose of the constitution is to give guidance in such conflict; it is a sort of final level of appeal. However, as we shall see in the next section, formal guarantees can never secure prosperity and well-being in society.

The Discursive Perspective

Jürgen Habermas has made a critique of systems theory where he rejects the idea that a meaningful description of social development could be made independent of value judgement and consideration of ideology and power structure. More specifically, he rejected the comparing of atoms and cells in biology with human agents in society. First of all he rejected it because human agents have meaning and purposes in themselves, while atoms serve the purpose of others. Society, therefore, is not a system with boundaries; rather it is an open sphere for public debate (discourse). Following the same line of argument, Habermas rejected the teleology perspective of systems theory. Society has no purpose or meaning independent of the individuals. Society is an arena for discourse where individuals present their meaning and purpose (Holub, 1991, p. 106ff).

Another aspect of Habermas's critique of the systems theory is his rejection of the idea that society develops independent of human action. By claiming that something *inevitable* happens is to give it *absolute authority*. Thereby, systems theory ends up as a self-legitimating system, which in practice means that the present order of society can claim legitimacy. It is very close to creating a link between what *is* and what *ought*.

But there are dilemmas. Habermas's colleague, Karl-Otto Apel, on the one hand shares Habermas's critique of systems theory, but on the other hand makes use of systems theory arguments. Apel (1984) is searching for *intersubjective ethics* as a means of solving some of the collective challenges in society. He is also regarding the environmental threat as a collective challenge. However, environmental threats are a challenge brought to light by systems theory and it is a problem arising because there is a dilemma between how rational people act individually and the overall order that is created. In other words, society is *not* only an arena for rational discourse!

Constitutions are results of social and political development, but they also affect social and political development. Constitutions put constraints on some types of action and legitimise others. If we take the Norwegian example from the 1814 Constitution, it restricted immigration; it restricted some religious practices and some commercial activities. It also put some procedural constraints on political decision-making.

SOCIAL DELIBERATION

The liberal constitution emancipates the individual. If that process is reversed by organisations in the form that people are not responsible for their actions, do not meet the consequences of their actions, are intolerant, are insensible or are uninterested in their actions, this emancipation will not lead to prosperity. Society needs discourse, irregularity, opposition and people who will not obey authority – people *who go on discoveries*. These irregular activities create tension in society. Society needs a certain tension in order to develop. Competition can lead to this type of creative tension. These processes will, if they are in balance, stimulate creative learning. It is the function of the constitution to establish the rules of the social learning process.

It might be more complicated to understand the discourse and learning process than only to refer to a strict causality between the rules of the constitution and the nature of discourse. In fact, although constitutions lay down rules for discourse, discourse itself legitimises norms and rules (Dreyfus and Dreyfus, 1990, p. 70). Again we can talk about two visions – one in which the purpose of the legal process is to interpret the original meaning of the constitution (this is what normally has been referred to as legality); the other vision that has been advocated by, among others, Foucault claims that meaning is something that occurs during the discourse: *the discourse activates and legitimises meaning*, that is, there was no prior meaning to be interpreted.

Although there are well-developed theories for understanding the effect of constitutional constraints, we can think of the building of constitutions in each country as a learning process, a constant dialogue or discourse. The constitutions of a country cannot be adopted by another country because they are more than only the words that are written on a paper. A constitution is the total amount of experience, tacit knowledge, norms, customs and attitudes that have developed within a nation. They are also related to different institutional frameworks, social structures and different interpretations.

Two countries might have the same laws to allow for tolerance, but it might mean something very different in a society where the debate is open and friendly compared with one where basic institutions or beliefs restrict the actions and behaviour of people. On the other hand, there are reasons to believe that a liberal constitution which promotes liberal institutions in society will, over time, encourage the development of liberal attitudes, customs and behaviour. There is learning going on, and it might be both constrained and encouraged by the constitutions. There are, however, historical examples of liberal regimes that have turned into totalitarianism, and totalitarian regimes that have turned liberal relatively quickly:

> *From the long-term perspective, the constitutional state does not represent a finished structure but a delicate and sensitive – above all fallible and revisable – enterprise, whose purpose is to realize the system of rights anew in changing circumstances, that is, to interpret the system of rights better, to institutionalize it more appropriate, and to draw out its content more radically. This is the perspective of citizens who are active engaged in realizing the system of rights. Aware of, and referring to, changed contexts, such citizens want to overcome in practice the tension between social facility and validity. Although legal theory cannot adopt*

this participant perspective as its own, it can reconstruct the paradigmatic understanding of law and democracy that guides the citizens whenever they form and idea of the structural constraints on the self-organization of the legal community in their society. (Habermas, 1998, p. 384)

Discourse is supposed to lead to rationality, since the assumption is that the better, more rational argument will win approval. Conditions for this creative process are, however, that an actual dialogue takes place, that people are willing to learn and to accept the better argument. We might refer to this as qualities of the learning arena and qualities of the learning individual. An alternative to discourse is authority. When authority is used, there is no dialogue. On the other hand, even a constitution presupposes some norms and constraints on actions. Constitutions are both the result of and give the structure to the discourse. In social development, structural elements such as the constitution are central because it influences both the *content* and the *form*. Social development occurs constantly independent of whether the constitution is in focus or not. One might perceive the constitution as a double-edged sword. It cuts both ways: either it is used actively, or one attempts to avoid it. In both cases, actions taken have to refer to some sort of meta-structure.

The Individual and the Legal and Administrative System

I have tried to attribute different perspectives on social order to different visions for the constitution and legal system. Roughly speaking, the naturalist position comes close to a natural law idea. The legal system builds on the rule of law principles and is founded on fundamental, moral obligations of law to the preservation of individual rights. The rationalist position on social order comes closer to the conceptualisation of law that we find in the positivist law theory. Law is its own social system which primarily establishes itself as an inertial referential system of legal structures. I have presented the humanist position as some sort of anti-law position. Here the idea of constitutional constraints and non-domination of law is the essential idea. Finally, I have argued that the discursive position sees law in a deliberative perspective. Law and constitution are inherently integrated into the social structure and should be understood as the tendency to social deliberation. I will now link this to the administrative system.

ADMINISTRATIVE SYSTEM

In the classical description of the bureaucracy, the bureaucratic process is to implement decisions made by the legal and political system as accurately as possible. While Max Weber described this bureaucracy, his intention was to develop ideal types for research purposes, not to describe the actual functioning of bureaucracy. However, this ideal type does have some elements of truth; there is an element of insensitivity, of inflexibility and authority in bureaucratic action. The literary description given by Kafka in his novel *The Castle* shows how impossible it is to get inside, get into dialogue or even get an idea of who is in charge within the bureaucracy. K. (he does not even have a full name, indicating the impersonality of the situation) is only encountered by a person bringing messages. And this person has no responsibility, does not answer questions or even argue in favour of decisions. Towards such a bureaucracy, the individual is without any real chances. The individual falls into despair.

Zygmunt Bauman, in his book *Modernity and the Holocaust* (Bauman, 1989), presents Holocaust not as a historical and ideological problem, but rather as a result of modern systematic rationality. Bauman's main point is that the individual moral responsibility is lost in modern bureaucratic systems. He writes:

> *One of the most remarkable features of the bureaucratic system of authority is, however, the shrinking probability that the moral oddity of one's action will ever be discovered, and once discovered, made into a painful moral dilemma. In a bureaucracy, moral concerns of the functionary are drawn from focusing on the plight of the objects of action. They are forcefully shifted in another direction – the job to be done and the excellence with which it is performed. (Bauman, 1989, p. 159)*

The administrative system is the *Thesis* within *Nomos*. Van Gusteren has even called it a part of the planning paradigm, that is, a rational, central rule approach to social change. It is the idea of vertical rationality: decisions are made in the political body on top of the bureaucracy, and these decisions are implemented efficiently. But because administrative laws are numerous, badly systematised, vague and changing constantly, legal uncertainty is the result (van Gusteren, 1976, p. 86). Therefore, van Gusteren concludes, administrative laws are not suitable for policy implementation. However, the last years have seen a change in the organisation of the public sector, and these changes have brought public administration closer to the organisation forms we find within the market economy.

On the one hand, there has been a tremendous growth both in the total number of tasks and the relative share of the creation of the gross national product produced by the public sector. On the other hand, there has been a drive towards efficiency, privatisation and reorganisation that has changed the face and nature of public administration.

If we look at the organisational changes, there has been a tendency towards decentralisation, use of decrees, emancipation of lower levels of bureaucracy, management by objectives, less political control, and more influence by users. Public administration has moved into new areas of society and, at the same time, privatisation has moved into traditional public areas. Management ideas of the private sector have influenced the public sector, and more and more it is difficult to discover the real difference between public and private organisations. The effect of this has been, among others, that law-makers have no guarantee of how the public administration chooses to implement political decisions.

What effect has this had on the relationship between the individual and public administration? First of all, public administration is so vast that no one has a complete perception of how it operates. Secondly, some analysis points out that these changes have created a grey zone between public and private activities where the legal conditions are unclear.

NEW TASKS AND THE REVOLUTION IN PUBLIC ADMINISTRATION

The state has different tasks. One group of tasks is related to enforcement of law, implementation of authority and interference in private conflicts. Courts, police and military activities are for this reason centralised functions with a strong hierarchical structure. There are other functions, such as distribution of welfare, production of services or production of benefits, that most states are involved in. These activities are different from both the need of political priorities and the possibility to compete in a market economy.

The classical description of government activities was related to the idea of common good, that is, benefits that the market will not provide because either it is impossible to restrict the demand (free-rider problem) or it is difficult to establish a competing supply (because of falling unit cost of production). In practical life, most government activities are either what we can call semi-collective goods, or purely private goods that the government chooses to provide because the government gives them priority.

Although government has chosen to provide different goods and services, they do not need to have the same close control over all these activities. One of the criteria that have changed in recent years is the view on the need to have centralised political control over all government activities. A more extensive use of the market process has emerged. In order to select activities, there are two criteria: is there a qualified demand and is there the possibility of establishing competing supply? These supply and demand conditions are important for the possibility of using the market process.

I have chosen to select government activities in relation to the need of centralised political prioritising and the possibility to use market forces. This gives us Table 10.1.

If we look at the changes that have happened within government organisation, we can identify some tendencies between tasks and choice of organisation form. The classical rule-led hierarchy that Max Weber described as the typical bureaucracy with its accurate implementation of the wishes of the legislative power (Weber, 1920, p. 144) does to some extent still operate within areas where the need for political control and prioritising is high and the possibility to use market forces is low. At the other extreme there is the market organisation, which more and more is chosen in areas where the need for political control is low and the market system operates. Examples of this last type are production of commodities and, to an increasing extent, the production of services. In the case of, for instance, hospitals – which in Norway are government-run – there is a growing debate whether to split the two functions of producing and financing hospital services: government might finance the services, while it is left to the market system to produce the services. Similar arrangements are tried in other areas and they reflect different organisation forms.

Table 10.1 Public tasks in relation to the need of political control and the possibility to use market forces

	Limited possibility to use market forces	Great possibility to use market forces
Little need for political control	the state as service provider	the state as producer of commodities
Big need for political control	the state as distributor of welfare	the state as protector and promoter of culture and values

There are border areas where it is difficult to privatise and at the same time there is need for – but little will to – public prioritising. These are areas where different sorts of decentralised administration and mixed organisations such as private organisations with some public responsibilities, or public authorities, are used. When government activities are organised according to traditional hierarchical bureaucracy, rules and political control as well as openness and equal standards are sufficient measures. However, these measures have little effect when the administration is organised as a market organisation. It lies in the structure of the market organisation that they are allowed to organise their work themselves. Control has to be related to results of their work, not procedures. Rule of law will likewise have to be related to rights, more than procedural guarantees. This means in short that the changing face of government organisation towards market organisation implies that the measure of rule of law to a lesser extent is related to procedural guarantees and to an increasing extent is related to individual rights. Negative rights are often called natural rights, while positive rights are often called welfare rights.

The level of welfare rights tends to be a result of what we can call political culture. Different societies have different expectations about welfare rights. Welfare rights may, for the same reason, take many different forms. In recent years, we have seen an increase in phenomena that we can call political priorities: that politicians guarantee a specific group of people some specific services. However, there is a legal debate over the legality of these priorities. It is also an important aspect to consider that such political priorities tend to be implemented in areas of public administration where the needs are easy to specify.

Political priorities tend to be biased, due, among other things, to structural differences in public tasks. The same could be said about the possibility to define collective goods and to implement procedural guarantees. When government activities are organised in the form of market organisations, individuals will have to be emancipated by strengthening natural rights. Service quality is a result both of competition and commitment and, although it is not a rule of law instrument like procedural rights, it does have some aspects that lead to improvement of service and therefore of the perceived quality of life.

In the instrumental vision, the assumption is that certain procedures will guarantee specific ends. The important end in question is the rule of law, that is, how the individual experiences the *comfort and safety of a good society.* This is a rather broad conception of the rule of law. This implies that a lot of measures contribute to the well-being of society, and that a discussion of the rule of law cannot be isolated from these other activities.

In the evolutionary vision, rule of law was a consequence of limited government, division of power and procedural rights in the law-making process. To secure individual rights and the rule of law, individuals were given rights against the administration, such as the right to participate, to openness, to welfare goods and to political priorities.

The question related to legitimacy and justice is mainly a question about who decides over the rules, the extent of the public administration and of the administrative laws. With reference to the expression of Bauman, we might say that in order to avoid *Holocaust* we must ensure that the oddity of bureaucracy is always discovered, that is, there has to be some mechanism by which the bureaucratic action is exposed. It might be exposed by internal control, but more and more as the public sector takes on new tasks and changes its organisation form, the exposure will be in the market and by those individuals who are affected.

Conclusion

In this chapter I have tried to establish a relation between social structure, social systems and legal order. My argument is that knowledge formation in society is in two ways linked to this discussion: (1) as visions of social system and order are based on different knowledge, and (2) that the actual system and order have impact on knowledge formation in society. I have tried to show that an attempt to formulate a relationship between social structure, social system and legal order (including both constitution and administrative system) has to comply with the fact that there are different and competing visions for these orders and systems. I have tried to identify four such visions:

- natural perspective: natural law, evolutionary perspective on order and market;
- rational perspective: positivist perspective on law, public administration as execution of legal decisions;
- humanist perspective: anti-law, constitutional constraints on political power, human flourishing, dialogue;
- discursive perspective: social deliberation.

Although these are opposed and contested positions, there are still a lot of cross-references and exchange of insights between them. In the next chapter I intend to build on this framework in order to discuss knowledge and democracy.

CHAPTER 11 *Knowledge and Democracy*

Introduction

I argued in the Introduction that my intention is to try to understand what knowledge is, how it is developed and what is does. I further argued that knowledge is a neutral concept. There might be knowledge that I disagree with. I might regard it as wrong or false, but it might still be knowledge. Knowledge is what is (socially) regarded as a right understanding of things. Knowledge is not merely an opinion. Saying it is social also implies that there are warrants to knowledge. The social process somehow sorts out what is knowledge in relation to lies, fantasies, deliriums or meaninglessness. Neither is knowledge mere fact. Facts are not knowledge. Facts become knowledge when they are subject to some sort of interpretation. One could say that knowledge is facts plus meaning, but that would be too simple. Knowledge is something we know, or we think we know. Knowledge is a meaning-related phenomenon. Knowledge is not the same as truth. Saying that there are socially warranted understandings of things that we hold as knowledge does not mean that they are true. However, as knowledge is distinguished from mere fantasies or opinions, there has to be some sort of *truth procedures* or *validity procedures* in order for something to be knowledge. So if claims and statements are not knowledge, there have to be (social) procedures that sort out mere fantasies from knowledge. It opens discussion on false consciousness, the need for critical theory and the need for democratic dialogue.

This conception of knowledge has many advantages. Firstly, it allows us to differentiate knowledge from other things such as beliefs, culture, routines, skills, opinions, truth and facts. All these can be discussed in relation to knowledge, many of them are based on knowledge, but none of these are knowledge itself. Secondly, this concept of knowledge brings us above the type of dualism that has been predominant in management and economic discourses on knowledge. These dualisms between local and universal knowledge, implicit and explicit knowledge, scientific and practical knowledge, have, as I see it, done more harm to developing knowledge about knowledge than to illuminate the field. It has created some either/or discussions that conceal the social nature of knowledge. Thirdly, this concept of knowledge that I try to argue for here allows us to discuss the cost of knowledge, investment in knowledge, trusting knowledge, cheating on knowledge or lying. It is also a concept that can help us understand why we always see new knowledge or need to make new investment in knowledge. As knowledge is related to the world and to facts that are constant, but also to our understanding of an interpretation that is shifting, knowledge has the characteristic that it is never fixed. What role does democracy play in this process?

NEGOTIATING KNOWLEDGE

Based on the arguments above, one could say that that knowledge is negotiated in the social field. Look at the following statements taken from current public debate:

- One should not allow abortions after 12 weeks' pregnancy.
- One should not allow abortion at all.
- Prostitution should be forbidden.
- Private people should not be allowed to produce and sell drugs.
- There should be kindergarten opportunities for all children from two years of age.
- There should be at least 40 per cent women representation on company boards.
- Fossil fuel creates global warming.
- More people get poorer and poorer.
- State budget deficit is negative for the economy.
- People should exercise more.
- It would be good for society if more people were vegetarians.
- The war on terror has been successful.

Although one might sympathise or agree with one or all of these statements, and many of them are supported by experts and researchers, none of them are true. They are all assumptions, opinions, and many of them, accepted as true, are even made into law. They are what I see as *negotiated truths*.

The concept of knowledge I argue for here allows us to distinguish between what is regarded as truthful in society and what opinions individuals hold. For example, in the Ibsen play *An Enemy of the People*, Dr Stockmann, the main character, holds an opinion contrary to knowledge in society. He happened to be right in his opinion and people in general were wrong. Ibsen tried in this play to show the limits to democracy, what he termed *the compact majority*. My concept of knowledge is completely in line with a situation like the one Ibsen portrays: the prevailing, social knowledge might be wrong and individual opinions might be right. Therefore, in relation to the majority in society, or the socially accepted truths, the individual will always have to be able to challenge what is regarded as knowledge in society. Discussion of democracy in relation to knowledge therefore implies that we are interested not only in the process of decisions, but also in what decisions democracy makes.

Paine and Burke on Revolution or Evolution

The debate between Thomas Paine (1739–1809) and Edmund Burke (1729–1797) can be used as an introduction to different theories of democracy. They represent two rather different interpretations of the tradition that brought the idea of democracy to the forefront of political development during the last two hundred years.

The first of these was the libertarian tradition, with arguments mainly on economic development and political liberty. The core of this tradition was natural rights and natural liberty, which meant limited government, liberal laws, economic and personal freedom. Hobbes was an exponent of this idea. It was one of the guiding ideas of the founding period of the United States of America, and in particular a tradition that was identified with the anti-federalists. Democracy meant limited government. Paine represents this idea.

The second position was the so-called republican tradition. In the republican tradition, people's rule should be a safeguard against despotism. The position builds heavily on John Locke: civil rights are guaranteed by the state. In England, democracy had meant exactly that, a safeguard against the despotism of Cromwell. People's rule and a weak king should safeguard a peaceful social development. Individual rights formed the ethical basis of this order. Individuals had a right to consent, a right to be involved in decisions that affected them. Society was for the individual a means, not an end. Legitimacy of the political process was related to how individuals were affected. In the American Constitution, the right to revolt against oppression was deliberately expressed. Burke represents this idea.

THE FRENCH REVOLUTION

The French still celebrate the storming of the Bastille on 14 July 1789. Habermas argues that the French Revolution represent a historical turning point that leads us into the modern era (Habermas, 1987). However, the interpretation of this event raises discussions and these discussions bring visions and views that were present even in the early period after the event. The debate between Paine and Burke covers many of these issues.

It is interesting to note that Paine and Burke were both Whigs in Britain, and that they fought on the same side in favour of American Independence. Paine had left for America in 1774 and in 1787 he came to France, where he stayed during the revolutionary period. For a short period in 1792 he was elected member of the National Assembly, and surprisingly he joined the moderate Georgines. Burke stayed all the time in Britain. The reason why he was involved in the Revolution was a letter he received on 4 November 1789 from Chames-Jean-Francois du Ponte, where the development in France was described. At the same time he learned that The Revolution Society (a club of supporters of the British Revolution of 1689) had taken official contact with the revolutionary National Assembly and that Dr Price had glorified the Revolution in a speech to the society. Burke was embarrassed and angry and wrote a 360-page reply to du Ponte. His thoughts were presented in Parliament on 9 February 1790 and published as *Reflection on the Revolution in France* in November 1790. Paine replied in his book *Rights of Man: Being an answer to Mr Burke's attack on the French Revolution*. It was published in two parts in February 1791 and February 1792.

THE RELATIONSHIP BETWEEN THE BRITISH REVOLUTION IN 1688 AND THE FRENCH IN 1889

Burke finds it incorrect to compare the French Revolution with that of the British in 1688. The British Bill of Rights had, according to The Revolution Society, implemented three principles that could be compared with that of the French Revolution: (1) the right to choose government, (2) the right to expel the state leader for incompetence, and (3) the right of the people to choose their own policy and form of government (Burke, 1988, p. 99).

Burke rejected the idea that this was the intention of the Bill of Rights. He argued that the overthrow of James I was not part of a general right to overthrow government, but some corrective action of the development that had violated 'the original contract between king and people' (Burke, 1988, p. 113). The preceding practice under the reign of William to have regular parliamentary meetings and 'constant inspection of parliament' had as its purpose 'not only for their constitutional liberty, but against the vices of administration' (p. 113). This is, according to Burke, something very different from a general right to overthrow the king:

> *The ceremony of cashiering kings, of which these gentlemen talk so much at their ease, can rarely if ever, be performed without force. It then becomes a case of war, and not of constitution. (p. 116)*

And Burke continues:

> *The Revolution (1688) was made to preserve our ancient indisputable laws and liberties, and that ancient constitution of government which is our only security for law and liberty. (p. 117)*

The British Revolution was, accordingly, not a change of the past, but rather a necessary action to protect the heritage of the principles of old political regime. Freedom is, according to Burke, a result of old, well-established institutions and norms that have evolved during a historical process and not a result of some constructed declaration of rights.

> *It has been the uniform policy of our constitution to claim and assert our liberties, as an entailed inheritance, derived to us from our forefathers, and to be transmitted to our posterity; as an estate specially belonging to the people of this kingdom without any reference whatever to any other more general or prior right. (Burke, 1988, p. 119)*

Burke has a vision of the state as a constrained structure, subordinate to its heritage rules and customs. Paine, on the other hand, gives an ironic comment to this:

> *Mr. Burke on the contrary, denies that such a right exists in the nation (the three fundamental rights) either in whole or in part, or that it exists anywhere; and, what is still more strange and marvellous, he says 'that the people of England utterly disclaim such a right, and that they will resist the practical assertion of it with their lives and fortunes'. That man should take up arms, and spend their lives and fortunes, not to maintain their rights, but to maintain they have not rights, is an entirely new species of discovery, and suited to the paradoxical genius of Mr. Burke. (Paine, 1977, p. 62)*

Paine advocates universal rights and represents an unconstrained vision of the constitution. He rejects the conservative idea of inherited rules as some sort of legitimacy:

> *The vanity and presumption of governing beyond the grave. (p. 64) [Therefore:] Every age and generation must be as free to act for itself, – in all cases. (p. 63)*

CAUSES OF THE REVOLUTION

Burke has a rather different impression of the revolutionary process in France than Paine. He writes (and this is at an early period, before the horror has been manifested):

> *Everything seems out of nature in this strange chaos of levity and ferocity, and of all sorts of crimes jumbled together with all sorts of follies. In viewing this monstrous tragic-comic scene,*

the most opposite passions necessarily succeed, and sometimes mix with each other in the mind: alternate contempt and indignation: alternate laughter and tears, alternate scorn and horror. (Burke, 1988, p. 93)

Contrary to this, Paine idealises the Revolution:

The mind can hardly picture to itself a more tremendous scene than what the city of Paris exhibited at the time of taking the Bastille, and the two days before and after, nor conceive the possibility of its quieting so soon. At a distance, this transaction has appeared only as an act of heroism, standing on itself: and the close political connection it had with the revolution is lost in the brilliancy of the achievement. But we are to consider it as the strength of the parties, brought man to man, and contending for the issue. The Bastille was to be either the price or the prison of the assailants. The downfall of it included the idea of the downfall of Despotism; and this compounded image was become as figuratively united as Banyans Doubting Castle and Giant Despair. (Paine, 1977, p. 74)

Burke regards the Revolution as a result of manipulation, not of will:

By following those false lights, France has bought undignified calamities at a higher price than any nation has purchased the most unequivocal blessings! France has bought poverty by crime! (Burke, 1988, p. 124)

He regards this process as a struggle between visions and ideas, where the wrong ideas have won. He regards France, with its 25 million people, as a very rich country; he regards the hunger and famine in 1787–88 as a result of natural causes independent of regime, and that agriculture, although centralised by the church, was efficiently run. For that reason, the Revolution would only lead to lower prosperity, not higher. (In fact, some historians reckon that France as a nation was poorer in absolute terms a hundred years after the Revolution than before.) Burke has a very interesting comment when he says that it seems that the new revolutionary leaders are less willing to see changes and gradual social development than those of the ancient regime.

Paine is far more personal in his description of the Revolution. He can see no possible way that the old regime could have been reformed:

It was not against Louis the XVIth, but against the despotic principles of government, that the nation revolted. These principles had not their origin in him, but in the original establishment, many centuries back; and they had become too deeply rooted to be removed, and the augean stable of parasites and plunderers too abominably filthy to be cleaned, by anything short of a complete and universal revolution. (Paine, 1977, p. 69)

While Burke says:

… by inspiring false ideas and vain expectations into men destined to travel in the obscure walk of laborious life, serves only to aggravate and embitter that real inequality, which it never can remove; and which the order of civil life establishes as much for the benefit of those whom it must leave in humble state, as those whom is able to exalt to a condition more splendid, but not more happy. (Burke, 1988, p. xx)

Burke's reference to the natural order is of great importance: the revolution destroys the natural order, that is, it destroys the constructive elements in the social process, while it does not change those fundamental phenomena that are the real cause of the problems (such as despotic rulers and inefficient economies).

Paine has no understanding of this argument. He compares the French Revolution to the American Revolution and regards it as the guardian of good forces and intentions. He thinks that the French soldiers that fought in America had brought the revolutionary ideas back to France. Therefore he agrees with Burke that the economic and social conditions in France were not the direct cause of the Revolution.

IDEAS AND CONTENT OF THE REVOLUTION

According to Burke, the revolution would lead to fewer rights since the constraints on political actions were removed. There was the danger of majority tyranny. What is the use of a constitution that gives rights as long as it has the authority to violate rights? He takes the example of property rights: 'Few barbarous conquerors have made so terrible a revolution in property' (Burke, 1988, p. 216). He is not convinced the expropriation was justified by the claim that the original acquisition of property was unjust: 'If prescription be once shaken, no species of property is secure ...' (Burke, 1988, p. 260). The road from confiscation of property to other violations of rights is small.

Paine says that Burke has no understanding of constitutionalism: 'As Mr Burke has not written on constitutions, so neither has he written on the French revolution' (Paine, 1977, p. 115). He refers to the division of power and other constraints given by constitutions as guardians against tyranny:

> A constitution is a thing antecedent to a government, and a government is only the creature of a constitution. The constitution of a country is not the act of its government, but of the people constituting a government. (Paine, 1977, p. 93)

We can interpret Paine as holding the opinion that the constitution is prior to the political process and therefore defines the political activity. Burke is very pessimistic on behalf of the revolution. As long as the social structure is destroyed, society will dismantle, rule of law will disappear, the economy will collapse and there will be a military coup. (This was a rather prophetic saying in 1790.)

On the other hand, he warns about too simple an analysis of the situation and the process by which society is able to live with different types of problems. That is why the revolution overshoots the problems that they are supposed to solve. They suppose that people will revolt against all sorts of injustice. In fact:

> We tolerate even these: not from love of them, but for the fear of worse. We tolerate them, because property and liberty, requires that toleration. (Burke, 1988, p. 273)

In a civil society, this tolerance is necessary. If people are impatient or have too idealised visions of the social development, this tolerance is in danger. The revolution has got this wrong. They look at conflicts and problems as something that can be solved once and for all. In fact, they have to develop over time:

> *But to form a free government, that is, to temper together these opposite elements of liberty and restraint in one consistent work, requires much thought, deep reflection, a sagacious, powerful and combining mind. (Burke, 1988, p. 374)*

As an ironic comment, Burke says:

> *They who destroy everything certainly will remove some grievance. They who make everything new, have a chance that they may establish something beneficial. (Burke, 1988, p. 374)*

Paine, on the other hand, has a global vision of the revolution, as a movement that started in America, moved to France, and that will spread from there:

> *I see in America, the generality of people living in a style of plenty unknown in monarchical countries, and I see that the principles of its government, which is that of the equal Rights of Man, is making a rapid progress in the world. (Paine, 1977, p. 147)*

He predicts that democracy will move into Europe:

> *... government by representation are making their way in Europe, it would be an act of wisdom to anticipate their approach ... (Paine, 1977, p. 168)*

The ancient regime has no value; it is only a blind way from the natural development towards democracy:

> *But what we now see in the world from the revolutions in America and France, are renovation of the natural order of things, a system of principles as universal as truth and the existence of man, and combining moral with political happiness and national prosperity. (Paine, 1977, p. 166)*

The consequence of these ideas is the end of politics. Paine's visions are great. He imagines a united Europe:

> *An European Congress, to patronise the progress of free government, and promote the civilization of nations with each other, is an event nearer improbability, than once were the Revolutions and Alliance of France and America. (Paine, 1977, p. 169)*

GENERAL POLITICAL PHILOSOPHY OF BURKE AND PAINE

One gets an impression of Burke's political ideas in the following comment:

> *You will see that their whole care was to secure the religion, laws and liberties, that had been long possessed. (Burke, 1988, p. 119)*

And he continues:

> *This policy appears to me to be the result of profound reflection; or rather the happy effect of following nature, which is wisdom without reflection, and above it. (p. 119)*

Burke calls *Rights of Men* 'political metaphysics' (p. 119) and he contrasts that to what he calls 'The real Rights of Men' (p. 149), which is not something constructed; 'it is a thing to be settled by convention' (p. 150). He says that two phenomena must be kept apart: the structure of society that makes the formation of natural order possible and the particular order that emerges. He refers to the first as 'wisdom without reflection', the same thing that is later called tacit knowledge. F.A. Hayek calls this view 'the empirist evolutionary tradition'. And he says about it:

> To the empirist evolutionary tradition [...] the value of freedom consists mainly in the opportunity it provides for the growth of the undesigned, and the beneficial functioning of a free society rests largely on the existence of such freely grown institution. (Hayek, 1960, p. 61)

Against this vision, he contrasts the revolutionary ideas as 'speculative and rationalistic' (Hayek, 1960, p. 54). About them, he remarks that they:

> assumes that man was originally endowed with both the intellectual and moral attributes that enabled him to fashion civilisation deliberately.... (Hayek, 1960, p. 59)

Paine's argument against Burke is that he:

> ... tells them, [...] that a certain body of men, who existed a hundred years ago, made a law, and that there does not now exist [...] a power to alter it. (Paine, 1977, p. 65)

Paine thinks Burke is unaware of the difference between the rights of the individual prior to the social construct and rights given by the social/political system. If 'Society grants him nothing', nor can it remove anything. On the other hand, as we enter the civil society, we to some extent exchange our natural rights with civil rights. The revolutionary regime is no social contract; individuals do not obey any political structure; it is a regime based on reason. In fact, in the society of reason, Paine's vision is that the political process will disappear. What will emerge is a conflict-free utopian society.

Four Traditions of Democratic Thinking

Both Paine and Burke ended up dissolute – the former because the revolutions turned in a direction quite different from what he had expected, the latter mainly for two reasons: he was accused of being an agent for the British king, and he was disillusioned by his native country Ireland, which joined the revolution. However, their dispute illustrates some of the tensions in democratic theory. The debate on the French Revolution illustrated a deep tension in democratic thinking between individual autonomy and the range of political decisions. One can discuss this as different perspectives on democracy as a decision-making process.

Thomas Sowell has discussed different decision-making processes in relation to different types of decisions (Sowell, 1980). In his analysis, he tries to decide which process is the most efficient to solve different types of conflict. The main types he discusses are illustrated in Table 11.1.

Table 11.1 Forms of reconciling conflict

	Voluntarily	Compulsory
Formal	Contract	Political decisions
Informal	Social relations	General obligations

Table 11.1 has parallels to Hirschman's (1970) discussion of exit, voice and loyalty, and Rorty's (1989) discussion of contingency, irony and solidarity. This is what Putnam (2001) calls *bowling alone*. In a formal, voluntary situation, such as a market encounter, contract, exit and irony are possible as the agents are free to make exchange or not. Social relations of a voluntary kind appeal to loyalty and solidarity. It is a situation where social capital becomes apparent (Putnam, 2001). However, in compulsory situations, both formal and informal, contingency and voice define the relation.

In the following I will shortly discuss four such theories: libertarian, republican, communitarian and deliberative. The libertarian has already been illustrated by Paine; the republican has been illustrated by Burke. I will also present the communitarian position, which has some of its roots in the thinking of J.J. Rousseau. Finally, I present the deliberative perspective, which has J. Habermas as one of its main exponents. I will try to show how they represent different perspectives on democracy as knowledge development processes.

The Libertarian Idea of Democracy

The libertarian perspective dates back to Hobbes (Skinner, 2010). As we saw above, Thomas Paine was very influenced by such libertarian ideas, but we have also seen that his reasoning holds many romantic ideas of democracy. Libertarians have in modern times mainly been concerned with two levels of social activity: on the one hand individual action, on the other hand the larger social order. Political authority and political organisation lie in between these two levels; it is conscious power but on the level of the great society. Libertarians in general, and Hayek in particular (Hayek, 1988, essay 5), have been quite uncomfortable with this level. It is a collective body with characteristics of individuals or organisations (making goals, decision-making and planning) but it operates on the level of the great society, in the complex order of social development (where goals, decision-making and planning are meaningless concepts).

Libertarians are therefore critical to conservative bourgeois society, as are neo-Marxists, but their criticism is quite different. While neo-Marxists would criticise bourgeois values as an obstacle to ideal freedom (in a non-dominant, ideal discourse situation), libertarians would criticise the same values only to the extent that they reduce individual autonomy towards the political order.

This libertarian position is quite consistent. Individuals are the sole ends of social activity. If an authority outside or above the individual is accepted, either in the form of an objective principle or in the form of steering and direction, individual liberty will be in danger. The history of liberalism is the history of the individual's fight against oppression, and this guardian against oppression might also apply to democracy. Even early American liberals had seen the danger of the rule of the majority. Famous is the observation by Alexis de Tocqueville after his 1831 journey to America that tyranny of the majority is a real danger. De Tocqueville refers to the individualistic tradition of liberalism and he sees no qualitative difference between the opinion of the majority and that of a single individual, and therefore he neither sees any particular legitimacy of the former in regard to the latter (De Tocqueville, 2000, p. 227).

Hayek (1960) and Popper (1945) have developed philosophical ideas on democracy along these lines. However, it is mainly in the Kantian form of individual rights and rational norms that the liberal ideas have influenced politics and law. In its modern form, the public choice school could illustrate this tradition. The essence of this view is that democracy is an *exchange process*. Exchange is made between autonomous individuals. The autonomy of these individuals is decided outside the social process. At the time individuals enter the social arena, they are already rational individuals with preferences. They enter the social arena in order to take individual advantage of social cooperation. Legitimacy is created through consent. Political authority is exchanged against personal liberty in order to obtain collective benefits. Optimisation of individual utility is therefore the main criteria for social change.

The ideas expressed through this exchange theory are often understood as the theory of *natural individual rights*. The idea is that individuals have certain natural rights that protect their individuality and guard them against collective action that has not been accepted through exchange or consent.

PUBLIC CHOICE

The public choice school discusses the relationship between the economic system and the political system. James Buchanan had, before developing the public choice theory, studied the work of, among others, the Swedish economists Wicksell and Lindahl's work on public finance (Buchanan and Tullock, 1965). It showed that these economists were aware of the complex effects different policies would have on the market. Buchanan argued that people in principle make the same kind of decisions whether they operate in the market economy or in the political market: they try to maximise individual utility. The difference between the two is their difference in structure and the difference between buying power and voting power.

In Buchanan's analysis, which has many different implications, one conclusion seemed to be that what we will have to do is not to choose between different policies, but to choose between different decision-making processes. The message from the public choice school was that some decisions should be fixed in the constitution, others decided by political bodies and the rest left to the market. It is the nature of the problem, and not the individual problem, that will be decisive for which decision-making process should be used.

LIBERTARIAN DEMOCRACY AND KNOWLEDGE

In libertarian democracy, decisions have to comply with the interests of the individual. It is likely that political decisions will only be relevant in areas of broad, collective interests. Knowledge development is likely to be influenced by the fact that individuals exist from decisions they disagree with.

The Republican Idea of Democracy

The republican idea of democracy also has long, historical roots (Skinner, 2008). One distinction that differentiates it from the libertarian perspective is what Isaiah Berlin (1989) discussed as *negative* and *positive* rights. The republican idea of democracy is to try to balance these two perspectives. The negative rights perspective is close to the libertarian idea of democracy. The positive rights idea is close to the romantic/communitarian idea of democracy. Republican democracy tries to balance these two.

These are two different conceptions of the liberal idea. On the one hand there is the Kantian heritage of rationality. This heritage is concerned with the structure of society. The perspective is to lay down a set of general rules that will function as a frame of reference and as a structure of communication between independent individuals. Based on such a framework, individuals will choose to cooperate or to remain individualised as they please (Berlin, 1989). Cooperation will therefore be a natural phenomenon, demonstrating the utility of individuals. We might call this perspective *instrumental rationality* (Nozick, 1993, p. 133).

Opposite to this Kantian perspective we have a large tradition of thought which includes those who do not accept the Kantian perspective that autonomous individuals cooperate within a rational general framework. This tradition would argue that the framework is a result of a social process, that shared values have led to the development of these rules, that although rules might be general, they are interpreted and get meaning only within a society of shared values, so that the interesting question that the Kantians do not address is how these shared values develop.

The difference here is both substantial and related to different perspectives. This means that there might be areas where both perspectives apply. But it means that a theory that combines the two perspectives should be able to explain both how values emerge and develop and how they develop into the sort of general rules that make the open society possible. Such a theory should be able to give democracy a meaningful function in society since democracy should be the mechanism by which shared values are converted into general rules.

In the discussion of the revolution above, Burke held this view. Here I will refer to Hume and Hayek, who had some of the same ideas (Hume, 1989; Livingston, 1991). The sceptical/organic theory of David Hume to some extent meets the challenge that the dichotomy of the rational Kantian and the romantic Rousseauean traditions are raising. Liberal values are essential to the formation of a liberal, democratic social order. However, social values are generated in the small face-to-face society, which can be a threat to the open pluralistic society and to civilisation. Therefore, Hume (1974; 1989) has maintained that the values and rules that shall govern the liberal society are not a result of a social process, rather they are obvious, abstract and rational, and universal constructions. But how could they be, since all values are a result of social processes?

David Hume made the observation that many things in life are difficult to explain but easy to practise. As a sceptic, he disregarded all attempts of rational construction of social theory. As an empiricist, he knew that knowledge is something that we receive through our senses and our social life. His alternative to rationalism was related to the practical aspect of human life, which is to be able to live in two different worlds at one and the same time: on the one hand we live in a small tribal world, the world we know from friends, neighbours and family, and on the other hand we are part of a broader social order and live in the great, open society.

Hume did not try – or even regard it as interesting – to deduce the great society from the small one. On the other hand, he saw that the two levels of social existence had their own logic of existence. The great, open society is a result of an organic development, a sort of natural selection or evolution process. It is the result of interplay, or complexity, of forces with some underlying selection mechanism. It is through such a process that language developed, not as a deliberate plan and not as a democratic decision or rational construction, but through a spontaneous development within a social, historical and geographical context.[1]

Hayek has, in his elaboration on this Humean prospective, tried to argue that the general, abstract rules that make the great society possible are a result of this organic process and not of deliberate legislation. Hayek is therefore critical of the idea that democracy shall have the right to make law and to overrule these general, naturally developed structures. At the same time, Hayek argues that these general rules and values are part of our cultural heritage. If they are, one should suppose that even a democratic process would observe and respect these rules and values. Hayek's suspicions towards democracy might therefore be regarded as based on idiosyncratic premises and the historical experience of misuse of democratic power, rather than on logic or as a consequence of his philosophy. David Hume had very little, if any, experience with democracy, but his idea of civil society includes a strong involvement by individuals. Society is only meaningful as related to individuals, never for its own sake.

In the Humean model, one therefore must accept two rather different levels of social existence: on the one hand the great, open society, on the other hand the small, intimate society. Each one of us lives in both at one and the same time, and we practise and use many of the general institutions, rules and values without being able to explain their development and origination. We practise and use them because they seem useful and lead to coordination and peaceful development or because we were educated that way.

At the same time we live in the small trivial world, where we make our first-hand experiences. To Hume, this is an interesting arena and an essential part of social practice. Our focus should therefore be on how this smaller structure is maintained and developed. Hume's observations here are different from that of the romantics. Hume is concerned with the natural tendencies of the small society. His approach is observation and understanding, not construction and evaluation.

Hume supposes that in some very general respect, we are all equal. Culture makes us different, but on the bottom we are all humans and share some basic characteristics. The essence of Hume's theory is to be able to divide between the universal, natural and general human characteristics, and those that are merely a result of social and cultural learning. Hume was therefore interested in the basic nature of human cooperation, which in his view is more fundamental than different cultural elaborations.

There are two dimensions in the thought of David Hume that help us overcome the conflict between the rational and the romantic approach to political society.

---

1   David Hume's thoughts are easily available for instance from his section 'Of political society' in his Enquiries (Hume, 1777, p. 205). In his discussion on political society he argues that general rules are necessary for the maintenance of society and the political structures exist only because they are useful to society. At the same time he is concerned with individual liberty and the small structures in society. He writes: 'Constancy in friendships, attachments, and familiarities, is commendable, and is requisite to support trust and good correspondence in society' (Hume, 1777, p. 209).

Firstly, individuality contains two elements, one from nature (where we are all equal) and one from culture (where we are different) and that the structure of society should observe both nature and culture. Secondly, society is functioning and developing on two levels, on the small, intimate level and on the great abstract level of the open society. In this Humean model, democracy is a practical matter, not a philosophical problem. Democracy is not the essence of existence, only a practical means to solve the social and political problems that are a natural consequence of social life.[2] Furthermore, democracy is to be performed within some defining limits in order to be liberal. There has to be some utility from the political process. It should be linked to individual utility as if it was an exchange process and secures the protection of the individual domain. In the Humean perspective, some institution and cultural differences would be accepted and tacit knowledge and tacit consent might be regarded as part of the political process. According to Hayek, the ethical content of the natural order is a result of how it has been formed; the formation of the order influences the meaning and content of the order. And the main feature of this formation process is that no single human will have had any decisive effect on this formation.

REPUBLICAN DEMOCRACY AND KNOWLEDGE

Republican democracy takes, in comparison with the libertarian position, a more active role in developing society, but still under consent from its citizens. Democracy is seen as important in creating conditions for human development. The idea here is dualistic: on the one hand there is society as a framework for the individual (as an abstract social order), on the other hand there is society as subjective engagement and flourishing (the local, tribal order). Knowledge development is here a division of labour between public and private knowledge.

The Communitarian Idea of Democracy

A different perspective on democracy developed alongside the libertarian and republican idea. Although the idea might have emerged over some time, Jean-Jacques Rousseau can be seen as the father figure of this tradition. We might call it the *communitarian tradition* of democracy. Communitarian will here be used as a term to characterise the idea opposite to the exchange theory, that is, the idea that society means something to individuals, that individuality is created in interaction with other people and that liberty is positive and related to self-realisation.[3] For Rousseau, democracy was more than a decision procedure. In his book *Social Contract* he developed his idea on the *general will* (Rousseau, 2011). This general will was to be realised within the political and social order.

Rousseau did not attach this idea of general will to democracy in particular; however, it is clear that realisation of social and political development according to his ideas are dependent on a common order, within which individuals can realise their individual needs, and this presupposes consent by the individual. Rousseau introduced *learning* as

2   This is in striking contrast to the idealistic tradition of T.H. Green, where democracy is something sacred. Hume's perspective implies that other values, such as individual freedom, are prior to democracy.

3   Hayek calls this tradition 'naive' (1960, p. 17; 1979, p. 134).

something dependent on the social process. He regarded the social process as a learning process and society as a learning arena. He perceived social development as a process where involvement by the individual would result in realisation of the general will. People would eventually be educated and socialised in a way that would reduce tension and conflicts.

These ideas of Rousseau anticipate a romantic democratic tradition of the mid- and late nineteenth century. Although it was not a homogenous tradition, it involved both an ideological mobilisation for democracy, a merger of democratic and socialistic ideas and an identification of democracy with nationalism. In its more politicised form, democracy became both the means of socialisation (education) in the sense of realisation of socialism (democratic socialists) and realisation of national identity (identified as the general will).

I classify all of these tendencies under the term *communitarian tradition*, and I see a parallel between these nationalistic tendencies in the last century and other tendencies that anticipates contemporary political philosophy or political movements. There is an American tradition, like the populist movement of the last century (Birch, 1993, p. 105), via the pragmatic theory of John Dewey up to John Rawls' theory on justice. There is also a continental tradition based on Rousseau and found in the idea of Engels of socialism as self-realisation, and the *small work* democracy of Masaryck and Havel (Pavlik, 1993), and likewise in the French tradition of Bergson and Lévinas. And there is a romantic tradition in Britain, with philosophers such as Green and Bacharac's theory from the 1960s on participation democracy and democracy in organisations as well as civic culture theory. It has a strong reference to the hermeneutic tradition in philosophy, not least in the interpretation of Charles Taylor (1971). This is not a classification according to genealogy and the theories and authors referred to here have very little in common except this reference to individual self-realisation through social interaction.

I will argue that the communitarian perspective has elements of what we could call a romantic tradition of democracy, and that it has a specific conception of the relation between the individual and the collective order represented by the political body. As an illustration of this, one might see the parallel in the romantic poetry of Lord Byron expressing non-hedonistic love. Love is in this context not self-expression nor pleasure-seeking; rather it goes beyond this since the individual self is put in second place. The individual obeys the force of love and is concerned with the well-being of the other. In Husserl's terminology (more than one hundred years later), one might say that the imminent becomes transcendent (I become It).[4] In political terms, romanticism mean that the collective is more than and cannot be reduced to individual utility and is therefore not a result of an exchange process. The collectively expressed order bears some qualities that are an important part of individual identity and its perception of the meaning of life.

COMMUNITARIAN DEMOCRACY AND KNOWLEDGE

Communitarian democracy has stronger elements of loyalty, solidarity and obligations than is the case with libertarian and republican democracy. Knowledge here is social knowledge that individuals comply with. They strive at forming identity and common understanding.

---

4   See George Naknikian; Introduction to Husserl, in Husserl (1964). Schusterman (1994, p. 400) Individuality is created in the encounter between the individual and society.

The Deliberative Idea of Democracy

Deliberative democracy has developed as a concept in the perspective of communicative theory (Bohman and Rehg, 1997; Elster, 1998; Dryzek, 2002) Habermas is among those who have been critics to the communitarian idea of democracy for prioritising local, contextual knowledge over universal principles. In his critique of Taylor (1971), he argues that the type of hermeneutic construction of knowledge that happens in a context disregards the need for universal principles and reason (Habermas, 1997).

Discourse theory elaborates on the fact that at the moment when a discourse starts, some contents have already been recognised, such as: the right to speak (if not, there will be no discourse), and the right to object and the willingness to listen and consider a better argument (if not, the discourse will be a meaningless activity and a waste of time). In the same mood, advocates of the neo-Aristotelian theory of human flourishing have argued that a good society in a normative sense has to be a liberal society in a liberal sense, since human flourishing indicates both human well-being (as an end) and human liberty (as a procedure). The argument of ignorance is more subtle. The argument says that since we are all ignorant about the complexity of the social process, social well-being can only be a result of the best utilisation of the dispersed individual knowledge. In order to be able to utilise this knowledge, individuals have to be free (which is a procedural right) to act and choose (since that is the only way individuals are able to activate their knowledge). Human well-being, which is a function of wealth (an end), will increase as individual freedom increases.

Against the ignorance argument John Gray (1989) holds that there is very little proof that the growth of knowledge and wealth is correlated with well-being and happiness. The functionalist assumption of the ignorance argument is not sufficiently proved. First of all, there might be truths that are obvious and should not be a matter of individual choice. If these truths were of a collective goods type, that is, if they were of a nature where each individual would be better off if all the others respected this truth while you disregarded it yourself, we might end up with a free-rider problem unless some authority was able to protect the truth. Secondly, to the extent that certain truths were protected in this way, how can we be sure that the mechanism of choosing truths is in itself correct.

The discourse argument, even if it has been elaborated, continues a long tradition of ideas that the social order in some way or another can be decoded by consent among individuals. In the discourse, or consent, tradition, the assumption is that society is a rational construction by individuals. It is supposed that society is founded by a contract, consent or a promise of individuals, while all these features are social practices and presupposes that society already exists. Contract or agreement can only emerge in an environment with a lot of shared understanding. As this understanding is prior to the discourse, the discourse or contract theory itself is unable to contribute anything to the understanding of this process. In fact, it has to be accepted that society is not a social construction, but a rather complex structure of tacit and rational knowledge, the emergence of which we have a limited knowledge.

Democracy is first of all a decision-making procedure in society. How this procedure is related to particular ends is among the subjects we will discuss here. One way to solve this is to argue that democracy should be closely related to liberal values and is inconceivable outside a liberal regime. Liberal values have their own origin. Attempts to implement democracy in non-liberal countries will therefore fail. Habermas argues that the intention to reach mutual understanding is the main way of developing co-action in communicative processes.

DELIBERATIVE DEMOCRACY AND KNOWLEDGE

Deliberative democracy tries to balance the argument of the republican and the communitarian idea of democracy. The main point is that deliberative democracy theoretically builds on a different epistemology than the two other theories. In deliberative thinking, one of the main ideas is that rationality comes for public deliberation. Under conditions of *communicative rationality*, democracy is able to balance the need for universal knowledge and more specific and contextual decision-making.

Comparing the Four Perspectives

The challenge to individuals is to be able to live both in the small tribal world of families and close social relations and with the extensive division of labour and observe all the abstract learned rules that make civilisation and the open society possible. *The fatal conceit*, according to Hayek, is to perceive the great society in the same terms as the small world of the tribe (Hayek, 1988). This can be illustrated with the concept of social justice: social justice is a tribal phenomenon, taken from a situation where people are collectively concerned with each other because they know each order and each other's needs. However, social justice cannot mean the same in the large, extended order where only general rules apply since we do not know each individual and his or her needs. When social justice is applied to this extended order, it can lead to oppression.

Communitarianism and romanticism is identified by liberals with this *constructivist fallacy*.[5] Firstly, libertarians fear that romantic ideas will be understood as legitimacy for state action on issues that should be left to individuals. Romanticism is identified with the middle level of social order, between individual action and the extended order: the constructed social order. Romanticism reduces pluralism and tolerance. In this way, it is feared that romanticism will lead to oppression. Secondly, libertarians fear that the romantic attitude will lead attention away from the great society, which is so important for welfare and development, and also that it will reduce tolerance on the individual level.

This is why general (universal) norms are necessary in the life-world, since otherwise it would be self-concealing. This is the rational argument in support of universality, developed by Kant and restated by Hayek (1976, p. 26) and even by Skirbekk (1993, p. 222) in his attempt to save the Habermasian discourse from intolerance. The Humean position is that universality (nature) is regarded as part of the constitution of individuals and that rules and norms are constructs that, though they are general, are not constructed that way, but rather have developed that way through social evolution. Both arguments – the one on political practice, the other on individual attitude – have given romantic ideas a low rating in liberal milieus.[6]

---

5   See John Gray (1989, p. 164) and Hayek (1988, p. 48).

6   Michael Oakeshott, although more a conservative than a liberal, might illustrate this tension. On the one hand he criticises what he calls rationalism in politics (1967, p. 35) since it does not observe the complex cultural and ethical

As far as I can see, there is a lot of sense in some of the romantic ideas, particularly on learning and learning conditions in society. I also believe that libertarians are too naive in their understanding about the moral and ethical basis of a free society and the formation of norms, some aspects of which I think are better understood within the romantic tradition. Democracy presupposes communication and consent. It also presupposes individual rights that enable the individual to take part in the communication process. Democracy is therefore not only an exchange process. There is some ethical basis for consent and communication and therefore also for democracy. The classical liberal tradition would argue that the rights that are presupposed in a democracy are the so-called negative rights, rights that protect the individual (Nozick, 1974). These are rights such as property rights, the right to speak and the right to make a contract. It is logical that these rights have to exist if democratic decisions based on consent should be made. On the other hand, the inconsistency of this tradition is that the protection of these negative rights is about the only objective of the political authority, so no political process is needed. Only in the case where unanimous decisions are made can collective action through the political process be legitimised (Nozick, 1974). However, in such a case where there is some unanimous attitude or opinion, political decision-making would be unnecessary. It follows from this type of reasoning that libertarians have problems in identifying the scope and meaning of the political process and therefore also the function of democracy.

DEMOCRACY AS A LEARNING ARENA

We could argue that ethics and democracy are a two-way process: on the one hand, ethics, like natural rights, is an important precondition for the political process; on the other hand, individuals are learning ethical values through their involvement in the political process. We should be concerned with how the democratic process is organised since it has an important influence on the attitude, norms and values of individuals. Democracy can in this sense be understood as a learning process. Democratic activity on a local level can increase mutual understanding and tolerance. In general, communication leads to less conflict, more mutual concern and less suspicion, more exchange of ideas, variety of experience and less intolerance. Local democracy might be related to schools, organisations, firms or neighbourhoods, and how these should be developed.

Also, one could point at the fact that in the history of liberalism, some of the strongest liberal forces have come from groups (religious and ethnic) who have defended their right to be different (as a group). The liberty for groups to be different calls for a pluralistic system of parallel politics. It calls for tolerance between groups, not necessarily within groups. Identity means that the individual identifies with certain interests, values or characteristics of other people. The important thing to address in this connection is that identity cannot be an exogenous factor, since it develops within the social context. If the two phenomena of self-realisation and identity are seen in relation to each other, we can talk about self-realisation through group identity.

John Dewey (1927) has argued that negative rights are not sufficient to shape true democracy. In his opinion, positive rights are needed in order to mobilise and activate individuals in the political process. Government should construct the social condition

---

structure of society; on the other hand he criticises (1967, p. 51) political participation and other processes that might utilise this tacit knowledge as collectivist and against freedom.

to allow participation. Liberals, on the other hand, have argued that positive rights will eventually lead to more government, more equality, less freedom and less individuality. Douglas Rasmussen (1989) argues that human flourishing is meaningless without a fundamental right to liberty (that is, a negative right to realise your own goals) and that this right is fundamental in any discussion on self-realisation. Another argument is offered by Rorty, who argues that Dewey's conception of politics is related and perhaps meaningful within the modern, homogeneous and innocent bourgeois context of the early twentieth century but rather meaningless in a post-modern pluralistic society. Rorty (1982) argues that the construct of Dewey will in the post-modern context mean bureaucracy. The idyllic idea of local democracy will end up in some bureaucratic procedure. So the question is, can we retain the positive values of local participation and communal life without violating the right to liberty (which is a right to be different) and to avoid bureaucratisation of society?

In order to understand the Humean perspective, we have to introduce the concept of *sympathy*. As already referred, Hume operated with two main sources to human values: natural tendencies and cultural heritage. Among the natural tendencies is sympathy. Sympathy is part of human nature. This means that the idea of rational exchange between individuals has to include this element of sympathy.

Hume argues that individuals are able to sympathise with others. We are able to take the effect of our action on others into account. Thereby, an exchange is part of a relationship. David Hume, and more consciously Adam Smith, argued that sympathy is not the same as benevolence. We do not necessarily want to do the best for our fellow citizens. We might accept that others are less well off than ourselves. But we will not tolerate naturally that they are so as a deliberate effect of our own action. Sympathy is a form of identification. It anticipates in a sense the Kantian moral imperative, but not in a normative sense. We are as humans able to comprehend the effect of our own actions on our fellow citizens.

This means that in a dialogue situation (discourse) individuals are both participants and spectators. A simple dialogue presupposes a minimum moral regime. Individuals have to observe the structure of this regime in order to participate in the dialogue. Furthermore, they will through their participation become aware of other ideas, other opinions and other meanings than their own. This again is part of a learning process that will increase knowledge and stimulate creativity. But sympathy is not enough to avoid greed or brutality. Individuals are concerned with their own interests, but identify with the interests of others. Social conditions, as well as other factors, might lead to greed and selfishness. So a system of disciplinary elements and moral and ethical sentiments are needed.

An interesting problem arises when we introduce sympathy into the exchange model. What effect will sympathy have on the assumptions and functioning of the exchange model? Naturally, it will make the model both more realistic and less simple. This might be the reason why it has not been done. So I take the liberty to suggest some possible effects.

Firstly, sympathy means that when we evaluate the effect of our action we take into account the reaction of others. The learning process in the market therefore is not only related to our own situation. Secondly, as a result of the learning process, action that through experience tends to lead to misery for others will be avoided. Thirdly, sympathy means that the exchange process is more complicated and has a longer-lasting effect than a pure theory of exchange would suggest. Concern for others is therefore not an extra-exchange phenomenon, but is included in the exchange process.

One of the main characteristics of the Humean theory of democracy is to regard democracy not as a metaphysical phenomenon, nor to regard it as extra-social or extra-individual. Democracy is a natural (although not in the philosophical sense) part of individual life. Decision-making by consent and through a process where the concern of others is taken into account is as natural as any other social activity. Since the concern of others is defined as part of individual action, no conflict or problem of defining this process as different from other processes occurs. This in itself is an important achievement, since it solves one of the main problems in liberal political theory.

Still, there is a limit to public involvement in the domains of the individual. Society is an artefact and is constructed for the sake of the individual, allowing them to remain individuals. So society can never replace individuals or individuality. Society is constructed for utilitarian reasons. Formal decision-making shall create a disciplinary system for individual action. In doing so, the consent of individuals is important, but equally important is the question of the scope and legitimacy of the political process.

One of the fundamental rights is to remain individual. In its rationalistic form, political processes are regarded as conflicting with this basically individualistic foundation. Therefore democracy is interfering with freedom. In the Humean perspective, there is no such individualised heaven of pure rights. Rights are artefacts, just as morals are. They are all part of a social process that has given us institutions, mediums of exchange and mediums of communication. It is meaningless to overlook these features of society. So individuals are as dependent on society as society is on individuals. The two are not in conflict, since society is giving legitimacy to individual rights and morals. The Humean perspective is that an individual, in order to remain individualised, has to have a domain, in the same way as the political process, since it has a utilitarian function, has to be defined.

There is in this Humean perspective no fixed solution to the question of how big government should be or how extensive individual rights should be. A society might be liberal in one sense and still not very liberal in another sense (as de Tocqueville remarked after his experience in America). On the other hand, there is a striking difference between this Humean perspective and that of the romantic tradition in which John Dewey called for democracy all the way from the personal family level to the great society. In the Humean perspective, democracy has a distinct and limited task, while the informal exchange in society takes care of many of the learning aspects that Dewey wanted to formalise.

Conclusion

I have briefly presented four perspectives on democracy. The discussion has argued that in order to be able to participate in democratic processes, more than negative rights are needed. People have to be empowered to take part in the democratic process. Libertarians have maintained that individual freedom and personal choice are a central part of the argument on why markets are superior to planning (Hayek, 1988). The creative force of the market comes from the utilisation of individual knowledge, which can only be coordinated and activated through an unplanned, free process. The same is valid for the political process. Knowledge in society is never centralised, but exists in the mind of each individual. A creative process of dialogue and competition brings out this knowledge, which would have been unavailable in a central planned system.

Table 11.2 Knowledge creation and structures in different areas of society

	Structural	Social	Functional	Individual
Institutional	Knowledge development mainly related to institutional development and legal structures	Institutionalisation of knowledge development in the social realm	Functional institutional forms of knowledge development are likely to be used, for instance in created, hybrid markets	Institutionalisation of the individual is a contradiction; however, it is used as a coordination mechanism
Social/political	Structuration of the social domain probably has some explanatory power in relation to knowledge development	Knowledge development in the area of social dialogue, public discourse and political processes	The combination of functional with social processes is a contradiction; however, social and political processes might have functional features on knowledge development	The social and individual represents an antagonism; however, one can argue for the social impact on the individual action and knowledge development
Organisational	Structural and formal (structural/ functional) features knowledge development in organisations	The social domain might be understood as processes for knowledge development	Knowledge development in a functional environment, such as in business and between businesses	Perspective here could be the relation between organisation and individual as a structuring of knowledge development and action
Personal	This is basically a meaningless position, but some form of behaviourist position could see the person in a structural perspective	This position is an antagonism in terms but can be understood as how social norms for behaviour are internalised	This position will see personal-level action and knowledge development as structured by functional causes, such as needs	Collaboration related to meaning construction, knowledge development and reflection at a personal experience level

These two arguments stand against each other in the political debate. Should we construct a political regime that guaranteed positive rights (the good life) for everybody, or should we only accept negative (protective) rights and let individual action and choice decide the outcome of the process?

I have argued here that the question is not as simple as that. The situation in society where there are only so-called negative rights is one where there is a minimum moral regime. Within this moral regime, we are allowed to practise all our virtues.

We are allowed to develop sentiments. We even develop these sentiments as part of the social process. The correct question to be asked is whether certain sentiments (of a positive kind) should be more important than others (of a negative kind).

The important perspective to consider is that since even sentiments develop, how far should we go in regulating the social process, and thereby limiting development and change? A too strong moral regime would have such an effect (Skirbekk, 1993, p. 222). Modernisation presupposes critical discourse, variety of experience and plurality. These qualities contradict a too naive social construction in the life-world.

The table below tries to summarise the different knowledge development processes we have discussed. It shows the plurality of knowledge development that a liberal sociality have to balance.

Core dimensions in Table 11.2 are that of structure–process and collective–subjective. These dimensions give some guidelines on how to perceive collaborative processes. The core argument that Table 11.2 is intended to illustrate is that knowledge development in society interplays with different knowledge development processes. Knowledge is the result of mediating and testing arguments across different domains, and thereby is dependent on a plurality of social forms.

Concluding Reflections

In this book I have discussed knowledge as a new, natural resource. This refers to the growing debate on knowledge society and knowledge economy. My contribution to this debate is to argue, firstly, that in order to understand knowledge society and knowledge economy, we need to have a deeper understanding of what knowledge is and how it is developed. Secondly, I argue that knowledge is inherently a social phenomenon. That implies that knowledge is a rather complex thing to understand. Thirdly, I have intended to show that in order to study knowledge and knowledge development, our theories also have to reflect the complexity of the phenomenon we study.

My thesis is, as I declared in the introduction, that knowledge development is a complex, often long-term, process. In knowledge society, although knowledge is a main resource for development, we should not expect to have knowledge about everything. This is not and should not be possible. We should be more concerned with the processes of producing knowledge, because we are so dependent on them. That requires more and deeper understanding of knowledge development processes in different areas of society. To understand these processes is complex. There are not only different theories of knowledge development; there are also, as I will show, different theories of theories of knowledge development.

I have therefore tried to take a broad approach to the issue of knowledge development in society. I started in Part I to argue that there are some foundations for understanding knowledge development that are important to clarify. Firstly, I tried to argue for a non-relativistic interpretation of sociology of knowledge. I believe that this literature tells us important things about social epistemology. Secondly, I found it relevant to discuss the concepts of individual/society relations. I identified three positions: pure logic of choice, pragmatic socialisation and subjective reflectivity – which all tell us something important about how individuals perceive their social relation. Thirdly, I defined communicative rationality and discussed conditions for rational dialogues. This is an important process in the social deliberation that defines knowledge.

In Part II of the book I have tried to discuss how knowledge develops in different social fields. I discussed knowledge development in science and in modernist art, and how it has affected and has been affected by society. I discussed the development of economic thought and how this has led to a dualism in understanding economics. Furthermore, I have discussed social development in the perspective of Max Weber's theory. I think these studies demonstrate firstly that knowledge development is a complex process and happens over time. Some knowledge takes a long time to develop. Also, that these deployments are often unexpected and unwanted.

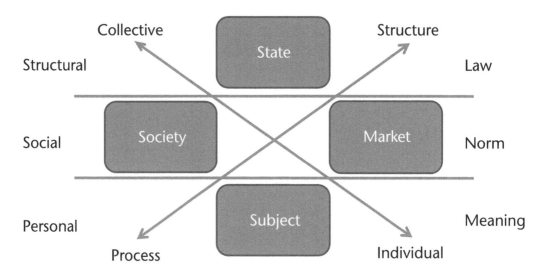

Figure C.1 The basic model with three layers: personal, social, structural

In Part III of the book I have therefore turned to the social and institutional systems of structuration in society. I have defined four perspectives on ethics: naturalist, rationalist, humanist and discursive. I have also defined four perspectives on development of the social and legal system: natural, rational, humanist and discursive. Finally I have discussed perspectives on democracy, again defining four positions: libertarian, republican, communitarian and deliberative.

It could be tempting to argue that libertarians hold a naturalist perspective on ethics and legal order, that communitarians hold humanist perspectives on the same issues, similar to republicans and deliberative positions. However, I think that is too simple to assume. The argument of my discussion is that we can see many and different combinations of arguments, which adds to the complexity of describing knowledge development. My intention has not been to answer the question: how should society develop knowledge? Rather, it has been my intention to establish some concepts that can help us understand the complexity of knowledge development in society.

I have tried to show how the opinions and ideas in the minds of people are influenced by structural dimensions in society. We should be concerned with to what extent structure creates monopolies of power, for example in the form of expert knowledge. Also an important issue is to what extent society is transparent and allows knowledge to be exchanged. This has an impact on issues such as to what extent the Internet should be supervised, or to what extent intellectual property rights should be granted. There is a need for differentiation in society. At the same time a central question is how knowledge made at a local level in a local context is transformed through the social system into more general knowledge. How do we secure the flow of knowledge between social layers?

The argument in the book is that we need to develop a theoretical framework for understanding knowledge development in society that is able to handle the complexity of this development. This book is an attempt to make this argument, although it does not go as far as presenting such a framework. However, I think I have presented some input for such a framework. I have argued that in order to theorise on knowledge development, we need to have concepts that do not restrict our understanding of knowledge development. I have also tried to show the limits to knowledge development. Some knowledge is held by a person or kept within the personal domain. What I have tried to underline is that we are dependent on the quality of knowledge that society makes. In knowledge society, and when knowledge becomes an important resource, we should be more concerned with how knowledge is developed. The biggest threat to the knowledge society is manipulation of knowledge.

Knowledge development in the social field happens in very complex ways. It is in many cases the plurality of institutions and the differentiations of social field that leads to knowledge development. Unwanted knowledge sometimes is necessary, in order to achieve innovation and wanted knowledge. The complexity of these processes is of a kind that supports further investigations and more sophisticated frameworks than are presented here in order to understand them.

I have argued for a liberal, plural society, but also for perspectives on social justice. I have compared four visions of social order: the naturalist perspective, the rationalist perspective, the humanist perspective and the discursive perspective. I have further presented four perspectives on democracy: libertarian, republican, communitarian and deliberate democracy. My intention is not to argue for one against the others. I believe that all these perspectives say something important about knowledge development and the liberal society. My point is to open a debate where we can have a deeper and more nuanced discussion on knowledge development and social and political order. What I bring to this debate is the necessity to look at how the social and political order has an impact on the kind of knowledge that is developed, and the validity, rationality and truthfulness it represents.

References

Adamson, Glenn and Jane Pavitt. 2011: *Postmodernism: style and subversion, 1970–1990*. London: V&A Publishing.

Adorno, Theodor. 1958: *Der essay als form*. Franfurt am Main: Suhrkamp Verlag.

Adorno, Theodor. 1991: *The cultural industry*. London: Routledge.

Adorno, Theodor. 1994: *Philosophy of modern music*. New York: Continuum.

Adorno, Theodor. 2001: *The cultural industry*. London: Routledge.

Adorno, Theodor. and M. Horkheimer. 2010 [1944]: *Dialectics of enlightenment*. London: Verso.

Adorno, Theodor., W. Banjamin, E. Bloch, B. Brecht and G. Lukács. 1977: *Aesthetics and politics*. London: Verso.

Alchian, Armed A. and Harold Demsetz. 1988: Production, information costs, and economic organization. In Barney, Jay B. and Ouchi, William G. (eds) *Organizational economics*. San Francisco: Jossey-Bass Inc. Publishers.

Alchian, Armed A. 1977: Uncertainty, evolution and economic theory, in Alchian, A.A. Uncertainty, evolution and economic theory, (1950). In *Economic Forces at Work*. Liberty Press, 1977. pp. 15–37.

Amable, B. 2003: *The diversity of modern capitalism*. Oxford: Oxford University Press.

Amin, Ash and Partrick Cohendet. 2004: *Architectures of knowledge: firms, capabilities, and communities*. Oxford: Oxford University Press.

Amin, Ash and Joanne Roberts. 2008a: *Community, economic creativity, and organization*. Oxford: Oxford University Press.

Amin, Ash and Joanne Roberts. 2008b: The resurgence of community in economic thought and practice. In Amin, Ash and Roberts, Joanne. (eds) *Community, economic creativity and organizations*. Oxford: Oxford University Press.

Apel, Karl-Otto. 1984: *Understanding and explanation: a transcendental-pragmatic perspective*. Cambridge, Mass.: MIT Press.

Arendt, Hannah. 1958: *The human condition*. Chicago: Chicago University Press.

Argyris, Chris. 1965: *Personality and organization*. Harper and Row, New York.

Argyris, Chris. 1982: *Reasoning, learning and action*. Jossy-Bass Publ, London.

Argyris, Chris. 2004: *Reasons and rationalizations – the limits to organizational knowledge*. Oxford: Oxford University Press.

Argyris, Chris and Donald A. Schön. 1996: *Organizational learning II*. Reading: Addison-Wesley Publishing Company.

Attali, Jacques. 2013: *Histoire de la modernité*. Paris: Robert Laffont.

Auster, Paul. 1997: *The art of hunger*. London: Penguin Books.

Ayer, A.J. 1947: *Language, truth and logic*. London: Victor Gollancz Ltd.

Badiou, Alain. 2001: *Ethics: an essay on the understanding of evil*. London: Verso.

Badiou, Alain. 2005: The adventure of French philosophy. *New Left Review*, 35, Sept/Oct.

Badiou, Alain. 2012: *In praise of love*. London: Profile Books, Ltd.

Bandura, Albert. 1986: *Social foundations of thought and action: a social cognition theory*. Englewood Cliffs, NJ: Prentice Hall.

Barney, Jay B. 1991: Firm resources and sustained competitive advantage. *Journal of Management*, 17, 1, 99–120.

Barney, Jay B. and William G. Ouchi (eds). 1988: *Organizational economics*. San Francisco: Jossey-Bass Inc. Publishers.

Baron, James N. and David M. Kreps. 1999: *Strategic human resources: framework for general managers*. New York: John Wiley & Sons, Inc.

Bataille, George. 2006 [1957]: *Eroticism*. London: Marion Boyars.

Baudrillard, Jean. 2005: *The conspiracy of art*. Cambridge, Mass.: The MIT Press.

Bauman, Zygmunt. 1989: *Modernity and the holocaust*. Cambridge: Polity Press.

Bauman, Zygmunt. 2007: *Consuming life*. Cambridge: Polity.

Becker, Gary Stanley. 1996: *Accounting for tastes*. Cambridge: Harvard University Press.

Bell, Daniel. 1973: *The coming of the post-industrial society*. New York: Basic Books.

Bell, Daniel. 1996 [1978]: *The cultural contradictions of capitalism*. New York: Basic Books.

Bell, Daniel. 2001: From class to culture. In: Daniel Bell (ed.) 2002: *The radical right*. New Brunswick: Transaction Publishers.

Berger, P., G. Davie and E. Fokas. 2008: *Religious America and secular Europe? A theme and variations*. Aldershot: Ashgate.

Berger, Peter and Thomas Luckmann. 1991 [1966]: *The social construction of reality: a treatise in the sociology of knowledge*. Harmondsworth, UK: Penguin Books.

Bergh, Trond and Tore J. Hanisch. 1984: *Vitenskap og politikk, linjer i norsk sosialøkonomi gjennom 150 år*. Oslo: Aschehoug.

Bergson, Henri. 2004: *Matter and memory* (Reprint of The Macmillan Co., New York, 1912 edition). Dover Philosophical Classics.

Berlin, Isaiah. 1976: *Vico and Herder: two studies in the history of ideas*. London: Chatto & Windus.

Berlin, Isaiah. 1989: *Four essays on liberty*. Oxford: Oxford University Press.

Bershady, Harold.1973: *Ideology and social knowledge*. New York: John Wiley & Sons.

Binmore, Ken. 2005: *Natural justice*. Oxford: Oxford University Press.

Birch, Anthony. 1993: *The concepts and theories of modern democracy*. London: Routledge.

Blackburn, Simon. 2011: *Truth: a guide for the perplexed*. London: Penguin.

Blom, Phillip. 2008: *The vertigo years: change and culture in the West, 1900–1914*. London: Orion Books, Ltd.

Bloor, David. 1983: *Wittgenstein – a social theory of knowledge*. Basingstoke: Macmillan.

Bloor, David. 2005: *Durkheim and Mauss revisited: classification and the sociology of knowledge*. In Stehr and Meje (2005).

Bohman, J. and W. Rehg (eds) 1997: *Deliberative democracy*. Cambridge, Mass.: MIT Press.

Boltanski, Luc and Eve Chiapello. 2005: *The new spirit of capitalism*. London: Verso.

Bourdieu, Pierre. 1990: *The logic of practice*. Stanford: Stanford University Press.

Bourdieu, Pierre. 1993: *The field of cultural production*. Oxford: Polity Press.

Bowles, Samuel. 1998: Endogenous preferences: the cultural consequences of markets and other institutions. In *Journal of economic literature*, XXXVI, March.

Bradbury, M. and J. McFarlane. 1991: *Modernism 1890–1930*. London: Penguin Books.

Brandl, Johannes. 2010: http://plato.stanford.edu/entries/brentano-judgement/.

Breton, André. 2010 [1924]: *Manifesto of surrealism*. Michigan: University of Michigan Press.

Brooker, Peter. 2007: Early modernism. In Morag Shiach: *The modernist novel*. Cambridge: Cambridge University Press.

Brown, Johns Seely and Paul Dugrid. 1991: Organizational learning and communities-of-practice: towards a unified view of work, learning and innovation. *Organizational Science*, 2, 1.

Bruner, Jerome 1990: *Acts of meaning*. London: Harvard University Press.

Buchanan, James. 1977: *Freedom in constitutional contract – perspectives of a political economist*. College Station, TX: Texas A&M University Press.

Buchanan, James M. 1990: *Europe's constitutional future*. London: IEA.

Buchanan, James M. and Gordon Tullock. 1965: *The calculus of consent*. Michigan: Ann Arbor Paperbacks.

Buck, N., I. Gordon, A. Harding and I. Turok. (eds) 2005: *Changing cities – rethinking urban competitiveness, cohesion and governance*. London: Palgrave.

Burk, Edmund. 1988 [1790]: *Reflections on the revolution in France*. Harmondsworth: Penguin Books, Ltd.

Burns, T. and G.M. Stalker. 1961: *The management of innovation*. London: Tavistock.

Burrell, Gibson and Gareth Morgan. 1979: *Sociological paradigms and organizational analysis*. Farnborough: Ashgate.

Caldwell, Bruce. 1982: *Beyond positivism, economic methodology in the twentieth century*. London: Georg Allan & Unwin.

Castells, Manuel. 1996: *The rise of the network society*. Oxford: Blackwell Publishers.

Chalmers, A.F. 2007: *What is this thing called science?* New York: Open University Press.

Chipman, Lauchlan. 1988: *Comments on Letwin and Ryan, in traditions of liberalism*. Australia: Center for Independent Studies.

Chisholm, R. 1977: *Theory of knowledge*. New Jersey, Englewood Cliffs: Prentice-Hall, Inc.

Choo, Chun Wei. 2006: *The knowing organization: how organizations use information to construct meaning, create knowledge and make decisions*. Oxford: Oxford University Press.

Christensen, Clayton M. 1997: *The innovator's dilemma*. Boston: Harvard Business School Press.

Clark, John Bates. 1899: *The distribution of wealth: a theory of wages, interest and profits*. New York: Macmillan.

Coase, Ronald H. 1937: The nature of the firm. *Economica*. 4, 16 (November), 386–405.

Cohen, R. and R. Seeger. 1970: Ernst Mach, physicist and philosopher. *Boston Studies in the Philosophy of Science*. Vol. VI.

Cohen, Susan G. and Diane E. Bailey. 1997: What makes team work: group effectiveness research from the shop floor to the executive suite. *Journal of Marketing*. 23, 3.

Coleman, Jules L. 1975: Market contractarianism and the unanimity rule. In: Paul, Miller and Paul (eds). *Ethics and economics*. Oxford: Basil Blackwell.

Comte, Auguste. 1988 [1830–1842]: *Introduction to positive philosophy*. Cambridge: Hackett Publishing Company, Inc.

Cook, S.D.N. and J.S. Brown. 1999: Bridging epistemologies: The generative dance between organizational knowledge and organizational knowing. *Organization Science*, 10, 4 (July–August), 281–400.

Cooke, Phillip. 2002: *Knowledge economies: clusters, learning and cooperative advantage*. London: Routledge.

Cooper, Robert and Gibson Burrell. 1988: Modernism, postmodernism and organizational analysis: an introduction. *Organizational Studies*, 9/1: 91–112.

Copleston, Frederick. 1985: *A history of philosophy: volume viii: modern philosophy: empiricism, idealism, and pragmatism in Britain and America*. London: Burns, Oates & Washbourne.

Craig, Megan. 2010: *Lévinas and James: toward a pragmatic phenomenology*. Bloomington, Indiana: Indiana University Press.

Critchley, Simon. 2009: *Ethics-politics-subjectivity: essays on Derrida, Lévinas and contemporary French thought*. London: Verso.

Croce, Benedetto. 1909: *Aesthetic as science of expression and general linguistic*. London: Macmillan and Co., ltd.

Cummings, Robert. 1975: On functional analysis. *Journal of Philosophy*, 20.

Cunningham, R.L. (ed.) 1979: *Liberty and the rule of law*. College Station, TX: Texas A&M University Press.

Cutcliffe, S.H. and C. Mitcham (eds). 2001: *Visions of STS: counterpoints in science, technology, and society studies*. New York: State University of New York Press.

Danchev, Alex. (ed.) 2011: *100 artists' manifesto*. London: Penguin Classic

Dawkins, Richard. 1976: *The selfish gene*. New York: Oxford University Press.

De Tocqueville, Alexis. 2000 [1835]: *Democracy in America*. Chicago: Chicago University Press.

DeGré, Gerard. 1943: *Society and ideology*. New York: Columbia University Bookstore.

Deleuze, Giles. 1991: Coldness and cruelty. In: Deleuze and Sacher-Masoch. 1991: *Masochism*. New York: Zone Books.

Deleuze, Giles and Felix Guattari. 2011: *Anti-Oedipus. capitalism and schizophrenia*. London: Continuum.

Derrida, Jacques. 1987: *The truth in painting*. Chicago: The University of Chicago Press.

Desai, Meghnad. 1994: Equilibrium, expectations and knowledge. In: J. Birner and R.V. Zijp (eds). *Hayek, co-ordination and evolution*. London: Routledge.

Devenport, T.H. and Prusak, L. 2000: *Working knowledge*. Boston: Harvard Business School Press.

Dewey, John. 1927: *The public and its problems*. New York: Holt.

Dewey, John. 1980: *Art as experience*. New York: Perigee.

Dilthey, W. 1976: *Selected writings*. Cambridge: Cambridge University Press.

DiMaggio, Paul J. and Walter Powell. 1991: The iron cage revisited: institutional isomorphism and collective rationality in organizational fields. In: Powell, Walter and DiMaggio, Paul J. (eds). *The new institutionalism in organization analysis*. Chicago: The University of Chicago Press.

Ditz, Gerard W. 1980: The protestant ethics and the market economy. *Kyklos*, 33, 4, 623–57.

Dreyfus, Hubert L. and Stuart E. Dreyfus. 1990: What is morality? A phenomenological account of the development of ethical expertise. In Rasmussen, David (ed.) 1990: *Universalism vs. communitarianism: contemporary debates in ethics*. Cambridge MA: The MIT Press.

Drucker, Peter. 1993: *Post-capitalist society*. New York: HarperCollins.

Drucker, Peter F. 1999: Knowledge-worker productivity: the biggest challenge. *California Management Review*, 41, 2 (Winter).

Dryzek, John S. 1996: Critical theory as a research program. In: White, Stephen K. *The Cambridge companion to Habermas*. Cambridge: Cambridge University Press.

Dryzek, John, S. 2002: *Deliberative democracy and beyond: liberals, critics, contestations*. Oxford: Oxford University Press.

Durkheim, Emile. 1997: *The division of labor in society*. New York: The Free Press.

Durkheim, Emile. 2000 [1893]: *De la division you travail social*. Nordic edition 2000: About the social division of labor. Copenhagen: Hans Reitzels Forlag AS.

Durkheim. Emile. 2005 [1897]: *Suicide*. London: Routledge.

Durkheim, Emile, and Marcel Mauss. 1963 [1903]: *Primitive classification*. Chicago: University of Chicago Press.

Dux, Günter. 2005: Toward a sociology of cognition. In Stehr, Nico and Volker Meja (eds). Op. cit.

Eccles, Tony. 1996 [1994]: *Succeeding with change: implementing action driven strategies*. London: The McGraw Hill Companies.

Eikeland, Olav. 2008: *The ways of Aristotle – Aristotelian phrónêsis, Aristotelian philosophy of dialogue, and action research*. Bern: Peter Lang.

Eikeland, Olav and Davide Nicolini. 2011: Turning practically: broadening the horizon. *JOCM*, 24/2.

Elster, Jon. (ed.) 1998: *Deliberative democracy*. Cambridge: Cambridge University Press.

Elster, Jon. 1989: *The cement of society: a study of social order*. Cambridge: Cambridge University Press.

Emery, F.E. and E.L. Trist. 1960: Socio-technical systems. In C. W. Churchman and M. Verhulst (eds) *Management science and techniques*, 2, Pergamon, 1960, pp. 83–97.

Ennals, Richard and Björn Gustavsen. 1999: *Work organisation and Europe as a development coalition*. Amsterdam: John Benjamins.

Etzioni, Amitai. 1961: *A comparative analysis of complex organizations: on power, involvement, and their correlates*. New York: The Free Press.

Etzkowitz, H. and L. Leydesdorff. 2000: The dynamics of innovation: from national systems and "mode 2" to a triple helix of university–industry–government relations. *Research Policy*, 29, 109–23.

Fairclough, Norman. 1993: Critical discourse analysis and the marketisation of public discourse: the universities. *Discourse & Society*, vol. 4.

Fayol, Henri. 1916: *Administration industrielle et générale; prévoyance, organization, commandement, coordination, contrôle*. Paris: H. Dunod et E. Pinat.

Fetzer, John. 1996. *Changing perceptions of Thomas Mann's Doctor Faustus: criticism 1987–1992*. Rochester, New York: Camden House.

Feyerabend, Paul. 2010 [1975]: *Against method*. New York: Verso Books.

Figura, Starr and Peter Jelavich. 2011: *German expressionism: the graphic impulse*. New York: Museum of Modern Art.

Florida, Richard. 1995: Toward the learning region. *Futures*, 27, 5, 527–36.

Florida, Richard. 2002: *The rise of the creative class: and how it's transforming work, leisure, community and everyday life*. New York: Basic Books.

Florida, Richard. 2005: *The flight of the creative class*. New York: Harper Business.

Flyvbjerg, Bent. 1993: Aristotle, Foucault and progressive phronesis; outline of an applied ethics for sustainable development. In: Winkler, Earl and Coombs, Jerrold (eds) *Applied ethics – a reader*. Oxford: Blackwell.

Foss, N.J. 2005: *Strategy, economic organization, and the knowledge economy*. Oxford: Oxford University Press.

Foss, N.J. and P.G. Klein. 2012: *Organizing entrepreneurial judgment: a new approach to the firm*. Cambridge: Cambridge University Press.

Foster, John. 1991: *The immaterial self*. London: Routledge.

Foucault, Michel. 1973: Power. In: J.D. Faubion 1994: *Essential works of Michel Foucault 1954–1984*, 3 (Essential Works of Foucault 3). Harmondsworth: Penguin Books, Ltd.

Foucault, Michel. 1983: *This is not a pipe*. Berkeley: University of California Press.

Foucault, Michel. 1986: Kant on enlightenment and revolution, *Economy and Society*, 15, 1, 88–96.

Foucault, Michel. 1989: *The archaeology of knowledge*. Translated from the French by A.M. Sheridan Smith. London: Routledge.

Foucault, Michel. 2011: Preface. In: Deleuze, Gilles and Felix Guattari (eds) *Anti-Oedipus: capitalism and schizophrenia*. London: Continuum.

Frege, Gottlob. 1961 [1934]: *Die Grundlagen der Arithmetik: eine logisch-mathematische Untersuchung über den Begriff der Zahl*. Hildesheim: Georg Olms.

Friedman, Milton. 1953: *Essays in positive economics*. Chicago: University of Chicago Press.

Friedman, Milton. 1955: Leon Walras and his economic system. *American Economic Review*, 45, 1955.

Friedman, Milton and Rose Friedman. 1980: *Free to choose*. Harmondsworth, Middlesex: Penguin Books Ltd.

Frisch, Ragnar. 1962: *Innledning til produksjonsteorien*. Oslo: Univesitesforlaget.

Frisch, Ragnar. 1964 [1929]: *Statistikk og dynamikk i den økonomiske teorien*. Oslo: Universitesforlaget.

Fromm, Erich. 1991 [1956]): *The sane society*. London: Routledge.

Fuller, Steve. 2002: *Knowledge management foundations*. Boston: Butterworth Heinemann.

Gadamer, Hans-Georg. 1977: *Philosophical hermeneutics*. Berkeley: University of California Press.

Gadamer, Hans-Georg. 2006: *Truth and method*. London: Continuum.

Galbraith, John Kenneth. 1958: *The affluent society*. New York: Houghton Mifflin Company.

Gay, Peter. 2009: *Modernism*. London: Vintage Books.

Geertz, Clifford James. 1973: Thick description: toward an interpretive theory of culture. In: Clifford Geertz *The interpretation of cultures: selected essays*. New York: Basic Books, pp. 3–30.

Geertz, Clifford James. 2000: *Local knowledge: further essays in interpretive anthropology*. New York: Basic Books.

Ghoshal, Sumantra. 2005: Bad management theories are destroying good management practice. *Academy of Management Learning and Education*, 4, 1, 75–91.

Gibbons, Robert. 1998: Incentives in organizations. *Journal of Economic Perspectives*, 12, 4, 115–32.

Gibbons, M., C. Limoges, H. Nowotny, S. Schwartzman, P. Scott, P. and M. Trow. 1994: *The new production of knowledge: the dynamics of science and research in contemporary societies*. London: Sage.

Giddens, Anthony. 1984: *The constitution of society*. Cambridge: Polity Press.

Giddens, Anthony. 1995 [1990]: *The consequences of modernity*. Cambridge: Polity Press.

Gillespie, R. 1991: *Manufacturing knowledge: a history of the Hawthorne experiments*. Cambridge: Cambridge University Press.

Glaser, B.G. and A. Strauss. 1967: *Discovery of grounded theory: strategies for qualitative research*. Sociology Press.

Goffman, Erwing. 1974: *Frame analysis: an essay on the organization of experience*. London: Harper and Row.

Goldman, A. I. and D. Whitcomb. 2011: *Social epistemology: essential reading*. Oxford: Oxford University Press.

Goldsmith, M.M. 1985: *Private vices, public benefits, Bernard Mandeville's social and political thought*. Cambridge: Cambridge University Press.

Goldsmith, M.T. 1999: *The future of art: an aesthetics of the new and the sublime*. New York: State University of New York Press.

Göranzon, Hammarén and Richard Ennals. 2006: *Dialogue, skill and tacit knowledge*. Chichester: Wiley.

Granovetter, M. 1983: The strength of weak ties: a network theory revisited. *Sociological Theory 1*, 201–233.

Granovetter, Mark. 1985. Economic action and social structure: the problem of embeddedness. *American Journal of Sociology*, 91 (November), 481–510.

Gray, John. 1989: *Liberalisms*. Oxford: Oxford University Press.

Gray, John. 1992: *The moral foundations of the market institution*. London: IEA.

Gray, John. 2009: *False dawn: the delusion of global capitalism*. London: Garnta Publications.

Grundmann, Reiner and Nico Stehr. 2012: *The power of scientific knowledge: from research to public policy*. Cambridge: Cambridge University Press.

Gustavsen, Bjørn. 2004: Making knowledge actionable: from theoretical centralism to distributive constructivism. *Concepts and Transformation*, 9, 2, 147–80.

Gwartney, J. and Richard Wagner. 1988: *Public choice and constitutional economics*. London: Jai Press Inc.

Haavelmo, Trygve. 1993: *Økonomi, Individ og Samfunn*. Oslo: Universitetsforlaget.

Habermas, Jürgen. 1968 [1971]: *Knowledge and human interests*. Boston: Beacon Press.

Habermas, Jürgen. 1974 [1964]: *Theory and practice*. London: Heinemann.

Habermas, Jürgen. 1976: The analytical theory of science and dialectics, (from 1963) in Theodor W. Adorno et al. (eds). *The positivist dispute in German sociology*. London: Heinemann.

Habermas, Jürgen. 1988 [1983]: *Moralbewusstsein und Kommunikatives Handeln*. Frankfurt am Main: Suhrkamp verlag.

Habermas, Jürgen. 1987: *The philosophical discourse of modernity*. Cambridge, MA: The MIT Press.

Habermas, Jürgen. 1989 [1981]: *Theori des Kommunikativen*, English translation by Thomas McCarthy: *The theory of communicative action: lifeworld and system: a critique of functionalist reason, vol 2*. Boston: Beacon Press.

Habermas, Jürgen. 1991 [1962]: *Strukturwandel der Öffentlichkeit: Untersuchung zu eiener kategorie der bürgerlichen Gesellschaft*, Norwegian translation: *Borgerlig offentlighet*. Oslo: Gyldendal.

Habermas, Jürgen. 1997 [1981]: *Theori des Kommunikativen*, English translation by Thomas McCarthy: *The theory of communicative action: reason and the realization of society, vol 1*. London: Polity Press.

Habermas, Jürgen. 1998 [1992]: *Handelns Faktizität und Geltung: Beiträge zur Discurstheorie des Rechts und des democratischen Rechtsstaats*, English translation by William Rehg: *Between facts and norms – contributions to a discourse theory of law and democracy*. Cambridge. Mass.: The MIT Press.

Habermas, Jürgen. 2001 [1984]: *On the pragmatics of social interaction*. Cambridge. Mass.: The MIT Press.

Habermas, Jürgen. 2003 [1999]: *Truth and justification*. Cambridge. Mass.: The MIT Press.

Habermas, Jürgen. 2007 [1968]: *Knowledge and human interest*. Cambridge: Polity Press.

Habermas, J. and Ratzinger, J. 2005: *The dialectics of secularization: on reason and religion*. San Francisco: Ignatius Press.

Haddock, A., A. Millar and D. Pritchard (eds). 2010: *Social epistemology*. Oxford: Oxford University Press.

Hall, P. and D. Soskice (eds). 2001: *Varieties of capitalism*. Oxford: Oxford University Press.

Hanna, Robert. 2009: http://plato.stanford.edu/entries/kant-judgment/.

Harris, H.S. 1960: *The social philosophy of Giovanni Gentile*. Urbana: University of Illinois Press.

Hart, H.L.A. 1961: *The concept of law*. Oxford: Clarendon Press.

Havel, Vaclav. 1989: *Ansprachen aus anlass der verleihung*. Frankfurt am Main: Verlag der Buchhändler-Vereinigung.

Havel, Václav. 1990 [1986]: *Living in truth*. London: Faber and Faber.

Hayek, F.A. 1937: Economics and knowledge, *Economica* IV, pp. 33–54.

Hayek, F.A. 1944: *The road to serfdom*. Chicago: University of Chicago Press.

Hayek, F.A. 1945: *The use of knowledge in society*. Reprinted in Hayek, F.A. (1976). *Individualism and economic order*. London: Routledge and Kegan Paul.

Hayek, F.A. 1949: The facts of the social sciences. In: Hayek, F.A. (1976). *Individualism and economic order*. London: Routledge and Kegan Paul.

Hayek, F.A. 1960: *The constitution of liberty*. London: Routledge.

Hayek, F.A. 1967: Notes on the evolution of systems of rules of conduct. In: Hayek, F.A. *Studies in philosophy, politics and economics*. London: Routledge and Kegan Paul.

Hayek, F.A. 1973: *Law, legislation and liberty*. (Vol. I). London: Routledge and Kegan Paul.

Hayek, F.A. 1976: *Law, legislation and liberty*. (Vol. II). London: Routledge and Kegan Paul.

Hayek, F.A. 1976a: *Individualism and economic order*. London: Routledge and Kegan Paul.

Hayek, F.A. 1976b: Economics and knowledge (1937). In: Hayek, F.A. (1976). *Individualism and economic order*. London: Routledge and Kegan Paul.

Hayek, F.A. 1976c [1952]: *The sensory order*. Chicago: Chicago Press.

Hayek, F. A. 1978: *New studies in philosophy, politics, economics and the history of ideas*. London: Routledge and Kegan Paul.

Hayek, F.A. 1979: *Law, legislation and liberty*. (Vol. III). London: Routledge and Kegan Paul.

Hayek, F.A. 1988: *The fatal conceit*. London: Routledge.

Hegel, G.W.F. 1966 [1807]: *The phenomenology of mind*. London: George Allen & Unwin.

Hegel, G.W.F. 1967 [1821]: *Philosophy of right*. Oxford: Oxford University Press

Hirschman, A. 1970: *Exit, voice, and loyalty*. Cambridge: Harvard University Press.

Hislop, Donald. 2005: *Knowledge management in organizations*. Oxford: Oxford University Press.

Hodgson, G.M., M. Itho and N. Yokokawa. 2001: *Capitalism in evolution: global contentions – East and West*. Cheltenham: Edward Elgar.

Holbek, Jonny. 1988: *The innovation design dilemma: some notes on its relevance and solutions, i Kjell Grønhaug og Geir Kaufmann (red.) Innovation: A Cross-Diciplinary Perspective*. Oslo: Norwegian University Press.

Holmström, Bengt and Paul Milgrom. 1991: Multitask principal-agent analysis: incentive contracts, assets ownership, and job design. *Journal of Law, Economics & Organization*, 7, 553–81.

Holub, Robert, C. 1991: *Jürgen Habermas: critic in the public sphere.* London: Routledge.

Holzner, Burkart. 1968: *Reality construction in society*. Cambridge, Mass.: Schenkman.

Holzner, B. and Marx, J.H. 1979: *Knowledge application: the knowledge system of society*. Boston: Allyn and Bacon, Inc.

Honneth, Axel. 1982: Work and instrumental action. *New German Critique*, 26, 31–54.

Honneth, Axel. 1992: Kampf um Anerkennung: zur moralischen Grammatik sozialer Konflikte. In Danish by Arne Jørgensen: *Kamp om anerkendelse: sociale konflikters moralske grammatikk*. København: Hans Reitzels Forlag.

Hope, V.M. 1989: *Virtue by consensus, the moral philosophy of Hutcheson, Hume, and Adam Smith*. Oxford: Oxford University Press.

Hoppe, Hans Hermann. 1989: *A theory of socialism and capitalism*. Massachusetts: Kluwer.

Hoy, Calvin. 1984: *A philosophy of freedom*. London: Greenwood Press.

Huber, George P. and William H. Glick. 1995: *Organizational change and redesign: ideas and insights for improving performance*. New York: Oxford University Press, Inc.

Hughes, H. Stuart. 1979 [1958]: *Consciousness and society: reorientation of European social thought, 1890-1930*. Brighton: The Harvester Press Ltd.

Hume, David. 1974 [1777]: *Enquiries concerning human understanding and concerning the principles of morals*. Oxford: Oxford University Press.

Hume, David: 1989: *Of the original contract, in essays political, moral and literary*. Indianapolis: Liberty Classic.

Humpal, Martin. 1998: *The rot of modernist narrative: Knut Hamsun's novels Hunger, Mysteries, Pan*. Oslo: Solum forlag.

Husserl, Edmund. 1964: *The idea of phenomenology*. Hague: Martinus Nijhoff.

Husserl, Edmund. 1970 [1937]: *The crisis of European sciences and transcendental philosophy*. Evanston, Ill.: Northwestern University Press.

Husserl, Edmund. 1999 [1929]: *Cartesian meditations*. Dordrecht, The Netherlands: Kluwer Academic Publishers.

Huxley, Thomas H. 2005: *Evolution and ethics*. Fairfield, IA: 1st World Library.

Isaacs, William. 1999: *Dialogue and the art of thinking together*. New York: Currency.

Jacobs, Jane. 1984: *Cities and the wealth of nations*. New York: Random House.

James, William. 1978: *Pragmatism and the meaning of truth*. Cambridge, Mass.: Harvard University Press.

Jameson, Fredric. 1977: Reflections in conclusion. In: Adorno et al. (eds). *Aesthetics and politics*. Op. cit.

Jameson, Fredric. 1991: *Postmodernism: the cultural logic of late capitalism*. Durham, NC: Duke University Press.

Janik, A. and S. Toulmin. 1973: *Wittgenstein's Vienna*. New York: Touchstone.

Jashapara, Ashok. 2011: *Knowledge management: an integrated approach*. Harlow: Pearson (Prentice Hall).

Johnsen, H.C.G. 1991: Mot en liberal argumentasjonsteori. *Norsk filosofisk tidsskrift*. September.

Johnsen, H.C.G. 2002: Discourse and change in organizations. *Concepts and transformation*, 7(3): 301–321.

Johnsen, H.C.G. 2009: Strategi for økt konkurranseevne – grunnleggende sett et valg av verdier. In Kalsaas, Bo Terje (red.). *Ledelse av verdikjeder: strategi, design og konkurranseevne*. Trondheim: Tapir akademisk forlag.

Johnsen, H.C.G. 2010: Cultural and market – an unsettled relation. In: Harald Knudsen, Joyce Falkenberg, Kjell Åge Grønhaug and Åge Garnes (ed.) *Mysterion, strategike and kainotomia*. Oslo: Novus £publishing.

Johnsen, H.C.G. 2010: Scientific knowledge through involvement – how to do respectful othering. *International Journal of Action Research*, 6, 1.

Johnsen, H.C.G. 2011: Discourse and change in organizations. In Ekman, M., Gustavsen, B., Asheim, B.T. and Pålshaugen, Ö. (eds). *Learning regional innovation – Scandinavian models*. Basingstoke: Palgrave Macmillan.

Johnsen, H.C.G. 2013: How socially engaged research makes knowledge. In Hva er innovasjon? Perspektiver i norsk innovasjonsforskning. Bind 2: Organisasjon og medvirkning – en norsk modell? Oslo: Cappelen Akademisk.

Johnsen, H.C.G. and R. Ennals. 2012: *Creating collaborative advantage*. Farnham: Gower.

Johnsen, H.C.G. and R. Normann. 2004: When research and practice collide: the role of action research when there is a conflict of interest with stakeholders. *Systematic Practice and Action Research*, 17, 3, 207–35.

Johnsen, H.C.G., J. Karlsen, R. Normann and J.K. Fosse. 2009: The contradictory nature of knowledge: a challenge for understanding innovation in a local context and workplace development and for doing action research. *AI & Society*, 23, 85–95.

Johnson, G.A. (ed.) 1993: *The Merleau-Ponty aesthetic reader: philosophy and painting*. Evanston, Ill.: Northwestern University Press.

Johnson, Paul. 1991: *Modern times*. New York: HarperCollins.

Joyce, James. 2000: *Occasional, critical and political writing*. Oxford: Oxford University Press.

Kelsen, Hans. 1967: *Pure theory of law*. Berkeley: University of California Press.

Kettner, Matthias. 1993: Consensus formation in the public domain. In: Earl Winkler and Jerrold Coombs. 1993: *Applied ethics: a reader*. Oxford: Blackwell.

Kirzner, Israel. 1992: *The meaning of the market process*. London: Routledge.

Knausgård, Karl Ove. 2013: Litteraturen og det onde (Literature and Evil). *Samtiden*, 1.

Knorr-Cetina, Karin. 1984: The fabrication of facts. In Stehr, Nico and Meja, Volker (eds) *Society and knowledge: contemporary perspectives in the sociology of knowledge*. London: Transaction Books.

Knorr-Cetina, Karin. 1999: *Epistemic cultures: how the sciences make knowledge*. Cambridge, Mass.: Harvard University Press.

Knudsen, Harald. 1998–2001: Bind 1 (1998): Reisen for teorias skyld (Vol 1: Traveling for the sake of theoriea); bind 2 (1998): Teoribygging i Praksis (Vol 2: Theory building in practice); bind 3 (2001): Mentor (vol 3: Mentor); bind 4 (2001): Sirenene (vol 3: Sirenes). Høyskoleforlaget, Kristiansand.

Kojeve, A. 1980 [1939]: *Introduction to the reading of Hegel*. New York: Basic Books.

Kotter, John P. 1996: *Leading change*. Boston, Mass.: Harvard Business School Press.

Kotter, John P. and James L. Heskett. 1992: *Corporate culture and performance*. New York: The Free Press.

Kreps, David M. 1990: Corporate culture and economic theory. In: Alt, James E. and Shepsle, Kenneth A. (eds). *Perspectives on political economy*. New York: Cambridge University Press.

Kreps, David M. 1997: The interaction between norms and economic incentives. Intrinsic motivation and extrinsic incentives. *American Economic Review*, 87, pp. 359–65.

Krugman, Paul. 1991: Increasing returns and economic geography. *Journal of Political Economy*, 99, 3 (June), 483–99.

Kuhn, Thomas S. 1970 [1962]: *The structure of scientific revolutions*. Chicago: Chicago University Press.

Kuhn, Thomas S. 2000: *The road since structure*. Chicago: Chicago University Press.

Kunda, Gideon. 1992: *Engineering culture: control and commitment in a high-tech corporation*. Philadelphia: Temple University Press.

Kuran, Timur. 1995: *Private truths, public lies: the social consequences of preference falsification*. Cambridge, Mass.: Harvard University Press.

Lachmann, Ludwig. 1994: *Expectations and the meaning of institutions*. London: Routledge.

Lakatos, Imre. 1987 [1959]: *The methodology of scientific research programmes*. Philosophical Papers.

Landauer, Susan. 1996: *The San Francisco school of abstract expressionism*. Berkeley: University of California Press.

Lange, Oskar. 1936: On the economic theory of socialism. *Review of Economic Studies*, 4, 1936–37, nos. 1 and 2.

Latour, Bruno. 1987: *Science in action: how to follow scientists and engineers through society*. Cambridge Mass.: Harvard University Press.

Latour, Bruno. 1993: *We have never been modern*. Cambridge, Mass.: Harvard University Press.

Lave, Jean and Etienne Wenger. 1991: *Situated learning*. Cambridge: Cambridge University Press.

Law, John. 2004: *After method: mess in social science research*. London: Routledge.

Leibenstein, Harvey. 1987: *Inside the firm: the inefficiencies of hierarchy*. Cambridge, Mass.: Harvard University Press.

Lévinas, Emmanuel. 1993 [1972]: Humanisme de l'autre homme. In Norwegian: Den annens humanisme. Oslo: Gyldendal

Levison, Arnold B. 1974: *Knowledge and society: an introduction to the philosophy of the social sciences*. Indianapolis: Pagasus.

Leydesdorff, Loet. 2006: *The knowledge based economy*. Bacon Raton, Florida: Universal Publishers.

Livingston, D. 1991: Hayek as Humean, *Critical Review*, 2, 2.

Locke, John. 1963 [1690]: *Two treatises of government*. London: Mentor Books.

Lomasky, Loren. 1987: *Persons, rights and the moral community*. Oxford: Oxford University Press.

Lorenz, E. and B-Å. Lundvall. 2006: *How Europe's economies learn: coordinating competing models*. Oxford: Oxford University Press.

Luhmann, Niklas. 1995: *Social systems*. Stanford, CA: Stanford University Press.

Luhmann, Niklas. 2004: *Law as a social system*. Oxford: Oxford University Press.

Luhmann, Niklas. 2008: *Love: a sketch*. Cambridge: Polity Press.

Luhmann, Niklas. 2012: *The theory of society, vol. I*. Stanford, CA: Stanford University Press.

Luhmann, Niklas. 2013a: *Introduction to social systems*. Cambridge: Polity Press.

Luhmann, Niklas. 2013b; *Systems theory*. Cambridge: Polity Press.

Lukács, Georg. 1971: *The theory of the novel*. London: Merlin Press.

Lukács, Georg. 1977 [1937]: Realism in balance. In Adorno et al. (eds). *Aesthetics and politics*. Op. cit.

Lunden, Eldrid. 2008: *Modernism, or literary populism – an essay about Arne unfairly and Knut Hamsun*. Oslo: H. Aschehoug & Co.

Lundvall, Bengt-Åke. 2002. *Innovation, growth and social cohesion: the Danish model*. Cheltenham: Edward Elgar.

Lyotard, J-F. 1984 [1979]: *The postmodern condition: a report on knowledge*. Minneapolis: University of Minnesota Press.

Machlup, Fritz. 1984: *Knowledge: its creation, distribution and economic significance*. Princeton: Princeton University Press.

Mackintosh, Robert. 2005. *From Comte to Benjamin Kidd*. (First published 1899) London: Elibron Classics.

Maehr, Martin L. and Douglas A. Kleiber. 1985: Motivation and adulthood. In: *Advances in motivation and achievement*, 4. Greenwich, Conn.: JAI Press.

Mailer, Norman. 2004: *The spooky art: thoughts wed writing*. New York: Random House.

Mandeville, Bernard. 1988 [1716]: *The fable of the bees – or private vices, public benefits*. Indianapolis: Liberty Press.

Mannheim, Karl. 1979 [1929]: *Ideology and utopia: an introduction to the sociology of knowledge*. London: Routledge and Keegan Paul.

March, James G. 1988: *Decisions and organizations*. London: Basil Blackwell.

March, James G. and Levitt. 1988: Organizational learning. In: March, James G. (ed.). *Decisions and organizations*. London: Basil Blackwell.

Marcus, Laura. 2007: The legacies of modernism. In: Morag Shiach (ed.). *The modernist novel*. Cambridge: Cambridge University Press.

Mares, Edwin. 2011: *A priori*. Ithaca: McGill-Queen's University Press.

Marshall, Alfred. 1920 [1890]: *Principles of economics*. London: Macmillan and Co., Ltd. Eighth edition.

Marx, Karl. 2000: *A critique of the German ideology*, Written: Fall 1845 to mid-1846, First published: 1932 (in full) Source: Progress Publishers, 1968, Language: German, Transcription: Tim Delaney, Bob Schwartz, Brian Basgen. Online Version: Marx/Engels Internet Archive (marxists.org), 2000.

Marx, Karl. 2001 [1867]: *Capital: a student edition*, Edited and introduced by C.J. Arthur. London: Electric Book Co.

Marx, Karl and Friedrich Engels. 2005: *The communist manifesto*. Chicago, IL: Haymarket Books.

Maurseth, Per. 1990: Anton Martin Schweigaards politiske tenkning. *Norsk Historisk Tidsskrift*, 1990: 1.

McCarthy, E. Doyle. 1996: *Knowledge as culture: the new sociology of knowledge*. London: Routledge.

McGinn, Colin. 1997: *The character of mind: an introduction to the philosophy of mind*. Oxford: Oxford University Press.

McKelvey, Bill. 2002: Postmodernism vs. truth in management theory. In: Ed Locke (ed.). *Modernism and management: pros, cons, and alternatives*. Amsterdam: Elsevier.

Mead, George Herbert. 1962 [1934]: *Mind, self, and society*. Chicago: Chicago University Press.

Merleau-Ponty, M. 1989 [1962/1945]: *Phenomenology of perception*. London: Routledge.

Merton, Robert, A. 1951: *Social theory and social structure – towards the codification of theory and research*. Glencoe, Ill.: The Free Press.

Merton, Robert, A. 2005 [1945]: The sociology of knowledge. In: Stehr and Meje.

Miller, Gary J. 1992: *Managerial dilemmas: the political economy of hierarchy*. Cambridge: Cambridge University Press.

Mintzberg, Henry. 1994: The fall and rise of strategic planning. *Harvard Business Review*, January–February.

Mintzberg, Henry, Bruce Ahlstrand and Joseph Lampel. 1998: *Strategy safari: a guided tour through the wilds of strategic management*. New York: The Free Press.

Montesquieu, Baron De. 1975 [1748]: *The spirit of the laws*. New York: Macmillan.

Morris, Frances. 2006: *Tate Modern: the handbook*. London: Tate Publishers.

Moulaert, Frank and Farid Sekia. 2003: Territorial innovation models: a critical survey, *Regional Studies*, 37, 3, 289–302.

Mulkey, Michael. 2005: Knowledge and utility: implications for the sociology of knowledge. In: Stehr and Meja.

Nagel, Ernest 1979 [1961]: *The structure of science, problems in the logic of scientific-explanations*. London: Routledge and Kegan Paul.

Nelson, R, and S. Winter. 1982: *An evolutionary theory of economic change*. Cambridge, Mass.: Harvard University Press.

Newell, S., M. Robertson, H. Scarbrough and J. Swan. 2009: *Managing knowledge work and innovation*. Basingstoke: Palgrave Macmillan.

Nobles, R. and D. Schiff. 2004: Introduction. In: Luhmann, N. (ed.). *Law as a social system*. Oxford: Oxford University Press.

Nonaka, I. 1988: Creating organizational order out of chaos: self-renewal in Japanese firms. *California Management Review*, Spring.

Nonaka, I. and Takeuchi, H. 1995: *The knowledge creating company: how Japanese companies create the dynamics of innovation*. New York: Oxford University Press.

Nowotny, H., Scott, P. and Gibbons, M. 2001: *Rethinking science: knowledge production and the public in an age of uncertainty*. Oxford: Polity Press.

Nozick, Robert. 1974: *Anarchy, state and utopia*. New York: Basic Books.

Nozick, Robert. 1977: Austrian methodology. *Synthese*, 36.

Nozick, Robert. 1993: *The nature of rationality*. New Jersey: Princeton University Press.

Nozick, Robert. 2001: *Invariance*. New Jersey: Princeton University Press.

Oakeshott, Michael. 1967: *Rationalism in politics and other essays*. London: Methuen & Co. Ltd.

Olivencrona, Karl. 1971: *Law as facts*. London: Stevens & Sons.

Oppenheimer, Franz. 1975 [1914]: *The state*. New York: First Life Edition.

O'Reilly, Charles. 1991: Socialization and organizational culture. In: Straw, Barry M. (ed.). *Psychological dimensions of organizational behavior*. New York: Macmillan Publishing Company.

Orwell, George. 1957: *Inside the Whale and other essays*. London: Penguin Books.

Ostrom, Elinor. 1990: *Governing the commons: the evolution of institutions for collective action*. Cambridge: Cambridge University Press.

Outhwaite, William. 1997: *Habermas: en kritisk introduksjon*. København: Hans Reitzels Forlag.

Paine, Thomas. 1977 [1791–92]: *Rights of man*. Harmondsworth: Penguin Books, Ltd.

Pålshaugen, Øyvind. 2010: *Passasjer hos Derrida, Platon, Aristoteles*. Oslo: Scandinavian Academic Press.

Pareto, Vilfredo. 1923, reprint 1983: *The mind and society: a treatise on general sociology*. New York: Harcourt, Brace and Company.

Parker, Rachel and Louise Tamaschke. 2005: Explaining regional departures from national patterns of industry specialization: regional institutions, politics and state coordination. *Organization Studies*, 26, 12, 1787–1807.

Parsons, Talcott. 1937: *The structure of social action*. New York: McGraw Hill.

Parsons, Talcott. 1971: *The system of modern societies*. New York: Prentice-Hall.

Paul, E., F. Millar and J. Paul. (eds). 1985: *Ethics and economics*. London: Blackwell.

Pavlik, Jan. 1993: Philosophy, 'parallel polis' and revolution: the case of Czechoslovakia. In: Barry Smith (ed.). *Philosophy and political change in Eastern Europe*. Illinois: Monist Library of Philosophy.

Peeters, Benoît. 2010: *Derrida: a biography*. Cambridge: Polity Press.

Pels, Dick. 2005: Mixing metaphors: politics or economics of knowledge? In: Stehr, Nico and Volker Meja (eds). Op. cit.

Perloff, Majori. 2003: *The futurist moment*. Chicago: University of Chicago Press.

Pettigrew, Andrew M. 2001: Management after modernism. *British Journal of Management*, 12, Special Issue, 61–70.

Pettit, Philip. 1993: *The common mind*. Oxford: Oxford University Press.

Pettit, Philip. 2010: *Republicanism: a theory of freedom and government*. Oxford: Oxford University Press.

Pigou, A. 1932: *The economics of welfare*. London: Macmillan.

Pinkney, Tony. 1989. Introduction. In: Raymond Williams (ed.). *Politics of modernism*. London: Verso.

Piore, M. and C. Sabel. 1984: *The second industrial divide: possibilities for prosperity*. New York: Basic Books.

Polanyi, Karl. 2001 [1944]: *The great transformation*. Boston: Beacon Press.

Polanyi, Michael. 1966: *The tacit dimension*. New York: Doubleday.

Polanyi, Michael. 1958: *Personal knowledge: towards a post-critical philosophy*. Chicago: University of Chicago Press.

Polanyi, Michael and Harry Prosch. 1975: *Meaning*. Chicago: Chicago University Press.

Popper, Karl R. 1945: *The open society and its enemies*. London: Routledge and Kegan Paul Ltd.

Popper, Karl. 1979a [1972]: *Objective knowledge: an evolutionary approach*. Oxford: The Clarendon Press.

Popper, Karl. 1979b: *The growth of scientific knowledge*. Frankfurt am Main: Vittorio Klostermann.

Porter, Michael E. 1990: *The competitive advantages of nations*. London: Macmillan.

Porter, Michael E. 1998: *On competition*. Boston: Harvard Business School.

Porter, M.E. and Kramer, M.R. 2011: Creating shared value. *Harvard Business Review*, January, February.

Posner, Richard A. 1983: *The economics of justice*. Cambridge, Mass.: Harvard University Press.

Powell, W.W. 1990: Neither market nor hierarchy: network forms of organization. *Research in Organizational Behavior*, 12, 295–336.

Powell, Walter W. and Paul J. DiMaggio. 1991: *The new institutionalism in organization analysis*. Chicago: University of Chicago Press.

Prendergast, Canice. 1999: The provision of incentives in firms. *Journal of Economic Literature*, 37, March, 7–63.

Pritchard, Duncan. 2014: *What is this thing called knowledge*. London: Routledge.

Proust, Marcel. 1997: *On art and literature*. New York: Carroll & Graf Publishers, Inc.

Prusak, L. and E. Matson. (eds). 2006: *Knowledge, management and organizational learning: a reader*. Oxford: Oxford University Press.

Putnam, Hilary. 2004: *Ethics without ontology*. Cambridge, Mass.: Harvard University Press.

Putnam, Robert D. 2001: *Bowling alone: the collapse and revival of American community*. New York: Simon & Schuster.

Quine, Willard Van O. 1951: Two dogmas of empiricism. *The Philosophical Review*, 60, 1 (January), 20–43.

Rabinowicz, Wlodzimierz. 1979: *Universalizability: a study in morals and metaphysics*. London: D. Reidel Publishing Company.

Rancière, Jacques. 2011: *The politics of aesthetics*. London: Continuum.

Rasmussen, A.J. 2012: *Arena-modernisme*. København: Gyldendal.

Rasmussen, Douglas. 1987: Economic rights versus human dignity. In: Rasmussen and Sterba (eds). *The Catholic bishops and the economy: a debate*. New Brunswick: Transaction Books.

Rasmussen, Douglas. 1989: *Morality and modernity: a critique of Jürgen Habermas's neo-Marxist theory of justice*. The Heritage Lectures. The Heritage Foundation.

Rasmussen, Douglas. 1990: Liberalism and natural end ethics. *American Philosophical Quarterly*, 27, 2, April.

Rasmussen, Douglas and Douglas Den Uyl. 1991: *Liberty and nature*. Illinois: Open Court.

Rawls, John. 1971: *A theory of justice*. Harvard: Harvard University Press.

Rawls, John. 1996: *Political liberalism*. New York: Columbia University Press.

Rehg, William. 1998: Translators introduction. In: Habermas, Jürgen (ed.). *Between facts and norms*. Cambridge, Massachusetts: The MIT Press.

Rehg, William. 2009: *Cogent science in context: the science wars, argumentative theory, and Habermas*. Cambridge, Mass.: MIT Press.

Richardson, John. 2010: How political was Picasso? *The New York Review*, 25 November.

Ricoeur, Paul. 1976: *Interpretation theory: discourse and surplus of meaning*. Fort Worth, Texas: The Texas Christian University Press.

Ricoeur, Paul. 1992: *Oneself as another (Original title: Soi-même comme un autre)*. Chicago: University of Chicago Press.

Robbe-Grillet, Alain. 1965: *Two novels – Jealousy; In the labyrinth*. New York: Grove Press.

Robbe-Grillet, Alain. 1989 [1963]: *For a new novel*. Evanston, Ill.: Northwestern University Press.

Robbins, Lionel. 1984 [1932]: *An essay on the nature and significance of economic science*. London: The Macmillan Press.

Rodrigues, Mario João. 2002: *The new knowledge economy in Europe: a strategy for international competitiveness and social cohesion*. Cheltenham: Edward Elgar.

Rokkan, Stein. 1966: Numerisk demokrati og korporativ pluralisme: to beslutningskanaler i norsk politikk. In: S. Rokkan. 1987: *Stat, nasjon, klasse*. Oslo: Universitetsforlaget.

Rorty, Richard. 1979: *Philosophy and the mirror of nature*. Princeton: Princeton University Press.

Rorty, Richard. 1982: *Consequences of pragmatism*. Minneapolis: University of Minnesota Press.

Rorty, Richard. 1989: *Contingency, irony and solidarity*. Cambridge: Cambridge University Press.

Ross, Alf. 1946: *Towards a realistic jurisprudence*. Copenhagen: Nyt Nordisk Forlag.

Rousseau Jean-Jacques. 2011: *Basic political writings*, translated and edited by Donald A. Cress. Indianapolis, IN: Hackett Pub. Co.

Ryle, Gilbert. 1990 [1949]: *The concept of mind*. London: Penguin Books.

Sacher-Masoch, L. 1991 [1870]: Venus in furs. In: Deleuze and Sacher-Masoch (eds). *Masochism*. New York: Zone Books.

Sanchez-Burks, Jeffrey. 2005: Protestant relational ideology: the cognitive underpinnings and organizational implications of an American anomaly. *Research in Organizational Behavior*, 26, 265–305.

Sandel, Michael. 2010: *Justice: what's the right thing to do?* New York: Farrar, Straus and Giroux.

Sandel, Michael. 2012: *What money can't buy: the moral limits of markets*. New York: Farrar, Straus and Giroux.

Sartre, Jean-Paul. 1946: *L'existentialisme est un humanisme*. Paris: Nagel.

Schein, E.H. 1985: *Organizational culture and leadership: a dynamic view*. San Francisco: Jossey-Bass.

Scheler, Max Ferdinand. 1973: *Selected philosophical essays*. Evanston, Ill.: Northwestern University Press.

Schlicht, Ekkehart. 1998: *On custom in the economy*. Oxford: Clarendon Press.

Schön, Donald. 1983: *The reflective practitioner: how professionals think in action*. New York: Basic Books.

Schumpeter, Joseph. 1976 [1942]: *Capitalism, socialism and democracy*. London: George Allen & Unwin Ltd.

Schumpeter, Joseph. 1978 [1950]: *History of economic analysis*. Oxford: Oxford University Press.

Schumpeter, Joseph. 2008 [1911]: *Theorie der wirtschaftlichen Entwicklung* (transl. 1934, *The theory of economic development: an inquiry into profits, capital, credit, interest and the business cycle*). London: Transaction Publishers.

Schütz, Alfred. 1972 [1932]: *The phenomenology of the social world*. London: Heinemann Educational Books.

Searle, John R. 1969: *Speech acts: an essay in the philosophy of language*. Cambridge: Cambridge University Press.

Searle, John R. 1995: *The construction of social reality*. London: Penguin.

Searle, John R. 1999: *Mind, language and society: doing philosophy in the real world*. London: Weidenfeld & Nicolson, in association with Basic Books

Searle, John R. 2004: *Mind: a brief introduction*. Oxford: Oxford University Press

Seip, Jens Arup. 1988: *Politisk ideologi, tre lærestykker*. Oslo: Universitetsforlaget.

Seirafi, Kasra. 2012: *Organizational epistemology: understanding knowledge in organizations*. Heidelberg: Springer.

Selznick, Philip. 1957: *Leadership in administration: a sociological interpretation*. Evanston, IL: Row, Peterson.

Sen, Amartya. 1970: *Collective choice and social welfare*. London: Holden Day.

Sen, Amartya. 1970: The impossibility of the Paretian liberal. *Journal of Political Economy*, 78.

Sen, Amartya. 1976: Liberty, unanimity and rights. *Economica*, 43.

Sen, Amartya. 1983: Liberty and social choice. *Journal of Philosophy*, 1.

Sen, Amartya. 1985: *The moral standing of the market*. In: Paul, Millar and Paul, op. cit.

Sen, Amartya. 2009: *The idea of justice*. Harvard, Mass.: Harvard University Press and Allen Lane.

Senge, Peter M. 1990: *The fifth discipline: the art and practice of the learning organization*. London: Random House.

Shusterman, Richard. 1994: Pragmatism and liberalism between Dewey and Rorty. *Political theory*, 22(3), Aug., 1994, pp. 391–413.

Skinner, A. 1990: The shaping of the political economy in the Enlightenment, *Scottish Journal of Political Economy*, 37, May.

Skinner, Quentin. 2008: *Hobbes and republican liberty*. Cambridge: Cambridge University Press.

Skinner, Quentin. 2010: *Liberty before liberalism*. Cambridge: Cambridge University Press.

Skirbekk, Gunnar. 1993: *Rationality and modernity*. Oslo: Scandinavian University Press.

Skjervheim, Hans. 1959: *Objectivism and the study of man*. Oslo: Universitetsforlaget.

Sloterdijk, Peter. 2012: *The art of philosophy*. New York: Colombia University Press.

Smith, Adam. 1976a: *An inquiry into the nature and causes of the wealth of nations*. Oxford: Oxford University Press.

Smith, Adam. 1976b: *A theory of moral sentiments*. Indianapolis: Liberty Press.

Smith, Berry. 1986: Austrian economics and Austrian philosophy. In: *Austrian economics: historical and philosophical background*. New York: New York University Press.

Snow, C.P. 2010 [1959]: *The two cultures*. Cambridge: Cambridge University Press.

Solana, Guillermo (ed.). 2009: *Lágrimas de Eros (Tears of Eros)*. Madrid: Musseo Thyssen-Bornemisza/ Foundation Gaja.

Sombart, Werner. 1902: *Der moderne Kapitalismus. Erste Band: Die Genesis des Kapitalismus*. Leipzig: Duncker & Humbolt.

Sombart, Werner. 2001: *Economic life in modern age*. New Brunswick: Transaction Publishers.

Sørensen, Øystein. 1988: *Anthon Martin Schweigaard*. Oslo: Universitetsforlaget.

Sowell, Thomas. 1980: *Knowledge and decisions*. New York: Basic Books, Inc., Publishers.

Sowell, Thomas. 1987: *A conflict of vision*. New York: William Morrow and Company, Inc.

Spencer, Herbert. 1970 [1850]: *Social statistics*. New York: Robert Schalkenbech Foundation.

Spencer, Herbert. 1978 [1897]: *The principles of ethics, vol 1 and 2*. Indianapolis: Liberty Press.

Spencer, Herbert. 1981 [1884]: *The man versus the state*. Indianapolis: Liberty Press.

Spender, J.C. 1997: Making knowledge the basis of a dynamic theory of the firm. *Strategic Management Journal*, 17, 45–62.

Stehr, Nico. 1994: *Knowledge societies*. London: Sage.

Stehr, Nico and Volker Meja (eds). 1984: *Society and knowledge: contemporary perspectives in the sociology of knowledge and science*. New Brunswick (USA): Transaction Books.

Stehr, Nico and Volker Meja (eds). 2005: *Society and knowledge: contemporary perspectives in the sociology of knowledge and science*. New Brunswick (USA): Transaction Books

Taylor, Charles. 1971: Interpretation and the study of man. *Review of Metaphysics*, 25, 1 (Sept.), 3–51.

Taylor, Frederick Winslow. 1911: *Principles of scientific management*. New York and London: Harper & Brothers.

Thomassen, L. (ed.). 1988: *The Derrida-Habermas reader*. Edinburgh: Edinburgh University Press.

Thyssen, Ole. 1998: *En Mærkelig Lyst: Om iagttagelse af kunst*. København: Gyldendal.

Tönnies, Ferdinand. 1979: *Gemeinschaft und Gesellschaft. Grundbegriffe der reinen soziologie*. Darmstadt: Wissenschaftliche Buchgesellschaft.

Toulmin, Stephen. 2001: *Return to reason*. Cambridge, Mass.: Harvard University Press.

Tsoukas, Haridimos. 2005: *Complex knowledge: studies in organizational epistemology*. Oxford: Oxford University Press.

Ullmann-Margalit, Edna. 1977: *The emergence of norms*. Oxford: Oxford University Press.

Ullmann-Margalit, Edna. 1978: Invisible hand explanations. *Synthese*, 39, October, 1978.

van der Ven, A. and P.E. Johnson. 2006: Knowledge for theory and practice. *Academy of Management Review*, 31, 802–21.

van Gusteren, H.R. 1976: *The quest of control*. London: John Wiley & Sons.

Vanberg, Viktor. 1994: *Rules and choice in economics*. London: Routledge.

Vaughn, Karen. 1980: John Locke's theory of property: problems of interpretation. *Literature of Liberty*, Spring, 1980.

Virilio, Paul. 2003: *Art and fear*. London: Continuum.

von Bertalanffy, Ludvig. 1968: *General system theory*. New York: George Braziller.

von Wieser, Friedrich. 1967 [1914/1927]: *Social economics*. New York: Sentry Press.

Wallace, Jeff. 2007: Modernist and the art of fiction. In: Morag Shiach (ed.). *The modernist novel*. Cambridge: Cambridge University Press.

Walsh, Kiron. 1991: Quality and public services, *Public Administration*, 69.

Warner, Stuart D. 1989: Anarchial snares: a reading of Lockes' second treatises. *i reason papers*, Spring, 1989.

Warren, Mark. 1992: Democratic theory and self-transformation. *American Political Science Review*, 86, 1.

Warren, Mark. 1996: The self in discursive democracy. In: White, Stephen K. (ed.). *The Cambridge companion to Habermas*. Cambridge: Cambridge University Press.

Waspshott, Nicholas. 2011: *Keynes Hayek: the clash that defined modern economics*. New York: W.W. Norton & Company, Inc.

Weber, Max. 1920 [1904]: *Die protestantische Ethik und der Geist des Kapitalismus*. Tübingen: J.B. Mohr. Norwegian translation from 1972: *Den protestantiske etikk og kapitalsimens ånd*. Oslo: Gyldendal norsk forlag.

Weber, Max. 1947: *The theory of social and economic organization*. Oxford: Oxford University Press.

Weber, Max. 1978 [1920]: *Economy and society*. Vol. 1 and 2. Berkeley: University of California Press.

Weick, Karl E. 1995: *Sensemaking in organizations*. Thousand Oaks, CA: Sage Publications.

Wenger, Etienne. 1998: *Communities of practice: learning, meaning, and identity*. Cambridge, Mass.: Cambridge University Press.

Whitley, R. 2006: Innovation systems and institutional regimes in Europe. In: Lorenz, E. and B-Å. Lundvall. 2006: *How Europe's economies learn: coordinating competing models*. Oxford: Oxford University Press.

Wilczynski, J. 1982: *The economics of socialism – principles governing the operation of the centrally planned economies under the new system*. London: George Allen and Unwin.

Williams, Raymond. 1989: *Politics of modernism*. London: Verso.

Williamson, Oliver. 1985: *Economic institutions of capitalism*. New York: The Free Press.

Winch, Peter. 1985 [1958]: *The idea of a social science and its relation to philosophy*. London: Routledge and Keegan Paul.

Wittgenstein, Ludwig. 1921: *Tractatus Logico-Philosophicus*. London: Kegan Paul.

Wittgenstein, Ludwig. 2001: *Philosophische Untersuchungen*, the German text, with a revised English translation by G.E.M. Anscombe. Oxford: Blackwell.

Wolin, Richard. 1992: Carl Schmitt the revolutionary habitus and the aesthetics of horror. *Political Theory*, 20, August.

Zaltman, G., R. Duncan and J. Holbek. 1973: *Innovations and organizations*. New York: John Wiley & Sons.

Znaniecki, Florian. 1940: *The social role of the man of knowledge*. New York: Columbia University Press.

Index

administrative system 215, 225, 233, 234, 237
Adorno, Theodor 10, 19, 28, 52, 158, 175, 184
aesthetics 177–82
Alchian, Armed A. 135, 222
American pragmatism 15, 20, 22, 29, 84
Amin, Ash 5, 46, 88, 128, 140, 160
Antigone myth 42–3
Apel, Karl-Otto 84, 93, 231
Arendt, Hannah 7, 158, 171, 180n
argumentation theory 92, 208, 209
Argyris, Chris 7, 43, 130, 137, 146
art and market 167, 179, 180
Aschehoug, Torkel 107
associated economy 4
Auster, Paul 176
autonomy of art 167, 183, 184n, 185
avant-garde 168n, 173, 174, 180, 181
Ayer, A.J. 32

Bacon, Francis 77
Badiou, Alain 178n, 179n, 189, 211
Barney, Jay B. 129, 133, 140
Baron, James N. 136, 221
Bataille, George 179
Baudrillard, Jean 169, 178, 179, 180
Bauman, Zygmunt 178, 184n, 234, 236
Bell, Daniel 6, 25, 129, 150, 155, 158–60, 168n, 181
Berger, Peter 8, 16, 18–25, 29, 157, 160n,
Bergson, Henri 42, 170, 171, 252
Berlin, Isaiah 194, 195, 250, 223, 229, 249
Bershady, Harold 25, 26
beyond dualisms 7, 138, 147
Binmore, Ken 194, 196, 203, 205, 208, 213
Bloor, David 16, 44, 192n
body–mind problem 30
Bourdieu, Pierre 10, 19, 23, 46, 74, 84, 180, 185

Breton, André 174, 175n
British revolution 241, 242
Buchanan, James M. 97, 104n, 193n, 200, 211, 219, 227, 228, 248
Burke, Edmund 227, 240–49
Burrell, Gibson 85, 119, 168n, 180, 184n

capitalism 3, 79, 102, 117, 149–60, 168, 178, 206, 226
capitalist justice 197, 206
Cartesian dualism 77–90
Castells, Manuel 6, 25, 54
Choo, Chun Wei, 128
Coase, Ronald H. 104n, 105, 134, 210
Coleman, Jules 47, 193n, 209n
collaboration 68, 97, 98, 161–3
common good 4, 108, 189–95, 200–211, 230, 235
communicative rationality 10, 12, 28, 29, 51–70, 83, 131, 142, 154, 261
communitarian democracy 251–2
Comte, Auguste 6, 78, 92, 99, 225
concept of the market 95, 96, 113
conformity 4, 40, 58, 66, 131, 135, 177n, 227
conservative 106n, 107, 150, 155–9, 181, 230, 247, 254n
constitution 138, 232, 233, 244
  of the self 39
  of society 12, 123, 215
constitutional constraints 230, 232, 233, 237
consumerist society 167, 169, 178,
contemporary society 158, 163, 167, 170n, 177, 178n, 179n, 181, 215
Cooke, Phillip 4, 5, 179, 180
creative economy 150, 154, 155, 156n, 158, 159, 164, 181
critical theory 6, 10, 17, 19, 22, 53, 83, 88, 93, 153, 239
Croce, Benedetto 175, 180